Practical Ethics in
Sport Management

Practical Ethics in Sport Management

Angela Lumpkin,
Sharon Kay Stoll and
Jennifer M. Beller

McFarland & Company, Inc., Publishers
Jefferson, North Carolina, and London

All photographs are by Jennifer M. Beller
unless otherwise noted.

LIBRARY OF CONGRESS CATALOGUING-IN-PUBLICATION DATA

Lumpkin, Angela.
Practical ethics in sport management / Angela Lumpkin,
Sharon Kay Stoll and Jennifer M. Beller.
p.   cm.
Includes bibliographical references and index.

ISBN 978-0-7864-6398-5
softcover : 50# alkaline paper ∞

1. Sports — Management.   2. Sports — Moral and ethical aspects — United States.
I. Stoll, Sharon Kay.   II. Beller, Jennifer Marie.   III. Title.
GV713.L86 2012   796.069 — dc23   2011040261

BRITISH LIBRARY CATALOGUING DATA ARE AVAILABLE

Front cover design by Bernadette Skok (bskok@ptd.net)

Manufactured in the United States of America

*McFarland & Company, Inc., Publishers
Box 611, Jefferson, North Carolina 28640
www.mcfarlandpub.com*

Table of Contents

Preface

This book provides the latest information and practical applications of ethical leadership for aspiring sport management professionals. Since on a daily basis sport leaders and managers face a plethora of ethical challenges, the ethical values and principles essential for decision making and action are discussed in detail. Based on these values and principles, the reader will learn the process for making morally reasoned decisions within the context of sport. After establishing a foundation for practical ethical leadership and management, the book focuses on specific ethical issues in sports. The conflict between sportsmanship and gamesmanship will be explored to determine how and why the former is increasingly being replaced by the latter. Ethical leadership will be discussed as a means to address violence in sports and ameliorate the problems associated with it. To ensure that racial and gender equity exists and thrives in sports, practical ethical decisions and actions are required of sport leaders and managers. This book discusses practical application ethics at all competitive levels and addresses issues such as the use of performance-enhancing drugs, academics, and commercialized sports. Specific examples will demonstrate how principle-centered leaders, morality, and ethical decision making are vitally important to the future of sports.

This book draws from experience, expertise, and practical application of how moral reasoning should pervade sports at all levels. It examines in depth the major ethical issues topically as well as specifically within competitive levels. Sidebars explain more complex concepts and provide real-world examples to engage students in the content. Students are challenged to apply moral reasoning to realistic ethical dilemmas as they learn the importance of ethical leadership in sports.

Each chapter includes the following pedagogical features:

- Chapter objectives to focus students' attention on the major content.
- Boxes with additional research information to expand knowledge and understanding.
- Summaries at the end of each chapter to emphasize the most important information.
- Reflective questions throughout each chapter to emphasize key points.
- Examples from sport situations at all levels for analysis.

1

Fundamentals of Ethics and Leadership in Sport Management

- What are ethics? What is moral reasoning within the study of ethics?
- What are ethics as applied to leadership?
- What is a practical ethical approach?

Introduction

You are in the grocery store and walking through the produce aisle deciding what to purchase for the next day's meals. You notice one of the shoppers testing the grape selection. She carefully selects the best grape of each bunch and pops those grapes into her mouth, savoring every bite. You are a little taken aback by her behavior, but since the produce manager is standing not more than five feet away and very aware of what she is doing, you think it is probably okay. You guess that since grapes are there to be sold and market managers want their product to be purchased, the store must approve of testing the quality of grapes before purchase. Perhaps it is good for business (see Box 1.1).

Box 1.1 Tom Morris

Tom Morris gave this exact scenario in a radio broadcast and asked for viewers' opinions. The large majority of people thought that it was perfectly acceptable to eat the grapes. Morris taught at Notre Dame for 15 years in the philosophy department, left academia became an ethical consultant for business and management and continues to be an active scholar as well as popular writer in ethics and philosophy. His work *If Aristotle Ran General Motors* (Morris, 1997) is an excellent teaching tool on the importance of knowing the works of classical ethicists and how that knowledge could make a better worker, manager, owner, and company. Morris seeks to make philosophy interesting, intelligible, and practical to the ordinary person.

But the more you think about the grape taster, the more you wonder—should we test grapes just because we can? Perhaps stores put out the grapes in unsealed packages so the potential buyer can test ahead of time? You wonder...

That evening at dinner with a group of your sport management friends, you brought up the story of the grape-testing buyer at the store. Interestingly, you got different reactions from individuals in this group. Jareem said that it is unethical to eat grapes without purchasing them. What if everyone ate a grape? There would be no grapes left. Megan said that it was okay because grapes are a lead item, an item that is sold at a lost value in order to lead customers to the store. The items are there to get people to purchase them. Store owners expect people to taste them, and they often have lost lead items that they know they will not make any money on, but which draw people into the store to buy more grapes or other items. Good-looking, fresh produce is like that—it looks so good you want to taste it and even though people may eat a few and there is a loss from those eaten grapes, the store owner makes it up because after selecting the grapes the buyer will most likely purchase another item or two that is marked higher. Thus the grapes not only increase sales but also increase profits. So, it is okay to eat that grape. Micah said no one cares if you take a grape, it is okay to take a little extra of whatever you want—that is the way the world is.

You asked them, is this an ethical issue?

Jareem said yes, of course it is—if you take the grapes you are stealing. You did not buy them; you are taking them—you are stealing. Megan said she did not think it was an ethical issue and it definitely was not stealing, because tasting grapes is really a non-moral issue, meaning that it is outside the realm of ethics. A non-moral issue is about non-moral values like success, money, or getting ahead. A non-moral value is about objective, social worth. Since the store owner knows you will sample and presents the grapes for you to taste, since they are not packaged, then you are being asked to taste. The grocer is hedging that you will taste and thus you will buy more, thus it's not an ethical issue at all. Micah said ethics has to do with the big things in life like the Enron scandal or the American International Group (AIG) Bailout Scandal with hedge funds and faulty accounting practices of Andersen and Morgan Stanley (see Box 1.2). Tasting grapes is not about ethics—it just is not an important or big issue.

What do you, the reader, think? Is this an ethical issue?

BOX 1.2 THE DANGER OF BEING SMART

The four examples Micah referenced have to do with the downward slide of the U.S. economy starting in the 2000s. The Enron scandal, revealed in October 2001, eventually led to bankruptcy of the Enron Corporation, an American energy company based in Houston, Texas, and the dissolution of Arthur Andersen, which was one of the five largest audit and accountancy partnerships in the world. In addition to being the largest bankruptcy reorganization in American history at that time, Enron undoubtedly is the biggest audit failure of all time. According to McLean and Elkid (2004) in their book *The Smartest Guys in the Room*, Enron executives' actions spiraled out of control resulting in the scandal. From late 1997 until its collapse, the primary motivations for Enron's accounting and financial transactions seem to have been to keep reported income and reported cash flow up, asset values inflated, and liabilities off the books. The AIG scandal, as stated by William Greider, is about coveting, greed, and hubris (Greider, 2010). The Morgan Stanley Scandal relates to illegal and unethical practices of its highest ranking real estate executive in China in which he secured transactions by offering case or gifts to Chinese officials. Some of his partners were Chinese government investment funds (Barboza, 2009).

Ethics as one of the branches (see Box 1.3) of philosophy is the study of right and wrong. Notice that the words used here are: *study* and *right* and *wrong*. What do these words really mean? Study is a deliberate activity. It is done on purpose. Study means that we actually want to understand the problem at hand, and we are going to dedicate ourselves to getting to the heart of the matter. Study means that we will go about it in a systematic, logical, and hopefully rational manner. Thus to study ethics is to take time to ferret out the issues and to think about how to solve them. Study also means that even before we take on these pesky issues, we have spent time trying to understand how to address the issues. We also should have a thought-out blueprint and plan that gives some direction, focus, skills, and tools. What does it mean to have the skills and tools to do the job?

BOX 1.3 APPLIED PHILOSOPHY

Philosophy, as defined by the late Robert Dyal, philosophy professor at Kent State, is the deliberate and rational attempt to understand the sum and whole of one's existence in both their subjective and objective realms with a view for effective living. His point was that philosophy is not just sitting around with your buddies having a brew and arguing about the philosophic coaching of Chris Petersen of Boise State versus the philosophy of the late Bear Bryant at Alabama, whose story is told in *Junction Boys* (Dent, 1999). Bryant was known for his brutal tactics in which he wanted to run off players and usually did so in a less than moral fashion. Rather, philosophy is a purposeful study in which we deliberate, reflect, and read about the issues. To know the issues, we have to read, be immersed in the facts of the issues, and know the literature. Philosophy does not limit itself to what can be studied — we could make a concerted, important study of the differences of coaching philosophy of Petersen and Bryant — but that would entail a detailed study of coaching philosophy and ethics in general to ferret out best practices, and a study of the historical practices of each coach's record. Philosophy asks us to examine the subjective and the objective focus of the issue — nothing is out of the purview of study. If we wanted to examine Bryant or Petersen, we would need more than newspaper clippings — we would need as much first-person material about them as possible as well as interviews of the coaches, assistant coaches, and players to understand their philosophies which, would need to be examined in light of the best practices in coaching. Best practices, according to philosophy, would be based on standards and guidelines and mission statements of coaching organizations. Remember that all of this is done to gain "effective living." If Dyal had an error in his definition, it would be in not using the adjectives "thoughtful and ethical living." It is possible to be very effective and be completely unethical.

Philosophy has four branches of study: metaphysics, epistemology, logic, and axiology. Metaphysics is the study of the *real* issues of life; the great, big, awesome issues of life — why am I here? Am I a spiritual being? Does God exist? R. Scott Kretchmar (2005) has argued that most of the questions in the field of sport are based in soft metaphysics — meaning that rather than the great, big, awesome issues of life, these are the softer issues: Who am I as a sport manager? What do I believe as a sport manager? Epistemology is the study of knowledge: This branch is essential to communication: what do I know? How do I know? What is to be known? We will talk more about this later. Logic is the study of language. Finally, axiology is the study of values. In axiology, there are two sub-branches: aesthetics and ethics. Aesthetics refers to that which is beautiful and that which is ugly. Ethics is the study of right and wrong.

Let's suppose I want to fix the brakes on my car. I can't fix the brakes if I do not know what a brake does, how it works, what are the acceptable standards of the brake functioning, who made it, any specific problems that occur with these sort of brakes, and how brakes are fixed. Of course, I could just take the car to the shop and let them fix it — which most of us do — let someone else deal with it. Often this works, and many times it does not. If I get an unscrupulous mechanic or an incompetent one, I do not get the brakes fixed, or I end up paying too much money. In all the cases above, I place myself in jeopardy of brake failure. Every one of us deals with this sort of issue every day. Do we just continue to be ignorant and stick our heads in the sand, or do we make an effort to figure out what the issues are and how should I handle them?

In this text, we will make a concerted effort to study ethics in a way that makes ethics a useful, practical tool as you progress into your sport management roles. We will make a concerted effort to study the process of reasoning about ethical issues in sport management.

What then is an ethical issue? Ethics is the study of right and wrong. Right and Wrong. What do these words mean?

For all of time in western tradition, these words — right and wrong — have been used to describe ethical conduct. Aristotle (see Box 1.4) said that ethics is the study of

Each interaction we have with another person has a moral consequence. We must be concerned with our actions, intentions, and motives as they affect other people on and off the field of play.

right conduct (Aristotle & Sachs, 2002)—implying that there was wrong conduct, and there was a preferred and better way to conduct oneself. Aristotle was not only concerned with what one actually does—the human action of right or the human conduct of doing right—but he was also interested in our plan—our motives and intentions—in deciding right and wrong action. He argued that wrong action is directly linked to our good or bad motives and intentions. A motive is what drives our final action, our conduct. Our intentions are the plan that we put together to fulfill our motive, and that which fleshes itself out is our final action.

BOX 1.4 DELIBERATE RATIONALITY IN ETHICS

Aristotle, in *Nicomachean Ethics* (Aristotle & Sachs, 2002) and *Eudemian Ethics* (1935), sorted out the nature of ethics and set the tone for the western tradition. Of course, his work was also highly affected by Plato; it is said that all of Western tradition philosophy is but a footnote to Plato. According to Aristotle, we study ethics in order to improve our lives and we ought to seek a virtuous life—a life built on specific virtues (actions based on values) that improve our lot as well as those around us. Aristotle follows Socrates and Plato in taking the virtues to be central to a well-lived life. Like Plato, he regards the ethical virtues (justice, courage, temperance, and others) as complex, rational, emotional, and social skills. What we need, in order to live well, is a proper appreciation of the way in which such goods as friendship, pleasure, virtue, honor, and wealth fit together as a whole. This all can only occur through upbringing, habits, and the ability to see each and every time which course of action is best supported by reason. However, to do so cannot happen solely by learning the rules—for following rules is highly limited. We have to practice deliberately emotional and social skills to have well-being.

For example, let's suppose you are in a sport marketing class with your best friend. You see her deliberately cheat. By the rule of the class and your university, you are supposed to inform the professor if you see someone cheating. You are sure she cheated and you know the rule, but you hesitate. You start to think about this situation. You begin to rationalize. If you follow the rule, your friend may be kicked out of the program. Also the peer pressure gets greater, because if you follow the rule your peers may think you are "selling out your friend" to gain a better standing with the authorities. If you follow the rule, the rest of your peers will probably think you are a "brown nose"— that is, if you follow the rule, you may suffer more from turning in your friend than you would gain. You then decide that it is not worth it to turn in your friend because it not your problem, it is the professor's problem; it is your friend's problem; it is the university's problem; you do not want to get involved. It is through this sort of thinking about the issue that you weigh the forthcoming action. Most of us are mercenaries— we will weigh the costs and benefits (i.e., what do I gain from this action?). If we were saints (and there are a few out there), we probably would not consider the costs and benefits because we just know what is right and intuitively make a decision and act upon it. But even the saints may be mercenaries at some time in their lives (unfortunately our own humanity becomes a vice). The point here is that motives drive decisions which then affect how we are going to handle the problem.

But who decides what is right and what is wrong? Actually you do, we all do—as have all people from the beginning of time when two people met each other and they had to decide how to act and treat each other. Do I take a stick and hit the other person? Do I laugh at the other person because he or she is funny-looking to me? Do I take what that person has and keep it for myself? Do I share what I have with that person? Do I shove the person out of the way, so I can get where I am going? Do I wait my turn? Do I lie? Do I cheat? Do I do what I want and violate everyone around me? Or do I consider others in my decisions and actions? Historically, for 4,000-plus years, we as people have decided what is right and what is wrong through either intuition or experience. Lawrence Kohlberg once said that right conduct is really housed in three questions: What is the right thing to do? Why is it right? And what sociomoral perspectives underlie and support the decision process (see Box 1.5) (Kohlberg, 1981).

Box 1.5 Lawrence Kohlberg

Lawrence Kohlberg, late of Harvard University, spent his life studying moral conduct and moral behavior of children and adults. He started his academic career wondering about Jean Piaget's earlier work on moral development of children. How does a child learn moral behavior? For Kohlberg, moral refers to actions that are affected by and directed toward others. Kohlberg brought forth some basic principles following and building on the work of Piaget as well as the philosophy of Aristotle and others that moral development is a universal, bottom-up process, and all of us go through different stages of development. Some of us progress further than others through our experiences, upbringing, education, and reasoning. Though Kohlberg's work was often criticized as being male-centric — because it originally was done only with males — his work is still an important starting point in understanding moral development.

Thomas Jefferson reportedly said that law is socialized ethics, meaning that the standard of right and wrong is decided by the social institution. This definition works, sort of—until a social institution becomes corrupt. Then the law becomes corrupt. Consider the example of legalized slavery in this country. Until 1863, slavery was legal, and if an individual tried to stop slavery he or she was considered a law breaker. If an individual tried to help a runaway slave escape, the person could be arrested and tried for conspiracy and theft. Laws sometimes fail us because the social institution of government can fail us in making ethical decisions. This becomes a quandary: how do we get to what is right? Social standards can be helpful, but remember Kohlberg's formula: What is right, why is it right, and what socio-moral historical perspectives support the decision? Consider the third tenet: What socio-moral historical perspectives support the decision? This argument tells us that we have over 4,000 years of western tradition to give us perspective, which we have a duty to know and understand (see Box 1.6). The great Spanish cultural philosopher George Santayana said that we are condemned to repeat the past if we do not know history. We cannot regard ethics in a vacuum of time and space. We are linked to our traditions, culture, history, philosophy, politics, and economics past and present, thus to make an informed decision means that we have to be versed in what has happened in the past and present. Our rich western tradition gives us much information and perspective to help us make informed ethical decisions about what is right and what is wrong. Therefore in deciding what is right and why is it right, we rely on our informed knowledge.

BOX 1.6 EASTERN TRADITION

This is not to say that the Eastern tradition cannot be helpful. However, the majority of our literature, law, and culture have been heavily influenced by ancient Greek, ancient Roman, Scholastic, Renaissance, and Western Europe tradition including history, philosophy, and religious study. Perhaps this is an artificial perspective, because today Eastern and Western traditions are interlaced and often not so very different.

Thinking about what is the right thing to do and why it is right is called moral reasoning. This is the systematic process of evaluating personal values and developing a consistent and impartial set of moral principles to live by, which is not an easy task.

Thinking is not an automatic process; rather, it requires self-discipline, time, knowledge of personal beliefs, and a systematic approach. Thinking about difficult issues and placing yourself in cognitive dissonance is also necessary to increase your moral development (see Box 1.7) (Kohlberg, 1981). Unfortunately, most of us are so involved in personal and professional activities that thinking about fundamental moral issues seems unimportant.

BOX 1.7 COGNITIVE DISSONANCE

Lawrence Kohlberg (1981) argued that for changes to occur in our reasoning process we must be cognitively stressed or in cognitive dissonance. This means that our way of thinking about something or valuing something must be challenged. Suppose all of our lives we have known that apples are ripe only when they are red, and then we are introduced to green apples. We are persuaded to taste and eat a green apple that is ripe — we now have a different view. Our point of view is now in dissonance — out of harmony — with what we know (cognition). Apples can be ripe when they are red or green. The same is true for most of our value systems — if we can be persuaded to be open to new possibilities, we may be cognitively placed in dissonance — or thinking that is in disharmony to what we know and believe. The key here is that we are open to a different way of thinking and are ready to learn and challenge what we know and value.

As you will learn in this text, ethical issues are very important because they affect what you do in all aspects of your field. As sport managers, you will work in a world of competition in your own job as well as the culture of where you will work. Your ability to make ethical decisions will have a direct effect on your concept of fair play, which represents the position that all individuals have the same chance for success. Your ability to make ethical decisions will have a direct bearing on almost every action that you take in your job. The quest in this text is to address certain ethical issues and offer some basic tools to help you think about what is right and why it is right.

Thomas Lickona (Lickona, 1993), a student of Kohlberg and the founder of the Center for 4th & 5th Rs, argues in his seminal text, *Educating for Character* (1993), that developing the tools that we need in making decisions or acting is directly linked to our valuing and knowing. Valuing is the actual process of internalizing relative good and knowing is the actual understanding of why these values are important.

Moral Knowing

In situations of ethical dilemmas, to know is called moral knowing. In this text, we will use the word "moral" for the actual reasoning process that affects ethical standards in the workplace. In common usage, ethical and moral are often interchangeable; however, in a formal sense moral refers to the personal decision-making process that involves a consideration of and concern for others as well as for each of us. Ethical refers to the standards of conduct written by the members of a professional organization. Ethics is the practice of following these standards. In a professional organization, the members agree explicitly or implicitly to follow these standards. If a member violates the standards, other members can charge that member with unethical practice, and if the behavior is egregious enough, the member might be expunged from the organization. We will discuss some of the ethical issues later in this text.

Moral reasoning, however, is a personal attempt to distinguish right from wrong and good from bad. Morality in the theoretical sense is associated with values and principles that are to be evaluated, understood, and fleshed out before one chooses or engages in a particular course of action. This is a personal, intentional activity.

Moral knowing, as one of the phases of moral reasoning, is the cognitive phase of learning about moral issues and how to resolve them. It is the ability to know that a moral dilemma exists, to know what you believe and value concerning the dilemma, to know how to look at the bigger picture surrounding the dilemma, and finally, to know how to reason through the dilemma to find the right thing to do. All of us learn early that it is wrong to take something that belongs to another. However, we also learn cognitively by watching others and listening to the arguments that others make about actions. Moral knowing is directly affected by our intentional study of our western traditions, history, and philosophy.

Moral Valuing

Moral valuing is the basis of what we believe about ourselves, society, and others around us. Valuing asks such questions as: What is most important to me? Is my gain more important than others'? Valuing is the personal relative worth that we place on an objective or a behavior. It is unique to each of us and yet is also affected by what others think is important. For example, I may think that performance is more important than results in playing a game whereas you think the end result is more important than the performance. I may think money is more important than love, whereas you may think love is more important than money.

Moral valuing takes into consideration empathy, self-control, humility, and conscience as each of us directs actions toward others. There is currently debate as to how we learn empathy, self-control, and humility, and how conscience is developed. For this text, we will not delve deeply into the science of each, rather we will argue that without empathy (see Box 1.8), self-control, humility, and a developed conscience our moral behavior will grossly, negatively affect everyone with whom we work or whom we know. Individuals who do not have these capabilities are usually thought of as sociopaths or psychopaths. We come to value through experience, education, and important role models in our lives.

BOX 1.8 EMPATHY

Sharon Lamb of the University of Massachusetts, Boston has written extensively on the development of morality in children. In one of her earlier works (Lamb, 1990), Lamb argues that children, in fact all primates, are born with a sense of empathy — and unfortunately in our modern world, they are actually taught not to be empathic. She argues that we must take an active role in teaching children and reinforcing a basic primate essence of empathy. This is an important point especially in our competitive society, for as children we learn not to be empathic in our games of chance and competition. Henri Nouwen (Nouwen, 1998) was one of the most significant writers on spirituality of the late twentieth century. In his work, he clearly spoke to the learned importance of humility in being a human as well as being a leader. Nouwen, after a successful career as a philosopher, theologian, writer, and speaker, took upon himself the humbling experience of caring for and serving the least of us: the mentally disabled at L'Arche en Trosly, France, the first of 130 communities where people with developmental disabilities live with assistants.

To Act

Moral action is our outward intentional behavior that we manifest contingent on our values and cognitive processes. Know that there is a LARGE difference between behavior and moral action. We may have all sorts of mindless behaviors in which little actual thinking occurs, such as putting on a seat belt or watching television. However, moral action depends on our competency about moral issues and our values. What exactly do we believe, and do we know it well enough to take action? Moral action also depends on our "will" to do what we believe. Do we have the courage and the will to accomplish what we believe? And finally, moral action depends on our daily habits. Is "doing the right thing" something that we value enough that it becomes a habit in our life? Do we actually think about what we do?

To Know, to Value, to Act in Application

The three phases — to know, to value, and to act — work in concert to help us make moral decisions, including the case of the grape taster. Is it wrong to taste the grapes, why is it wrong, and what socio-moral perspectives support the decision that we make?

Can we say simply: It is wrong to taste grapes because the grapes are not ours? Or can we say: It is right to taste grapes because others do it or the store owner appears to allow it? Because there is conflicting information in the grape taster's case, how would we go about reasoning through the case? As you remember, Kohlberg said that we have to address our three questions. What is right? Why is it right? What socio-moral perspectives support the decision process?

One technique that can be used simply to determine what is right and why it is right is to universalize the action and/or reverse the action. Universality and reversibility are two practices that come to us through our rich historical traditions. Aristotle spoke of this process as did other scholastics from Aquinas (1911) through the utilitarians Mill and Bentham (Bentham, 2003). Universality means to apply it to all cases within the context. For example, the question would be: Would tasting the grapes to make sure of their quality apply to all articles or goods in the grocery store? Would it be permissible to walk down the aisle of the mayonnaise jars and pop the lids on several of the different products, stick in a finger and pull out a dollop to taste? Would it be permissible to shuck several ears of corn, take a bite out of each and then discard the ones we do not think meets our standard of being sweet enough? Or would it be permissible to pop a can of beer, take a swig and then put the can back on the shelf?

All of these are examples of universalizing the case. In all of the instances above, we would say it is not permissible to taste the mayonnaise or the corn or the beer, which helps answer the questions: **What** is right or, the reverse, why is it wrong? Tasting destroys the property and wastes the product — and essentially takes something which is not ours, which again answers the question: **Why** is it right or wrong?

Another technique to help in deciding what is right and why it is right is reversing the case. This means: would we want the same behavior applied to us if the grapes were our property? If we were selling this product, would we want people to sample away and not purchase the grapes? We may permit it because we do not want to lose the customers, but we probably don't especially like it. If too many people sample the grapes, we lose money. No business can continually lose money and stay in business, thus answering the question: **Why** is it right or wrong? Thus the grape taster should probably re-evaluate her practice of tasting her way through the grapes and consider the universality and reversibility principle in relation to her purchasing practices of tasting before buying even IF everyone seems to engage in that practice.

Requirements of Moral Reasoning

Be advised that conflicting views are commonplace, and our case of the grape taster is only one of numerous cases that you will face daily. The grape testing may seem to be a rather trivial point; however, little decisions over a long period of time affect our moral reasoning and our moral behavior (see Box 1.9). Whatever position you take on moral issues, you will find that not everyone accepts your arguments.

BOX 1.9 GLADWELL

Malcolm Gladwell (2002) in his text, *The Tipping Point: How Little Things Can Make a Big Difference*, reiterates in popular common fashion what Aristotle said in his work — every action, no matter how seemingly trivial, sets a pattern of events whether it is in our own character development or in how we treat others. Little things make a difference.

Because conflicting views are commonplace, you and your friends may never resolve them. Other positions may be right and you may be wrong, or you may be right and they may be wrong. Because the purpose of moral reasoning is to seek moral truth to guide day-to-day conduct and to regulate social institutions, discussions about moral issues may result in arguments. Such arguing is not necessarily bad, as some people may believe. Moral arguing may help you reach agreement through a systematic reasoning process. Arguing is not so good if it is irrational or if the persons engaged in it are unreasonable. At the same time, such unreasonableness may be helpful it if is used to make progress in discovering moral truth. Arguing does not necessarily mean fighting or even heated disagreements. Rather, argumentation is attempting to demonstrate that some beliefs are true based on the truth of other beliefs.

What we do know is that the actual discussion and articulation of these moral issues is imperative for the growth of our moral brain as well as our moral selves (Tancredi, 2003). Recent research in neuroscience has found that a specific portion of the frontal lobes compose the elite machinery geared toward social interaction and maintaining order through social morality. This portion of the brain is now often called the moral brain. We also know that articulation, discussion, and reflection are very, very important. This reality is also why as future professionals in the field of sport management, discussions about ethical issues, ethical practice, and ethical missions — the purpose of why a company exists — should be at the heart and soul of who you are, what you do, and how you do it. Every business should focus on these important issues, and the professionals within it should be involved in active and continued discussion (see Box 1.10).

BOX 1.10 ADMINISTRATORS AND ETHICS

In an earlier work, Stoll and Beller (2004) discuss this important issue of discussion and reflection. Stoll argues that administrators are plagued daily by moral issues and ethical dilemmas, and if sanity is to exist, there must be a clear vision of what they believe and a mission that carries through. They give a specific guideline of how this can be done through operations and perspective.

Before we continue, other tools exist that may help us flesh out the power of social moral perspectives that help us answer the knotty questions of what is right and why is it right. As you remember, we discussed earlier our 4,000 years of tradition that can help inform us (see Box 1.11). Below are three of these social-moral perspectives that we can use in our decision making process: our ability to be impartial, consistent, and reflective.

BOX 1.11 VEIL OF IGNORANCE

These perspectives are the basis of rational thought about decisions of ethics. Continually from Aristotle to the present, philosophers, historians, social critics, lawmakers, politicians, and others use these tools to make arguments for their position, or they should. Perhaps we are all limited in how impartial we can truly be. John Rawls (2005), the eminent social philosopher, argued for what he termed "Veil of Ignorance" to derive principles of Justice. He was well aware of our limitations as human beings because we would act in our own self-interest, but by his prescribed action of placing ourselves behind a "Veil of Ignorance" we might be able to realize our limitations and thus our place in society. With just this minimal assumption about human nature (we rationally act in our own self-interest) and assuming that no one knows his or her eventual social position, we will come up with these two principles of Justice (Justice as Fairness): A society is just if it provides the most extensive set of liberties possible to everyone in the society and if it contains ways to balance social inequalities and provide equal access.

Requirements of Moral Reasoning

Impartiality

Being impartial in determining any issue is always difficult and perhaps impossible. Merleau-Ponty (1962), the existential writer most aligned with body/mind perspectives, said that we "drag our existence" with us. Humans tend to seek their own personal pleasure. Our value system is bombarded with intuition, emotion, and a myriad of values from science, logic, sense experience, and authoritarian perspectives (Lewis, 1990).

What is difficult is quieting your own wants and attempting to develop an impartial reasoning system. To do so means to become concerned with other points of view. Since we all must live in the world with other people, we must come to realize that our wants and desires must be tempered by how those wants and desires affect other people. In developing a reasoned view, we must grow beyond, "What's in

Each participant, coach, and sport manager must make decisions about right and wrong. We must learn to reflect and be impartial and consistent in our moral knowing, valuing, and doing.

it for me?" Rather, our goal should be to consider the ramifications of each decision in relation to other people who may be affected by our action. This becomes even trickier in the sport management world because profit will veil and darken our perspective — more about this later.

Interestingly, most of us expect better behaviors from our friends. We expect them to be altruistic even if we are egotistical. For example, most of us choose friends who demonstrate certain altruistic virtues (a particular moral excellence that promotes the general good or a special manifestation of specific moral values). That is, we choose friends for certain basic virtues, such as fairness, honesty, and truthfulness, and we usually trust our friends and believe that they will not fail us.

Would you choose friends you know would lie to you, cheat you, or steal from you? Probably not! Of course, the same virtuous traits you find imperative in your friends are traits that you want others to think you demonstrate. Most of us want others to know us as being honest, truthful, responsible, and altruistic, and to think of us as being fair and concerned for others, even if we are not.

To be fair means developing an awareness of others' feelings and needs. Being fair also demands imagining and understanding others' interests and the effect of our actions on their lives (Frankena, 1973). To be otherwise is to risk friendship or companionship and loss of our own civility.

From a moral point of view, being fair or impartial is attempting to be free from bias, fraud, or injustice. Being fair and impartial is trying to be equitable and legitimate, or not taking advantage of others. Such qualities are essential in making decisions about moral issues. Without such qualities, all decisions become biased and centered on the good of one, or what is considered good for one. If you wish to be considered fair, or if you wish to hold traits esteemed by others, you work toward impartiality in your reasoning. Obviously, you will fail because of your own mortality ... but the point is to at least try.

Consistency

To reason morally, you must also be logical and consistent. Being logical is the essence of moral reasoning, which involves an exact process. To be consistent when making moral decisions, past and present decisions must be taken into account. If you hold two positions that contradict each other, both cannot be truthful or acceptable. We often are measured through our actions, and actions should follow some sort of consistent pattern. If you say you will do something, people will look for you to do it. If you do not, they begin to doubt your word and your action. Also, consistency refers to how you treat others — is the treatment the same over time, or is the treatment different by degree or by temperament or by whom the treatment is directed toward?

Reflection

You must resolve your moral and ethical dilemmas through reflective judgment based on clear moral and non-moral values. Reflective thinking is exercising careful judgment in all moral issues, based on your moral and non-moral values. Unfortunately, few of us exercise reflective thinking. Often, we take a stand on an issue because we are biased by our own cultural, sociological, or biological presuppositions. Our non-moral values drive our decision-making process. These values are the "thing" of life, or the objectively based measures of life. Success, money, power, fame, adulation, and admiration are all non-moral values. How much weight we put on the non-moral values may distort and disable our ability to make moral decisions. Earlier, we spoke of being mercenary. A mercenary is one who does whatever she does for the benefit that she gets from it. Many of us sell out our moral values for the non-moral gain that we will receive. We cheat on an exam (we violate the moral value of honesty) because we want a better grade (non-moral value). We cheat on our spouse (honesty) because we want the physical or emotional experience of sex. We lie to our friends (honesty) because we want to seem important. We steal (honesty) because we want the money (non-moral value).

So how does all of this work in the field of sport management? Let us consider another case that is closer to this subject than our grape taster. This case exists at a majority of colleges and universities across the U.S.

Gender Equity

XYZ University believes that it meets the requirement of gender equity in its distribution of funds for men's and women's sports. There are an equal number of sport teams for men and women. There are an equal number of coaches for men's and women's teams. The men's teams are football, cross country, golf, tennis, track and field, and basketball. The women's teams are volleyball, cross country, golf, tennis, track and field, and basketball. The budget for the men's program, including football, is approximately three times as large as the women's. However, if these budgets are calculated without football, the budgets are approximately equal. Football, as the number one revenue sport, brings in about 60 percent of the operating revenue. Without this revenue, there would be no funds available to support programs for the non-revenue sports. Therefore XYZ university school states that equity exists.

1. Do you agree?
2. What are the issues in this case?

In a traditional ethical inequity inquiry, the emphasis has always been on rationally determining moral issues, which in turn justifies our choices to behave in certain ways. Specifically, critical, reflective thinking means exercising careful judgment or observation about an issue. Critical means to be accurate, exact, and precise about an issue, take into account all sides of an issue, and determine its present and future implications. Use critical thinking to examine the different sides of the gender equity issue at XYZ.

Case One: Equity exists.
Case Two: Equity does not exist.
Case Three: Equity does not exist, but inequity is acceptable in this case.

Which of the three cases is true? All three cannot be true.

Rebuttal to Case One: Does equity exist? If equity is defined as equal access to all goods for all people, equity does not appear to exist. If the primary purpose of athletics is for education, then the university has a duty to provide experiences that meet the educational purpose. And, if education by law and tradition in the U.S. should be available to all in an equitable fashion, and if football uses or has access to twice as much funding as the women's programs, equity cannot exist.

Rebuttal to Case Two: Equity does not exist. As with case one, the statement must be true. Equity does not exist.

Rebuttal to Case Three: Inequity is acceptable in this case, since without football there would be no other programs. This scenario may be true, or it may not. Put another way, this argument for inequity rests on justification of unequal distribution of goods to men because without men there would be no football and without football there would be less money for all other programs.

This appears to be logical — football brings in the money, therefore without football there would be no program; however, this argument does not take into consideration all of the attending collateral issues. For example: What is the cost of all of the programs? From where is revenue generated? Which programs are the most expensive? Which are the least expensive? Are coaches paid an equitable salary or even an equal salary?

In general, football is the most expensive sport and spends more money than all the other sports combined. If football didn't exist, most college athletic programs could be supported by student fees, donated scholarships, and ticket sales. It then becomes a circular argument.

To have an athletic team is always a choice, and deciding to have a football team is a choice. However, this choice directly affects gender equity as well as team equity for every other men's and women's team (see Box 1.12).

BOX 1.12 BLAIR VERSUS WASHINGTON STATE UNIVERSITY

This very argument was used in a case won by Sue Durrant and colleagues against Washington State University. Durant and her colleagues sued Washington State University over gender equity. Washington State argued that it met gender equity as long as the football team was taken out of the equation. The case went to the Washington State Supreme Court, which ruled that WSU chose to have a football team and since it did so, then it was obligated to meet the gender equity demands of Title IX. Washington State in response became an example of positive gender equity programs when it instituted more teams for women, especially crew, and increased funding and coaches' salaries for women coaches (Libraries, 2006).

Even though gender equity is supposedly required by law, the way football is supported is inequitable. Therefore men in football are special. This argument rests on the assumption that men have more of some quality than women. More of what? We aren't sure of the answer to this question. Culturally and institutionally, funding of football programs is inequitable. If we can access the quality that men have more of, then we may have the reason why inequity is acceptable. A different supporting argument to

Case Three might be: "But without football there would be no other programs." The reply might be: "Why have, therefore, a program that by its very nature unfairly discriminates against others? Should we have programs that benefit only one class of athletes, or one class of people?"

The counter to this statement is that without football, there are no funds and no programs. Would we not advocating the demise of sport, period (see Box 1.13)?

BOX 1.13 FOOTBALL SALARIES

Football is a difficult case in point. Budgets for Bowl Championship Subdivision (BCS) schools range anywhere to $38.5M for football at Ohio State, as compared to BCS aspirant Boise State at $4.5M. Salaries for football coaches are astronomical, such as $4.1M for Alabama's Nick Saban for a total of $32.8M over an eight-year contract. Boise State's Chris Peterson who wants to play Alabama for the championship, has a salary of $2.5M. Boise State in 2010 was the team challenging the thinking of the BCS selection system with a budget an eighth of that of Ohio State, and with a budget that is largely coaches' salaries.

This may also be true, and it may not be true. It is certain that distribution of funds will change what sport is today. The change may be good, and it may be bad; however, change is necessary if we truly want equity. As we write this, the University of California at Berkeley has cancelled two teams, baseball and men's gymnastics, and rugby was reduced to a varsity club sport. The goal was to save $4M. However, the school decided not to touch the funding of any of the other programs in which men's football and men's basketball head coaches make over $1.5M each, not counting the salaries for assistant coaches.

Such scrutiny may or may not bring about new enlightenment. As you can see, we may all agree about the issues after critical reflection, or we may find that we disagree. It is possible that several different theories may survive the reflective process. We have no guarantee that our means to finding the truth through moral reasoning will support only one view. Even if we do find different views, however, we will have begun to understand how to defend your moral positions; and you may learn about yourself and your beliefs.

Summary

In this chapter we have discussed practical applications of ethics in real-world experiences. We have learned that even little decisions and seemingly unimportant actions play an important role in the development of our moral lives, which directly affects our ethical decision making. We also know that to make a moral decision there are certain tools that can help us: What is right? Why is it right? What socia-moral perspectives support the decision process. We also know that a moral environment is highly affected by reasoning morally. We only grow through discussion, argument, and reflection about the issues at hand. Certain social-moral perspectives can also help us in making those decisions. As we continue our discussion about ethics in sport management, we will find that these basic questions inform what we do and how we make decisions.

References

Aquinas, T. (1911). *The Summa Theologica of St. Thomas Aquinas.* Notre Dame, IN: Ave Maria.

Aristotle and Rackham, H. (1935). *Athenian Constitution. Eudemian Ethics. Virtues and Vices.* Cambridge, MA: Loeb Classical Library.

Aristotle and Sachs, J. (2002). *Aristotle's Nicomachean Ethics.* Newburyport, MA: Focus.

Barboza, D. (2009, March 1). Morgan Stanley's Chinese land scandal. Retrieved from http://www.nytimes.com/2009/03/02/business/worldbusiness/02morgan.html

Bentham, J. (2003). *The Classical Utilitarians: Bentham and Mill.* Indianapolis, IN: Hackett.

Dent, J. (1999). *The Junction Boys: How Ten Days in Hell with Bear Bryant Forged a Championship Team.* New York: Thomas Dunne.

Frankena, W. K. (1973). *Ethics* (2nd ed.). Englewood Cliffs, NJ: Prentice Hall.

Gladwell, M. (2002). *The Tipping Point: How Little Things Can Make a Big Difference.* Boston, MA: Back Bay.

Greider, W. (2010, August 6). *The AIG Bailout Scandal.* Retrieved from http://www.thenation.com/article/153929/aig-bailout-scandal.

Kohlberg, L. (1981). *Essays on Moral Development: Vol. 1: The Philosophy of Moral Development.* San Francisco, CA: Harper and Row.

Kretchmar, R. S. (2005). *Practical Philosophy of Sport and Physical Activity* (2nd ed.). Champaign, IL: Human Kinetics.

Lamb, S. (1990). *The Emergence of Morality in Young Children.* Chicago: University of Chicago Press.

Lewis, H. (1990). *A Question of Values.* San Francisco, CA: Harper and Row.

Libraries, W. S. (2006). Cage 711: Sue M. Durrant. Pullman, WA.

Lickona, T. (1993). *Educating for Character.* New York: Bantam.

McLean, B., and Elkind, P. (2004). *The Smartest Guys in the Room: The Amazing Rise and Scandalous Fall of Enron.* New York: Penguin.

Merleau-Ponty, M. (1962). *Primacy of Perception.* London: Routledge.

Morris, T. (1997). *What If Aristotle Ran General Motors?* New York: Henry Holt.

Nouwen, H. (1998). *Reaching Out.* Grand Rapids, MI: Zondervan.

Rawls, J. (2005). *A Theory of Justice: Original Version.* Cambridge, MA: Belknap Press of Harvard University Press.

Stoll, S. K., and Beller, J. M. (2004). "Ethical dilemmas in college sport." In R. Lapchick, *New Game Plans for College Sport* (pp. 75–90). Westport, CT: Praeger.

Tancredi, L. (2003). *Hardwired Behavior: What Neuroscience Reveals About Morality.* New York: Cambridge University Press.

CHAPTER 2

The Process of Making
Morally Reasoned Decisions in Sports

- What are the usual approaches in sport leadership today?
- What are the limitations of these usual approaches?
- What are values and principles, and how do they affect ethical choices?
- Why would a principled ethical leadership approach be more successful than other theories of leadership?

Introduction

You are the new assistant athletic director in charge of marketing at Smalltown University, known for its competitive athletic teams. You have worked hard to secure this position and were lucky to get it in this downturned economy. In the job interview for the position, you were asked if you were competitive and creative. You answered that you were and that you looked for the challenge of being a leader at Smalltown. When you arrive at Smalltown, you can feel a true esprit de corps about the athletic programs: One for all and all for one. Everyone seems directed toward and believes in the mission of the athletic program: Success on the court and in the classroom.

At Smalltown, the cheerleaders and the pep band are a large part of the aura of game nights. At your first home women's basketball game, you are seated next to the athletic director and the president of Smalltown. Fan support is tremendous, and the crowd is loud and boisterous. When the opposing team is introduced: the home cheerleaders hold signs that say, "YOU STINK!" "HEY THERE, DON'T BE BLUE ... FRANKENSTEIN WAS UGLY, TOO!" and "GO HOME!" The fans love it.

You sneak a peek at the athletic director and the president—they are clapping, cheering and laughing, too. The game begins and both teams seem to be well matched with good coaching and skilled play on the floor. At the first time out, the pep band runs onto the floor and does a quick maneuver that places the brass instruments facing directly into the visiting team's huddle. It is doubtful that the players can hear their coach or that the coach can yell over the noise.

You again look toward the athletic director and president—no response. During the visiting team's free throws, a group of students apparently organized by a band member uses large black dots on white cardboard that they move back and forth and up and down to cause vision problems for the opposing players. During play, the band hurls a constant barrage of profane chants toward the opposing team with sexual and homophobic undertones. The game concludes and the home team wins by two points.

After the game, you mention to the athletic director that you thought the band and cheerleaders were out of line. The athletic director says, "I thought you were a competitor. We want to win and our mission is to be successful. Gaining an advantage is the name of the game. This is what the fans want. The media and the professionals, plus the big schools, are all doing the same thing. How can you expect the fans at Smalltown to be any less competitive?" He then tells you to lighten up, and surely you knew what you were getting into when you took the job at Smalltown. "If you don't want to do your job, someone else will."

After the game and after you have licked your wounds, you go out with your group of sport management friends and bring up what you saw and the athletic director's response. You think the whole scenario was unacceptable and you worry that if you disagree with the practice any longer, you will be terminated.

Jareem tells you that there are three issues here: (1) the behavior of the fans and the culture established by the cheerleaders and pep band; (2) the complicity of the athletic director and president; and (3) the expectations of the athletic director about your behavior and loyalty to the program. "Which do you want to discuss?"

You respond, "All of them, but how about the first one, the behavior of the fans—am I being too conservative, or is this the way of the world?"

Jareem says of course it is unacceptable and you should challenge the athletic director about it. Yes, you are only one voice, but one voice is enough to make a difference. The whole thing is a lack of good ethics throughout the athletic department.

Megan tells you that the fan behavior is common practice and no one really cares, so why should you? What you saw is no different from what our players at Smalltown suffer at Bigtown when they play there. Besides, she says, "You have worked too long to get this job, enjoy it, do what you are told, and you probably will get ahead much faster."

Micah tells you that this is the way business works. "No one expects anyone in the business world to be ethical. The fans were probably drunk. The cheerleaders were having fun with the opposing team and the band was just into it. It wasn't personal. Don't make something bigger out of this than it is." He recommends you get your own dots to use during the game, and then chuckles. "It's not your job to police the athletic department, you are supposed to be a team member—just do what you are told."

Megan: "How could the fans be drunk? Aren't they monitored on the way in?"

Micah: "What ball games do you go to? Most of the people I know have had a few too many before they show up at the game—the security seems to always miss these guys."

Your oldest friend, Jeremy, asks, "Did you stop and think about what you were getting into before you signed that contract? The mission of the athletic department at Smalltown is rather clear. What did you expect?" He quotes the mantra of the old sage, "Don't complain about where you got, when you didn't plan ahead. A good leader knows what they believe, when to act on it, and how it affects others."

What do you the reader think? What advice would you offer about what occurred at Smalltown?

What Is a Good Leader?

The issue at hand has much to do with the basic values of what makes a good leader and what does not make a good leader. Leadership comes in many different varieties; however, here we will address "good" leadership — that is, leadership that is directed toward a mission of excellence in which all individuals involved are better human beings for the experience. Historically, many great leaders have existed who were malevolent dictators who murdered and butchered millions of people — Mussolini, Hitler, Genghis Khan, and Pol Pot, to name just a few. There have also been other great leaders who changed the face of mankind through their grace, love, kindness, and ability to motivate others to do good in a moral sense — Gandhi, Jesus Christ, and Mother Teresa.

Few of us will be of the caliber of either group in their intensity, motive, or action. What we do know is that leadership can be efficient and effective without being good; the task is how does one become a "good" leader who is also efficient and effective? So what is a good leader in a moral sense?

Dupree (2004) said that good leaders liberate their followers and the followers become better people for the experience. Good leaders influence people to work enthusiastically toward goals that benefit the common good (Hunter, 1998). Leadership comes in many different varieties (see Box 2.1), but "good" leadership is directed toward a mission of excellence in which all individuals involved are better human beings for the experience. What does the "good" represent in good leadership? In ethics, we use the words "good" and "bad" to designate our motives and intentions. As we learned in Chapter 1, a motive is the drive behind our actions. Motives are usually thought out and reasoned as to why we do what we do. Motives are labeled good if they are driven by morality — or improving the lot of others through increasing whatever moral values exist. The motive thus will take into consideration what is known as moral values. For this text we will consider three prime moral values to guide our decision making process: justice, honesty, and beneficence. Moral values are different and unique from non-moral or social values. Moral values are the relative worth that we place on human relationships and all human acts, intentions and motives that affect or impinge on others. Relationships are the determinants of how you value morality. Do I value you as someone of merit? How do I treat you? What importance do I place on my dealings with you? Do I treat you fairly, or do I cheat to gain an advantage for myself? Am I honest with you, or do I lie to you for my own betterment? Do I respect you, or do I disrespect you? Do I harm you, or do I protect you? Again, moral values are the relative worth that is placed on some behavior. Moral values are internal, subjective, and immeasurable in an objective sense. They are traits or dispositions that you esteem and portray. Moral values are usually esteemed in America because human relationships would be difficult to maintain without them.

BOX 2.1 LEADERSHIP STYLES

Many different types or styles of leadership exist in the literature. Each of these may be found in any corporation, athletic department, business enterprise, or educational setting. For example, Goleman (2000) discusses the Authoritative leader who mobilizes people toward a vision and often serves as a catalyst for change; the Participative or Democratic leader who involves others in the decision-making process and builds consensus; the Coaching leader who facilitates individual development, performance, and unique strengths; the Delegating or laissez-faire (affiliative) leader who assumes that highly motivated and competent team members are capable of getting tasks accomplished on their own; the Pacesetting leader who sets high standards for performance as long as the high expectations are not excessive and unending; and the Coercive or autocratic leader who demands immediate compliance. Historically there are numerous other types of leadership styles in the literature: the Bureaucratic leader who is very structured and follows the procedures as they have been established (Weber, 1948); the Charismatic leader who leads by infusing energy and eagerness into their team members; the Autocratic leader who is given or who seizes the power to make decisions alone, having total authority; the Laissez-faire leader (Lewin, Lippitt, & White, 1939) who gives no continuous feedback or supervision because the employees are highly experienced and need little supervision to obtain the expected outcome; the Servant leader (Greenleaf, 2002) who facilitates goal accomplishment by giving team members help when they need it in order to be productive; the Transactional leader (Burns, 2003) who is given power to perform certain tasks or reward or punish for the team's performance; and the Transformation leader who motivates the team to be effective and efficient (Burns, 2003).

What Are Moral Values?

Moral values, unlike non-moral values, have to do with these important contextual points where people come into contact with other people. A non-moral value is the relative worth that we place on objective experiences or things. It is relative in the sense that what you think is valuable may have no effect on others or what another person may think has value. Some may value a new red sports car, while others may value a Land Rover. You may value a Keith Urban tee-shirt; I don't even know who Keith Urban is. Examples of non-moral values are money, fame, power, position, and winning. They are not moral in the sense that they are not people, intentions, motives, deeds, or traits of character that affect other persons. These values are usually "things" or extrinsically based.

However, these non-moral values will drive and affect every moral decision you make. Non-moral values and the non-moral good they bring determine how you make moral decisions. In America, capitalism rewards those who value material goods, success, and winning, all powerful values. The moral question, however, is: How important is winning? Is winning more important than how we treat others? If winning or other non-moral values are "the bottom line," moral values may be seen as useless or silly. As a Division I athlete said, "Hey, it's nice to talk about morality, and I'm as moral as the next guy, but the only thing that matters is winning. I'll do whatever it takes to win, even if I have to knee him in the groin or kick him in the head." Or, "Nobody cares about number 2. Winning is all that matters" (Stoll & Beller, 1992a).

It is the tension between non-moral values—success, fame, fortune, winning—and moral values (honesty, justice, and beneficence) that causes ethical dilemmas to occur. Fortunately, or unfortunately, how we decide which moral values to use to guide our decision-making process is not simplistic or easily done.

Selecting Moral Values

For this text, we are going to limit our discussion of moral values to a specific few. Moral values are numerous and varied, including honesty, honor, truth, respect, sincerity, integrity, justice, duty, cooperation, and so on. The trickiness of working with moral values is deciding which is more important or which can be the basis for making a "good" leadership practice. The very choice of using the adjective "good" in relationship to leadership means that we have an obligation to be concerned with how we treat others. What are the basic and most important ways that we should treat other humans? If we examine certain general, historical, and cultural parameters that can be found in the Holy Bible, the Pali Canon, the Koran, and most societal ethics, we will find some explicit, simple, common and shared values. That is, in all of the above sources certain values surface: justice, honesty, and beneficence. These shared values have a universal appeal because they are imperative to the very nature of human relationships, without which morality does not exist (see Box 2.2).

BOX 2.2 THE NUMBER OF FIRST PRINCIPLES

How many moral values and principles are there? Moral values are varied as we have discussed. Your task is to limit your values so that you can develop a workable set of principles. Too many universal values and principles may conflict with each other; however, only one moral value like love and its accompanying principle of "love your fellow man" may be too general, too abstract, or too vague to be useful in making moral determinations. Therefore more than one is preferable, but more than five is probably ineffective. Writers on the subject of universal principles agree somewhat on the content. Most favor principles based on justice, freedom, and beneficence or non-maleficence. For example, Frankena (1973) reduces the universal principles to (1) distributive justice and (2) beneficence. Fox and DeMarco (2000) state that the universal principles are: (1) Do No Harm, (2) Do Not Be Unfair, and (3) Do Not Violate Another's Freedom. Lickona (1991) calls for only two universal principles: (1) respect for others and (2) responsibility.

Fox and DeMarco (2000) state two general conditions for establishing moral principles that you can apply to both examining your values and developing principles. Principles must be explicit and simple (no abstraction, just basic concrete statements). In developing principles, simplicity is imperative because difficult moral questions must be made easy to understand. Complicated principles affect your efficiency in deliberation and judgment of moral issues; too complicated a principle and you may never resolve the problem.

Sport managers who lead using principles of honesty, justice, and beneficence help educate and set the environment in which participants, coaches, and other sport enthusiasts play by both the letter and intent of the rules (courtesy Michael Everett).

Principles must also be shared, common, and universal (that is, the principles you choose are actually cited by people in many different societies and cultures in various ways.) Common principles are shared by the world's major religions, cultural laws, and knowledge of basic human nature. Because of the universal nature of the principle in relation to other people, the wider the acceptance, the stronger the ability to settle disputes. Realize, however, that universal agreement about a principle is not the complete test. History has shown that some cultures have accepted deviate behavior as the norm. For example, the people of Germany seemed to accept Hitler's genocide of the Jews, which would imply that genocide of Jews was acceptable. Principles must pass various tests of reasonableness and rationality.

The reasonable and rational tests center on: Are your thoughts coherent? Do your thoughts support your convictions? Are you willing to test your reasons by taking others into account? Are you willing to place your principles against the tests of impartiality, consistency, and reflection? Can you submit your principles to the scrutiny of others?

Justice: Moral Value One

Numerous types of justice exist; we will limit our discussion here to three: (1) distributive; (2) procedural; and (3) compensatory. Distributive justice involves the perceived fairness and distributions of benefits and burdens relative to outcomes. Procedural justice involves the perceived fairness of the policies, procedures, and agreements used to determine outcomes. Compensatory justice involves the perceived fairness of making good on a harm or unfairness that a person or persons may have suffered in the past. Interestingly, the types of justice interact in decision-making.

The total relationship of these types of justice is inherent in moral reasoning and moral decision-making in leadership. For example, organized sport organizations have procedural manuals giving the organization direction and focus. These procedures state what is acceptable and unacceptable. If these guidelines are violated, sanctions are imposed in the way of penalty and/or punishment. Organizations have policies and procedures in place for just about every action that occurs. Policies and procedures exist for hiring, evaluation, promotion and termination of employees, for the everyday maintenance of the facility, and for dealing with fans at sporting events. The types and conditions of these policies usually exist to guarantee equity, fairness and safety in opportunity and use within an organization. As such, justice serves as the moral value guiding the decision-making process to develop these policies and procedures.

Distributive justice can be seen in the passing and implementation of Title IX legislation, while compensatory justice involves awarding monetary relief or some form of goods for past misconduct. That is, distributive and compensatory justice must be considered in issues of equity, which refers to gender and racial opportunity, plus opportunity for persons with disabilities. Theoretically, distributive justice is based on integrity for doing the just and equitable right thing. Equitable does not necessarily mean being treated equally or the same in this case. Suppose that you and Joe are both swimmers. You swim for health reasons. Joe is an able-bodied swimmer; you, however, are a paraplegic. If you and Joe are treated the same, there would be no special accommodations for you. You would have to access the facility the same as Joe — no wheelchair ramps and no hydraulic devices to lower you into the pool. In this case it is not fair for you and Joe to be treated the same. For justice to exist, we must realize that equal does not always mean just. Rather, equal must mean that each of us has an equal chance for a good life (Frankena, 1973). This does not mean that justice demands that all lives must be equally good in a non-moral sense, that is, distribution of money, wealth, goods, winning, and success. Rather, justice asks that we treat others equally in the sense that they have the proportionally same contribution to the goodness of their lives in a moral sense. It does not mean that once a certain minimum has been achieved by all, you must distribute all your goods to help others meet the same competitive standard that you have achieved. To do so would be unproductive and possibly fanatical.

Honesty: Moral Value Two

Honesty is the condition or capacity of being truthful or trustworthy in dealing with others. Honesty is dealing fairly and uprightly in speech and action. The moral value of honesty is based on the premise that the actor or agent will not lie, cheat, or steal. (Moral actor or moral agent is common terminology referring to the person who is acting, based on motives and intentions.) For example, the honest person accepts policies, procedures, guidelines, rules, and laws as a necessity. However, if we believe that the rules, guidelines, policies, or actions from them are dishonest or even unjust, we have a responsibility to challenge the policy, procedure, and practice.

For example, let us return to the scenario which began this chapter. You, as the new assistant athletic director, with your personal set of moral values, are being challenged by ethically questionable practices and behaviors that appear to be supported by the athletic department. It appears that the athletic department has not come to grips with certain practices and behaviors as violating the moral principles and purpose of the program. They defend the action as being acceptable under the guise of "competitive." However, since you didn't really look into the mission of the program or have a discussion about the meaning of competition, you are caught in an ethical dilemma one that has several corollary issues — the cheerleaders' and band members' behaviors, the effect on the fans, and the resultant effect on the total athletic program and the institution. You also are confronted with the first and most personal ethical dilemma: should you continue to disagree with the practices of the athletic department and risk losing your position? You also know that if you challenge this behavior, you risk being "blackballed" from further employment in other athletic programs.

Beneficence: Moral Value Three

Beneficence is the condition of (A) not doing harm, (B) preventing harm, (C) removing harm, and (D) doing good. Considering the perspective of competition in this country, we have taken a moral leap by including this value. In the international sense, beneficence might be called "Fair Play," the act of giving to another above and beyond the call of game play, or the act of common civility. For example, in the 1952 Olympic Games, the Italian bobsledder, Carlo Monti, was winning the event, with one team left to compete. Monti also knew that the times had been improving steadily as the competition went on due to ice conditions. At that time, sleds were alike and one part could be interchangeable with another team's sled. When Monti heard that the last team had a broken brake, he removed the brake from his sled, immediately returned to the starting line and gave the opposing team his brake. The opposing team won using Monti's brake. The international "Fair Play" award was given to Monti for his devotion to the concept of fair play. In this situation, Monti decided that the real goal of the competition was that everyone should be able to compete and that he didn't want to win by a forfeit. He wanted to win based on the caliber of his ability, not because of a broken brake. For him, more harm would have been done by a forfeit than by a possible loss, since competition should be the goal, not winning by default which harms the whole purpose of competition. He therefore interceded and helped his competitor replace the brake. He lost the race but he held to his belief about the good that comes from competition and the harm that comes from not doing good.

This moral value is challenged daily in the world of competition and sport. It has been argued that beneficence is too high a standard for true competitors, rather the goal should only be "non-maleficence," that is not doing evil. We argue in this text that if our standard of harm is lowered to this level of avoiding evil, we open the door to a host of evils that will follow. To be beneficent in competition will stretch us and challenge us to "actually" do the good and right. Being beneficent challenges us to actually accomplish the doing of the knowing, valuing, and acting triangle that we discussed in Chapter 1. How does beneficence come into play with our assistant athletic director's ethical dilemma?

Considering the nature of the behaviors of the fans, band, and cheerleaders, we see the tension between "being competitive" and the value of beneficence. Beneficence does *not* dictate that we are wimpy about our performance — that is, not challenging our opponents whether in the board room or on the field of play. However, the amount of harm done must be considered. In this athletic administrator's dilemma, obviously the profanity and in-your-face behaviors are causing harm to the opponents, but harm also occurs to the individuals who chose to perform and condone these acts. If sporting activities exist for the good of the institution, the fans, the students, and the community, then being a party to harmful acts does little for the purpose or the mission of the program.

From Values to Principles

Negative Versus Positive Principles

We offer three moral values that can act as first principles — reasoning tools to help us make ethical decisions as leaders. We have tried to apply these values in a competitive environment. Now we should develop a set of universal principles to follow in our leadership lives.

A principle is technically a statement (in the negative) of our values and beliefs from which all other rules are developed. For example, if I say that I believe that honesty is an imperative moral value, then the principle to follow would be: I will not lie. Let's apply the concept of writing in the negative to the three moral values we selected for our example.

Justice: Principle One — Do Not Be Unfair or Unjust

We mean fair in the sense of simply treating people by both the same set of standards and the more difficult concepts of distributive justice, procedural justice, and compensatory justice. This principle simply stands as a measure of fairness. This principle or First Rule should be applied to everyone it touches. Such a perspective opens a wide array of questions when dealing with equity questions and rule interpretations. Often we confuse the notion of fairness with being equal or the same. However, equal, if strictly applied, would not bring about an equal result. For example, let us assume that we have a rule that states that all people will be treated exactly the same. Suppose that a set of stairs leads into a building and all people are expected to climb the stairs in the same fashion. However, you are in a wheelchair. When you approach that set of stairs, the same rule does not apply because you cannot navigate those stairs in your chair. Hence, the notion of same does not bring about equal treatment. Instead we have a concept of equality — meaning that we should all have the same opportunity to enter the building.

Honesty: Principle Two — Do Not Lie, Cheat, or Steal

The moral value of honesty is framed within three possible negative precepts of lying, cheating, and stealing. Lying is verbal dishonesty. Cheating is being dishonest in action after giving your word, implicitly or explicitly, or making a promise. Stealing is taking something that belongs to someone else.

Lying is more than not "telling the truth," because truth is often relative by time, place, and perspective. Two people who see the same automobile accident will not see the same truth of what occurred. One might see how fast the cars were approaching. The other might see the gender of the drivers. One might swear that he saw what caused the accident and the other might swear that what he saw was not what the first saw. Truth is relative to our perspective. However, we all know when we choose to alter what we believe the truth to be. Lying is purposefully altering what we believe the truth to be.

Cheating is always about breaking an implied or explicit promise. One promises to be faithful to a partner. When one of them chooses to be unfaithful, it is called cheating. In college classrooms, there is an implied promise given to do one's own work. When a student plagiarizes, or takes information from another student's paper or work, that student breaks the implied promise and is known as a cheater.

Stealing is the actual act of taking another's property. It is usually the direct action of taking an objective product from another to keep as one's own.

Beneficence: Principle Three — Do No Harm or Be Uncivil

We have written this principle to take into consideration the four tenets of beneficence: (A) doing no harm; (B) removing harm; (C) preventing harm; and (D) doing good. We are using this principle as the concept of being civil to others and showing common decency. The concept is that you treat others with a certain sense of decency in which you do no harm, you remove harm, you prevent harm, and you attempt to do good.

The difficulty of being beneficent in this case is to know what harm actually is — how is harm defined and how is it measured? The harm can be physical, emotional, or psychological. Physical harm is usually easier to measure for we can see the bruises, the battery, and the broken bones. The effect can be measured in health care costs, or time lost from a job. Emotional or psychological harm is much more difficult to measure. One of the problems of childhood bullying is that the present emotional trauma of the bullying action can cause long-term trauma of that bullying on the individual.

We all could do harm without even knowing that we did it; our ignorance could mask our action. The harm that is usually the source of the problem is intentional harm done to another. This argues that we must be aware of what causes harm and be vigilant to work to do none of it ourselves, to remove it when we see it, and if we can prevent it, to do so.

Doing good is the actual intentional action of helping others.

Applying the Principles

In our athletic director scenario, which of the aforementioned principles apply? At least two apply and probably all three: justice, honesty, and beneficence.

To apply the principles, you need to ask yourself some particular questions.

1. Is justice being served in the athletic director's scenario? Does good competition have a chance to survive or exist when the external conditions are such that equal or fair play cannot occur? If the opposing coach cannot coach, is fair or equal play occurring?
2. Is beneficent action occurring in this situation? Are the people involved holding to the concept of doing no harm, preventing harm, or doing good? Should the band and cheerleaders hold to a higher degree of civility because of their representative positions for the school? Should the athletic director and president be concerned with civility and holding the cheerleaders and band members to a higher standard? Are the fans being civil in their actions?
3. Is civility occurring around the court? Should opposing teams be treated with common decency? Would you want to be treated civilly in the same situation? Why should the standard be different at a basketball game?

Stacking the Principles

If you have more than one principle, they may at times conflict; for example, which is more important, not telling a lie or being just? In the three principles we have written, list which is the most important, second-, and third-most important? Now, use an example in which two of your principles will conflict, such as Do Not Lie and Do No Harm. Decide how you will resolve the problem.

Mary is your good friend. You are both competitive dance skaters. Mary is always highly sensitive about her personal attire; in fact, Mary is sensitive about any negative comments directed toward her. You realize this and understand that though Mary may be too sensitive, she is worth the effort to be a friend. Mary buys a new competitive dance costume that is very expensive. She wears the outfit for a special dress rehearsal in which you and she are preparing to compete, though in different levels. She thinks the costume is gorgeous. When Mary sees you, she tells you about her expensive outfit and how beautiful she thinks it is. In your heart of hearts, you think her choice is just about the ugliest thing you have ever seen. You think it is the wrong style, the wrong color, the wrong length, and the wrong everything for Mary. Mary asks you what you think of the outfit.

Considering the four principles, Mary is asking you to make a moral decision concerning at least two of them, "Do Not Lie and Do No Harm." What would you do?

1. Would you tell Mary the truth, and bear the consequences of her response? Or,
2. Would you tell a little white lie, and tell Mary the outfit is okay? (Would it make any difference if you both were competing in the same event?) If you chose number one, perhaps you believe that the principle of "Do Not Lie" is more important than "Do No Harm." In this perspective, you believe that honesty is the most important value. You decide that truth is more important than Mary's feelings.

If you chose number two, then you may think that being kind is more important than being honest. You took into consideration Mary's sensitivity and think that honesty really is not that important. What is the more right action, not being unkind or telling the truth? In stacking principles, though, you are forced to decide which is more important.

Or perhaps you believe that the issue is a matter of taste, which is a non-moral issue. Therefore you chose number two because in the sense of social tact it is permissible to tell a little white lie (Stoll & Beller, 1992a).

The purpose of moral reasoning is to use a rational, impartial, reasoned system to find solutions to moral questions. When you decide your stacking order, you are bound or obligated to follow this order. Does this mean at all times? Yes, it does unless you can find specific exceptions.

Suppose in this case you argue that "telling the truth" is really hurting Mary. Should you be so bound to a principle that it becomes more important than the person? Perhaps, but principles without context many times cause wrong actions and inconsistencies. In stacking your principles, you need to ask yourself if this moral question is an exception to your principles. If "Do Not Lie" is your most important principle, does it remain so at all times or does this become an exception? Is telling a friend what you see as the truth about a skating outfit an exception to your principle? Reason and rationality tell you that to all principles and ordering of principles there must be exceptions. However, what merits an exception?

3. Suppose that in the skating scenario, you chose an alternative approach. Is there a way to address both honesty and beneficence equally? If you can find a way to place both values on an equal plane, this may be an acceptable alternative and the best solution. You are able to take into consideration both principles and may even argue that the principle.

When you order your First Principles, you decide which is the most and which is the least important. When conflict arises, ordering or stacking principles will suggest which principle is more important. You must also take into consideration, when ordering your principles, if an exception exists. This ordering, though, must remain the same and consistent through all situations. If not, your ability to reason critically and find

Once sport managers have identified the principles that will guide their leadership practices, they must have the courage to follow those principles even when others do not see their value. These principles should guide program direction on and off the field of play.

alternative solutions (the very nature of moral reasoning) becomes greatly diminished and mired in confusion.

From Principles to Rules

As a principle-centered leader, your First Principles will act as basic guides in developing day-to-day rules, which are subordinate to First Rules. The word "rules" in this case can be explicit (like actual written game rules) or implicit unwritten rules (like personal moral guides on being a friend, parent, or spouse). You expect your friends to be trustworthy, loyal, and honest. You expect your partner to be loyal, responsible, and monogamous. Examples of other day-to-day written and perhaps unwritten rules, sometimes called ethics, include professional ethics, business ethics, and medical ethics.

The terms ethics and morality are often interchangeable, but generally we use the word "ethics" to apply to those standards of conduct that groups of people expect from each other. A lawyer is expected NOT to sleep with his clients; a physician is expected to use best practices in the care of his patients; a business is expected to make sure that their products do NO harm; an engineer is expected to follow the accepted and proven guidelines of engineering and developing a product — to do otherwise is unethical behavior.

Unfortunately, daily examples occur when individuals are pushed by the non-moral values of success, fame, fortune, or the bottom line in making decisions, and often an unethical breach occurs. The examples of this are limitless. A classic example is the Challenger tragedy when engineers decided to "fly" the Challenger shuttle when they knew that the O ring was not safe in subzero temperatures (Boisjoly, 2006). When the Challenger shuttle exploded a minute after takeoff in 1985, the ensuing investigation found that ethical breaches occurred throughout the process. Another classic example is the Ford Pinto Scandal. The Pinto's design allowed its fuel tank to be damaged easily in the event of a rear-end collision, which often resulted in deadly fires and explosions. The scandal was heightened when it was alleged that Ford was aware of this design flaw, but refused to pay the minimal expense of a redesign. Ford supposedly decided it would be cheaper to pay off possible lawsuits for resulting deaths than pay for the redesign (Corporate Narc, 2010). In the world of sport management, the scandals usually revolve around violations to NCAA rules, and during any given year one can find example after example. Most of the examples hinge on violating a rule to gain an advantage to win.

Summary

Thus far, you have discovered that reasoning strategies are highly important to solve moral issues in sport. Before you continue, review the precepts of moral reasoning. Critical inquiry is based on rationally determining moral issues. A critical, reasoned inquiry demands accurate, exact, and precise thinking. A reasoned inquiry also takes into account all sides of an issue in its past, present, and future sense. To reason demands that you follow the three tenets of moral reasoning, that is, to be impartial, consistent, and reflective.

In developing your reasoned inquiry, your personal philosophies also come into play. What you believe and who you are colors how you act. That is, your values, both moral and non-moral, are the deciding factors in your moral inquiry. Values determine your principles and your obligations. If you can reason through your values and determine a consistent value system, you will be on your way to a moral standard that can withstand internal and external scrutiny. Once you have discovered your values, you write your universal principles. These First Rules stand for you in developing your personal and professional rules or guides.

What did you decide in the athletic administrator's scenario? Would you have kept quiet and followed the status quo? Would you have stepped up and challenged the status quo? Was there a way in which you could address the moral dilemma offered without finding yourself out of a job? What solutions would you offer to the scenario?

Jeremy: "I think it's really important to figure out what your purpose is as an athletic department. I mean if you watch some of the behaviors of fans out there, I'm not sure that it's the best thing for athletes. I mean, would we accept that kind of fan behavior in the classroom? Let's suppose we don't like the competition of one of our peers, how about we all dress up in some crazy outfit, put on some paint, and when he is taking his test we stand over him shouting at him and cursing him."

Micah: "What are you talking about? The basketball court is not the classroom — what happens on the court is like the 'ethos' of the game. Ethos meaning the character — I listened in philosophy of sport class. It is what is expected out there."

Jareem: "But the behaviors of the fans are way over the top. I think we will have our hands full as sport managers with crowd control. If the university is supposed to be about education, should we really have fans that border on being thugs?"

Micah: "Thugs!!! The fans know when to control it — it's just good fun out there."

Jeremy: "I'm not so sure. Maybe it is time we started to think about why we have sport and athletics."

References

Boisjoly, R. M. (2006). *Ethical Decisions: Morton Thiokol and the Space Shuttle Challenger Disaster*. Retrieved from Online Ethics Center for Engineering and Research: http://www.onlineethics.org/cms/7050.aspx.

Burns, J. M. (2003). *Transforming Leadership*. New York: Grove.

Corporate Narc. (2010). Retrieved from http://www.corporatenarc.com/fordpintoscandal.php.

Dupree, M. (2004). *Leadership Is an Art*. Moberly, MO: Crown.

Fox, R. M., and J. P. DeMarco (2000). *Moral Reasoning: A Philosophical Approach to Applied Ethics*. New York: Harcourt.

Frankena, W. K. (1973). *Ethics* (2nd ed.). Englewood Cliffs, NJ: Prentice Hall.

Goleman, D. (2000). "Leadership that gets results." *Harvard Business Review, 78(2)*, 78–90.

Greenleaf, R. (2002). *Servant Leadership: A Journey Into the Nature of Legitmate Power and Greatness*. Mahwah, NJ: Paulist Press.

Hunter, J. C. (1998). *The Servant: A Simple Story About the True Essence of Leadership*. Roseville, CA: Prima.

Lewin, K., R. Lippitt, and J. White (1939). "Patterns of aggressive behavior in experimentally created 'social climates.'" *The Journal of Social Psychology, 10*, 271–299.

Stoll, S. K., and J. M. Beller (1992a). *Division I Athletes: Sportsmanship Qualities*. Unpublished manuscript, Center for ETHICS*, University of Idaho, Moscow.

Weber, M. (1948). *From Max Weber: Essays in Sociology*. Abingdon, Oxon, Oxford, England: Routledge.

CHAPTER 3

Ethical Values and Principles versus the Challenges Facing Sport Managers and Leaders

- What is the relationship of values and principles to a personal mission statement?
- What are the conflicting social values that challenge a principled mission?
- What is a principle-centered leadership mission?

Introduction

You are in a sport marketing class with your peers when your professor offers you a scenario titled "Finders, Keepers, Losers, Weepers." Your assignment is to work with your peers to find a solution and explain how and why you addressed the dilemma posed.

You are the owner of a sophisticated line of women's sport clothing, known as Sport Tight (ST for short). Your line has been the best in the business for decades and your company and you are known for quality products and business practices. However in the past year, sales have declined from what you perceive is shoddy, yellow advertising or besmirching your products by your closest competitor, BRZ lingerie. BRZ has maligned your reputation as well as your established products and now reigns as number one in this market. As luck would have it, one of your designers brings you BRZ's fall production models. She states that she found the layout in a design class she was taking at the local college. After investigation, she realizes that one of BRZ's people apparently inadvertently left it behind. She excitedly notes that the material is dated and appears to be the latest prototype model for the forthcoming season. She also states that from what she can glean, your company can outdo BRZ easily and win back the lost market share. What do you do based on your stated principles?

A. *Keep the model, tell your designer to be quiet about what she found, and develop a new strategy based on what was found. Losers are weepers. All's fair in love, war, and the sport apparel business. And obviously, BRZ has sloppy, as well as unethical, business practices, which now have caught up with them. It's payback time!*

B. *Tell your designer to return the model to BRZ, emphatically stating that you will have no part in clandestine snooping and warning her that her behavior borders on stealing.*

C. *Tell your designer to return the model, but only after you analyze it thoroughly. You're not a thief, but you're not stupid either.*

D. *Toss the design in the trash. BRZ is a totally unethical business and the managers are not above using this scenario to accuse you of being a thief. You don't want to deal with it—it's better just to get rid of the design. Tell your designer to be quiet.*

E. *Any alternative options.*

You meet with your peers—*Jareem, Megan, Micah and Jeremy*—*to discuss the scenario. You ask them, what would you do?*

Micah, the realist, argues for choice A—finders keepers, losers weepers. "BRZ has been unethical and has blemished the good name of ST for several years now. BRZ's corporate officers are known to be total thieves and have gotten away with it for years. They are miserable human beings who do whatever they can to get ahead. They deserve what they are getting. It's the right thing to do. Besides, that's the nature of competition—when you can get an advantage use it for your benefit. Don't be weak!"

Megan interrupts and states, "BRZ deserves what it gets but you don't want to be a thief either. Just because BRZ is a thief doesn't mean that ST should be a thief, but at the same time—what harm would it do to just take a peek? Business is supposed to be about competition and if you can, through luck, get an advantage, go for it. There is no harm done, but only good will come from it." She argues for letter B—Tell your designer to return the model to BRZ, emphatically stating that you will have no part in clandestine snooping, and warning her that her behavior borders on stealing.

Jareem shouts, "Wait a minute, everybody. You guys are justifying unethical behavior because BRZ is unethical. Is that what you want to do? Are you going to make your decision based on what someone else is doing? This scenario isn't just about BRZ, it's also about ST. In the scenario wasn't there something about ST's mission and what they have stood for all of these years? If its mission is what it says it is, then ST cannot in good conscience do anything but return the model and not look at it.

Micah says, "Jareem, there is nothing in this scenario about mission statement. To quote, ST is 'known for quality products and business practices....' That's not about a mission."

Jeremy cuts in, "Wait a minute; I think Jareem is onto something here. Isn't ST's business practice really about who it is? Isn't what a business does and how it does it sort of define who it is? I mean, it's like character—who we are should always be played out in what we value, think, and do. If ST is about quality practices, then isn't that a mission?

Micah says, "Not really, it's just about what it does when it sells a product. It's like when you compete in a ball game. Let's suppose you always follow the rules, but then you play a pick-up game with some dude who is constantly cheating. The game changes—it's now about who can cheat the most. BRZ is unethical, so they are asking for it. Besides, a mission statement is not that important, well maybe it's important. It's important for the sign on the front door, but it has to be useful. Ethical practices and moral missions only work in a perfect world, and the BRZs of the real world don't play the same game. Besides, BRZ probably has some high and mighty mission statement, but its executives sure don't play by the rules — and that's the way that life is."

You break into the conversation, saying, "Micah's got some good points here. BRZ is unethical, and they are known for their unethical practices. I think that maybe Scenario D would be the best choice. Just throw it away and don't do anything, and tell the designer to keep quiet. If we look at it, won't we be influenced by what we saw, and isn't that a form of stealing? Aren't we already in trouble, since our designer picked it up and brought it to us? Now we are a part of a conspiracy if we go any further."

Jareem says, "Yes, we are in a bad situation here. We don't know if our designer looked at the design or not, and we don't know what BRZ is up to. But we do know what we value and what we believe, and I think that's the most important issue here. It's really not about BRZ, it's about us and who we are."

Megan speaks up, "You know, guys, I think this is a very good example of how hard it is to actually follow a set of ethical principles in the real world. In our classes, we have studied about the importance of knowing what we value and then writing principles about these values. However, in this scenario we are willing to chuck our principles that we wrote and do what just seems the best choice. It appears that we are all about retribution rather than following our own principles (see Box 3.1). Also, it seems to me that these principles should be our guiding light and that we as ST should have a very focused idea of who we are. If we are about good business practices and good products, what do you think our mission would be?"

BOX 3.1

Retribution is the practice of returning an offending action to the originator of the offense in the same form. The exact Latin (*lex talionis*) to English is, "The law of retaliation." The root of this principle is that one of the purposes of the law is to provide equitable retribution for an offended party. It is a punishment identical to the offense. Legal cases which follow the principle of *lex talionis* have one thing in common: prescribed and fitting punishment. This concept can be found as early as Hammurabi's code in 1780 BC: "if a person causes the death of another, the killer will be put to death." Forms of retribution can be found in Judaic law and Islamic law, but is mitigated by later legal systems, especially Roman law which moved toward monetary compensation as a substitute for vengeance.

Jareem says, "Well, if we have a set of ethical principles wouldn't those principles and the values of them be a part of our mission?"

Micah counters, "The public wants to know about how good our product is, not if we are 'civil.' They want to know that we put out a good product and stand behind it. The people who work for us want to know that our business climate and culture (see Box 3.2) is a place where they can be productive and make a good wage."

> **Box 3.2**
> Ethical climate refers to the "feel of the organization" and to activities that have ethical content. It also refers to those aspects of the work environment that constitute ethical behavior. The ethical climate is the feeling about whether we do things right or whether we behave the way we ought to behave according to what we say we believe. Victor and Cullen (1988) suggested that ethical climate includes correct behavior as well as how to handle ethical situations in organizations. A premise of this is that the social conduct of an organization plays a major role in determining whether employees and management behave ethically. The climate can be affected by a variety of management styles (Wimbush & Shepard, 2010).

Megan: "But wouldn't our principles define all of what you just said? Wouldn't our principles set a culture and climate that is respectful, honest, fair, and civil? Wouldn't our principles also define a business practice in which the products that are developed are for the common good, in which the common good is the heart of what you do—I mean like being respectful of that common good? And wouldn't you want your products to reflect honest production and honest distribution—meaning that what you produce is done honestly, which means no cutting corners? Doesn't it also mean that our work is our work and not stolen from another business? Wouldn't we want our product to be sold for a fair price? So I do believe your principles and values affect your product and practices."

Micah: "I think you are getting a little abstract here. BRZ has been getting away with unprincipled behavior for years. Their product is questionable in every way but people buy it because they don't know any different and ST is suffering. ST had better step up to the plate."

Jareem: "I think Megan's right but I think there's more to it. I think the scenario tells us that ST does have a mission statement and if I were writing it I think it would say something like, 'The purpose of ST is to provide a quality product at a fair market value. ST is a company based on certain ethical principles developed from specific moral values. Our community is built on the principles of honesty, fairness, respect, and civility to our employees and our customers.'"

Micah: "Okay, but come on—what has that got to do with the assigned ethical scenario? We are supposed to be deciding how we would answer, not pontificate on mission statements."

Jeremy: "Yes, but how do you decide an ethical dilemma? Do you just wing it at the moment and in a fit of passion make a decision that may affect you for the rest of your life?"

Micah: "Look, I took a class in cognitive psychology and there is a lot of information out there that says that is exactly what we do. We do make judgments very quickly and the process is so quick that it's intuitive. We see and we act: And my gut reaction in this scenario is to pay BRZ back. I bet that the majority of people out there would do the same thing" (see Box 3.3).

> **Box 3.3 Moral Intuition**
> There is an influx of research and data through the study of neuroscience. Moral psychologist Joshua Greene (Greene & Haidt, 2002) used functional Magnetic Resonance Imaging (fMRI) to see what happens in our brains when we respond to moral dilemmas. His subjects were told they could push a person in front of a train in order to save five

others, or throw a switch to the same end. Almost everyone believed it was okay to flip the switch but not okay to push someone. Greene found that those who refused to push had greater activity in parts of the brain associated with emotion than they did in parts of the brain associated with cognitive processing. By contrast, those who were willing to push showed more cognitive activity. Greene interpreted the results as more of a cognitive response. Greene implies that we therefore function often at a more intuitive level.

Jeremy: "Wait a minute. I took the same class—it is true that intuition is a powerful force, but intuition is informed by our experiences and our cognitive development. We are moral agents, but arguing that making a moral decision is on the fly is not exactly the whole of it. Discussing ethical issues is important, and how we discuss them is also related to how we think and learn. Our cognitive development is highly affected by our growth and development (see Box 3.4). It's just too easy to say that moral decision-making is nothing more than intuition. That's why the mission statement is an important part of helping us make moral decisions. We need to take time to figure out who we are, what it is we do and how we do it. A mission is just that: Who is ST? What do they do? And how do they do it? I think Megan is correct; ST's mission would have to be close to her definition: 'The purpose of ST is to provide a quality product at a fair market value. ST is a company based on certain ethical values. Our community is built on the principles of honesty, fairness, respect, and civility to our employees and our customers.'"

BOX 3.4 COGNITIVE MORAL DECISION MAKING

Neuroscience and the use of fMRI experiments have informed us that the process of making moral decisions is more complicated than we know. The brain function and the development of the brain are affected by how we use the brain.

A life spent in mediation, prayer, and serving others develops a brain that is healthy and functioning for long periods of time. The Nun Study (Snowdon, 2001) is rather clear that such is the case. In contrast, a life spent in doing evil to others, lying, cheating, and manipulating has a negative effect on the growth of the moral brain. The brain grows in relation to what it is asked to do. Thus the brain is affected when it is not asked to reflect and think (Tancredi, 2003). What is interesting is that we often do make snap, intuitive judgments; however, the more that the brain is developed by thought, mediation, and practice, the more thoughtful that intuitive response. Micah is correct, we do make intuitive calls, and those decisions are often in a snap moment. However, there is also an inhibitor response that affects the snap response, and that inhibitor is affected by our cognitive and moral growth.

Micah: "Okay, I'll play along but the consumer or our clients want to know concretely what this means. I was listening in those ethics classes and didn't the professor talk about these powerful social values of hard work, dedication, sacrifice, intensity, and teamwork? And didn't that professor also say that competition is a powerful factor which probably supports these social values more than moral values? If that's true, then we need to infuse some social values into that mission statement."

Jeremy: "I agree, but don't we have to be very clear that these social values must be informed by moral values? The professor said, 'You can be a very hard-working rapist,' which means that one can have very strong social values while doing immoral action."

Micah: "Okay, but that's another one of those jumps. Our clients are decent sorts, and so are we. We are not talking here about rape, we are talking about productivity. How do we weave productivity and social values into our mission statement?"

Jareem: "I don't think we have to because they are there. I think we take the mission statement and tweak it just a little: 'The purpose of ST is to provide a quality product at a fair market value. ST is a company based in the values of honesty, fairness, respect, and civility to our employees and our customers.'"

Megan: "As much as I don't like agreeing with Micah, I agree. I think we need more but I don't know if I have the answer. Wouldn't we have to think about this for a while and have our employees think about it and give their input? I mean, it's not just management's mission, it's a company mission, and don't we want our people to actually be a community?" (see Box 3.5).

Box 3.5

Stanley Hauerwas (2001), in his provocative text *Community of Character*, uses the story of "Watership Down" to teach us the importance of stories for social and political life. By paying close attention we can learn about the social ethic of a community through the stories that are told. The fabric of the community rests in the individuals who live and work in that community. If a community enables individuals to be moral individuals, they will grow and thrive. If the community is one in which principles guide its story, then the individual people within that community will also have rich, principled lives.

Micah: "Here we go again—this assignment is not about actually doing a mission and we don't have employees. We are just a study group doing an ethics assignment."

Jeremy: "You are both right. A true mission statement needs input from all concerned parties. I remember reading that a 'community of character' only occurs if everyone is involved, and everyone understands and believes in the purpose and mission of the organization. Disenfranchising people often leads to more problems. Our goal here is to answer the scenario, however, what ST has been and what it practices is how we have to answer the scenario."

Principles, Mission Statements, and Leadership

Thus the debate continues; how does one answer these important questions when they arise? In the authors' experience, we know that if you are ever fired from a position, it will probably be because of a lack of ethical character or a perception of a lack of ethical character. We also know that programs not built on moral principles and a moral mission will self-destruct over time, encompassing all the individuals related to the company, and affect all their lifetime personal stories.

How Do We Develop that Mission? What Is the Process for Accomplishing that Task?

A mission usually is about developing a direction. The mission should be "unreachable," but the goals are realistic as long as there is careful planning. It is the clear and

A mission statement should reflect an organization's values. A truly great mission inspires individuals to want to follow and to be a member of the leadership community in all levels of sport governance.

careful planning that is important. In ST's case, the principles by which the company directs itself gave a focus to its mission. What does the company want to be? What does the company want others to think of when they think of ST? But we must remember that a company is about people; it is people who set the moral tone and the moral mission.

A mission should be short in the number of words used. It should have meaning to all of the organization's members and should state in very clear terms what it is to be a part of that company. A company's values should also direct our attention to the quality of the company's product as well as the quality of the individuals who lead and serve in the company. That is where the rubber truly meets the road. If a company's mission states that it has integrity, then everyone in the company is obligated to work toward integrity — to be free from corruption, and to be whole individuals who believe in the combined qualities of the company and what this means for every individual within the company. A truly great mission inspires individuals to want to follow and to be a member of the leadership community.

A Mission to Inspire Others

David Packard of Hewlett-Packard was interviewed as an old man and was questioned about his theory of leadership. What was it that inspired others to follow him?

Packard did not respond. The interviewer thought the old man had drifted off to sleep, so she repeated the question. Packard looked at her slowly and said, "I don't know that I have a theory. My friend Bill Hewlett and I just always did the things we loved to do, and we were so happy that other people wanted to join us" (Senge, 2002). Packard didn't force anyone to come along. His passion and commitment inspired others to join him. True vision and true commitment will inspire others to follow.

The path to success for any person or group must be based on more than intuition or just a gut reaction. The end product does not always tell the story, and without a well-conceived and well-articulated mission, it is easy to become derailed and to make bad decisions that may affect the rest of our lives. The development of a mission statement built upon sound principles (values) provides an opportunity to progress toward success. The mission articulates the beliefs of the leadership, and the belief system should be grounded in ethical/moral values that will promote individual growth for all. Leadership that promotes the development of individual growth is necessary to optimize group performance (Dupree, 2004; Greenleaf, 2002; Senge, 2002). Perhaps in our scenario ST should consider employing the methodology of servant leadership since its values tend toward a servant mentality.

Servant Leadership

A servant leader is a bottom-up view of leadership. Servant leadership occurs on and off the field. These leaders build relationships with subordinates that will ultimately enable them to identify their talents and abilities as they relate to the organization's mission and purpose.

The modern era concept of servant leadership first emerged with Robert Greenleaf's 1977 work *Servant Leadership*. Following the tradition of virtue ethics and the work of Aristotle (Aristotle & Sachs, 2002), St. Paul (Harrington, 2008), St. Augustine (Augustine, 2009), and St. Thomas Aquinas (Aquinas, 1911), Greenleaf explains that servant leadership begins with the notion that one wants to serve others (Greenleaf, 2002). The servant leader transforms his or her thought process to align with the needs of others rather than with personal desires. The servant leader must change his/her thinking from "what is it that I want?" to "what is it that is needed?" Further, servant leaders perceive their role from the perspective of what impact their actions have on others. The servant leader asks, "do the people who are served, grow as people? Are those served healthier, smarter, more free, more able to make decisions on their own, and do they also want to serve others?" (Greenleaf, 2002). Such a belief and mission nurtures those in the group and the servant leaders empower their subordinates to achieve and succeed beyond personal expectation.

Since Greenleaf's original work, many authors have endeavored to identify the characteristics possessed by the servant leader. Servant leaders have been shown to display integrity, respect, responsibility, honesty, and an ability to empower others and to develop relationships that are communal in nature (Farling, Stone, & Winston, 1999; Hunter, 1998; Laub, 2004).

Servant leadership is a bottom-up view of leadership. The leader builds relationships with subordinates that ultimately will enable them to identify their talents and abilities. The leader assumes the responsibility for providing autonomous opportunity for the subordinates to manifest these talents within the organizational framework. As the subordinates grow in ability and their achievement levels improve, the organization will ultimately prosper and experience gains in productivity (VanMullem, 2009).

Hence, as the leader strives to create a mission for the group, he/she should have first decided the moral, core values that define him/her. In ST's case, the values have been decided — ST is known for "quality business practices." Quality business practices rest on fair business practice and honest dealing. Quality business practice defines how the client is served as well as how the company associates are treated. It fosters a community of trust, fairness, and honesty and respect — a community of integrity. With these basic moral values, ST defines itself.

Considering these values, the leader at ST must also consider his or her actions in relationship to the style of leadership that he or she chooses to employ. We believe that the best style of leadership is one in which every individual grows to his or her potential and every voice has value. Yes, someone needs to be in charge to give direction, but a servant leader leads in such a way that every individual grows. The late legendary basketball coach John Wooden defined leadership as more than forcing people to do what you say. He likened that sort of leadership to being a prison guard. A prison guard can get people to do what he wants. But a good leader inspires others to believe in the leader's philosophy. According to Wooden, a good leader has a mission that inspires others to follow and to do good works. If the only thing that matters is the end results, there probably will be a vacuum of values, which usually results in unethical practice.

A leader must grasp the servant-minded mentality needed to comprehend the concept of servant leadership, a mentality focused on identifying and meeting the needs of those they lead. In other words, the leader is meeting the physical or psychological requirement for the well-being of human beings (Hunter, 1998). Therefore the key to servant leadership is an understanding that great leaders are servants first. They have a belief system that every person is important to the group and has something to offer (Greenleaf, 2002). Servant leadership is about developing trust, and there is no more effective way of displaying trust than proving yourself as a servant first. Greenleaf (2002) stated that a servant leader is defined by one's ability to influence others based on the following three questions: (1) do they grow as persons?; (2) do they become healthier, wiser, freer, and more likely to become servants?; and (3) will the less fortunate not be further deprived?

The decision to develop moral values for a mission statement will support a servant or principled leadership perspective. In ST's case, the values are already there waiting to act as the bases for a servant leadership mission.

Trust Including Honesty

Trust is the glue that binds a leader to his followers (Hunter, 1998). Without trust nothing will happen. A leader must earn the trust of his/her followers first, which then flows outward to the company's clients (Greenleaf, 2002).

In the nature of a servant leader (Dupree, 2004), the leader must not only develop trust but must also affect trust by giving powers to others (see Box 3.6). A true servant leader trusts that the followers can also lead. The servant leader therefore steps back and permits others to lead, recognizing and believing in the strengths of others with their unique abilities and talents. This action of stepping away is a difficult display of leadership for a society built around the hierarchical structure of authority. Casting an iron fist and instilling a sweeping fear among subordinates may provide a quick result but ultimately may do more harm than good (VanMullem, 2009). However, how do the subordinates view their leader? Will they become more productive and efficient and strive for perfection, based on their leader's style? According to Hunter (1998) authority is about you as a person, based on your characteristics and the influence you build with people. A servant leader builds authority through service and sacrifice.

BOX 3.6

Max DuPree (2004), author of *Leadership Is an Art*, who according to Greenleaf was one of the clear thinkers about servant leadership, argued that leaders have to know what they believe and have the confidence to get others to follow them. DuPree's writing on leadership was valued by Greenleaf for his clarity of thought and because Herman Miller furniture is a standard of rare quality, a business where every voice has merit. Herman Miller is consistently recognized as one of *Fortune Magazine's* "Most Admired Companies," having placed at the top of the list for furniture companies for 18 consecutive years up through 2011. The company is also noted for its dedication to a people-focused employee culture, following a servant leadership concept.

Commonly, the concept of servant leadership is confused with providing goodwill. However, the service of a servant leader is action based on belief and ability to help others grow as people. Servant leadership is deeply personal and expresses a genuine compassion for other human beings (Dupree, 2004).

Respect and Responsibility

Lickona (1993) discusses two universal moral laws as the core of universal public morality — respect and responsibility — both of which can be measured by how they promote the good of the individual and the good of the whole community. Respect and responsibility are necessary for health, personal development, interpersonal growth, a democratic society, and a peaceful world.

A value is something of relative but undeniable worth. This value can be a moral value. In Chapter 2 we discussed in detail three of these moral values as universal first principles: justice, honesty, and beneficence. However, there are other moral values, including but not limited to respect and responsibility. A moral value is intrinsic behavior directed towards other humans and carries an obligation to act based on our beliefs or principles. In other words, this is our common decency towards others (Stoll et al., 2009). In contrast, a non-moral value is an extrinsic object, a means to a good life, such as a car or money (Stoll et al., 2009). We value them, give them worth, and consider them very important. However, they are not moral values. A servant leader values people; he or she demonstrates this by displaying respect for each individual. When we give people respect and value them, we do not hurt them (Lickona, 1993).

One of the most important ways in which a servant leader can demonstrate respect for those he or she leads is in the ability to listen. Greenleaf argued that listening is an attitude that shows genuine interest in another. If we can manifest this attitude to truly listen, we have a greater capacity to understand (Greenleaf, 2002).

The act of listening builds rapport and trust in followers. It is a disciplined effort to silence all internal conversations, a true extension of ourselves towards other human beings (Hunter, 1998). In all of us, there is an internal need to be understood; the act of listening is one step towards understanding another person. By listening, a servant leader can build strength in the speaker (Greenleaf, 2002). When a person senses that he or she has been understood, respect develops.

The servant leader will demonstrate respect towards his/her followers by treating them with dignity, practicing active listening, and setting a positive example. A servant leader will demonstrate responsibility by helping others.

The leader has a responsibility to the personal growth of the individual. A leader is accountable for his or her actions. If the leader takes a vested interest in his/her followers, he or she can ignite gigantic leaps in the personal growth of the individual (Greenleaf, 2002).

An environment built on respect and responsibility with passionate leadership and love is the bedrock of a servant leadership. Becoming a positive influence and developing an enduring leadership style begins with humility.

Integrity

Integrity is about the beliefs, attitudes, and behaviors that go into how we make decisions and conduct ourselves in our day-to-day lives. It is who we are in the workplace and at home. Integrity is the quality of one's character, the virtue of habit, and having a commitment to the values of community. Integrity is the total package (Stoll et al., 2009). A good role model leads with integrity.

A component of integrity is the moral value of honesty. An honest individual is free from deception and dedicated to telling the truth (Hunter, 1998). Therefore, the total package for a servant leader is upholding strong moral character values and leading by example through service and sacrifice. This is a leader leading with integrity.

Justice

Stoll and colleagues (Stoll, et al., 2009) have stated that many people in highly competitive situations do not know what is right from what is wrong and that the competitive environment of sport as it is currently practiced is not teaching or developing moral character. Most of us learn about what is right and wrong from our role models, the environment in which we live, and our cognitive experiences about the nature of rightness and wrongness. All of this is also affected by the personal outcomes to us. We measure what we think is fair by watching what happens to others and ourselves; we also decide if we are going to follow the rules by the same measure: do others follow the rules and do these rules really work? We decide if we are going to be fair if we were treated fairly in the same sort of context (VanMullem, 2009). This notion of how we are treated and our experiences will affect our organization, our members within the organization, and everyone connected with the organization (Jordan, Gillentine, & Hunt, 2004).

In summary, proving one self as a servant leader is not an easy task. A servant leader focuses on the good of many rather on the good of the self. The act of caring for others and being able to serve each other is the building block of a good society (Greenleaf, 2002). Therefore a servant leader will demonstrate and embody certain character traits built around an honorable nature, which is truthful and knowing what is the right. A servant leader is focused on doing right, inspires others to do right and is courageous in doing right.

Developing a Mission — Summary

With the moral values defined and addressed, ST can write a mission statement. Just as Megan stated earlier in this chapter, the mission statement should focus on those values. "The purpose of ST is to provide a quality product at a fair market value. ST is a company based on certain ethical values. Our community is built on the principles of honesty, fairness, respect, and civility to our employees and our customers." Such a mission statement has a clear message based on a proven set of values that will keep ST in business. But what about that pesky scenario—what would you do, considering the mission of ST?

References

Aquinas, T. (1911). *The Summa Theologica of St. Thomas Aquinas.* Notre Dame, IN: Ave Maria.

Aristotle and H. Rackham (1935). *Athenian Constitution. Eudemian Ethics. Virtues and Vices.* Cambridge, MA: Loeb Classical Library.

Aristotle and J. Sachs (2002). *Aristotle's Nicomachean Ethics.* Newburyport, MA: Focus.

Augustine; M. Dods, Trans. (2009). *City of God.* Brockton, MA: Peabody.

Dupree, M. (2004). *Leadership Is an Art.* Moberly, MO: Crown.

Farling, M., M. L. Stone, and B. E. Winston (1999). "Servant Leadership. Setting the Stage for Empirical Research." *Journal of Leadership Studies, 6,* 49–72.

Greene, J., and J. Haidt (2002). "How (and Where) Does Moral Judgment Work?" *Trends in Cognitive Sciences, 6,* 517–523.

Greenleaf, R. (2002). *Servant Leadership: A Journey into the Nature of Legitmate Power and Greatness.* Mahwah, NJ: Paulist.

Hauerwas, S. (2001). *Community of Character.* South Bend, IN: University of Notre Dame Press.

Hunter, J. C. (1998). *The Servant: A Simple Story About the True Essence of Leadership.* Roseville, CA: Prima.

Jordan, J. S., J. A. Gillentine, and B. P. Hunt (2004). "The Influence of Fairness: The Application of Organizational Justice in a Team Sport Setting." *International Sports Journal, 8,* 139–149.

Laub, J. (2004). "Defining Servant Leadership: A Recommended Typology for Servant Leadership Studies." *Proceedings of the Servant Leadership Research Roundtable.* Retrieved from http://www.regent.edu/acad/global/publications/conference_.

Lickona, T. (1993). *Educating for Character.* New York: Bantam.

Senge, P. (2002). Afterword. In R. K. Greenleaf, *Servant Leadership* (pp. 350–355). Mahwah, NJ: Paulist.

Snowdon, D. (2001). *Aging with Grace: What the Nun Study Teaches Us About Leading Longer, Healthier, and More Meaningful Lives.* New York: Bantam.

Stoll, S. K. (1989). *Moral Reasoning in Sport.* Moscow, ID: University of Idaho, Department of Health, Physical Education, Recreation, and Dance.

Stoll, S. K., J. M. Beller, P. VanMullem, D. Brunner, and J. Barnes (2009). "Servant Leadership in Coaching." In U. M. Markarov, N. V. Lutkova, and K. A. Kozjemiakin, *Sport Games: Present and Future, Vol. 2* (169–175). Saint Petersburg: Lesgaft, P. F.

Tancredi, L. (2003). *Hardwired for Morality: What Neuroscience Says About Morality.* New York: Cambridge University Press.

VanMullem, P. W. (2009). "An Online Intervention to Improve the Moral Reasoning of NAIA Coaches." (Unpublished doctoral dissertation.) University of Idaho, Moscow.

Victor, B., and J. B. Cullen (1988). "The Organizational Bases of Ethical Work Climates. *Adminstrative Science Quarterly, 33,* 101–125.

Wimbush, J. C., and J. M. Shepard (2010). "Toward an Understanding of Ethical Climate: Its Relationship to Ethical Behavior and Supervisory Influence." *Journal of Business Ethics, 13,* 637–647.

CHAPTER 4

The Conflict between Sportsmanship
and Gamesmanship in Sports

- What is the difference between sportsmanship and gamesmanship and how will these drive your leadership?
- What is the effect of gamesmanship strategies on being a principled leader?
- What is acceptable and unacceptable in using gamesmanship strategies as a sport leader?

Introduction

The problem for any leader is being able to follow one's ethical mission in ordinary circumstances; it becomes more difficult when placed in the context of timely and important issues (see Box 4.1). This chapter will focus on one very important and compelling value that will stress and challenge every ethical leader in sports: Gaining advantage whether it is in the sport management profession or in the sport marketplace. In a highly competitive market, the sport manager who has a principled mission will soon learn the complexities of following that mission when the real world values success and monetary reward more often and more lucratively. In sport management, the dilemma is also stressed by social values within the industry itself, for example, the notion of sportsmanship. There are few if any sport organizations that don't pay some respect to the importance of sportsmanship, including the National Collegiate Athletic Association (NCAA), National Association of Intercollegiate Athletics (NAIA), National Federation of State High School Associations (NFHS), and even professional teams. However, what is said of sportsmanship often is not what we do. Rather, we in America appear to value gamesmanship much more than sportsmanship. For clarification, gamesmanship is the ability to use rules to gain an advantage. It is pushing the rules to gain an advantage without actually openly violating the rule, though the rule usually is bruised and battered. Gamesmanship appears in many different forms throughout sport and the sport culture. In this chapter, we will discuss a variety of gamesmanship tactics to gain advantage whether on the court or in the boardroom.

BOX 4.1 SPORTSMANSHIP: DOES IT EXIST?

Forgive us for using the word sportsmanship. Many individuals are offended by the use of this word, clearly preferring "fair play" or "sportspersonship." We checked the majority of ruling organizations in this country and over 1,920,000 hits occur on Internet sites which are still using the word "sportsmanship." Therefore, since the majority of organizations still use it, we will use the term here. Few people can identify exactly what moral values, principles, or rules sportsmanship is supposed to portray. Historically, sportsmanship derives from our English heritage and is an unwritten moral rule based on the virtues of fairness and honesty. It used to be considered requisite to playing a game. Interestingly, a group's values may not be consistent within the group and each person within the group may have a different understanding of what that word means. The word sportsmanship is often misunderstood. Sportsmanship also is written into playing rules today under the rubric of unsportsmanlike conduct. The word itself is probably a dying entity. Some prefer the term "Fair Play," which has over 12,600,000 hits on the Internet. The Canadian government developed the Fair Play Commission to educate and address issues of sportsmanship, or as they describe it, fair play within sport. In a general search of the sites for the NCAA, NAIA, and NFHS, the language is direct and explicit about sportsmanship and fair play. For example, the NCAA states that its core purpose is to govern competition fairly and in a sportsmanship-like manner (NCAA 2011), while the NAIA states that there is an expectation of ethical, committed scholarship, sportsmanship, and leadership (NAIA, 2011). Of course, the notion of sportsmanship and fair play sits at the very heart of what sport and competition is supposed to be about, and the use of the terms will be found in most sporting organizations, for without fair play the very concept of "playing an activity" does not exist. Warren Fraleigh (1984) argued in a seminal work about fair play, *Right Actions in Sport*, that a game no longer exists if one pushes the rules to the limit or cheats to gain the advantage; Sigmund Loland (2001) also argued for this position in his work, *A Moral Norm System*, saying there must be an accepted value structure of following the rules and playing fairly for a game even to exist.

Will sportsmanship or gamesmanship be the value to drive your leadership? Where is the line of ethical practice between sportsmanship and gamesmanship when managing games or activities for the public? Where and what strategies are acceptable for home-court advantage and which cross the line into unethical practice?

Gamesmanship in Practice

You and your sport marketing peers go to a basketball game at the Coliseum. The game is close and in the waning moments of the fourth quarter the home team is in the lead by two points. They try to slow down the game. Their strategy obviously is to use the shot clock to win. The opposing team in response begins to intentionally foul to stop the clock and force the other team to have to shoot free throws to score. The strategy works. The opposing team is able to recover the rebound on the missed free throw, pass it out, and their star player shoots a successful three-pointer as the buzzer sounds.

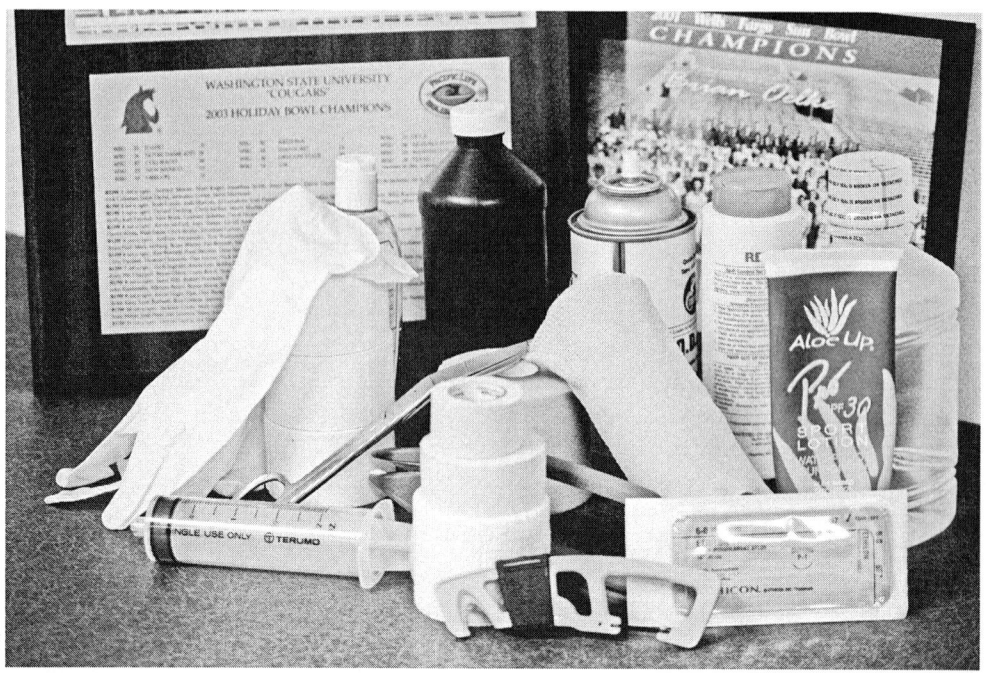

Competition is all about gaining an advantage. In sport many individuals use whatever means possible within and outside the rules to gain an advantage. Principled leaders work to instill values that support the ideal nature of competition.

At a local sports bar after the game, you are rehashing the game with your peers, when the discussion turns to intentional fouls. Jareem, always the idealist, states that using a strategy of intentional fouling is nothing less than cheating. "The rules are clear that certain actions are against the rules and when someone uses the rules to gain an advantage it is clearly cheating."

Micah, the realist, says, "You have got to be kidding!! Everyone knows that intentional fouling is the game. You foul openly—you want the foul, you accept the penalty. That's where the strategy lies. When the opponent misses the free throw, you get the rebound and bingo, you got an advantage. And besides, what about the other team, rather than play they chose to slow down play and use the clock to get an advantage. By your logic, are they cheats also?"

Jareem says, "Yes, they are—both teams are cheating the game. Rather than put their skills out there, they use some sort of deceitful strategy to win. The game should be about being the best that you have to offer. You should want to play to the best of your ability, and you should want your opponent to play to the best of his/her ability. Then winning really means something. Wasn't it A. Bartlett Giamatti, the commissioner of Major League Baseball (MLB), the guy who banned Pete Rose from MLB for gambling on games which he managed, who said something about being obedient to the letter and spirit of the rules so that winning is sweeter still?" (Giamatti, 1988).

Micah laughs, "Little buddy, I worry about you. Did you ever play the game? Games are about strategies as much as they are about motor skills. The game isn't just about how often we can hit the basket; it's also about how well we can outwit and outplay the opponent. There is so much more to the game than just dribbling and shooting" (Hamerslough, 2011).

Jareem says, *"Yeah, but the game has really changed and it's not the pure game anymore. Now it's about how well you can 'waylay' the opponent. The pros are nothing more than big beefy guys pushing around other big beefy guys. It's just not fun to watch. The only pure game of basketball is watching either the women play or high school kids play."*

Megan interrupts, *"Are you making some sort of snide sexist remark about women playing basketball?"*

Jareem: *"No, not in the least. I think the women basically play a pure game. They don't beat themselves up. They truly know how to play what the game is supposed to be."*

Megan: *"When was the last time you watched a woman's game? It is pretty brutal out there. I don't think there is much difference today. However, I think your point about cheating is well taken and I do not think it is just about gender."*

Micah counters, *"Next thing you two will be telling me some drivel about gamesmanship being unethical. Gamesmanship is where it's at. Good players know how to gain an advantage and the only way to get that advantage at times is to push the rules a little. Intentionally fouling is an accepted form of pushing the rules. Everyone knows that the purpose of intentionally fouling is to change the tempo and hope that Lady Luck gives you the opportunity to capitalize on it. We accept gamesmanship as a strategy and a means to win!!"*

Jareem: *"Okay, so would you use the same strategy outside the game of basketball?"*

Micah: *"Maybe, but sport is different, everyone knows that!"*

Jareem: *"Let's suppose that you are the athletic director of Smalltown University. And with your hard work you have finally raised enough money for a new field house. All is going well until you realize that the local city officials have changed the number of handicap access permits from the original 10 slots. They are now demanding 20 places front and center. You have already promised these 10 parking places to your leading donors. Those 10 parking places were part of the deal for the donors; if you lose the places you worry you will lose their money. Most of these donors are hardnosed business folks and they expect perks with their donations. They want to be able to drive right up and walk in. One of the gentlemen has stated often that if he had to walk, he wouldn't come. So you decide to push the rules a little. You go to the authority in charge of mandating the 20 parking place rule and offer a little incentive, four season passes for five years. More passes are available; all the authority has to do is ignore the law and grandfather your field house in under the old law. The city official pauses — he tells you that with another four passes he can make the deal happen. You agree to give eight season passes for five years, and you keep everyone happy. Is this acceptable?"*

Micah: *"Sounds pretty smart to me. No harm, no foul. In business that's how the world works. You scratch my back, I scratch yours. The rules are to be bent to make things work."*

Megan: *"Whoa, wait a minute. This is a lot different from pushing the rules in basketball. I don't think it's the same sort of thing at all. Game rules are sure a lot different from a city ordinance or a federal law."*

Micah: *"What's so different about it? Rules and laws are made by people, and if people can figure out a way to gain an advantage by using the rule or not using the rule, what's the harm? I mean, shouldn't we consider the consequences of the action? In this case, everyone benefits. Without the boosters or donors, the arena won't be built. If the arena isn't built, a lot of money doesn't change hands. Contractors and builders don't make money. The economy suffers. Look at all the people who will have a job building the arena and all those people who staff and maintain the facility. Let's get real here; bending the rule helped a whole lot more people than those who suffered, if they suffered at all."*

 Megan: "Do you mean the people who need those handicap spots? Don't they count?"

 Micah: "Oh give me a break. Have you ever noticed that the handicap slots are always open? I mean at the grocery store, there are all of those handicap parking slots and the majority of them are open, and the rest of us have to park a city block away. And did you ever look at the people who use the handicap slots; most of them need to walk a little. Very few of the people using those slots are truly "handicapped" (see Box 4.2).

BOX 4.2 REVERSIBILITY AND UNIVERSALITY

 Generally we can say that one of the ways to understand a moral issue is to place oneself in the context of the situation. What would it feel like if it happened to you? Would you want this action to have the same effect on you, your loved ones, your family, or your friends? Another practice to follow is universality — would you want this action to become a universal norm, meaning that it is a rule for everyone, everywhere, and at all times? Reversibility places us in the shoes of the other, much like the concept offered by Buber (2008) in his I-Thou approach — by using the simple question, "Would I want this done to me?" Universality simply asks: would we want all humans to be treated this way?

 Jeremy enters the argument. "Wait, wait, wait. People with disabilities are to be valued. Wait, Micah, until you fall into that category — and I promise you, you will. Someday you will have an acute disability, maybe temporary, but you will need some help also, and those parking slots close up will mean a lot to you when it happens to you. The reason we have those assigned slots is because of a little law called the American with Disabilities Act (Justice, 2011). The point of that law is to treat individuals with disabilities with dignity and respect."

 Micah: "Individuals with disabilities? Now we have to be politically correct when talking about handicaps?"

 Jeremy: "I guess you could say politically correct, but I read Jonathan Mooney's (2007) book, The Short Bus, *and I think the author's point is well taken. When we speak of individuals with handicaps as individuals with disabilities, we take the time to realize that they are people and as people we owe them respect. Wasn't it Martin Buber (2008), Jewish theologian and existentialist, who said you should treat others as an extension of you? I think he called it the "I-Thou"* (see Box 4.3).

BOX 4.3 MARTIN BUBER

 In *I and Thou*, Buber (2008) introduced his thesis on human existence — others as an extension of oneself. Buber worked upon the premise of existence as encounter. He explained this philosophy using the word pairs of *Ich-Du* (I-Thou) and *Ich-Es* (I-It) to categorize the modes of consciousness and interaction through which an individual engages with other individuals, inanimate objects, and all reality in general. Philosophically, these word pairs express complex ideas about modes of being — particularly how a person exists and actualizes that existence. If we as human beings could move from the practice of objectifying others, the I-It, our humanity and concern for others would also increase. "I-Thou" is a relationship that stresses the mutual, holistic existence of two beings. Buber argued that seeing others as I-It devalued human beings and the meaning of all existence. Buber's work has been influential in numerous contemporary works and philosophies, including the notion of caring as an alternative moral value to respect, responsibility, justice, and honesty. First mentioned in the work of Carol Gilligan (1982) and then Martin Hoffman (2001) and Nel Noddings (2003), this perspective argues that caring is a higher level of ethics that is steeped in the importance of human relationships. Gilligan's original work, *In a Different Voice*, probably was the single most important work of the decade that forced a rethinking of the Kohlbergian (1981) model of justice as the essential point of understanding moral development.

Micah: "I hate to say this but you all are a bunch of bleeding heart liberals. Look, the point here is weighing the benefits. Think of this like a scale of justice. On one scale we have 10 parking slots for people who don't give money to the arena and who probably won't come to the games, weighed against the other side of the scale with 10 RICH people who give a ton of money and who will make this facility rise—and when the arena is built a whole lot of people get jobs. It is measuring the utility of the situation (see Box 4.4). If you put the good from both of these on a scale, my side weighs more. The harm is almost nonexistent here, but *good is done from using the parking slots to keep the donors happy. Money rushing in to build the arena and putting a lot of people to work is a whole lot of good. I also took an ethics class and remember reading that utilitarian ethics is all about weighing the consequences. Look, we have 99 percent good here and only 1 percent harm, and that harm can be mitigated and the law changed. This is good ethics and good business."*

BOX 4.4 CONSEQUENTIAL AND NON-CONSEQUENTIAL ETHICAL THEORY

Even though numerous varieties exist, ethical normative theory generally falls into two main classes: consequential (teleological or utilitarian) and non-consequential (deontological, deontic, Kantian) ethics. Utilitarian, teleological, and consequential ethics are not exactly the same. Although they basically believe in the concept of the greatest amount of good, the teleological is concerned with moral intention while the consequential is more concerned with the ultimate action for the amount of good. The deontic, as per Kant (1946), would argue that we should act as if every act should become a universal norm. This concept thus bears great weight on the moral agent, or moral actor, for our acts affect others in such a powerful degree that we should pay close attention to them and understand that we have a moral obligation to act in this universal fashion. In contrast, the consequential or utilitarian is concerned about the greatest amount of good that is done by the resultant action. For Mill (2002) this was a justice of utility that must be measured. For a good examination of these theories, see the original sources or these interpretations that are quite readable and understandable (Frankena, 1973, and Fox & DeMarco, 2000). Frankena does an excellent job of explaining the difficulty with weighing harm. In his very short seminal work, he argues that even though there may only be 1 percent harm and 99 percent good, when that 1 percent harm is directed toward you, it is not so easy simply to ignore it. His point is that harm is not an objective, measurable quality that we can measure with a measuring cup. Harm, even a slight amount, has ramifications. He argued for a mixed deontic approach.

Jareem: "Okay, you are just proving that we can use ethics to morally justify just about anything, and in this case you are justifying pushing the rules to get a benefit while only a few suffer. I took that same ethics class and as I remember it, the problem with utilitarian ethics is measuring harm. Can anyone really measure the amount of harm by an objective standard? That is, even one unit of harm that is done to me personally can't be weighed by you. You might say it is only 1 percent but to me it is more like 99 percent?"

Micah: "What? You have got to make that a little clearer!"

Jareem: "Okay let's say you are an individual who suffered polio and are on crutches, you know the kind of crutches that clasp around your forearms and you put your weight on your hands as you shift your weight to move your brace-lined legs. Let's say you are a philosophy professor who came to see one of your students play. You do pretty well in getting around and don't want to use a wheelchair. You drive to our new arena to go to the game. You drive to the handicapped access, but there is no access because the rich boosters have all the spots. So you have to park quite a distance away. It's raining. You have to struggle to get to the arena or choose not to go. When you drive by the rich boosters getting all the parking spots, you begin to take it all very personally. I bet you wouldn't measure it as 1 percent harm."

Micah: "Okay, so you got a point. But I doubt how often this scenario happens."

Megan: "It probably does happen, but our point here shouldn't be driven by the one scenario, we should be considering how we manifest our mission in what we do. I think this one scenario screams for us to consider not just harm done but we probably should also be considering the whole spectrum of the beneficence principle, 'Do no harm? Avoid harm and do good.'"

Micah: "I just don't see the problem here. You can't prove that there is any harm."

Jareem: "We know that a law is being violated through bribery, which has to amount to some harm."

Micah: "Bribery. What bribery, that's called incentive. Look, the law was originally for 10 parking slots. The city upped the number right in the middle of the process. One day it was 10 slots, the next day it was 20. I don't think that there is any harm here in following the former law—and I bet a good attorney would have gotten this grandfathered in before all the wheeling and dealing. This athletic director saved the program the cost of attorney fees and got the job done. I see that as a whole lot of good and very little harm."

Jeremy: "Unfortunately, Micah's argument appears to be quite logical; however, the case in point is not about what we would do. It's about what we should do (see Box 4.5). Jareem didn't give us any more information than the scenario, before answering this. I would want to know our mission as an organization. Does our organization believe in equal opportunity? Do we have an obligation to equal opportunity? What do we believe in? What do I as the CEO believe in? Do I think that all people should have equal access? If I do and if the organization has this standard, I think I am obligated to figure out a better solution. It isn't about expediency, it is about ethical conduct."

BOX 4.5 THE PROBLEM WITH WHAT WE DO AND WHAT WE SHOULD

Generally people want ethics to be useful. They want rules to exist and norms to be standardized so that everyone can just follow what we are supposed to do. However, ethics is not so easy; it is messy business. Decisions can be affected by a multitude of factors, and trying to ferret out the good and bad, right and wrong, is often frustrating and difficult. One thing that we should all remember is that ethical practice should not be based on what "we do" but on what we should be doing based on a clear mission and purpose. Often, we make ethical policy on past practice, or what "we have always done." However, this sort of practice of making ethical policy lies within a theory of ethics called situational ethics. Essentially this is building ethical practice on the basis of particular cases which are then used to determine policy. Usually, we would hear someone say, "Well, that's the way we have always done it." Just because it's always done "this way" doesn't mean that it is necessarily ethical. Past practice may be highly flawed in determining the nature of right and wrong. Historical examples are abundant (i.e., gender equity and racial equity) (see Frankena, 1973).

Micah: "A better solution? What better solution than the donors give the money and we build the arena? Again, no harm, no foul."

Jeremy: "In that same ethics class that we all took, weren't we told that one of the skills and tools of an ethical leader is to find solutions that would be a win-win situation? Is there a way to accomplish the task of keeping the donors happy and still comply with the letter and spirit of the law?" (see Box 4.6).

BOX 4.6 WIN–WIN SITUATIONS

Kretchmar (2005), in his thoughtful text, *Practical Philosophy of Sport and Physical Activity*, argued that most activity in sport has an ethical perspective, for whatever it is about this activity that has value or worth also has an ethical dimension to it. What is it about sport that has value? Why do we think it is so important? Kretchmar argued that this is the soft metaphysics of the activity, meaning the purpose of the activity. Metaphysics in philosophy is the study of reality. Metaphysics focuses on the meaty questions of life, death, God, essence, and being. Kretchmar argued that in sport and athletics there should also be some meaty questions though not of the level of general metaphysics. Rather he called it "soft metaphysics." What is the purpose of sport? Why do we play? Who are we as we play? He argued that once we find the answers to these "meaty" questions in sport or athletics, we will have an easier road to doing ethics. In his first text, he also argued that in order to do ethics: (1) we must become sensitive to moral issues; (2) we must understand the importance of self-respect; (3) we must look for win-win solutions; (4) we must respect and love our craft of sport; and (5) we should search for moral excellence (see Kretchmar, 1994).

Micah: "The spirit of the law?"

Jeremy: "Yes, the spirit is the overarching ethical value that informs the law. Thomas Jefferson said that the law is socialized ethics. We in America say we believe in equal access; we say we want everyone to have equal opportunity. We believe in justice and fairness for all—that's the spirit. It's when we place that spirit into law that we say that we not only believe in equality, we believe also that all of us have a responsibility to enforce that value and there will be consequences if we don't enforce the law. In the case of the handicap spaces, our athletic department could suffer a heavy fine. We would also suffer the consequences of the public knowing that we are basically pretty much hypocrites since our letterhead says we are an equal opportunity employer. That equal opportunity is more than just words on a sheet of paper."

Micah: "You pretty well make me look like a real schmuck! But you still haven't solved the problem of our big-buck donors—if we follow the law, we don't have the donors and we don't build."

Megan: "Surely there is some sort of alternative to this—like how could we make sure our donors don't have to walk and are afforded the specialness that they want? Is this really good ethics that some people get treated differently because they are rich?"

Micah, "Yeah that's right—we might all want to believe in equality but we all know that some people are more equal than others and our donors are an example of that. They have the benefit of a lot more money and don't want to be treated like the common masses."

Jeremy: "True, that is a problem in a free market society; some folks do make more money and some folks make less. Some have the financial ability to buy whatever they want and to influence others through their money. However, in our society the state, that's we the people, has a responsibility to make sure that certain needs are met, and one of those needs is opportunity. Our society doesn't guarantee equality. Our society doesn't say that we all have to have the same amount of money, or the same goods. Rather our society, in focusing on equal opportunity, does not mean the same but rather equal opportunity and equal access (Frankena, 1973). What we do say is that with equal opportunity, each of us decides what we will do with the opportunity. It is ours to decide. If I have the equal opportunity to go to college, then it is up to me to get an education and to see where I can take that. If I want to attend a public arena and watch a football game, and I can't walk or I am limited to a wheel chair, then as a person of disability I might have no access. I should have the same opportunity as an able-bodied person to have access."

Micah: "Look, I'm not against equal opportunity, but I am against the notion that we have to lose a whole ton of money and support because of a law that changed from one set of standards one day to another set of standards the next day."

Jareem: "Yes, that is problematic but we still need to consider the spirit of the law and what it says about us as leaders and about our mission. I want to know what alternatives are available."

Megan: "Right—didn't we learn in one of our classes that in ethical dilemmas we should look for the alternatives and think through the situation? Is there another way to address this situation so that we still follow the rule but still keep our donors happy?"

What Is a Solution?

Megan, Micah, Jeremy, and Jareem have a dilemma on their hands: how does one decide an issue with major consequences. A moral dilemma occurs when two values are in conflict. In this case, which is more important: the value of a law or the value of building a facility that will benefit so many different people. If they choose to follow the spirit and intent of the law, they may upset their donors and lose the monetary support that they need, and thus sacrifice building a facility that will benefit so many people in the long run. In the study of ethics, we know that all of our ethical decisions will be challenged by non-moral values — success, money, and fame. How should this dilemma be solved? Is there a reasoned process that could be followed which would help determine the best direction? Perhaps there are some basic steps to follow. For example, let us consider the following:

1. Step One: Are Any Moral Principles Violated?

Earlier in our text we chose three moral values but mentioned the possibility that others do exist. To refresh our memory, moral principles are the basis of our most fundamental obligations to others. Once established, these principles become guidelines that you can apply at all times. However, everything is not as simple as just developing a principle. If you violate any of your principles, then you must decide whether this action is an exception to the rule or whether your action is morally unacceptable. How do you know when a principle is violated? The answer lies in knowing what you believe, what you value, and what principles you have developed. If you do not know, you will have continual problems with making moral decisions. Your purpose in developing these principles is to foster a sport society that is just, honest, and beneficent. In the scenario about the boosters and accessible parking slots, what do you believe about the worth of the laws in setting criteria for parking at sporting events? Also, in this text we noted that it is important to determine a clear mission statement, and that mission statement must be steeped in moral values that give focus and direction to what we believe and who we are. In Step One, we can use some additional questions to give us direction.

   a. Should rules be followed at all times?
   b. Are there times when rules should not be followed?
   c. Are any moral principles being violated?

If we answer no to any of the above, we move to Step Two.

2. Step Two: Are Any Moral Rules Violated?

Numerous moral day-to-day rules follow directly from each principle that we have developed. These rules govern all behavior whether in sport settings or in the board room. These role-specific rules should guide us; if they do not, we need to address why they are exceptions. However, if we find that there is an exception or we can't follow our rules, then....

3. Step Three: Is This Case an Exception?

Rules may have exceptions, but the exceptions must be justified. The burden of proof of whether this is an exception means that we must show that there is a good, overriding reason for allowing this exception. For example, perhaps an exception occurs if a moral rule is in conflict with a moral principle. Examine a situation involving the moral principle, Do Not Be Unfair. An athlete has asthma and requires a specific drug to compete at the minimum level. The drug, however, is on the "banned drug" list of the governance body. The "banned drug" is a rule: Do Not Use This Drug. But the asthmatic athlete cannot compete in a distributive justice sense. This case is an exception. Therefore if many exceptions exist, perhaps the rule needs to be changed to, "Do not use this drug, unless authorized by a physician for medical conditions to meet minimal performance levels."

4. Step Four: Are the Rules Justified?

Sometimes rules are immoral. Just because a rule exists, doesn't mean that it is infallible. If a rule arbitrarily harms or is unjust, it is a bad rule. When we apply rules, we must ask whether the rule is a good rule. If the rule violates one of our moral principles, we may truthfully say that it is morally wrong, even though there appears to be a good reason for the rule. Throughout history there have been many unjust laws as well as unjust rules. Slavery was legal for centuries before becoming outlawed. It was illegal for women to vote, or for people of color to vote, until laws were overturned. The same is true of rule books in sporting organizations. Historically, we can find many examples of bad rules that were later overturned when the organization discovered after much angst that it was a bad rule. For example, in 1991 the NCAA rule book stated that a staff member of an institution could not provide transportation to an enrolled student athlete unless the student athlete reimbursed the institution or the staff member for the appropriate amount of gas expense. A coach or any athletic personnel could not give an athlete a free or reimbursed ride. Its original intent, motive, and spirit was basically good because the rule was to help make sure that student-athletes did not receive special favors. However, its resultant effect could have brought about bad actions. Suppose that athletic administrator A is driving through a rain storm and sees athlete B walking without benefit of umbrella or raincoat. If athletic administrator A gave athlete B a free ride, she is violating a rule. The NCAA had good reason for the rule, in that the governing organization was trying to keep a rein on unfair inducements or free gifts and benefits. However, the rule in this case was violating two moral principles, "Do Not Be Irresponsible" (letting a human being walk in a rain storm without benefit of protection, when we have protection to offer) and "Do Not Be Unkind" (offering someone a kind service when a kind service is needed). The rule in this case violated two basic moral principles; the rule appeared to be in error in its application to this situation, although maybe not under other circumstances. Today the NCAA does provide funds to a needy student for such things as coats and boots and could prevent the above scenario from occurring. However, the point here is that just because a rule exists does not mean that the rule is ethical, and we should be very diligent in examining rules as to their ethical motive, intention, and action.

5. Step Five: How Can the Rules Be Changed?

If the day-to-day rules are personal rules, action can readily be taken. However, if the changes affect a large social group, such as those made by sport governing bodies or, in our case, the local town council and local statute, a change may require political action, a demonstration, or a legislative move. If you cannot morally function within the rules and change cannot be effected, you may even be morally justified in breaking or violating the rule as long as it is done consistently, within the parameters of our moral principles.

Rules exist to help ensure that the game is played fairly. However, some rules may violate ethical principles. Violating these rules may be acceptable if you cannot morally function within the rules and change cannot be effected, as long as it is done consistently within the parameters of our moral principles.

Let's consider the case of the handicap parking slots. If you choose to use deception on the number of parking slots, you might use the following reasoning process.

1. Does your choice violate any of your moral principles? Yes, it does. It violates the principle of justice as well as the city ordinance and the principle of beneficence (do no harm) as well as the principle of respect. Because your choice does violate at least two principles, you move to question two.

2. Is this case an exception? Yes, you say. You argue that the good that will come from building the arena is more important than the rule, thus you write an exception which states: do not be unjust except in cases where being unjust does a greater good. Or, do not be disrespectful except in cases where being disrespectful results in a greater good.

3. Does the burden of proof state that it is an exception? Can you use this exception in all cases? At this point, you may become hard-pressed to meet the burden of proof. For the burden of proof asks if you can generalize this exception to all cases. Would you want others to follow the same line of reasoning? Would you want other leaders to apply this same exception? What might occur

if you do have such an exception to the rules? "Do not be unjust except in cases where being unjust does a greater good." Our problem now becomes defining the "greater good" and controlling the interpretation of the "greater good."

4. Should the rules be changed? If the exception is strong enough, the rules should be changed. Should the rules now state, "All laws should be followed except when it costs us money or when it costs our donors money," or "all laws should be followed except when it costs money or doesn't get an arena or building built." As you can see, such exceptions become difficult to formulate. Can you write your exception so that it can bear the burden of being universalized to the greater society? Probably not, and if not, what is the solution to this dilemma? In this case, perhaps working with the boosters to find a solution would be more helpful. Let's listen in on what Jeremy suggests.

Jeremy: "Why not ask the donors to help solve the problem? Suppose we went to them, told them our dilemma and offered them an alternative?"

Micah: "Like what? What would be an alternative to having your own parking space?"

Jeremy: "Suppose we offered them a free ride from a parking place away from the front of the building, and we had special student volunteers who picked them up and brought them right into the building. I could just see one of our athletic department golf carts with a sign on it: 'Donor Van.' With the donor's cell phone, the donor could call when he/she was driving into the lot and the 'Donor Van' would be there presto with a student volunteer available to help him/her in and out of the 'Donor Van.' If I were a donor, I would think that was pretty special."

Jareem: "I guess we will have to figure out a lot of alternative thinking to accomplish everything we are going to be dealing with as sport managers."

Micah: "Okay, I get your point here. You may have solved the problem with the parking spaces, but you didn't solve the problem of gamesmanship and intimidation in the game itself. All of us here will be involved in sport marketing in one way or another—selling a product means that we have to be creative to get people in the seats. People want their teams to win, and we all know as former athletes that sometimes we have to push the rules to get an advantage. You guys painted a scenario that is just too ideal to exist in sport today. Gamesmanship is where it's at. I just don't think there is any way around the fact that intimidation and gamesmanship is the game today."

Jeremy: "I agree with you and that is a problem."

Intimidation, Competition, and Sportsmanship

What Is Intimidation?

Much of what occurs today in gamesmanship practices has to do with acts of intimidation whether on the field or in the board room. The following is a discussion of the different influences of intimidation on gamesmanship. To begin, we offer a scenario of often-used language to discuss the meaning of sportsmanship.

At a meeting on sportsmanship, a professional football player was discussing what it meant to be a good sport. He argued that good sportsmanship is linked to how a player treats the opponent before the game, during the timeouts in the game, and after the game. Good sports shake an opponent's hand before and after the game. Good sports help the opposing player up after a good hit. Good sports follow the rules. Good sports win humbly and lose with little, if any, negative trash-talking to the opponent. Good sports value the game and what it means to play fair. In contrast to his fair play rhetoric, this specific professional player is portrayed by the media as an "in your face" opponent. When asked what the place of intimidation was in competition, his response was, "Hey, I'm a good sport between plays and when the game is over. But the bottom line of my job is to physically, mentally, and spiritually take the opponent out of the game." Our question: So then whom would he play against? His response was, "The second-string player, and then do the same thing to him." When asked, "If this is the case, why not go into the opponents' locker room before the game and just shoot the opponent? Then, you could play number two, or on second thought shoot him too, maybe shoot them all and then you would win for sure." His response was, "I would if it was legal, but it's not. The point is that we want to take the other guy out so that we can win. Football is about life and death, as long as everything is done within the rules. Look, it's not just me. It's everyone in my organization. My coach tells me to hate my opponent. My owner doesn't reward me with a better contract until I consistently obliterate the opponent. The fans at my stadium hurl insults and cups of hot coffee at my opponents. It's not a nice world out there. There's what we do — we intimidate to get an advantage just like our opponents try to do to us."

Intimidation

Should we purposefully use intimidation as a tool to win sporting events, either by the players, the coach, the marketing director, the athletic director, the band director, or even the fans? Should we physically, mentally, and spiritually want to take the opponent out of the game? Should we want to play the second-best individual, or perhaps the third-best? Should these tactics be used by leaders in whatever role they play in sport management, from the player to coach to executive?

Intimidation is the act of causing another individual to be cowed, to be fearful, to withdraw, and to bend to another's will. Intimidation is a polarizing activity in that it can occur under two divergent cases: purposeful or non-purposeful intimidation.

Purposeful Coaching Intimidation

We can purposefully cause another to be cowed; that is, we can purposefully decide, either by our actions or words, to cause other people to be afraid of us. While it has been argued that such behavior is questionable as a moral action, the issue will be addressed in this text more in-depth later.

Intimidation has long been used as a means to control the behavior of others. Coaches often use intimidation practices to motivate athletes to behave in certain ways —

that is, to be more aggressive during competition or to attend to and meet the responsibilities of being an athlete. The moral agent, in this case the coach, believes that intimidation will motivate the athlete to act in a certain fashion, through fear of what may otherwise occur. Typical intimidation methods can range from mild tactics such as glaring at the athlete or raising the pitch and tone of the voice, to stronger physical and emotional tactics, such as cursing, throwing objects, kicking, berating, grabbing the jersey or face mask, pushing the athlete, or spitting in their faces. In the psychology literature, these forms of motivation are typically called negative feedback. The constant negative verbal and physical assaults are typically used to "motivate" an athlete to perform his or her best. Often, however, these forms of negative feedback set a motivational climate that is outcome/ego oriented — one whereby the focus is on the individual in relation to the win, the goal, rather than a performance/task/mastery environment—whereby the focus is on individual performance goals and mastery of skills, strategies, and so forth. Positive motivation (positive feedback) tends to set a climate focused towards the performance/task/mastery environment. Thus, according to researchers, performance is best improved if the motivation climate is set using positive feedback.

The authors once asked a highly intimidating coach why he used such strong negative feedback practices to motivate, considering that most of the psychological research today supports the notion of positive motivation techniques — those that uplift the athlete—rather than negative motivation—those that tear away at the athlete's psyche. It has long been documented that though both techniques work, positive motivational techniques, in the long run, are better for the athlete, better for the coach, better for the sport, and even better for the fans. The coach responded that although the research might be true, negative motivation gets the job done quickly and with little investment of his time. We noted that in a baseball game during the seventh inning stretch, he used the "f" word 27 times. What exactly did that do — wouldn't the athletes become immune after about the tenth time? His response was, "A coach doesn't have the time or energy to be worried about who needs what form of motivation — positive or negative. Cursing and screaming gets the job done quickly and I can spend my time concentrating on strategy." He also noted that his method has been highly successful. History and tradition were in his favor. He has won numerous local, regional, and even national titles, and several of his athletes have been drafted into the professional league. Little doubt exists that his technique works. The question is whether positive motivation techniques may be as good if not more productive in motivating the athlete.

Of course, intentional intimidation can also occur in the office, in the hallway, in the stands, or wherever people are congregated. In the office, examples of intimidation can occur with the boss yelling at an employee for not doing his or her work in a timely fashion, an executive secretary berating an internship student for not doing the assigned work correctly, an athletic trainer screaming at a student trainer for not being quick enough in a response, or anyone swearing at or belittling a co-worker who does not meet our specifications for doing a job. In all cases, the actions are purposeful.

If intimidation is intentionally practiced, then the action becomes a moral issue. As noted in our first three chapters, if the moral agent has motive and intention to violate another, the agent's action becomes a moral issue. At this point we need to take intimidation and the practice of negative intimidation a step further.

Non-Purposeful Coaching or Leadership Intimidation

Intimidation can occur with no purposeful motive, intention or action of the moral agent. That is, the demeanor and professional position of many individuals, without any overt decision to be intimidating, may cause others to be intimidated. Because of college professors' professional demeanor, professional position, or even professional dress, college students often find their professors intimidating. Employees may be intimidated by their supervisors not because of any direct action, but because of the employees' perception of what the supervisors might or might not do, just because the boss is the boss. Children may be intimidated by an adult, not because of anything the adult did, but because of the adult's size, the depth and strength of their voices, or the manner in which they walk or wear their clothes. Athletes may often be intimidated by a coach because of his/her reputation. The reputation may be based on the success ratio of wins to losses, the coach's professional experience, or simply the coach's position. Perception is the key to the problem. The moral agent is perceived as an intimidating individual and thus the moral receiver behaves in a certain way, fears the agent, and may avoid contact with the agent at all costs. If the moral agent has no intention or motivation to intimidate, the resultant perception of the receiver is not the fault of the agent. Some could argue that if the moral agent knows that his/her position, dress, carriage, voice, size, or position intimidates others, that agent should seek out different practices. That is, if children are overtly intimidated by the size of the agent, the agent could speak gently to the child, kneel down to speak with the child, or be less brusque in physical actions. However, many times the moral agent has no notion that others are intimidated by them. As such, the moral agent is not responsible for the ensuing intimidation. But remember that each of us perceives our world and the motives and intentions of others differently. As such, what one of us may perceive of as intimidating in an individual, another may not. Because perception is an individual view of the world and our perception of another's motives and intentions is unknown, perception cannot be the basis for deciding moral issues.

Intimidation from the Player's or Worker's Point of View

Intimidation is also part of the bag of tricks that athletes use to gain an advantage over an opponent. An athlete will argue that if the opponent is intimidated, the feeling of intimidation will psychologically take the opponent out of the game. If the opponent is cowed then the athlete or moral agent will have an opportunity to gain the edge and win the game. This same practice can be used in the board room, classroom, locker room, or family. Many times it can be called by another title: bullying. It becomes a moral issue when it is intentional to do harm. It is not a moral issue if it is unintentional. Intimidation is a double-edged sword as well; it can again be purposeful or non-purposeful.

Purposeful Intimidation by the Athlete

Purposeful intimidation by the athlete is the direct motivation, intention, and action to somehow take the opposing player out of the game. Usually the purposeful activity revolves around psychological tricks such as preening or strutting before, during, or after the game. For example, a gymnast might practice psychological intimidation by purposefully and repeatedly doing her hardest trick before the meet begins so that the competition will worry about their ability to meet the challenge. Or a basketball player during warm-ups might make numerous difficult shots and strut his or her stuff, so that opponents will notice and have concern about that player's ability in the game.

Generally, purposeful psychological intimidation occurs through the art and science of trash talking. Though outlawed by most amateur sport ruling bodies, trash talking is as common as putting on a game uniform. Trash talking is the verbal act of berating the opponent. The athlete will chide the opponent on his lack of skill, physical size, competitive demeanor, or any other attribute that might be in question, "Is that all you got? My Mamma plays better than you!" "You suck!" The Hollywood movie *White Men Can't Jump* not only has a trash talking title, but is replete with every creative notion of how one can trash other players. Trash talking exists in youth sports, school sports, collegiate sports, and of course, by the time a player makes it to the pros that player has become an expert in using it. Women practice it, children practice it, and fans practice it. The question becomes: if it is common practice, why not let it exist? If it is so commonly practiced, is it really a moral issue?

Sport sociologist Keith Harrison (K. Harrison, personal communication, October, 2007) has argued that trash talking grew from the jive of the intercity playground. Some trace its origin from an inner city game called "Playing the Dozens," "Basing," or "Jonesing," whereby the goal is to use words and trash talking to gain an advantage. As a cultural practice, trash talking moved from the playground to the court and the field of play. Its purpose may be intimidation but Harrison argues that the trash talking is not about doing any type of physical or emotional damage. Rather, the African American athlete may use trash talking as a way of bringing the game up to a higher level. Athletes will argue that trash talking makes them more psyched to play the game, and if they are denied the use of trash talking, they will lose a motivational edge. Trash talking, in this sense, may actually be a way of celebrating the very act of competition. Harrison argues that trash talking has been outlawed because of its African American roots and that the outlawing is really a form of racism — denying the worth of a cultural practice. Harrison also notes that trash talking today is definitely not limited in practice to African American players; he tells us that many white players have now honed their trash-talking skills.

Eassom (S. Eassom, personal communication, October, 2007) notes that name calling or trash talking is only what we make of it. He states that just because a "crazy old man" down the road says nasty things to us, it doesn't mean that we have to listen, and there's nothing personal meant by it anyway. Just like ignoring the crazy old man, the athlete learns how to "not listen" or tune out the trash talking that occurs with sport.

In contrast to Harrison's and Eassom's points of view, Dixon (2007) argues that trash talking, with all the notion of cultural practice, is still words, and "words hurt."

He asks, "Have we learned nothing about hurtful words from the history of racism and sexism? Have we not learned that it is hurtful to call women and different ethnic groups names? Have we not learned that words are hurtful? And have we not as a culture learned that such words can be legally interpreted as sexual and racial harassment? Is it necessary to say hurtful words to play the game and to play it well? Is sport supposed to be about psychological games of hurtful words?"

Rudd and Stoll (1998) argue that trash talking is a moral issue because when trash talking is practiced individuals show disrespect toward others for their own personal gain. Hence, if the action of trash talking occurs and is purposeful, a moral dilemma occurs. The athlete has a choice whether to trash talk or not, and if the athlete chooses to trash talk, disrespect is shown.

Physical Purposeful Intimidation

If an athlete goes onto the court or field and intentionally acts to "take out" the opponent through a physical act, physical intimidation occurs. The direct purpose of physical intimidation may not be long-lasting injury, but just enough to make the opponent think twice before acting, to ring his bell hard enough and long enough that just a glint of fear exists. This issue of physical intimidation becomes cloudy when the practice of sport is about physical aggression (i.e., ice hockey, lacrosse, football, and today even basketball). The athlete uses the body against an opponent's body to gain the prize. The football player blocks and tackles; ice hockey, lacrosse, and basketball players all make contact (though basketball players can be penalized). Players involved in physical contact sports argue that the physical contact and the aggression of the game are what these games are about. "There's nothing better in sport, especially football, than the sound of two bodies hitting as hard as they can." "Lacrosse is about violence." "Wimps don't play ice hockey."

All of these comments may be true, and we concede that physical aggression and physical contact are integral parts of contact sports (see Non–Purposeful Physical Intimidation). However, if the athlete as moral agent intentionally tries to "take out the opponent," a moral issue is raised. If the intention is to take out the player, who plays then? The second-string person, the trainer? Or is playing not the point? If not, the only purpose would be to increase the chances for a win to occur. If playing games in sport is about using one's mental finesse and physical skill, it is illogical and unethical to want to decrease the opportunity to use one's best skills to play the game.

If the purposeful intention and motivation are to psychologically and physically take the opponent out of the game, a moral issue arises because the athlete is neither being just nor responsible in his/her action toward the opponent. It matters not what is accepted practice.

Non-Purposeful Athletic Psychological and Physical Intimidation

As with non-purposeful intimidation by the coach, the same can and does occur for the athlete. Athletes by their very nature can intimidate their opponents; that is, their size, demeanor, and physical skill may cause the opponent to be intimidated, with no motive and intention to do so. However, this case is not a moral issue because the athlete is not going about his or her activity with any purposeful negative motive and/or intention toward the opponent. It is true that the resultant action of a sport practice may intimidate, but in this sense the athlete is not responsible — as it is a matter of perception. Remember, in this case, the moral agent is not responsible for how an athlete interprets the final action. The world would be better if good motives and good intentions were interpreted as right action, but in sport many times they are not. For example, many years ago one of the authors was coaching high school gymnastics. As is the nature of a gymnastics meet, gymnasts from opposing teams were warming up by going through their routines. As the coach, I was waiting with my gymnast for another, very talented, gymnast to finish her beam routine. As she dismounted, I said to my athlete and to her, "That was a great routine, we wish you good luck today." The athlete never responded to me but did say to her coach, "What did she mean by that?" Her coach turned toward me in disgust and said, "Ignore them; they're just trying to psyche you out." However, there was no motive or intention to psyche out this young athlete. I truly enjoyed what I saw and truly wished her luck. My athlete, who watched and sort of participated in the drama, had a different perception of the unfolding events. She thought the coach was being rude and obnoxious, and said, loud enough for about everyone in the facility to hear, "Coach, why don't you punch out her lights!"

As pedagogists would say, this was a teachable moment. We talked about the situation and about the fact that good motives and good intentions are still good no matter how the other individual interprets the final action. Interestingly, the opposing gymnast must have been psyched out, because she was a good practice performer but a poor meet performer. She fell numerous times, which she had not done in practice, and her performance doomed her team's chances of winning — they lost that day. Perhaps the coach's negative perspective had an influence, perhaps my good motives and good intentions had an effect, or perhaps the athlete and her coach had some other psychological performance problem. I'll never know, but my athlete and I learned a great deal that day about non-purposeful intimidation. We had no control over the interpretation of an innocent, supportive remark. I do know that in all future meets for the next four years while I finished my tenure as a high school coach, I was careful not to make any comments to this team and, for that matter, all other opponents, which was a shame. We buckled under and played the game in which none of us made any positive comments or supporting remarks, or displayed any appreciation for another's skill. Sport took a real hit that day and I, my athletes, and our opponents were the worse for it.

Non-Purposeful Physical Intimidation

Injury and physical harm may occur to an opponent with no intention on the part of the offending athlete; in this case the same sort of thinking applies that occurs with non-purposeful intimidation. Injuries do occur. Physical contact does happen. Accidents do occur. However, if the motive and intention is not about causing injury, then the resultant action is not a moral question. Athletes take the risk; the chance is that an injury may occur. Playing sport is risky behavior. Sport is not for the faint of heart or the "wimps" of the world. The players go out and give it their best shot. They give their all. It's not about half-hearted activity. Players blocking in football do so with every fiber of their being. If one is blocking a shot in basketball, one does it with the whole self. When activity is physical and opponents are physical, the chance of injury always exists. The injury only becomes questionable as a moral issue if the motive and intention of the athlete is to "physically harm." This may seem like a bit of fancy rhetoric considering the physicality of many contact sports. Basketball players intentionally use their bodies, arms, and legs to "clear the boards." Football players intentionally use all of their strength, mass, and accumulating force to "hit" as hard as they can. Hockey players "check" with determination and gusto. However, it is a different concept entirely if the athlete does all of the above intentionally. One can intentionally go out to give the hardest hit ever without intentionally thinking that my job is to "crush" this guy's skull. Even through the activity might appear brutish, the resultant action may be innocent of intentional moral harm. However, there is a caveat. We know today that too much physical contact may cause "great" harm in the form of concussions.

Of course, one could always argue that any activity that celebrates aggression has a moral question mark next to its name. However, such an argument, if supported, would necessitate the end to numerous activities in which physical aggression is necessary to play the game. Perhaps it is so ... that all activities that abound with physical aggression should be banned. Perhaps, perhaps not. Hamerslough (2011) as well as McNamee and Parry (1998) have argued that violent sports have no place in moral activities.

External Forms of Intimidation

While intimidation occurs on the playing field between players, players and coaches, and coaches and referees, a major piece of the puzzle involves external intimidation. In this sense, we mean influences that affect the game that are external to the game. Under this category fall the influences and actions of fans, parents, coaches, administrators, media, and others who are not directly involved in the game play itself or on the field of play. The belief by many is that because they have bought a ticket, they not only have the right, but the obligation to their team, to influence the game through all sorts of intimidating practices. Mild forms of purposeful intimidation involve such practices as: (1) distributing very large, over-filled balloons to basketball fans so they can wave the balloons behind the bucket in an attempt to throw off the shooter's focus on the basket; (2) having the school band stand behind opposing players' bench during time-outs playing as loudly as possible; and (3) using fans moving *Playboy* centerfold pin-ups behind the basket to interrupt a player's concentration. Individuals practicing these actions argue that it is the coach's responsibility to teach players to ignore attempted distractions and that, after all, the opposing team's fans have the same opportunity to intimidate—in other words all is fair in love, war, and basketball.

While many sport enthusiasts argue that these forms of intimidation are just a natural part of the game as well as showing that one is "being a true fan," purposeful intimidation has taken on new, detrimental, obscene practices. For example, in a recent basketball game that one of the authors attended, the student section chanted the following for most of the game at the opposing team's and league's star: "One, two, three, four, Davis' mother is a whore. Five, six, and seven eight, Davis loves to masturbate." The chant became so loud that the public radio station broadcasting the game had to turn down the volume, as they could not broadcast the statements and language on a "family" radio station. The following morning the local newspaper also carried a column abhorring the student section's action, claiming the students were worse than the coach in verbal abuse. When administrators who were in attendance and heard the chants were queried, their response was, "They don't mean it; it's not meant to be personal; they are just supporting their team." However, the next day, the president of the university came forth with a call to the community to be civil. Interestingly, though, the tactic appeared to work. The player who received the most taunting was held to 18 fewer points than his season average and his team lost a close game.

External unethical intimidation, though, is not limited to practices during the game itself. For example, a high school coach decided that for his team to gain an edge over the cross-town opposing team in the district championship game, he needed to intimidate the opposing players. He called a local florist, hired a hearse and driver, and had delivered to each opposing player and coach a wilted, dead rose and a card that said, "Wishing you the worst in Saturday's game."

As future leaders in sport, you will deal with the temptation to use intimidation or gamesmanship strategies to gain an advantage. These strategies can occur on the field — from how the field is maintained or not maintained for the coming game, to how the locker rooms are supplied for the opposing teams. One of the more famous strategies was used by Paul Brown at Massillon, Ohio, who in 1928 trained his basketball team in a steam-filled gymnasium. When the opposing team showed up, they couldn't perform. Well, they could but not very well. Or the typical and often heard practices of growing the grass longer on the football field so that the opposing team can't run as fast. The list of possibilities for treating others, especially the opposing teams, as an I-It, rather than an I-Thou as Buber (2008) noted, includes making sure that visiting locker rooms have no water available, no toilet paper, or no heat in the dead of winter. If the goal is to follow a principled mission statement and treat others in a just, fair, honest, respectful, and beneficent climate, then thought must be given to how that is accomplished. One of the best ways to do that is to consider the opponents as an extension of you.

Jeremy: "If we want our opponents to do their best and if we want to be sportsmen, then we have a duty and obligation to treat them as we would want to be treated with respect. Unfortunately, the philosophy of gamesmanship really limits what we can and what we should do. Following your ethical mission is difficult when so many opposing forces work against you."

Micah: "So are you saying that the 'good foul' isn't good?"

Jeremy: "No, I'm not saying that the good foul is not good, I'm saying that when the fouling becomes so blatant that the game suffers and we suffer because of what we do — maybe we need to consider how important it is to get that advantage."

Micah: *"You gotta know that not many people are going to agree with this sort of thinking—it's pretty ideal."*

Jeremy: *"Maybe we need a few idealists out there."*

References

Buber, M. (2008). *I and Thou*. London: Hesperides.

Dixon, N. (2007). "Trash Talking, Respect for Opponents and Good Competition." *Sport Ethics and Philosophy, 1,* 96–106.

Fox, R. M., and J. P. DeMarco (2000). *Moral Reasoning: A Philosophical Approach to Applied Ethics*. New York: Harcourt.

Fraleigh, W. (1984). *Right Actions in Sport*. Champaign, IL: Human Kinetics.

Frankena, W. K. (1973). *Ethics* (2nd ed.). Englewood Cliffs, NJ: Prentice Hall.

Giamatti, A. B. (1988). *A Free and Ordered Space: The Real World of the University*. New York: Norton.

Gilligan, C. (1982). *In a Different Voice: Psychological Theory and Women's Development*. Cambridge, MA: Harvard University Press.

Hamerslough, W. (2011, October). "Is Sport a Moral Activity?" *Western Society for Wellness and Kinesiology, Keynote Address*. Reno, NV.

Hoffman, M. (2001). *Empathy and Moral Development: Implications for Caring and Justice*. New York: Cambridge University Press.

Justice, D. O. (2011). *Americans with Disabilities Act of 1990, As Amended*. Retrieved from http://www.ada.gov/pubs/ada.htm.

Kant, I. (1946). *The Moral Law: The Groundwork of the Metaphysic of Morals*. New York: Barnes & Noble.

Kohlberg, L. (1981). *Essays on Moral Development: Vol. 1: The Philosophy of Moral Development*. San Francisco: Harper & Row.

Kretchmar, R. S. (2000). "Moving and Being Moved: Implications for Practice." *Quest, 52,* 260–272.

Kretchmar, R. S. (2005). *Practical Philosophy of Sport and Physical Activity* (2nd ed.). Champaign, IL: Human Kinetics.

Loland, S. (2001). *Fair Play in Sport: A Moral Norm System*. London: Routledge.

McNamee, M., and S. J. Parry (1998). *Ethics and Sport*. London: E&FN Spon.

Mill, J. S. (2002). *Utilitarianism*. Indianapolis: Hackett.

Mooney, J. (2007). *The Short Bus: A Journey Beyond Normal*. New York: Henry Holt.

National Association of Intercollegiate Athletics. (2011). *History of the NAIA*. Retrieved from http://naia.cstv.com/genrel/090905aai.html.

National Collegiate Athletic Association. (2011). *About the NCAA*. Retrieved from http://www.ncaa.org/wps/wcm/connect/public/ncaa/about+the+ncaa.

Noddings, N. (2003). *Caring: A Feminine Approach to Ethics and Moral Education*. Los Angeles: University of California.

Rudd, A., and S. K. Stoll (1998). Understanding Sportsmanship. *Journal of Physical Education, Recreation, and Dance, 69(9),* 38–42.

CHAPTER 5

Violence in Sports

- What is violence?
- What are constitutive, proscriptive, and sportsmanship rules?
- Were some sport rules established specifically to attempt to prevent violent behavior in sports?
- Does violence include only physical acts, or does it involve psychological ploys, too?
- Why does violence in sports exist, and why is it condoned?
- How has the emphasis on winning influenced violence in sports?
- What are several controls that could reduce or prevent violence in sports?

You and your sport management friends are walking back from an ice hockey game at the university ice arena. Both Micah and Jeremy played ice hockey in high school and are explaining the finer points of the game to the rest of you. Micah informs everyone that he has two crowns for his two front teeth and then laughs heartily about how it was one of the great shots of all time. Jeremy mentions the number of concussions he has had and begins a contest of who was decked the most often in his career.

Megan, who is strolling arm-in-arm with Jareem, says, "You men just are unreal. You act like getting knocked out is some necessary condition to being manly. I personally think that your game is brutish and it's even worse than football."

Jareem: "Brutish? Football, brutish? Football is the greatest game ever created. It is a game grown in the civilization of American dynasty—if Vince Lombardi didn't say that he should have."

Megan: "The greatest game ever? The game to me is all about seeing how many guys can beat up other guys. There is absolutely nothing about the game that inspires character or the development of principled individuals."

Micah: "What are you talking about?"

Megan: "Last week in our sport marketing class Professor Jones gave us some information on what it means to be a principle-centered leader."

Micah: "What has that to do with our discussion right now? We are talking football here."

Megan: "Let me see. Didn't Professor Jones say that 'Principle-centered leaders are com-

mitted to and guided by enduring values like integrity and respect for others that lead to success when shared with followers.'?"

Jeremy: "Yes, so?"

Megan: "How do you play football and respect another human being when all you guys want to do is 'take the other guy out'?"

Jareem: "But that is respecting the other guy: You hit him before he hits you. You share the respect of a good hit."

Megan: "Share the respect of a good hit? How can you calmly stand there and say that it is permissible to 'hit' another human being? You of all people — you are the most conservative of all of us. You are the most ideal. In all our discussions for the past three years, you have argued and argued about principles. I mean, wasn't it you that wrote in our paper about mission and principles something like, 'Principle-centered leaders apply moral and ethical standards in determining what is right and wrong and good and bad. Principle-centered leaders personify universal virtues such as responsibility, compassion, and loyalty. Principle-centered leaders ensure that values and virtues become central to and the core of organizations and the passionate focus of everyone involved. Principle-centered leaders are individuals of character who let principles guide their actions and help shape the actions of others. The consummate goal of principle-centered leaders is to stand for and act upon what is good and right and influence their organizations to do the same.'"

Jareem: "Yes, I did. I believe that, too, but that has nothing to do with the greatest game of mankind. All four of us guys here played at one time. We love the game. The game is about physicality and contact."

Megan: "Oh, really. I just sat through four quarters or whatever it is in ice hockey of watching the four of you yell borderline obscenities at the other team. And I heard you, Jareem, yell, 'Kill the bum!' when one of their players made a goal."

Jareem: "Nobody is serious when they yell that stuff, it's just what goes on at ice hockey or even football games. It's not personal."

Megan: "Oh really, if you yelled that at Professor Jones when you got a C on that last test, I bet she would have 'taken it seriously.' I couldn't believe the way you acted throughout the game. Where was the idealist? Aren't you being a hypocrite?"

Jareem: "Hypocrite because I enjoy an ice hockey or football game?"

Megan: "Look, I have heard you argue about the ideal nature of sport and the ideal perspective of a principled leader. It would seem to me that violence just can't be a part of such a perspective?"

Jareem and Jeremy: "Violence? Are you trying to tell us that ice hockey is bad?"

Megan: "What I'm trying to tell Jareem is that he is being inconsistent in his philosophy. He has argued about what he perceives a principled leader to be, I think he would agree. I think that if Jareem wrote something about violence he would say, 'Principle-centered leaders never condone wanton violence in sports.'"

Jareem: "Yeah, I would write something like that— but playing a game of football or ice hockey is not about 'wanton violence.'"

Megan: "Oh really, when I watched the game today it seemed to me there was a lot of 'wanton violence' going on. I saw two guys take off their gloves and they were pretty well pounding each other. I also saw Micah standing up and sparring in the air like he was coaching them in how to take the other guy out. The fans were yelling and cheering—I couldn't believe the language, and there were some children down there in front of me. One of them was cursing, too—it looked to me like everyone was really into it. It reminded me of people who go to a NASCAR event and hope for a huge pileup."

Micah: "Yeah—that was a great fight. Did you see how many guys got into that one? I mean, both teams were on the ice duking it out. It was great!!! Wonder how many stitches Smelsky got after Evanovich nailed him with the stick?"

Jareem: "Megan's got a point here. I didn't think that was all right. I would agree that brawls aren't what the game is supposed to be. I do agree with what Professor Jones said the other day; she said that as leaders we have an obligation to 'teach, model, and reinforce the importance of playing by the letter (what is written in the rule book and policy manual) and spirit (the morally right intent) of the rules.'"

Micah: "Jareem, give me a break. You played the game. You know what the game is— it's supposed to be about mixing it up a bit. I played football in college—remember I was a walk-on my freshman year, and I can't count the number of times the coach told me to get a fight started before the game to inspire and motivate my team. That is the game!"

Jareem: "Really? I never was asked to do that. I don't think I could. I think it is important to respect my opponents. I also remember Professor Jones noting this in class last week when she was talking about honor as a leader. She said that we have an obligation to be respectful of opponents, officials, teammates, fans, and all others associated with sports. She also said, 'Principle-centered leaders structure organizations and operations to work toward adherence to a code of conduct that is honor-bound to always do what is right—by the letter and spirit of the rules.'"

Micah: "Look, I don't think that it's okay to let a brawl occur at a game like the one that happened a few years ago in a professional basketball game up in Detroit where the fans and players embarrassed themselves. That definitely wasn't right! But games in which the body comes into contact with another body—some 'mixing it up' will occur. That's just the way the game is played."

Jareem: "I don't know—Megan has got me thinking. Just what is violence?"

Megan: "Well, I just happen to have my sport ethics book here, so let me look up what it says."

Micah: "You carried your sport ethics book to an ice hockey game? You really don't get it."

Megan: "I actually had an assignment to watch the fans, the players, coaches, and officials for unethical behavior. I brought along the book to give me some inspiration. Let me see, here it is: **Violence** *is the use of physiological or psychological force to injure or harm another person, multiple individuals, or one's self. Violence typically involves physical pain or emotional distress caused by assaults, overly aggressive actions, bullying, fighting, and self-inflicted injuries. Physical and verbal violence is used to manipulate others to gain unfair advantages.*

Micah: "You had an assignment to watch the fans, players and coaches for unethical behavior? Did you see any?"

Megan: "I saw a lot—I sat with you! Let me see, what was that waving you were doing at the other team—oh yes, you only used one finger."

Micah: "That was a low blow—maybe you should go out for ice hockey."

Megan: "Look guys, I just don't get it—I mean I really don't—if this definition of violence is correct isn't much of what we saw tonight really violent behavior?"

Jareem: "Well, maybe. I have heard people argue that high-contact sports like football, rugby, ice hockey, and lacrosse when played by males are violent sports, but they really aren't."

Megan: "Oh, how's that?"

Jareem: "Well, there is a difference between contact allowed by the rules and violence. When I played football, I loved the physical contact. I mean I truly loved the hitting, blocking, and tackling."

Micah: "Yeah, buddy, now you are talking. There is nothing better than ringing a guy's bell!"

Jareem: "No, I don't mean intentionally hurting another guy. I just loved the contact and putting myself up against another guy's strength. I can't describe it."

Jeremy: "I get it. I really loved to play the game—I tackled a guy one time and when I hit him, he fell the wrong way and broke his leg. I heard it snap. I can still hear that sound—the snap and his cry. It was gosh-awful—I didn't take pleasure in causing that. But I didn't do it on purpose. It just happened."

Micah: "Not to be funny, but that's the breaks of the game. It is a sport in which guys get hurt. It just happens. You take a chance when you play a contact sport. You go into the game and know that you may get hurt—but that's just whether lady luck shines on you or not."

Megan: "But how is that sort of violence okay?"

Jareem: "I don't think that is violence. When unintentional harm occurs, it's not violence."

Megan: "But aren't you guys taught to hit someone really hard?"

Jareem: "Yeah, we are taught to go for it—but I never wanted to hurt anyone else. I just always enjoyed playing this contact game."

Megan: "But harm did occur, right? Why should we accept games that do harm to others? In our future professions, we probably will be managers of sporting organizations or possibly a manager of an ice hockey rink. We know that ice hockey is dangerous and that harm is a real concern, so aren't we responsible?"

Micah: "Excuse me, Megan, but no one, and I mean no one, is going to hire you to manage an ice arena. You don't have to worry about it."

Megan: "Micah, you are so funny, but the truth is all of us should worry about it. I don't think you guys really get it. I agree with Professor Jones. Let me read this to you. 'For some people, violence has become so pervasive in society, including as viewed electronically on television, in video games and movies, and in sports, that they have become desensitized to the point of accepting violence as a normal part of life. Similarly, violence in sport may have reached a point where some individuals no longer perceive actions or behaviors as violent. For example, sports fans understand that bench-clearing brawls in baseball and swinging elbows to get in position for a rebound in basketball occur outside the rules, yet they seldom classify such behaviors as violent.'"

Micah: "I wish you would put that book away—it's creepy that you carry a book to an ice hockey game."

Jareem: "I agree with Megan. Come to think of it, there is too much violence—maybe we are all becoming callous to it. We see so much of it. I was thinking about the number of concussions that I had in high school. I probably had at least five."

Jeremy: "Me, too. I don't think I ever told anyone about most of them. I was afraid that I would be taken out of the game."

Micah: "Look, we have all had concussions—it just happens. That doesn't mean that it is violence and we should do away with these great sports."

Megan: "I'm glad that people are becoming more educated about concussions. My brother played football and we all worried about the helmet-to-helmet collisions. It seems to me that the violence and contact is quite frankly glamorized. Shouldn't games be more than hits, concussions, and broken limbs?"

Jeremy: "Hey, I think that most fans would acknowledge that helmet-to-helmet collisions in football and hockey sticks used as weapons to cause injuries to heads and knees are malicious."

Megan: "Yes, I agree, but it seems to me that these occurrences increasingly are accepted as the way games are played. It also seems to me in watching you guys and everyone around me tonight that much of violence is justified on the basis of gaining competitive advantage, or it's all just fun—it's not personal."

Micah: "What! Of course it is about getting an advantage."

Jeremy: "Yes, we want to get the advantage, but I want to get an advantage through my skill, not by beating another guy up."

Jareem: "I don't either, but I also agree with Megan. Maybe we accept violence in sports because, well—we just do because we were taught to accept it. I don't want to admit it, but I had coaches and fans tell me to take another guy out. I have heard administrators tell me to do whatever it took to win—and that probably included a late hit or two."

Micah: "Wow, the perfect Jareem actually did something not ... well, perfect?"

Megan: "Maybe that's the whole point—it doesn't matter who we are. If we are involved in sport in America we are all affected and desensitized by what we see. Maybe we accept violence, and the more we see of it the more we think that's just the way it is. It is obvious that the electronic and print media exacerbate this problem by increasingly publicizing violent behaviors in sports that are psychologically, emotionally, and ethically abusive."

Jeremy: "Yeah, maybe we need to think about it more."

Micah: "Not me. I like hitting the other guy!"

What is the solution? Is violence a result of sport or does sport support violence? We, the authors, want to believe that violence may be the result but not the purpose. This chapter suggests that some constitutive, proscriptive, and sportsmanship rules were developed in response to overly aggressive and violent behaviors in sport. Moral principles based on a categorical imperative underlie these sport rules and are recommended as ways to prevent or reduce violence in sports. After a discussion about how violence affects sports, how and why violence is taught, condoned, and rewarded is examined. Recommendations for putting controls in place and offering moral education are suggested.

Types and Purposes of Rules in Sports

The absence of standardized rules in casual games frees participants to play without constraints, agree to a few control measures before games begin, or devise rules during the competition. Although this may seem appropriate for children's games or impromptu contests, organized, competitive sports (especially when fans are present, records are maintained, and championships can be won) require rules. Three types of rules—constitutive, proscriptive, and sportsmanship—were developed for sport competitions to standardize play, regulate behavior, and attempt to prevent harm.

Constitutive Rules

Constitutive rules guide play within a specific game and were developed out of the need to equalize competition. They govern factors such as length of games, number of players, eligibility of participants, and conduct of contests. These rules stipulate game-specific skills, strategies, and techniques, making football different from basketball and both dissimilar to baseball. Constitutive rules specify what actions by players and coaches are permissible during games.

Constitutive rules also place boundaries on players' actions by constraining behaviors to those deemed appropriate to the sport. For example, some constitutive rules in basketball specifically prohibit player-to-player contact to prevent violence by dictating how much touching and holding is allowed and when such actions will be punished with a foul or, for more severe violations, with disqualification. Baseball and softball rules specify when and how one may slide into an opposing player defending a base. Constitutive rules give structure to sports, helping make games fair for all. They standardize the competitive environment so that each player has an equal opportunity to excel.

Constitutive rules place boundaries on players' actions by constraining behaviors to those deemed appropriate to sport: length of games, eligibility, and number of players. Sport administrators are also governed by rules and must ensure that programs are administered following guidelines that specify participant ages, weight classes, skill and maturational levels, and academic performance of athletes in educational sponsored programs.

Sport administrators are governed by rules, too, since through governance organizations, they specify the ages, weights, skill levels, and maturational statuses of youth to help ensure fair and equitable competition. Sport administrators in interscholastic sport governing organizations regulate ages, genders, residences, and academic performances required of players competing in educationally sponsored programs. College athletic directors and their staffs help establish and enforce rules governing the eligibility and academic progress of athletes, recruiting practices, and financial aid. General managers and other front office personnel in professional sports are constrained by collective bargaining agreements and league rules. All of these constitutive rules help provide equitable competitive opportunities for everyone involved.

Proscriptive Rules

Proscriptive rules prohibit specific behaviors and expressly forbid specific actions, such as spearing in football and undercutting in basketball, often because of the high risk of injury. In some sports, scoring advantages and ultimately winning may be predicated on the utilization of one's body and equipment as weapons against opponents, resulting in pain, serious injury, and even death. Specifically, proscriptive rules were established to prohibit players from intentionally trying to harm opponents. For example, the National Football League (NFL) in 2010 cracked down on excessively violent hits by more strictly enforcing proscriptive rules and penalizing players with fines and suspensions for forcibly or violently hitting a defenseless player's head, neck, or face with the helmet or facemask. Also in 2010, the National Hockey League (NHL) established similar rules preventing intentional hits to the head, due to a rash of concussions.

Many proscriptive rules exist in response to stick-wielding hockey players, pitchers throwing at batters' heads, linemen using chop blocks, and teams engaging in bench-clearing brawls. Some proscriptive sport rules governing overly aggressive and violent behaviors are enforced because sport leagues do not want interference from governmental authorities. That is, sport leagues and governing organizations have imposed rules on their participants to control physically violent actions during competitions to keep these situations out of the courts. When fouls lead to injuries in the NFL, National Basketball Association (NBA), NHL, and Major League Baseball (MLB), league officials mete out penalties for violent actions. One reason for these penalties is that had some violent actions seen in sports occurred outside of sports, they would have been punishable by imprisonment or resulted in other legal sanctions. In one example of this happening, in 2004 NHL player Todd Bertuzzi pled guilty in a Canadian court to assault charges for his on-court assault of Steve Moore, which ended Moore's playing career. Violent behaviors are not restricted to the professional leagues, as youth, school, and college athletes imitate their heroes' and heroines' violent actions.

Sportsmanship Rules

Sportsmanship rules emphasize playing fairly and respectfully, such as abiding by the rules of the National Collegiate Athletic Association, athletic conferences, or athletic departments. Historically, sport administrators, parents, and others have claimed that sports build character and teach values and virtues like respect for others, cooperation, self-discipline, and teamwork. To achieve these outcomes, however, principle-centered leaders must ensure that positive goals are emphasized, and one way to do this is through sportsmanship rules. These rules seek to prevent behaviors that place winning above everything else, including opponents' welfare, and promote competitions between equally-matched opponents. Sportsmanship rules are designed to prevent ethically questionable and violent conduct.

Basketball players, for example, can be charged with "technical" fouls for arguing with officials or slamming balls against the floor when whistled for fouls or violations. Soccer officials can give yellow cards (warning) or red cards (ejection) for actions that are unsportsmanlike and often violent. Violent actions that break sportsmanship rules lead to disqualification and sometimes suspensions from subsequent games in an attempt to prevent their reoccurrence.

Without rules, games change. Rules establish parameters while constraining certain behaviors or requiring specific actions. Many rules have been established to control or discourage violent behaviors. Yet the societal emphasis placed on winning too often has resulted in blatant disregard for the welfare of opponents, as seen through violent actions.

Ethical Conduct or Not

It has been suggested that violence is so pervasive in sports that some players are indifferent when an opponent is injured. In fact, often the intent is to "take out" or debilitate an opponent as a desired goal in trying to win (see Box 5.1). Since it is difficult to judge intent to injure, officials are genuinely concerned whether some players may have this goal in mind when they violently hit opposing players during games. Sometimes it is the severity of the blow, while at other times violence may occur extraneously to the primary action in the game. When violent actions occur, officials are more likely to enforce penalties. But sometimes violent actions occur outside the vision of officials, such as in the midst of a pile-up after a tackle, behind the play, or when players are trying to recover a fumble. Players know, though, the dirty players who land blows after a play has been whistled dead to attack sensitive body parts. In fact, some players, especially in the NFL or NHL, take great pride in their reputations for excessive violence, especially if they are rewarded with lucrative contracts or individual recognition. These players want to be feared, are often paid more when they are feared, and believe this helps their teams win more games.

BOX 5.1 CHALLENGES TO BEHAVING IN MORALLY UPRIGHT WAYS

The values and virtues of principle-centered leaders are needed to ameliorate the increasing nexus between sport and violence. This linkage occurs when sport administrators, coaches, and players disregard the rules by intentionally circumventing them. A downward spiral of unethical behavior begins with cognitive dissonance leading to rationalization, moral disengagement, bracketed morality, and finally moral callousness as players and coaches no longer feel conflicted and claim their actions are sound strategy, not moral trickery.

Cognitive dissonance is the discomfort or tension felt when there is a discrepancy between what is known or believed and new information or interpretations (Kohlberg, 1984). When sport administrators and those under their supervision, including coaches and players, are confronted with new ideas or perceptions and asked to accommodate them, we often experience conflict with what we believe is right. Cognitive dissonance occurs when a pitcher who knows it is wrong is told by his coach to throw a pitch at the batter. Conflict for this pitcher increases when he is told by the coach that he will be benched if he does not comply with the directive. The importance and impact of whether to take the action conflict with whether to rationalize and explain away the conflict.

Rationalization is the process of trying to bring disparate expectations into accord or make possible actions seem reasonable. This may mean we concoct incorrect and sometimes unethical reasons to justify our feelings when taking actions or making decisions that previously we would not have done. Rationalizations for unethical behaviors in sports often include "This is how the game is played," "Everyone else does it," "There is no rule against it," "No one will be harmed," and "No one will ever know about it." Rationalizations are used to justify vicious body checks against the boards in ice hockey or slide tackles in soccer by trying to make a wrong action seem as if it were right.

Moral disengagement is when individuals disengage from moral reasoning (stop thinking about it) and act immorally without hurting their self-concept or self-esteem (Bandura, 1999). Moral disengagement normally occurs when people are physically, mentally, and emotionally exhausted, as frequently happens in competitive sports.

Bracketed morality occurs when sport administrators, players, coaches, and fans rationalize acting unethically in sport settings, even though we know these actions would not be congruent with our values outside of sports (Bredemeier & Shields, 1984). By suspending the moral principles of everyday life, bracketed morality allows for "game reasoning" to take over as we act differently within a competitive sport context based on the situation. When this occurs repeatedly, we view our actions as acceptable and become calloused when we behave in unethical ways. Sport administrators may bracket our morally by verbally assaulting an employee who has failed to fulfill a responsibility, yet act in morally upright and highly principled ways outside of the work environment.

Moral callousness describes how individuals associated with sport may display an absence of concern for the welfare of others when acting in morally bereft ways for personal gain (Kretchmar, 2005). Hardened feelings gain strength and serve as barriers for any regret or remorse for the harm caused to others by acting in ways that are selfishly beneficial and morally wrong, such as intentionally harming an opponent or sexually harassing an employee. As calluses become so hardened on our hands that we are prevented from feeling what we touch, moral calluses around our hearts keep us from feeling that our actions are morally wrong. The existence of moral calluses results in sport administrators, coaches, and players feeling no remorse when we harm others because we treat them as objects that can be manipulated.

Some violence in sports occurs when players choose to disregard the rules. They participate in and condone ethically questionable conduct to gain advantages. When a player does something that may not break the letter of the rules but certainly is marginally within the spirit or intent of the rules, the affected opponent may retaliate violently, either through physical attacks or psychological intimidation.

Often, people defend violent and ethically questionable conduct on the premise that a violent behavior is justified if opponents engage in violent behavior first. Regardless of the reason, is violence in sports deviant behavior? Many people seem ignorant of the purpose of sport when they say that behaviors they condone and cheer for are not violent but, rather, are used to gain advantages through clever or strategic coaching and playing. The rationalization becomes, "Because everyone else is doing it, I must do it, too, or get beaten." Does the fact that everyone else commits rule-violating actions make these actions fair, honest, or responsible? Others claim their actions do not exactly violate the precise wording of the rules. Even if this is true, do these actions infringe on the spirit of the rules?

Relativism is a philosophical theory premised upon the belief that truth and knowledge are subjective, and ethical truths depend on individual beliefs as well as the situation. Since to the relativist moral values are not absolute but rather vary depending on the people espousing them, relativism abounds in sport. This theory suggests that players, coaches, and sport administrators are free to define moral values in any way they choose. As a result, behaviors that others would classify as violent, against the rules, and unethical are engaged in with no regret or concern about whether others might be harmed. Relativism facilitates cognitive dissonance, rationalization, moral disengagement, bracketed morality, and moral callousness.

Another reason often given for engaging in violent behavior is retaliation. When players feel their opponents' behaviors toward them are unfair (i.e., a cheap shot), they may respond in-kind, leading to an escalation in violence. For example, if the pitcher on one team hits an opposing batter, is retaliation justified for the opposing pitcher to hit a batter, too? Or if an offensive lineman is trying to take out the defensive lineman using violent actions (such as a crack-back block), is the defensive lineman justified to reciprocate? The issue is, "Does an opponent engaging in violence actions, breaking the rules, or seeking to intimidate justify retaliation?" Often associated with retaliation is the action by some players who choose to initiate rule-violating behavior, hoping that they will not be caught by officials, but causing their opponents to retaliate and be penalized. This is fairly common in sports as officials often only see the retaliatory action, not the action that precipitated the retaliation.

One additional type of violent behavior in sport, namely hazing, deserves mention. Alleging that hazing builds team cohesion, coaches and players have engaged in hazing even though such behaviors have been banned in sports offered by high schools and colleges. When players are stripped of their clothing by coaches when they miss free throws and forced to run naked, hazing has become disrespectful, if not violent. When older players force their new teammates to strip and grasp another person's testicles from behind and walk in a chain, this is demeaning and physiologically and psychologically violent. The emotional and psychological scars from these incidences can last a lifetime. In other cases, players have been initiated onto the team through expectations to drink excessive amounts of alcohol, have been forced to run until they become sick or pass out, have been sexually assaulted, or have been physically beaten; this is not only violent treatment, but it is also against the law. Yet each of these incidents has occurred on sport teams.

Is Winning the Only Thing?

The importance placed on winning directly influences the extent of physiological and psychological violence in sport. That is, as winning increases in importance because of status and financial rewards, many players choose to use any means at their disposal, even violence, to win. This phenomenon is all too evident in the violent actions seen at all competitive levels of sports. When violence occurs in youth leagues, it is usually associated with coaches and parents who have over-emphasized winning or who are living vicariously through their child/athlete. Sadly, a few parents have assaulted coaches, officials, and even young athletes in their over-zealousness for winning, or when they believe their sons or daughters have been wronged. Thomas Junta acted violently when he fought with the father of an opposing player after their sons' ice hockey practice. Junta repeatedly hit the victim's head against the floor, causing his death. Sadly, their sons now are denied their fathers — one dead and the other imprisoned for involuntary manslaughter. Violence exhibited by players, coaches, parents, and fans in interscholastic sports also has escalated because of too much pressure to win. Coaches have physically attacked officials, parents, and opposing players. Some coaches, parents, and sport administrators condone and encourage players to rant and rave or throw things when they lose by castigating them for not caring enough about losing or doing whatever it takes to win. Violent actions directed against objects or opponents are likely to increase when athletes are taught that out-of-control outbursts are viewed favorably or do not result in negative consequences.

Since intercollegiate sport teams competing at the highest levels have become entertainment businesses, physiological and psychological violence has increased. Taunting of opponents leading to fights, intentionally breaking the rules to gain unfair advantages, and trying to intentionally injure highly skilled opponents are examples of violent behaviors driven by the belief that only winning counts. Many professional athletes claim they are expected to demonstrate violent behaviors, not care about their opponents, and not worry about the consequences of their actions. If professional athletes refuse to join in bench-clearing brawls on behalf of teammates or fail to punish, even if outside the rules, opponents who aggressively sack their quarterback or harm their star player in ice hockey, they may find themselves not playing or getting cut from the team. The norms of sport, especially when exacerbated by expectations of aggression, seemingly demand increased physical and verbal abuse at each higher level of competition.

Some players see their opponents as objects rather than people. By objectifying opponents, players become callous and seem to feel no remorse in injuring them intentionally. The aura of masculinity in sports often leads to athletes learning to "take out" the opposing player with hard hits or be perceived as weak. The ethos of winning layered upon expectations of masculinity in sports seems to demand unquestioned loyalty to the team's goal of winning and physical domination by whatever means are necessary. Some athletes say they would do anything to win—anything!

One unconscionable example of objectifying opponents occurred just before the 1994 United States Figure Skating Championships when friends of Tonya Harding conspired to and intentionally injured Nancy Kerrigan. The elimination of Kerrigan from the national championship in singles opened the door for Harding to win the title and qualify for the Olympic Games. The resultant media blitz surrounding the evolving saga included reports of Federal Bureau of Investigation interrogations that implicated Harding as a co-conspirator, a threatened $25 million lawsuit by Harding against the United States Olympic Committee if she was denied the right to skate in the Olympic Games, shared practice time on the ice with Kerrigan in the Lillehammer Winter Games, and Kerrigan's silver-medal performance surpassing Harding's eighth-place finish. In the quest for a national championship, an opportunity to skate for an Olympic gold medal, with the potential for earning millions of dollars in endorsements awaiting the next champion on ice, Harding condoned the attempted elimination of her closest competitor.

A disregard for the rules often leads to an objectification of an opponent as the enemy, someone to be overcome physically, mentally, and emotionally. Many athletes reveal that they do not wish to inflict career-ending injuries, just injuries that will force players off the field or court today so they can compete against lesser-skilled players and improve the likelihood of winning. Protective gear worn by football and ice hockey players may facilitate seeing opponents as objects because so little of the person is seen. Sometimes equipment is used as a weapon to inflict more severe injuries. Other players may view their opponents, and sometimes even teammates, as objects. For example, one intercollegiate volleyball player stated that she would kick a teammate in the head for telling an official that she had touched a ball, causing it to go out-of-bounds.

There is a clear connection between the emphasis on winning and belief in the legitimacy of more aggressive and violent behaviors. Has winning gained predominance because winners receive trophies, media attention, collegiate grants-in-aid, and popularity and may advance to higher levels of sport? Because these rewards are valued, in order to keep them coming players learn to do almost anything to win, including acting violently. In addition, as more violence is condoned and cheered for in sports, violent incidences increase. What is happening in sports when a high school pitcher throws a ball during a game at the head of an on-deck batter? The severe head injury suffered by the on-deck batter ended his promising athletic career, while the pitcher who committed this violent act was unpunished by his coach and advanced to the next level of competition. In France, a high school-aged tennis player's father spiked his son's opponents' drinks to make them sick and unable to play.

Violence is practically non-existent when sport is played informally without rules or high stakes financially. As more constitutive rules are established to govern competitions, proscriptive rules are enacted to curb actions that could harm opponents. Within competitive sports, some players display increased ethically questionable conduct. Sportsmanship rules legislate against this, yet some actions within the letter but outside the spirit of the rules continue. There is no doubt that more violent actions parallel the increased emphasis placed on winning and its associated rewards.

How Violence Affects Sports

Why Violence Exists

Several psychological and sociological theories have postulated about why violence is associated with sports. The **catharsis theory** suggests that acting aggressively in certain situations diminishes the likelihood of engaging in other aggressive actions in possibly less appropriate contexts. One example of how this theory applies to sport occurs when fans vent their anger or frustration on opponents and sometimes their favorite teams when actions on the field or court do not meet with their satisfaction. This cathartic release may free fans from engaging in aggressive or violent actions such as road rage or sexual assault. Another extension of this theory posits that some athletes may be drawn to contact and collision sports because they offer socially acceptable outlets for the expression or release of their aggressive and violent tendencies. Sometimes this aggression occurs within the rules and improves their performances. But sometimes too much aggression becomes violent and hurtful to opponents. The **behaviorism theory** states that aggression is learned. As a conditioned response, aggressive and violent behaviors are influenced by rewards and punishments. Contact and collision sports nurture violence through their structure and discipline as coaches stress conformity yet reward individualistic, hard-hitting, violent behavior. The **social learning theory** posits that violence occurs through imitation. That is, aggression is learned by viewing violence through the media, from the stands, or via electronic games that portray heroes as violent. Because athletes see that aggressive behaviors are accepted and rewarded, they mimic these successful behaviors. Young athletes by imitation learn from older players how to be violent because they will be handsomely rewarded for their violence. Box 5.2 includes another theoretical analysis of violence.

BOX 5.2 THE SEVEN P'S OF MEN'S VIOLENCE

Kaufman (1999) first describes the triad of violence, and Messner (2002) elaborates on this sociological theory that appears to be based on power as a primary characteristic of masculinity. The triad of men's violence against women, other men, and themselves, with each contributing to others, thrives in patriarchal or male dominant societies because of a nurturing environment of violence that is characteristic of some sports. Kaufman's triad of violence in sports includes what he labels as the Seven P's. He describes **patriarchal power** as the use of violence by the dominant male to maintain his status. Males' **sense of entitlement to privilege** is demonstrated through their belief that they are entitled to commit violent acts whenever and however they chose. The third P represents **permission** as violence of males is repeatedly celebrated in sport and by the media, the patriarchal nature of sport is glamorized, and aggressiveness and violence are rewarded. In the **paradox of men's power**, violence becomes a source of power and fear to intimate those who are weaker or more vulnerable, as power is used to dominate and control. Violence as a man's way of creating and maintaining emotional distance from others is called the **psychic armor of manhood**. This distance allows for a lack of empathy or feeling toward anyone who may be hurt through violent acts. Kaufman describes the sixth P, **psychic pressure cooker**, as how masculinity is associated with not showing emotions apart from anger. Since the cultures in many sports celebrate stoic manhood as characterized by power and control, if a male does not feel and demonstrate his power, such as through violence, he must not be a man. **Past experience** explains how males' attitudes toward violence are directly associated with growing up in households where they learn that violence is an accepted part of life. Some boys internalize violence as normative behavior because their survival depends on it. Kaufman and Messner agree that males' violence is more related to societal attitudes and stereotypes than to genes and hormones. While Messner argues that the majority of male athletes do not act violently toward women, there are males who as an expression of their masculinity sexually assault and act violently toward females. Messner stresses that sport encourages athletes to act roughly and violently against opponents, rather than show empathy. Messner also states that athletes are physically, psychologically, and socially conditioned to be tough and to play through pain. Some athletes injure themselves, sometimes permanently, by continuing to play despite suffering from severe injuries.

As Kaufman and Messner argue persuasively, some athletes engage in violence toward their own bodies. The most obvious example of this occurs when players disregard their injuries and play anyway even though they risk permanently debilitating themselves. Sometimes players do this because they do not realize or refuse to admit the severity of their injuries, and they are often encouraged to do this by coaches and parents. For example, players have continued to compete and practice after suffering concussions without realizing that without allowing the body to recover, subsequent blows to the head could cause death or life-changing negative consequences. Injuries to necks, backs, knees, shoulders, ankles, and other body parts can be severe enough to end careers if athletes continue to play instead of allowing for proper healing. When players are too eager to return to games, they may agree to the use of injections to block the body's natural warning of pain as a deterrent to movement or use. The risk of permanent injury increases exponentially when this occurs. Some players in wrestling, football, and other sports practice unsafe weight-cutting methods even though this heightens their risk of disability or death. Other players may choose to use performance-enhancing drugs to enhance how well they perform despite warning about their harmful side effects. When winning, keeping one's position on the team, or maintaining playing time replace sound judgment in dealing with injuries, irreversible physiological damage may result.

Violence occurs in sport because the rules or the rule enforcers permit it and because coaches and players fail to hold themselves accountable to the letter and spirit of the rules. We also know that if violence does occur, it always should be directed toward the activity and not a human being. Athletes at all levels quickly learn what they can and cannot do relative to how the game is officiated. For example, when a football player is not penalized for holding, he is more likely to keep holding because it helps his team. Legislating constitutive and prohibitive rules in an attempt to curb and eliminate violence from sport appears easy, yet many rules elude effective interpretation and enforcement. Do sport rules exist because people violate others' rights? Do sport rules increase in number because people ingeniously find ways around existing rules? Some coaches and players act as if they only believe in exactly what is stated in the rules and use every imaginable way around the intent or spirit of the rules. In sports, obscene language and gestures, verbal and physical intimidation, vicious hits intended to injure, psychological ploys, fights and brawls, and gamesmanship are commonplace, although most are of relatively recent vintage (see Box 5.3).

BOX 5.3 GAMESMANSHIP AND INTIMIDATION

Gamesmanship is pushing the rules to the limit without getting punished and using whatever methods possible to achieve the desired goal of winning. Gamesmanship may take the form of faking an injury to stop the clock so substitutes can enter the game so a game-winning field goal can be attempted, or to slow the fast-paced offense of the opposing team. **Intimidation** is another example of gamesmanship. Intimidation is the act of intentionally causing someone to be fearful, withdrawn, or coerced with the goal of rendering him/her too timid to perform in optimal ways. Some coaches use intimidating and threatening actions and words to try to motivate their athletes. Some players use physical intimidation against opponents, such as trying to injure an opposing player, and psychological intimidation, such as trash talking.

Given the American addiction for winning at all competitive levels of sport, players and coaches spend endless hours developing ways to gain advantages both within and outside the rules. A favorite ploy appears to be trying to see how much one can get away with and not get caught, even if these actions harm opponents. Rather than matching opponents' talents and strategies, too many games lapse into players and coaches seeking to gain advantages without being penalized. Short of having one official per player and endless whistles, flags, and ejections, can officials, as rule enforcers, prevent increases in unethical, violent behaviors?

Should those who write the rules specify the full meaning of the rule, including the spirit of the rule? In other words, should the rules include an explanation of why they were developed and how they apply to fair play? This might lead to officials consistently enforcing these rules, with increased and more severe penalties for infractions, and league officials at all levels matching the penalty to the severity of the violation while taking into account prior actions and the competitive level of sports.

Why Violent Behavior Is Taught

Some coaches teach their players to act in violent ways in order to gain competitive advantages over opponents. Coaches who emphasize winning over playing the game fairly may label behaviors as ways to gain strategic advantage, not overly aggressive and violent actions. Box 5.4 poses an interesting ethical dilemma.

BOX 5.4 VIOLENCE OR GOOD STRATEGY?

Near the end of a closely contested basketball game, a player on the team with fewer points intentionally and sometimes semi-violently (to ensure a call) fouls an opponent, hoping that the free throws will be missed, the rebound secured, and more points scored to try to win the game.

1. Is this cheating since there is an intentional rule violation in opposition to the spirit of the rules?
2. Is this acceptable gamesmanship since fouling is permitted within the letter of the rules?
3. Is this good strategy in seeking to win?

Violent behaviors often are learned from and modeled after those seen on the electronic media and praised in videotaped replays during sports reports, on ESPN's *Sportscenter* and other sports highlight shows, and on video boards in stadiums and arenas. Young athletes watching this aggressive contact are directly or subliminally learning that such violent actions are permissible and rewarded.

Volunteer, interscholastic, intercollegiate, and professional coaches who observe violence in sports portrayed through the media may in turn condone violent actions by their players. Parents and other fans callously perceive that such actions are simply the "way the game is played." One high school player's father modeled the use of violence in sports when he sharpened the straps and snaps on his son's football helmet in order to cause cuts and injuries to opponents. What lessons about violence did this father teacher his son?

Some coaches' bad behaviors, some of which could be classified as violent, are displayed during practices and games as they model how not to act. Players are often yelled at, struck by their coaches, and have their helmets jerked by their coaches. For example, in 2009, Texas Tech University's Mike Leach, University of Kansas' Mark Mangino, and University of South Florida's Jim Leavitt were accused of physically and verbally abusing players on their football teams, behaviors associated with their removal from their jobs. In 2010 football coaches Mike Stoops of the University of Arizona and Bo Pelini of the University of Nebraska were shown on television and videos (circulating nationally) verbally berating officials when they disagreed with their calls. University of Alabama's Nick Saban, Nebraska's Pelini, and other coaches have been shown during games verbally attacking their players. Collegiate basketball players also often feel the rage of their coaches who may grab them and verbally attack them for not performing as they were told. Contact and collision sports may contribute to heightened violence by coaches and players. Also, as role models, coaches' violence may signal to players that similar action is expected and condoned, especially if it contributes to winning.

The higher the competitive level, the more intense is the pressure exerted by coaches for players to perform in violent ways. Professional football players are often drafted and retained on the basis of how aggressively they play. The media praises the aggressive "hurts" put on quarterbacks or receivers by defensive players. James Harrison, Pittsburgh Steelers linebacker, and many other professional football players brag about their aggressiveness and how they try to crush their opponents. The NFL has fined Harrison repeatedly for vicious hits that led to injuries to opposing players.

Some players claim they use anabolic steroids and amphetamines because these drugs increase their aggressiveness and violent actions against opponents. These players often add that since opponents use performance-enhancing drugs, they believe they also must use them to stay competitive. When players observe dramatic changes in their teammates relative to strength and aggressiveness, they acknowledge that such gains are not natural and must be drug-enhanced. As a result, peer pressure to do whatever it takes to win may lead to increased use of performance-enhancing drugs. Coaches may ignore the enhanced body size, muscle mass, and endurance of players who use drugs to enhance their performances, or they may encourage their use by placing demands on players to get bigger, stronger, and more aggressive. Rather than educating athletes about the physiological and psychological risks, some coaches reward players who willingly choose to use performance-enhancing drugs.

Why Violence Is Condoned

Violence continues because fans enjoy it, the media glamorizes it, and it helps athletes win. Although rule books at every level of sports clearly describe basketball as a non-contact sport, this game has increasingly become more physical, even though only the most severe contacts are penalized. As a result, many basketball players wear pads to protect themselves from the sometimes violent contact with opponents. Fans want the officials to let the athletes play, advocating that pushing and holding are all part of the game in ice hockey, because many fans thrive on the violent action displayed on the ice. In professional ice hockey, fighting sells tickets and players' replica jerseys, and fans make heroes out of players whose primary roles are to intimidate and injure opponents.

Some people argue that violence is inherent to some sports such as ice hockey. In some cases an individual intends to "take out" another player. A downward spiral of unethical behavior begins, players and coaches rationalize that violence is a part of the game, and everyone becomes morally calloused, causing more violence and unethical behavior.

Fighting traditions in ice hockey are passed on through generations from fathers, uncles, and sometimes coaches to junior-level players. Some former players have made it all public by establishing camps for children to teach them how to fight on skates. Players as young as 11 years of age learn how to throw punches, grapple, and defend themselves in helmetless, bare-knuckled fights. Labeled as a "goon school" by the media, these camps reinforce and perpetuate the centrality of fighting to ice hockey, something that fans clamor for and cheer.

Society reinforces violence in sport. For example, Jack Tatum, a former professional defensive back in the NFL, received praise for describing in *They Call Me Assassin* his injurious exploits as he continuously intimidated and injured wide receivers. In 1978, in one of the most crushing hits ever in the National Football League, Tatum's violent hit broke Darryl Stingley's neck and left him a quadriplegic. Some have posited that the increasing popularity of auto racing is linked to the aggressive driving of its champions, which often results in violent pile-ups such as Dale Earnhardt's fatal crash in 2001. See Box 5.5 for some other examples of violence in sports. Sports in America reward the victorious with multimillion-dollar contracts and lucrative endorsement opportunities. When violent behaviors help advance an athlete and the athlete is rewarded, these actions will be repeated, regardless of who might be harmed in the process.

BOX 5.5 YouTube Videos on Violence in Sports

Baseball
- Bench-clearing brawl in baseball game between Boerne High School and New Braunfels Canyon High School resulted in five players being ejected. Retrieved from http://www.youtube.com/watch?v=Ad0AUw3FRbc&NR=1.
- University of Oklahoma and Oklahoma State University baseball brawl led to suspensions. Retrieved from http://www.youtube.com/watch?v=ltDZimdHk9M.
- Robin Ventura charged the mound after being hit by a pitch thrown by Nolan Ryan, resulting in a bench-clearing brawl between the Chicago White Sox and Texas Rangers. Retrieved from http://mlb.mlb.com/video/play.jsp?content_id=12745349.

Basketball
- University of North Carolina's Tyler Hansbrough was fouled hard by Duke University's Gerald Henderson while rebounding. Retrieved from http://www.youtube.com/watch?v=ZGHaLUgrzi4.
- Members of the Indiana Pacers and Detroit Pistons brawled on the court with each other and went into the stands and fought with fans. An important lesson stressed in the game suspensions handled out by the NBA was that regardless of the circumstances, players cannot go into the stands and fight with fans. Retrieved from http://www.youtube.com/watch?v=TI87Fr9Z0Vc.
- Detroit Shock's Cheryl Ford and Los Angeles Sparks' Candace Parker started a brawl in a Women's National Basketball Association game. Retrieved from http://www.youtube.com/watch?v=c4DucZ9Tr9A.

Football
- Coaches for two youth football teams in Pearland, Texas, got into a fight, resulting in the banning of their teams from the playoffs as the players suffered from the violent actions of their coaches. Retrieved from http://espanol.video.yahoo.com/watch/8408911.

- Houston Texans' Andre Johnson and Tennessee Titans' Cortland Finnegan were ejected from an NFL game for fighting. Each was fined $25,000 by the league. Retrieved from http://www.youtube.com/watch?v=PT3UqBIobcA.

Ice Hockey

- Kids on under-10 teams got into a fight on the ice. Retrieved from http://www.izlese. org/kids-mass-hockey-brawl-under-10-teams-big-fight1.html.
- Chicago Black Hawks' John Scott and Los Angeles Kings' Kevin Westgarth pummeled each other during their NHL game. Retrieved from http://www.hockeyfights.com/ fight-of-the-week/video/john-scott-vs-kevin-westgarth-nov-27-2010.
- Colorado Avalanche's Patrick Roy and Detroit Red Wings' Chris Osgood participated in a brawl during a NHL game that got really personal. Retrieved from http://www. hockeyfights.com/fights/5473.
- New York Islanders' Chris Simon viciously slashed New York Rangers' Ryan Hollweg. Retrieved from http://www.youtube.com/watch?v=RLmon0XoH3I.
- See also hockeyfights.com for videos of numerous other fights in ice hockey games.

Soccer

- Elizabeth Lambert of the University of New Mexico engaged in violent acts in a conference tournament game against Brigham Young University. Retrieved from http:// www.youtube.com/watch?v=UvEobeNfGcc.
- French soccer star Zinedine Zidane head-butted Italy's Marco Materazzi in the face in the finals of the 2006 World Cup. Retrieved from http://www.youtube.com/watch?v= vF4iWIE77Ts.
- A compilation of violence in international soccer matches. Retrieved from http://www. videobash.com/video_show/soccer-violence-and-fights-1892.

In addition to the impact of violence on sport, some athletes engage in violent behaviors off the field or court. For example, Lawrence Phillips helped his University of Nebraska team win its second straight national championship after his coach permitted him to continue on the team after a brief suspension even though he had physically assaulted a female athlete at that institution. Sexual assaults, barroom brawls, and drug-related shootings are among the incidents of violent behaviors of athletes, such as Kobe Bryant, Plaxico Burress, Adam "Pac-Man" Jones, Ray Lewis, Ben Roethlisberger, and Donté Stallworth. There are numerous cases of athletes involved with murder, drug dealing, rape, assaults with guns and knives, and other altercations. One wonders if the aggressiveness taught and reinforced through sports makes athletes more likely to engage in such violent actions or whether sport attracts individuals who are inherently more aggressive and violent. It may be, however, that athletes engage in violent behaviors less frequently statistically but that the media chooses to publicize their misbehaviors because of their perceived celebrity status.

Do fans condone and thus perpetuate violence in sport by purchasing tickets, watching televised sport, playing video games, and following their favorite teams in print? Do the electronic and print media glamorize and publicize violence because of its sensationalism? The likelihood of change remains doubtful because many fans are no more morally educated than most athletes. How can athletes be expected to behave morally when people throughout society fail to do so? Any overemphasis on winning perpetuates violence in sports. With only victories praised and rewarded, too many athletes learn and practice whatever immoral actions seem necessary to win.

In professional sports, expectations linked with winning demand that teammates enter the fray in defense of wronged teammates. (A common saying in sports is "I've got my teammates' backs.") Although such behavior may be considered manly, it certainly fails the test of honor. What moral questions arise if an athlete races onto a field or court and swings at people because of team loyalty or affiliation? Teammates may have no idea who threw the first punch or why; some seem not to care—anything for a good fight. Would these actions stop if management dictated that such actions would no longer be tolerated and would be punished? This has been an effective deterrent in minor league baseball; fighting in intercollegiate ice hockey is almost non-existent because players are automatically suspended if they fight.

Competing or striving to perform to the best of one's ability defines sport. However, should an athlete have the right to harm another person or to take an unfair advantage just to win a game? Many justify such practices, stating that only the winner gets the trophy, the front-page picture, and the chance to advance to the next level of competition. Violence pays dividends to those who practice it when it helps in winning games. Aggressive behavior in basketball, for example, intensifies when contact outside the rules is not whistled. Players adapt to what officials will permit and usually become as violent as allowed. When holding and pushing help athletes play defense more effectively, then opponents typically score less often. When these actions lead to victories and even championships, recognition and rewards follow.

Often, violent behavior is used to intimidate. When a defensive back flattens a wide receiver on a crossing pattern and stands over him taunting him, this action seems to say, "come into my space and you will have to pay the price." The overly aggressive athlete frequently is shown in a feature on ESPN's *Sportscenter*, markets himself equally aggressively to get endorsement deals, and demands a bigger salary because his violent play helps win games. The collegiate athlete who can use violence advantageously may enjoy benefits, such as the adoration of fans, unearned grades, and under-the-table payments. The interscholastic athlete who throws at a batter's head after giving up a home run or the runner who attempts to "take out" the second baseman when trying to break up a double play has already learned that rewards are associated with doing whatever it takes to win. Interestingly, sport rules over the years have been changed or enforced in ways that reward or fail to penalize such violent behaviors. As a result, many individuals involved with competitive sports do not believe that violent actions in sport are wrong because the only thing that matters is winning.

Violent actions are taught, condoned, and rewarded because of the importance placed on winning. Because many athletes believe that lucrative contracts, collegiate grants-in-aid, national acclaim, campus popularity, friendships, and other benefits accrue to the victorious, they may choose to display violent behaviors in order to attain these benefits. The expected norm in sports is to push the rules as far as possible to win because only then will lavish rewards be enjoyed. However, players, coaches, and sport administrators can learn that violence is wrong. They can be educated about "doing good by doing well."

The Impact of Violence on Sport

Moral reasoning focuses on the principles of justice, honesty, and beneficence. Playing fair and demonstrating integrity and respect preclude athletes choosing to disregard the rules. The moral reasoning process should guide athletes to know the rules and how they should be followed, to feel congruence between their values and the rules they have agreed to follow, and to act based on what is known and valued. There is evidence, however, that the moral reasoning of athletes is less consistent, impartial, and reflective than is that of non-athletes, and the longer athletes participate in sport, the lower their moral reasoning.

Violence undermines the values that potentially can be learned through sport and makes a travesty of the meaning of sport. Fair play demands an adherence to the letter and spirit of the rules to ensure equity for all. Cooperation suggests a willingness to work for the good of the whole, be it the game itself or one's team. Whereas athletes with propensities for violent behaviors primarily care for their personal status and success, the principled player will not intentionally inflict injury or harm an opponent to gain an advantage. Principle-centered coaches and leaders must require that this occurs. Coaches can demand and reward athletes who play by the letter and spirit of the rules. Conversely, coaches can punish players who break the rules and play with excessive violence.

Sports are games and activities directed toward the play experience in which organizational structure and rules have significant roles. The true meaning of sport requires a fair and just playing field with each opponent having an equitable chance for success. When any individual or team uses violent actions, the meaning of sport erodes. For example, is the athlete who holds an opposing player on the line of scrimmage or under the basket contributing to violent retaliation when this behavior is not penalized? The values and meaning of sport will thrive only when violence and other unethical behaviors are discouraged and prevented.

Recommendations

The inherent nature of sportsmanship in competitive sports carries with it a willingness to seek to win while being willing to accept defeat as a part of the game. While playing aggressively within the rules shows respect for an opponent, violent acts show disrespect for opponents and the game itself. How games are played is a measure of the integrity of players, coaches, and sport administrators (see Box 5.6).

BOX 5.6 CATEGORICAL IMPERATIVE

Immanuel Kant (Engstrom, 2009) laid the groundwork for deontological ethics by emphasizing that a categorical imperative should be used to guide all actions. A categorical imperative is a universally accepted maxim that holds regardless of the situation because it is based on undeniable moral principles and absolute, unconditional requirements. Applying this to sports, moral principles that would deter violence in sports could include the following:
- True sportsmanship requires playing to the best of one's ability within the letter and spirit of the rules. That is, a person obeys not only the literal words and their interpretation but also the intent of these words.

- Seeking to win is acceptable only if the letter and spirit of the rules are followed.
- An opponent is not the enemy but a worthy athlete deserving to be treated exactly as everyone would wish to be treated.
- Retribution, which means to give in return and especially punishment, is never acceptable regardless of the unfairness or violence of the initial action.
- Games are not played to intimidate; the ideal purpose of sport is a mutual quest for excellence through equitable and fair competition.
- Sportsmanship requires modesty and humility in victory, praise for winners, and self-respect in defeat.

A myriad of controls are needed to curb or eliminate violence in sports. In youth sport, league officials and coaches should teach and enforce sport rules and ethical values like respect for others. No violations by any player or coach should be tolerated; penalties should be swift and appropriate to the unethical or violent behavior. Any coach, parent, or fan who engages in violent behavior should be banned permanently from the bench or stands.

Interscholastic sports under the direction of school administrators and coaches should enact similarly stringent rules governing their programs. All sport, league, school, and team rules should be followed and additional ones enacted to prevent unethical, violent behavior. Coaches should be held accountable for teaching these rules and for the skill development of players, not the number of victories they tally. Coaches also should be held accountable for their players' behaviors. Parents and fans should be held to a strict code of conduct that requires them to behave responsibly or forfeit their right to be spectators. Players should be required to comply with constitutive, proscriptive, and sportsmanship rules, including those governing the letter and spirit of the sports they play; if they do not, they should be removed from their teams (see Box 5.7).

BOX 5.7 TO OBEY OR NOT OBEY THE RULES… THAT IS THE QUESTION

People obey rules when they
- Perceive that the benefits outweigh the risks.
- Experience peer, coach, or team pressure to comply with the rules.
- Believe the rules are legitimate.
- Adhere to their personal morality or values.

People disobey rules when they
- Believe they are unlikely to be penalized.
- Conclude that rule-breaking behaviors have become normalized.
- Believe ethical conduct is based on each person's moral code, so people can invent their own moralities.
- Lose faith in rules being applied fairly to everyone.
- Want to win at all costs (adapted from Callahan, 2004).

Intercollegiate athletes should be accountable for and required to adhere to sport rules and team guidelines for conduct. There should be less emphasis on the winning-at-all-costs attitude that too often leads to rule-breaking behaviors. Principle-centered institutional leaders, athletic directors, and coaches should consistently emphasize to athletes that choosing to play obligates them only to do the best they can within their abilities, not to resort to violent behaviors to win at all costs.

Colleges should place restraints on fans that seem to have an insatiable appetite for violent actions. This is more likely to occur if principle-centered leaders govern athletic programs and stipulate that coaches will be evaluated on the basis of players' athletic, academic, and social development, not the number of games won. In addition, principle-centered institutional leaders should hold fans, students, athletic administrators, coaches, and players to an ethical code of conduct that prevents violence by their sport teams.

Although controls at the professional level are more challenging given the emphasis on profit maximization and winning, they are nonetheless important and possible to implement. Because players' jobs are on the line, league and team management should dictate that violent behaviors will not be tolerated, and if they occur, they will be penalized swiftly and severely. It may take enforcing harsh penalties for one or two violent incidents to stress the seriousness of the commitment to eliminate violent actions, but clear messages will impede the spread of violence, such as briefly described in the examples in Box 5.8.

BOX 5.8 EXAMPLES OF VIOLENCE IN SPORTS

- In 1977, Los Angeles Lakers' Kermit Washington punched Houston Rockets' Rudy Tomjanovich during an NBA game. This vicious hit detached Tomjanovich's face from his skull and caused blood and spinal fluid to leak into his skull capsule. Washington was suspended for 60 days.
- In 1997, Golden State Warriors' Latrell Sprewell choked his coach, P. J. Carlesimo, during a team practice claiming that his coach had disrespected him. Sprewell's initial one-year suspension was reduced through arbitration to 68 games.
- In 2000, Boston Bruins' Marty McSorley struck Vancouver Canucks' Donald Brashear in the head with his stick during an NHL game. Brashear was knocked unconscious, experienced convulsions, and suffered a serious concussion. NHL Commissioner Gary Bettman suspended McSorley for one year.
- In 2004 during an NBA game, Indiana Pacers' Ron Artest entered the stands and shoved a fan who Artest claimed had thrown a cup of beer at him. Nine fans were injured during the brawl. Nine players including Artest were suspended for a total of 146 games.
- In 2005, Mark Downs, coach of a youth baseball team, paid an eight-year-old boy to hit an autistic teammate in the face with a ball so he would not be able to participate in a playoff game. Downs was found guilty of corruption of minors and criminal solicitation to commit assault.
- Also in 2005, after Coach John Crovo suspended a player for missing a high school softball game to attend a prom, the player's father, Mark Ricard, hit the coach six times with an aluminum bat.
- In 2006, Mitch Cozad, who was the backup punter at the University of Northern Colorado, stabbed his rival's kicking leg, hoping to take his position on the team. Cozad was sentenced to seven years in prison.
- Also in 2006, football players representing Florida International University (FIU) and Miami University (Miami) got into a bench-clearing brawl during their game. This resulted in game suspensions for 18 FIU and 13 Miami players.

• In 2010, Houston Texans' Andre Johnson and Tennessee Titans' Cortland Finnegan exchanged punches, leading to a bench-clearing brawl in their NFL game. Both players were ejected and later fined by the league.

An issue associated with violence by fans is the consumption of alcohol. Professional sport teams depend on the sale of alcohol as a significant revenue source. But drinking excessive amount of beer leads to reduced inhibitions and unethical actions, such as fights among fans, vulgarity that offends families with children, and throwing objects onto courts and fields, sometimes at players, officials, and coaches. Some fans attending Philadelphia Eagles games got so out of control that the team in conjunction with the city conducted Eagles Court at the stadium. The judge handed down quick sentences, such as forfeiture of season tickets, monetary fines, and confinement to the stadium jail until the game ended. Increased security guards and an enhanced video security system led to a significant reduction in unruly fans and the elimination of Eagles Court. Public safety officers are ubiquitous at professional sporting events to protect fans, players, coaches, and officials from random acts of violence. Public address system announcements state expectations for behavior and threaten removal from the event if fans are disruptive.

Although these recommendations may deter some violence in sport, a more effective means for change calls for a comprehensive program in moral education for coaches, players, parents, fans, sport administrators, and the media. This program should focus on values, moral principles, and moral reasoning. The principles and concepts of moral reasoning would challenge people's values and their commitment to them. Discussions about values and ethics are needed, and everyone involved in sports should commit to these. Coaches can have conversations with their teams about what are and what are not acceptable behaviors. A moral education program should completely refocus people's attention on values like justice, honesty, and beneficence that can be modeled in and learned through sport. Perhaps team captains before every game could publicly reaffirm the following statement on behalf of all players, coaches, and fans:

"We are here today to play each other to the best of our abilities and not to intentionally harm our opponents. We hope we are good sports and play by the letter and spirit of the rules. We challenge you to help us in this endeavor. We ask that you cheer us on to excellence. We ask that you neither boo us nor demean our playing or that of our opponents in any way. We ask you to help us be good sports."

Summary

This chapter exposes the ethical problems associated with violence in sport. The development of additional constitutive, proscriptive, and sportsmanship rules has occurred due to an increase in violence. As winning became the most important goal of sport, rules have expanded in an attempt to control violence and ethically questionable aggressive behaviors. Unless individuals in sports value the welfare of opponents, fair play, and integrity in sport, more rules will have to be written and more strictly enforced to close the loopholes currently being exploited.

Moral principles serve an essential role in guiding players, coaches, fans, and sport administrators to act in ethically responsible ways. An examination of sports shows a pervasiveness of violence that undermines the more positive outcome of following the categorical imperative. Possibly understanding why violence exists and is condoned, as well as its negative impact, will help curb or prevent violence. Sport administrators, officials, coaches, players, and fans should re-educate themselves morally if sport is to eliminate violence and replace it with ethical behavior.

There are always going to be the Micahs of sport who argue that "Hitting and taking out the other guy is the whole purpose." However, Jareem, Megan, and Jeremy also believe that perhaps sports should be played, governed, and administrated by people who think and believe that the quality of the activity is affected by how we play the game. Yes, some games involve contact but that doesn't mean that we should celebrate intentional harm or intentional violence. As one of our friends, a national rugby player, once said, "It is truly a brute that enjoys hurting another. Yes, violence exists in the game—but the violence is directed toward play and movement of the ball, never against another human being. The joy exists in the playing of a good, clean game."

References

Bandura, A. (1999). "Moral Disengagement in the Perpetration of Inhumanities." *Personality and Social Psychology, 3,* 193–209.

Bredemeier, B. J., and D. L. Shields (1985). "Values and Violence in Sports Today: The Moral Reasoning Athletes Use in Their Games and in Their Lives." *Psychology Today, 19(10),* 22–25; 28–29; 32.

Callahan, D. (2004). *The Cheating Culture: Why More Americans Are Doing Wrong to Get Ahead.* Orlando, FL: Harcourt.

Engstrom, S. P. (2009). *The Form of Practical Knowledge: A Study of the Categorical Imperative.* Cambridge, MA: Harvard University Press.

Kaufman, M. (1999). "The Seven P's of Men's Violence." Retrieved from http://octevaw-cocvff.ca/en/pdf/mantalk/7_Ps.pdf

Kohlberg, L. (1984). *The Psychology of Moral Development: The Nature and Validity of Moral Stages.* San Francisco: Harper and Row.

Kretchmar, R. S. (2005). *Practical Philosophy of Sport and Physical Activity* (2nd ed.). Champaign, IL: Human Kinetics.

Messner, M. A. (2002). *Taking the Field: Women, Men, and Sports.* Minneapolis: University of Minnesota Press.

Additional Readings

Feinstein, J. (2002). *The Punch: One Night, Two Lives, and the Fight That Changed Basketball Forever.* Boston: Little, Brown.

Jones, J. C. H., Stewart, K. G., and Sunderman, R. (1996). "From the Arena Into the Streets: Hockey Violence, Economic Incentives and Public Policy." *American Journal of Economics and Sociology, 55,* 231–243.

Leizman, J. (1999). *Let's Kill 'Em: Understanding and Controlling Violence in Sports.* Lanham, MD: University Press of America.

Leonard, J. (1997). *Smoke and Mirrors: Violence, Television, and Other American Cultures.* New York: New Press.

Tatum, J., and B. Kushner (1996). *Final Confessions of NFL Assassin Jack Tatum.* Coal Valley, IL: Quality Sports Publications. (Includes reprints of his previous books *They Call Me Assassin* and *They Still Call Me Assassin.*)

CHAPTER 6

Equity Issues in Sports

- What effects did integration have on African American athletes and coaches, ethically and unethically?
- What are the myths and realities about upward mobility through sport for African American athletes?
- Why are African Americans largely excluded from management positions in sport?
- What are the ethical and moral issues associated with racial equity in sport for African Americans, and how can these issues be ameliorated?
- How have societal attitudes influenced females' participation in athletics, and how have these attitudes related to ethical issues?
- What has been the impact of Title IX on sport opportunities for female athletes?
- Why are females seldom hired for sport management positions?
- What are the ethical and moral issues associated with gender equity in sport?

You and your sport management friends have just returned from a wrestling match at your university. The team won the match but in the midst of all that good news there appears to be some very bad news: you all have heard rumors that the wrestling team will probably be eliminated next year. The rumors are focused on the cause and you all enter into a heated debate: the worth and purpose of Title IX.

Micah starts the conversation. "I personally am tired of watching men's sports get cut all around the country because of Title IX. I am not saying that women should not participate; I'm asking why are the men's programs getting cut? Why do the men have to suffer to offer programs to women? Why doesn't equity work in reverse?"

Megan: "I don't like to see programs cut either, but universities are required by law to follow the mandates of Title IX. Let's see, in our sport management class what were those three interpretations of the law, something like: proportional scholarships, equivalent treatment, and accommodation based on interest and ability."

Micah: "Yeah, Megan, that's exactly the point. The reality is we have more men who want to participate but they can't because there aren't enough women who want to participate so men's programs are being cut. Just last week I read that BXY's gymnastics program was eliminated. Historically that program is one of the greatest gymnastics programs in America and it is being cut because of Title IX."

Jareem: "I don't think you can lay the blame on Title IX. I remember in our sport ethics class we learned that the purpose of Title IX was to give women more opportunities in all educational programs, meaning if a college received federal funding then it had to follow federal law. Originally, it was about all educational programs from law to medicine. Women could get into college, but they were limited to majors like education or nursing. Before 1970, few women could go to school and major in programs that were directed toward professions like pre-med or pre-law, because of quota systems — women just were not admitted. When Title IX was passed it opened educational opportunities for women and, as I remember it, the section of Title IX that included athletics was like an afterthought. Most people today think that Title IX is all about athletics but actually it is about education in general. I think it's a great law. My mother was able to go to veterinary school when 20 years before that, women were seldom veterinarians."

Micah: "Okay, so Title IX did a lot of good, but I think the interpretation of Title IX in reducing men's athletic programs to gain opportunity for women is just bad! There must be a better way."

Jeremy: "What do you propose? How would you solve the problem?"

Micah: "Isn't that easy? Just offer more programs for women. I heard that women's crew is a great way to increase numbers. Put in a women's team of rowers and you can increase the opportunities and not have to worry about getting rid of the men's programs."

Jeremy: "So where does the money come from to support all of these teams? In case you haven't heard, times are tough right now. Programs are really suffering. The money just isn't there."

Megan: "What? The money is there. Did you pay any attention to the amount of money paid out in the BCS series? Something like $17,000,000 per team. That is a whole lot of money."

Jareem: "But I heard that most of the schools, if they make it to the BCS games, spend most of it. There are some flush programs out there, but the majority of the schools are always crying poor."

Megan: "That's what really bothers me about men's sports — they never have enough money. Look at this very institution we attend. The head football coach makes ten times what the head women's swim coach makes, and the head swimming coach is a four-time Olympic gold medalist. The whole system is so far from fair that I just can't believe it. It doesn't matter what the law says — Title IX is just not carried out as it should be."

Micah: "Hey, nothing against the swimming coach, but come on — no one goes to the swimming meets, but everyone, including you, Megan, goes to the football games. That's where it's at!"

Jareem: "Megan's got a point. Shouldn't the coaches be paid an equitable wage?"

Micah: "Well, equitable doesn't mean equal. I learned that in the same ethics class that you guys always use to make your point. Equitable means opportunity, not equal. The university has the responsibility to offer equal opportunity — not equal experience. Maybe the swim coach deserves what she gets and since no one goes to their matches, it's a fair wage."

Jeremy: "Wait a minute, this is America. We say we believe in a fair wage for a fair amount of work. I used to date one of the swimmers, and she told me she is in the pool four to five hours a day and swims something like five miles per session. That's a whole lot of time working out. When I played football I didn't practice that many hours a day. I think Megan's point is well taken—there is something wrong with this equitable system."

Megan: *"I think if you looked at the assistant coaches' salaries in football you would find that they make more money than many of the head coaches in the women's sports."*

Micah: *"Look, football is the golden goose that laid the golden egg. You've got to expect those coaches to make big bucks. Hey, I heard our university president respond to this very situation when he was questioned in a press conference. Some reporter asked about the fairness of the salary of the football coach when a chemistry professor made less than one-tenth as much. The president said that he would pay the chemistry professor the same amount of money as the football coach when 20,000 people showed up to watch one of his chemistry experiments."*

Megan: *"Ha ha. You are so funny, Micah. You really don't have a reason for these disproportionate salaries except that men's football or men's basketball draws more fans. Just what did the football players or basketball players do to deserve all of this adulation that the women's swimmers don't do? Nothing, absolutely nothing different! The women swimmers work just as hard. They practice just as hard. They are phenomenal athletes. They sacrifice just the same. The only difference between the men's football team and the women's swimming team lies in the fact that we in America culturally and socially love football and are willing to spend big bucks to go to the games. For lack of a better way to describe it, there is just something sexy about football and men's basketball."*

Jareem: *"Actually you may have hit on something there—we in America seem to be truly in love with these men's sports and are willing to sacrifice everything else for them."*

Megan: *"I think you men might be your own enemies. Did you ever think that maybe if we didn't have football there would be enough money to field all of those teams that are being cut, including gymnastics, wrestling, baseball, volleyball, and soccer?"*

Micah: *"Cut football—are you crazy? Cut the greatest game ever played?"*

Megan: *"No, you don't want to cut that golden goose—except that golden goose eats his golden egg and then wants to eat everyone else's egg. It's not only the coaches' salaries, it's everything else that goes along with the perks of the program from equipment, travel, housing, support staff, and, of course, those 85 scholarships. Just think how many different women's sports have to exist to equal 85 scholarships. If you choose to have a football team, you actually reduce the chances for more men's sports."*

Jeremy: *"Right, it does appear that the problem is football. However, few administrators are willing to give up that golden goose—and truthfully, without the golden goose we wouldn't have the funds to begin with."*

Jareem: *"Maybe, but as we learned in sport finance class, sometimes the big bucks bring more problems than we expect. This university uses student fees as a means to supplement the athletic budget. If we reduced our costs and cut the football program, we just might be able to field a lot more teams."*

Micah: *"I don't believe this."*

You jump into the conversation. *"You know, the thing about sports in America is that it really isn't about fairness at all. As Bill Gates once said, 'Life is not fair.' And the football example we have been discussing is only one of many examples in sport where some people have more power than other people. It isn't just the differences in perception of importance by the sports that we play, it's also found in the perception of how we treat each other on and off the field. How many times have we heard, 'white boys can't jump,' or 'women can't play'; we are a society with lots of equity issues. We like to believe that racism or sexism doesn't exist—but unfortunately it does."*

Micah: "Oh please, everyone knows that sport is a place where race doesn't exist. Look at Michael Jordan—he truly is seen as a person without color—or Tiger Woods. These guys are beyond race."

Jareem: "That may be true for Jordan or Woods—but it is still true that racism exists. I remember reading Malcolm X, who argued that if you are born in America you are a racist. I know he wrote that a long time ago, but I have been thinking about it. Maybe we are all racists and sexists. Maybe it's something we should really think about. Maybe sport is not that perfect place where everyone is equal."

Micah: "Well, it's a lot better place than most other places. We all played on a lot of different teams with a lot of different races, and sport builds community."

Jeremy: "I agree, but maybe our communities have real issues in how we view race and how we treat each other. Maybe we need to study this more."

The conversation of Megan, Micah, Jareem, and Jeremy addresses the ethical dilemma of race and gender. What is equal and equitable in sport and athletics as you work in the field of sport management? How do you address the issues of equity? This chapter will focus on these important and troubling issues.

Sport is viewed as a meritocracy with the highly skilled, better prepared, and mentally tough prevailing. While this is an accurate assessment for white males, historically and socially it less accurately describes the status of African Americans and females in sports. Historically, hegemonic masculinity for the privileged white race excluded African Americans from competing alongside and against whites and characterized females as disinterested in sports and inferior in ability. In the absence of principle-centered leadership, African Americans and females were relegated to the backwaters and sidelines of competitive sports.

Principle-centered leadership requires mutual respect with just and fair treatment, but this type of leadership has not always been evident in the governance of and opportunities in sports. Prejudicial discrimination against individuals not a part of the dominant group excluded African Americans and females. As a consequence, white males enjoyed the prestige and rewards of sport achievement. Power and control held by white male sport administrators and coaches for decades perpetuated the perception that only they were talented, smart, or interested enough to deserve preeminence atop the world of sports. With few exceptions, the status quo didn't change until after the middle of the twentieth century. Even then, white males' predominance remained the standard with African Americans and females always considered the secondary or tertiary "other" by comparison. This chapter examines how African Americans and females have historically overcome unethical treatment and socially and gained more equitable opportunities in sports.

Racial Equity: African Americans in Sports

Fans of professional sports and most college sports as recently as the middle of the twentieth century would have seen only white athletes competing against each other, with African Americans excluded because of discriminatory practices, written and unwritten agreements, societal and cultural constraints, and prejudicial attitudes. The dominant white print media publicized the sport performances of whites almost exclusively, thus relegating the sporting achievements of African Americans to the black press. Segregated sports resulted in the establishment of African American sport opportunities like the Negro Leagues in baseball and the American Tennis Association. Limited also was recognition received by African Americans athletes attending historically black colleges. White males dominated almost all sports because of moral ignorance supported by racist educational and social systems and the absence of principle-centered leadership needed to redress indignities like racial epithets and exclusion from or discriminatory treatment in housing, restaurants, and transportation.

The predominance assumed by white males in sports reflected the power and control positions they held in government, education, business, and religion since the founding of the United States. Did such dominance signal a lack of justice, honesty, and beneficence toward all other groups? For example, why were African Americans not allowed to vote until 1865 when this right was extended to them by constitutional amendment? (In actual practice, many African Americans did not get to exercise this right until decades later.) Whites governed all levels of politics, dominated education (with separate but unequal schools and colleges existing for African Americans), managed almost all commercial enterprises, and perpetuated the status quo through social mores proclaimed from church pulpits. Firmly entrenched in positions of power, most white males accepted and acted upon the belief that non-whites were physically and intellectually inferior and undeserving of equitable treatment. How was educational, employment, and social discrimination morally defensible on the basis of one's racial heritage? To what extent does educational, employment, and social discrimination exist today?

Discriminatory treatment of African Americans based on preconceived ideas, unfair prejudices, and widespread biases raised many ethical concerns that intensified over the years. To prevent any erosion in hegemonic masculinity, most white sport administrators and athletes simply refused to allow African Americans, and sometimes other minorities, to join their leagues. For example, there was no written policy (only a "gentleman's agreement") that resulted in segregated professional baseball, yet no team owners signed any outstanding African American players for over half a century. When a few ethnic minorities tried to break through segregated barriers in sports, they often were verbally and physically assaulted and inevitably expelled. Without the economic and political power to challenge such exclusion, African Americans formed separate teams and competed under less than ideal conditions. While Negro Leagues stars like Cool Papa Bell and Oscar Charleston were never allowed to compete in Major League Baseball (MLB), their performances equaled or often surpassed those of white players playing with all-star teams in hundreds of barnstorming games against teams comprised of African American players.

Discriminatory practices and segregated sports set the stage for an examination of the numerous inequities endured by African American athletes. Historical, organizational, and societal events and perspectives in this section describe how such treatment violated ethical principles. Of particular importance are how slowly changes occurred and how these changes were driven more by economic considerations and social changes than because of respect for and beneficence toward African Americans. Although past discriminatory practices and the most egregious mistreatment have been eliminated, yielding conditions approximating equity, some recommendations for continued diligence are provided to address residual less-than-equal treatment.

Historical Perspective of Racial Inequity in Sports

In the twenty-first century, it is difficult to imagine the depth of racial discrimination experienced in the past by African Americans in the United States, including sports. Segregated swimming pools, sport competitions restricted to those between educational institutions that admitted only one race, and the "whites only" policies in MLB and the United States Lawn Tennis Association are illustrative of shameful snubbing. As a result, most sports fans are unaware of the remarkable achievements of Paul Robeson in football, Ora Washington in tennis and basketball, and Josh Gibson in baseball. Yet these African American athletes were as good as, if not better than, their white contemporaries. Only on the pages of African American newspapers were the outstanding performances of these and other athletes recognized. To most whites, these African American athletes were invisible or their performances were disparaged as inferior.

Before the middle of the twentieth century, African Americans seldom attained economic power, most having suffered the ignominy of slavery or remnants of this subservience. Enduring separate housing, menial jobs, and inferior educational opportunities, if any, African Americans were forced to accept discriminatory treatment without resistance or complaint. The few African Americans who challenged being mistreated and denied equal rights usually endured harsh repercussions. How did the exclusion of African Americans from all levels of competitive sports violate moral values? Did white sport managers fail to reason morally and thus act in unethical ways? Why was there an absence of principle-centered leaders showing respect toward and fairly treating African Americans?

From Exclusion to Limited Opportunities in Sports

The sons and daughters of African Americans through the 1960s, or later in some sections of the United States, continued to suffer the same exclusionary ignominy their parents did as recreation departments, private organizations, and country clubs excluded them from sport programs. The limited number and relative power of African Americans relegated them to forming competitions for their children or seeing them denied sport opportunities. Because most African Americans lacked financial resources to purchase sporting equipment and clothing, pay for instruction or coaching, and fund travel expenses, their children rarely had opportunities to play golf, swim, or attend sport camps. Children who never learned to ski, fence, and play tennis, golf, or ice hockey were unlikely to develop skills in these sports. Separation into sports by race and socioeconomic status resulted in few African American children on swimming, tennis, golf, and gymnastics teams. Lee Elder in golf and Arthur Ashe in tennis served as notable exceptions to the typical dearth of mixed race and African Americans in these and other sports.

Youth sport opportunities historically and today have differed in urban, suburban, and rural areas. Basketball, for example, has been touted as the most popular urban sport based on the limited equipment and space required and because of the individualized moves and fast-paced style of play associated with playgrounds. Basketball also has been characterized as the spot-shooting game of choice of mostly white males in rural settings, especially in Indiana, Kansas, and Kentucky. Suburban sports for youth reflect the higher economic status of families living there. Golf, tennis, swimming, other individual sports, and in recent years soccer and lacrosse are more likely to be available for the children in suburban locations because their parents can afford the costs.

School Segregation Gives Way to Integration

Within their segregated world, African Americans managed to offer their children limited sport opportunities in schools, albeit with fewer amenities than those enjoyed by the more economically blessed. In all-black schools, which were judged as unequal in the 1954 United States Supreme Court case *Brown v. Board of Education*, African American males competed in football, basketball, baseball, and track. Although segregated schooling became illegal and civil rights legislation starting in the 1960s worked diligently to guarantee everyone's rights, only gradually did integration in educational institutions occur. Subsequently, school consolidation and court-ordered busing changed the face of public, K-12 education.

Court-ordered busing sought to adjust the racial mix in schools, thus affecting athletic teams. Initially, African American males were not chosen for sport teams or not given playing time they earned by white coaches; soon, though, most coaches put racial biases aside and played the best athletes to improve the chances of winning. Through financial support for football, basketball, and baseball in integrated schools, many African American students enjoyed better facilities, equipment, and competitive opportunities than they had previously.

A significant consequence of integration was the closing of many former African American schools. Would a more reasoned approach have been to promote cultural diversity by placing students of all races in former all-white and all-black schools, rather than usually uprooting African American students from their schools? As a result of consolidation and the closing of many formerly all-black schools, numerous African American coaches lost their jobs; almost all white coaches at the now integrated but formerly all-white schools retained their coaching jobs. The movie *Remember the Titans* poignantly depicted a rare exception where acceptance of a successful African American head coach who replaced a venerable white head coach in football at a newly integrated high school was begrudging and volatile.

As competition for places on baseball, football, and basketball teams increased, fewer white athletes saw these teams as their only sport options because often their family circumstances allowed them to pursue sports like swimming, tennis, and golf often associated with private lessons and facilities. As a result of increased numbers of African Americans in team sports and some whites males selecting other (often individual) sports, many school teams began to segregate based on color. Today, many high school football and basketball teams have a much higher percentage of African Americans than do the schools' student bodies. What are some possible ethical issues associated with sports being mostly segregated by race, even when based on students' choices?

Integration of Intercollegiate Sports

Beginning in the late 1800s, a very small number of African Americans played on northern colleges' athletic teams, but they often experienced discrimination. These African Americans suffered mistreatment from teammates, had to sleep and eat in segregated facilities, endured physical and verbal abuse from opponents and fans, and often did not get to play when teams from the South refused to compete against them. The withholding of African Americans from games occurred in deference to the prejudicial attitudes and bigoted practices of coaches in Southern colleges. In placating the racism of the opposing coach and players, African American players were denied opportunities to display their talents and instead suffered humiliation and hurt from being considered second-class citizens. Even if African Americans were allowed to compete, they often suffered from the indignities of segregation from their teammates on trips (see Box 6.1). If they were permitted to stay in the same hotels, African Americans inevitably were paired as roommates with each other because of societal opposition to mixing the races. Did coaches' or athletes' discriminatory practices, including the refusal to compete against African Americans, retard their moral development? Were the actions of these coaches and athletes unethical?

BOX 6.1 DID THIS REALLY HAPPEN?

Mitchell Tatum, the only African American on the team, was the star halfback of Midwestern University, having gained a conference record of 1,572 yards rushing during his senior season. While earning All-America honors individually, he also led his team to the conference title and an invitation to play in the Sugar Bowl. In addition to his athletic achievements, Mitchell, who was studying music, had a 3.5 grade point average.

When the team bus arrived at the team's hotel from the airport, Mitchell's coach pulled him aside and introduced him to the music director (Dr. Cooper) of the famed Southern College (a local, historically black college) band. Dr. Cooper talked briefly with Mitchell before inviting him to his home for dinner and to see his famous instrument and music collections. Mitchell's coach gave his approval, and off they went to Dr. Cooper's house. After a delicious dinner and a few hours of conversation about music, Dr. Cooper invited Mitchell to spend the night since his coach had told him this would be allowed. After a hearty breakfast, Dr. Cooper drove Mitchell back to the team hotel just as the bus arrived to transport the team to the stadium.

Mitchell was really pleased with his 104 yards rushing in the Sugar Bowl but disappointed with his team's loss. In reflecting on his experiences, which were even more memorable because of the time spent with Dr. Cooper, he wondered why not a single teammate had asked him about his absence at team meals or the hotel. Then Mitchell realized that his coaches had arranged his time with Dr. Cooper so he and the team would experience no problems. That is, the team hotel refused to serve and house African Americans. (This situation is based on an actual experience of an African American athlete.)

This Actually Happened

The Indiana State University Sycamores under Coach John Wooden finished the regular season in 1947 with an 18–8 record and qualified for the National Association of Intercollegiate Athletics (NAIA) tournament in Kansas City. Wooden declined the invitation, however, because tournament officials refused to permit an African American to play in its segregated event. While Clarence Walker typically did not play much, Wooden stated that he was a member of the team, and they would only participate as a team. The following season, the Sycamores compiled a 27–7 record and were again invited to the tournament. Wooden again refused for the same reason. NAIA officials acquiesced and agreed to allow the entire team to play, making Walker the first African American to play in a national intercollegiate basketball tournament.

College coaches began to recruit African American athletes when they realized their talents could help their teams win, even though these individuals formerly were barred from admission and remained non-representative of student bodies. A seismic shift in recruiting practices occurred after the all-white University of Kentucky basketball team lost to the predominantly African American team from Texas Western College (University of Texas at El Paso today) in the 1966 National Collegiate Athletic Association (NCAA) championship game. In the aftermath of this game, many white coaches began to recruit African American athletes.

African American males traditionally have been expected to be star players; otherwise, they did not receive grants-in-aid or sit on the bench. That is, the few African Americans who were recruited were expected to excel athletically. These athletes had to accept limitations on their behaviors. For example, they were not allowed to date white women, even though few African American women were enrolled on their campuses; they were also expected to accept without retaliation or comment the numerous racial slurs directed at them. Was it ethical to demand that African American athletes accept these restrictions and such mistreatment? Why did coaches, teammates, and fans show little empathy for the plight of African American athletes? How did this reflect their values? What similar discriminatory treatment do African Americans have to deal with today?

The few African American athletes who initially were recruited to attend traditionally all-white institutions were strong students academically. Because they excelled in the classroom and on the field or court, they were welcomed or at least accepted in sports, although not in social settings. Even though more recruited African Americans attended schools that failed to prepare them for the academic rigors of college, often they did not receive academic assistance in college. Some coaches helped ensure the continued eligibility of African American athletes by enrolling them in easy courses that would not lead to degrees or by convincing instructors to give them passing grades. Whenever such actions occurred, did coaches break the contract with their players by denying them opportunities to get an education and earn degrees? Did college coaches care more about these athletes' physical talents than about them personally or their preparation for life after college without their sports? Were these coaches' behaviors helpful or ethical?

While traditionally white colleges benefited from the contributions of African American athletes, over the years historically black colleges saw their best talent lured away by coaches at larger, more prestigious colleges with promises of glamour, media exposure, and potential professional contracts. Contributing to this was the reality that historically black colleges did not have large grant-in-aid budgets, premier facilities, and other amenities to compete in recruiting the best African American athletes. By 2007–2008, the percentage of African Americans players on NCAA Division I football teams reached 46.4 percent; 60.4 percent of the NCAA Division I basketball players were African Americans (Lapchick, Calderon, Harless, & Turner, 2010).

African Americans seldom have been hired to coach by mostly white athletic directors at the larger, more prestigious institutions of higher education, despite the fact that the percentage of African American athletes increasingly exceeded the number of coaches of their race. For example, in 2007–2008, 5.1 percent of the head football coaches and 22.9 percent of the head men's basketball coaches were African Americans (Lapchick, Calderon, Harless, & Turner, 2010). African American assistant coaches on otherwise all-white staffs oftentimes are less frequently appointed as offensive or defensive coordinators in football or associate head coaches in basketball. What ethical issues, if any, are associated with the hiring practices in intercollegiate athletics in football and men's basketball?

Professional Sports

Jackie Robinson is credited with opening the door for African Americans in professional baseball in the modern era (1947). But only slowly did prejudicial attitudes and behaviors change and dissipate to more fully welcome African American athletes as equals. Although outstanding African American athletes like Kobe Bryant in basketball, Adrian Peterson in football, and Ryan Howard in baseball have signed multi-million dollar professional contracts, this does not mean that all African American athletes receive salaries that are comparable to equally skilled white athletes.

In the early years of integration in professional baseball, African Americans like Hank Aaron and Willie Mays lived and ate with African American teammates while socially segregated from their white teammates. Like Jackie Robinson, they were expected to passively endure physical and verbal abuse from opponents and fans if they wanted to keep their jobs and understood not to expect teammates or management to intervene on their behalf. Until recently, African Americans — not even future Hall of Fame stars like Julius Erving in basketball, Bob Gibson in baseball, and Jim Brown in football — could expect to earn endorsement and appearance incomes to match what was available to outstanding white athletes. Fortunately, most of these discriminatory practices have ceased.

For decades, African Americans knew better than to expect to be hired as coaches and front-office administrators in professional sports. Biased owners of professional sport teams may have secretly professed or demonstrated through their practices that African Americans were intellectually incapable of coaching or administering a sport. Although Al Campanis lost his job as vice president for player personnel for the Los Angeles Dodgers in 1987 because of his racist statement reflecting this perspective, African Americans have achieved limited advances into professional sport administration positions. To partially address this, the Rooney Rule in the National Football League (NFL) requires each team owner to interview at least one African American for each head coaching position. Are whites acting honestly when they justify discriminatory hiring practices based on prejudices and biases? Does beneficence call for sport administrators, coaches, teammates, opponents, and fans to treat all athletes equitably? How might moral knowing and moral valuing bring about greater equity in sports for African Americans?

Societal Attitudes

The socioeconomic status of African American athletes today is another limiting factor regarding sport opportunities. Some sociologists have suggested that the sports African American athletes choose to participate in are directly the result of what their families could afford. Private lessons in ice skating or gymnastics are virtually impossible when a family is on welfare or children are raised in single parent homes. Not surprisingly, sport teams offered by public agencies and schools, such as basketball and track, are much more likely to have African American athletes, whereas sport teams with associated high costs are not. In addition, in order to play soccer or tennis, children must have transportation to practices, lessons, and competitions as well as funds to buy equipment and uniforms and pay entry fees. With few exceptions, socioeconomic circumstances and opportunities directly influence choice of sport.

Societal attitudes are difficult to change. Many have lauded sport as a leader in integration of the races; others disagree, arguing that sport is so inconsequential that it only reflects what is happening in society. Box 6.2 looks at whether sports are a reflection or leader of society in changing attitudes and treating African Americans more equitably.

BOX 6.2

Sports as a Reflection of Society
- Most aspects of society have been resistant to changing discriminatory practices and exclusionary actions.
- Society historically viewed African Americans as stereotypically inferior and less intelligent.

Sports as a Leader of Society
- Sports espoused a race-neutral approach, thus helping eliminate racial discrimination.
- Sport allowed African American athletes equitable opportunities to prove their merit and skill before society treated African Americans fairly.

- Equitable treatment in all aspects of society began and became more pervasive only after laws mandated it.

- Role models of successful African Americans can be found throughout society.

- In an increasingly diverse world, equality of all races was viewed as essential.

- White coaches, athletes, and sport administrators accepted African Americans as equals and influenced progress in other areas of society.

- African American athletes served as role models for success before African Americans in other professions achieved similar status in society.

- Because of the desire to win and make more money, athletic talent counted more than race.

Role Models, Stacking, and Quotas in Sports

African American culture may disproportionately reward the athletic prowess of its sport heroes who are more likely to serve as role models than are doctors, lawyers,

educators, or business executives. African American males may choose to practice their sport skills more diligently than they focus on educational attainment because they are rewarded with status and they see their sports as tickets to better ways of life. The dream of a sports career is dashed for 99 percent of high school athletes of all races who will never sign professional contracts. Those who do achieve their dreams by signing professional contracts, an average of three to four years later find themselves out of jobs and often poorly educated.

The importance of having role models starts at a young age. Some adults may encourage or discourage children into almost self-fulfilling prophecies as they overtly or subtly tell youth about opportunities in

African American culture may disproportionately reward the athletic prowess of its sport heroes and heroines, who are more likely to serve as role models than are doctors, lawyers, educators, or business executives. Even though there are a large percentage of African Americans who play sports, there are still relatively few in coaching and leadership positions.

life. Boys growing up in families without fathers at home may seek male role models at school, primarily coaches. The bond that develops between the football, basketball, and baseball coach, who usually is white, and the athlete, who often is African American, may lead to a singular emphasis on sports.

During their school years, athletes choose heroes, usually of the same race, in their preferred sports, with these individuals serving as powerful role models of behavior, both moral and immoral. Typically, individuals assimilate the values of any group they join like a sport team because of the disproportionate amount of time spent together. Although parents and families may teach and model morally acceptable behavior, coaches or teammates might not. But it is often coaches and teammates whom the athletes imitate. How can role models in sports help shape the moral reasoning abilities and ethical conduct of young athletes? What are the moral, and sometimes immoral, values associated with sport teams? Has the non-moral value of winning displaced moral actions because those involved with sport fail to address the issues facing them in moral terms? What responsibilities do coaches have to develop moral values in their athletes? What responsibilities do coaches have to be moral and ethical role models to athletes on their teams?

Modeling also affects the selection of sports. Do few African American youth aspire to become quarterbacks because they subconsciously believe this is traditionally a white person's position? Have white coaches urged African Americans to play other positions, even though these athletes possessed the requisite physical skills and leadership abilities to play quarterback? Would something like the discriminatory treatment faced by the Miller boys in Box 6.3 occur today?

BOX 6.3 QUARTERBACKS ARE WHITES AND WIDE RECEIVERS ARE AFRICAN AMERICANS

The Miller boys and their father loved football. Regardless of the season, as soon as Mr. Miller got home from work, Wayne, Robin, Eric, and Jeremy urged him to play with them. All of the boys enjoyed catching their father's accurate spirals. The Miller boys admired their father for all the trophies he had won in football and especially for his all-star performances at Midwestern State University, where he had played quarterback. When Wayne, Robin, and Eric got old enough to join youth football leagues, each wanted to play wide receiver. As experienced recipients of their father's passes, they earned starting positions and performed well. Jeremy was different; he wanted to be a quarterback like his father. Each year he tried out for quarterback, and each time the white coach told him that his skills were more appropriate for a wide receiver or defensive back. Although Jeremy accepted this decision initially, he began to question it when some of his African American teammates hinted that he would never get to play quarterback as long as a white teammate could play that position. Mr. Miller encouraged Jeremy to try his hardest in whatever position he was assigned while coaching him at home on how to play quarterback.

When Jeremy tried out for the high school team on which Eric played wide receiver, he was determined to show he could play quarterback. The neighborhood Miller-to-Miller combination was unbeatable because the two boys had played together so much. Jeremy was told by the white coach that he was good enough to earn a spot on the team, but not as a quarterback. Again, it seemed to him that skin color, not skill, was the determining factor in who played quarterback. Mrs. Miller, a teacher at the high school her sons attended, began to inquire about why Jeremy was not allowed to play quarterback, especially because three white quarterbacks had been doing poorly. When Coach Dobbins heard about Mrs. Miller's questions, he informed her that African Americans possessed physical traits such as the ability to run faster and jump higher that made them superior wide receivers and defensive backs. African Americans, he added, were better at these reactive positions but less adept at thinking positions such as quarterback and linebacker. Everyone who knew football, he assured her, understood this was based on racial genetics.

In colleges where only African Americans enrolled, males for years had proven they possessed the physical and intellectual abilities to become top athletes and play all positions. But on integrated teams this changed. As a result, often athletes self-selected their positions by modeling their heroes who have historically played in positions requiring speed and reaction time rather than decision making and centrality to the action. Many coaches with prejudicial or misinformed attitudes like Coach Dobbins reinforced playing African Americans at positions requiring speed and reaction time.

Position allocation, or stacking, refers to a disproportionate concentration of African Americans in specific positions. As African Americans played on formerly all-white sport teams, they inevitably were wide receivers, running backs, power forwards, and outfielders. That is, African Americans were much more likely to play in reactive, speed, and strength positions. African American athletes still predominantly play in many of these positions. There are several possible explanations for stacking: (1) racist stereotypes about the physical, social, and personality attributes of athletes; (2) racial discrimination keeping some athletes from leadership, responsibility, and authority roles; (3) an economic assumption that African American athletes from lower socioeconomic circumstances do not have access to training and facilities needed to develop certain position-related skills; (4) self-selection by African American athletes into positions in which they perceive they have the greatest chance to achieve success; (5) possibility that African American athletes choose to emulate those of their race who have historically played in certain positions; and (6) a residual prejudicial attitude that African American athletes excel only at reactive positions. Because of one or more of these factors, African American athletes have often competed against themselves, not against whites, for some starting positions and opportunities to play.

Historically, quotas limited the number of minorities playing for a team at any time, thereby restricting sport opportunities for African Americans on interscholastic, intercollegiate, and professional teams. For example, in the 1950s and 1960s, the unwritten rule in the NFL was that no team would have more than ten African Americans on its 35-man squad. Another standard practice of white head coaches was that the number of African American players on a team had to be an even number because since players at that time shared rooms, they had to be paired based on race.

African American athletes often have claimed that the odds of retaining a place on a team with only average talent tipped heavily in favor of whites, as did earning playing time or starting positions. For many years it was believed by some athletes in the National Basketball Association (NBA) that coaches would start two African Americans at home to appease the local fans but start three African Americans on the road because they needed more of the best athletes to win games on the road. The injustices endured by African American athletes chronicle the discriminatory practices of coaches and sport administrators at the time. Has the idolizing of males of their race who have become professional athletes led many African Americans down a dead-end road where dreams of stardom and financial success are shattered? Has accepting position shifts and enduring quotas damaged African American athletes' self-esteem and limited their playing options? Have coaches treated African Americans athletes dishonestly? Is it ethical that earning a position on a team, playing any position, and being hired or not are based on the color of one's skin? Do selection of position based on where role models play, stacking, and quotas exist today?

African American Athletes as Portrayed in the Media

Until recently, the media condoned and perpetuated a second-class status for African Americans in sport. Although the African American press proclaimed the achievements of Buck Leonard and Ora Washington, most whites knew little about these outstanding athletes. The white print media praised Joe Louis, who fit its image of a modest boxing champion, while disparaging Jack Johnson, who refused to behave demurely, flaunting his wealth earned as the heavyweight boxing title holder. When Hank Aaron became the greatest home run hitter of all time, many in the media refused to lavish superstar status upon him, and racists sent him death threats.

In integrated sports, African Americans were conditioned to passively take orders from white coaches as the media praised those who "knew their place." Former Boston Celtics star Bill Russell suffered verbal attacks and criticism at the hands of sportswriters and broadcasters because he outspokenly lambasted prejudicial attitudes and behaviors. Tennis champion Arthur Ashe spoke out against apartheid in South Africa and racism in the United States. Jim Brown, running back of the Cleveland Browns, lashed out against racism while working diligently to help African Americans economically. These athletes were the exceptions as most African American athletes were unwilling to challenge the persistence of second-class status inflicted on them, possibly because they did not want to offend white owners, sportswriters, announcers, and fans.

Race may be the most important social construct in examining societal issues, with racism culturally ingrained and endemic in the United States for centuries. There is little doubt white males viewed themselves in the normative position or as the standard against which other racial groups should be measured. Stereotypical descriptions reinforced and perpetuated by the media resulted in African American athletes being ignored or disparagingly treated. For example, while white male athletes were praised for their outstanding sport performances resulting from hard work, diligent training, and intellectual acumen, African American athletes' exploits were inevitably credited to natural abilities such as speed, jumping abilities, and power. Despite the absence of empirical evidence to support these claims, up until recent years, the media overtly or covertly elevated in status white athletes over African American athletes through how they reported on and wrote about their achievements in sports.

Has the media perpetuated prejudice against and stereotyping of African Americans? What values have been reinforced by how the media has portrayed African American athletes? Can the media help make an athlete a star or preclude this based on the amount and type of exposure it provides? Does the media influence whether athletes attain celebrity status, which often translates into endorsement and appearance income? How does race influence how athletes are portrayed by the media? Is there a lack of equity in sport reporting by race?

Economics as the Pivotal Factor in Greater Equity in Sports

Branch Rickey is credited with breaking the color barrier in the modern era of MLB because he ignored the "gentleman's agreement" that disallowed African Americans in the major leagues. While Rickey was sympathetic to the mistreatment of African Americans, he was definitely concerned with attracting more African Americans fans to watch the Brooklyn Dodgers and winning more games. Rickey's strategy worked because Jackie Robinson withstood death threats, racial slurs, intentional attempts to injure him, and other indignities to break down the door for other African American players. Robinson and other African Americans on the Brooklyn Dodgers team (such as Roy Campanella and Don Newcombe) and on other teams increased the quality of play in MLB. One of the unintended consequences of signing African Americans by major league teams, though, was the demise of the Negro Leagues. So while MLB benefited from increased gate receipts because of the outstanding performances of African American players, the once thriving Negro Leagues (they ceased to exist in 1962) lost their stars and fans.

One of the ethical issues associated with the demise of the Negro Leagues was that major league teams often signed African American players without compensating their teams. While team owners were happy their players finally got opportunities to play with and against white players, they expected to be paid for the loss of their most talented players. When major league teams paid compensation when signing Negro Leagues players, this amount was much less than their values to the new team. Did management in MLB act ethically in signing away the best players? Were there any other ethical issues involved with the demise of the Negro Leagues following integration of MLB? For example, how were African Americans treated by teammates and opponents? Did fans treat them fairly? Did the media treat them with respect? Were African American players housed with their teammates, paid comparably, and judged fairly relative to playing time and baseball recognition, such as All-Star selection or post-season honors?

In 1946 Bill Willis and Marion Motley playing for the Cleveland Browns, and Kenny Washington and Woody Strode for the Los Angeles Rams broke the color barrier in the modern era of professional football to much less fanfare. Since professional football was much less popular than professional baseball at the time, most baseball players were from the segregated South, and more African Americans have played on integrated collegiate football teams, the integration of professional football occurred with less acrimony than it did in MLB. (In 1939 Jackie Robinson's backfield teammates at the University of California at Los Angeles were Washington and Strode.) Today, 67 percent of the players in the NFL are African Americans (Lapchick, Kitnurse, & Moss, 2010). While professional basketball has more African American players today (77 percent) (Lapchick, Kaiser, Russell, & Welch, 2010), it was the last of the big three sports in the modern era to integrate, with Earl Lloyd playing for the Washington Capitols and Chuck Cooper for the Boston Celtics in 1950. Did economic factors, changes in societal attitudes, or reductions in discriminatory treatment contribute to the dramatic increases in the number of African Americans playing professional football and basketball? Were African American players in these two sports treated respectfully, fairly, and beneficently? Did African American players enjoy equal opportunities with whites to succeed and excel in these sports?

The NBA, though, was the first league to have an African American head coach when Bill Russell was hired in 1966 by the Boston Celtics. In 2009–2010, 27 percent of the head coaches in the NBA were African Americans (Lapchick, Kaiser, Russell, & Welch, 2010). Frank Robinson became the first African American manager in MLB in 1975 when hired by the Cleveland Indians. Lastly in 1990, the Los Angeles Raiders hired Art Shell. (Shell was the second African American head coach in professional football because he was preceded by Fritz Pollard in 1922 with the Akron Pros.) In 2009, African Americans were 19 percent of the head coaches in the NFL (Lapchick, Kitnurse, & Moss, 2010). Are any ethical issues involved when there are significantly more African American players than African American head coaches? Are the white owners (there has never been an African American owner of an NFL team, and there is one African American majority owner in the NBA — who purchased the team from the first African American owner) prejudiced against hiring African Americans to coach their teams? Are African American assistant coaches less likely to be hired as offensive and defensive coordinators, the most frequent positions held by successful candidates for head coaching positions?

There has never been an African American commissioner in MLB (nine white males), NBA (four white males), and NFL (seven white males and one Native American). Box 6.4 provides data on the dearth of African Americans owners and individuals in the top leadership positions in each of these leagues. In addition, there has never been an African American president of the NCAA (six white males) or commissioner of a conference in Division I of the NCAA. Have discriminatory hiring practices resulted from the predominance of whites in leadership roles in professional and intercollegiate athletics? If prejudice exists, what can be done to address the unethical treatment of African Americans? Why has the myth persisted that African Americans are less capable of providing leadership in sports like basketball and football, where as players they are in the majority?

Box 6.4 NUMBER OF AFRICAN AMERICAN LEADERS IN THREE PROFESSIONAL SPORTS*		
	Major League Baseball (2009)[1]	*National Basketball Association (2009–10)*[2]	*National Football League (2009)*[3]
Owners (Majority)	0	1 (Michael Jordan)	0
CEO/Presidents	0	4	0
General Managers	3	3	5
Managers/Head Coaches	4	8	7

*[1]Lapchick, Kaiser, Caudy, & Wang, 2010; [2]Lapchick, Kaiser, Russell, & Welch, 2010; [3]Lapchick, Kitnurse, & Moss, 2010).

Double Discrimination in Sports

African American female athletes find themselves in a double bind of facing discrimination because of their race as well as their gender. Like their African American brothers, for centuries African American females were denied opportunities to compete in sports against and with whites because of the color of their skin. African American female athletes inevitably competed in segregated school- and college-sponsored track meets or basketball games or on teams offered at historically black schools and colleges. As one indication of their skills, in track and field competitions sponsored by the Amateur Athletic Union and at the quadrennial Olympic Games, African American female athletes often excelled. Seldom did they receive much recognition, however, because of their race and gender. As with other females, college-sponsored teams only gradually began to offer educational opportunities and grants-in-aid based on their athletic prowess to African American female athletes. However, by 2007–08 in NCAA Division I competition, African American females comprised 50.1 percent of the basketball players and 29.5 percent of the outdoor track and field athletes (Lapchick, Calderon, Harless, & Turner, 2010). There also are a small percentage of African American female athletes playing sports like volleyball, soccer, and tennis. What is the just distribution of sport opportunities for African American female athletes? Was it ethical that most African American female athletes chose track and field or basketball because these were the only sports available to them?

Dispelling Myths

Society has perpetuated several racial myths that need to be examined and dispelled before sport will equitably accept African Americans.

Myth 1: *African Americans are physiologically superior (that is, they can run faster and jump higher).* Have stereotypical biases about race and athletic performance led to this myth? Questions have been raised about the appropriateness of statistical design, validity, and sampling techniques in the few studies that suggest genetic superiority.

Are the high numbers of African Americans on interscholastic football, basketball, baseball, and track teams related more to opportunities than to genetics? Contrastingly, do fewer African Americans participate and excel in golf, tennis, swimming, figure skating, ice hockey, and gymnastics because the cost of private lessons, club memberships, and expensive equipment and facilities exclude youths from lower socioeconomic circumstances? Although certain bodily measures have shown differences between African American and white athletes in areas such as mesomorphy and vital lung capacity, it has not been proved that these variations directly affect athletic performance.

Myth 2: *African American athletes have the ability to play only reactive, rather than decision-making or leadership, positions on teams.* Do African American athletes have equal opportunities to play all positions, such as quarterback or pitcher? African Americans have historically been restricted to positions where reaction time is a valuable skill. When coaches shifted the positions of African American athletes, this may have reflected stereotypical or prejudicial attitudes that African Americans will succeed only in certain positions. Historically, stacking limited opportunities to develop the leadership skills needed to play quarterback, catcher, or point guard. Although African American athletes have demonstrated the skills required to play every position in football, baseball, and basketball, their percentages in "thinking" positions consistently remain less than their overall participation numbers.

Myth 3: *African American athletes are treated as equals of their white teammates.* Do African American athletes perceive they are treated the same as their teammates? Compared with white athletes, do African American athletes on average earn lower salaries, receive fewer and smaller endorsement opportunities and less media exposure, and occupy fewer positions on team rosters if they are not stars? Do white teammates, coaches, sportswriters, announcers, owners, and members of teams' management staffs ever utter racist comments? Do whites resist consciously or unconsciously any loss of power to or dominance over African Americans? Does justice and beneficence require that all athletes receive equitable opportunities and treatment?

Myth 4: *African American athletes use sport for upward mobility.* Have African Americans placed too much emphasis on athletics by chasing elusive dreams? While chasing the elusive media image of the sports superstar, too many youths squander educational opportunities. Because of different socioeconomic opportunities, however, African Americans seem disproportionately affected. Football coach Joe Paterno, former tennis champion Arthur Ashe, and others have argued that the myth of upward mobility for African Americans has channeled youths into viewing a sport career as the only goal worth pursuing, even though most will not achieve it. Without a professional contract or a college degree, the stark reality of a limited future hits abruptly and harshly.

Myth 5: *African Americans are intellectually inferior and thus not qualified for coaching or team management positions.* Have prejudicial biases restricted the opportunities for African Americans to be hired for leadership positions in sports? The "good old boys" network often leads to hiring coaches, scouts, general managers, and sport officials who are also white. Maybe those in the power positions feel better about hiring someone known or someone like themselves, rather than a lesser-known person of a different race. If athletic managers use objective criteria and conduct open job searches, will qualified African Americans continue to lose out on leadership positions? Are there any ethical issues or moral values involved in traditional hiring practices?

Racist behavior, founded on myths and prejudices, can be traced to a lack of moral reasoning, moral valuing, and an insufficient determination to change. Some people in sport have not been educated for justice and social responsibility. Values do not come to sport administrators and athletes through osmosis; values must be taught and reinforced by principle-centered leaders. Moral reasoning and moral valuing and appreciation and understanding of justice and social responsibility evolve through intentional and planned efforts to instill values in athletes and coaches. Needed are principle-centered leaders who can demonstrate moral values, guide others in living by these values, and instill values through experiences playing on sport teams.

Recommendations

As discussed in previous chapters, the moral values of justice, honesty, and beneficence offer hope for changing prejudicial attitudes and positively affecting behaviors of individuals involved with sports. Racial discrimination and equity are antithetical to each other. Justice demands that African Americans have equitable opportunities to (1) receive equal opportunities to play every position; (2) receive salaries, endorsements, and media exposure on the basis of merit; and (3) be hired for coaching and management positions on the basis of their qualifications.

Whites have opportunities to eliminate discriminatory treatment of African Americans. But an honest appraisal of interscholastic, intercollegiate, and professional sports reveals that equal employment opportunities and affirmative action directives have not fully permeated whites' stronghold in sports. Has this occurred because these directives may not have been valued by those who could make a difference?

Honesty enters the recruiting picture for college coaches. If recruiters reason and act ethically, will they honestly assess young athletes' potential for playing on their teams as well as the abilities of students to successfully earn degrees? Unrealistic promises lead to shattered dreams and continued exploitation of athletes' physical talents.

Beneficence goes beyond treating others fairly. Beneficence means showing kindness. The importance of treating others as one wants to be treated should not be limited by color. The beneficent person in sport will oppose and work to prevent the use of intentional and unintentional words or actions that cause hurt or harm. The beneficent person does no harm, removes harm, prevents harm, and does good because each of these is the right thing to do.

Racial discrimination and inequities cannot coexist with justice, honesty, responsibility, and beneficence. Principle-centered leaders understand, appreciate, and act on the basis of moral values, and ensure that sport eliminates color barriers. What do you believe about equitable treatment of African Americans in sport? Could you change your response to the first question and be able to live with it if you were an African

American? Could you universalize your beliefs to all people in all races and ethnic backgrounds? Are there any exceptions to your belief statements?

In addition, acting responsibly means being ethically accountable for the care and welfare of others, thus countervailing discrimination. Responsibility includes educating others about universal values and principles. Principle-centered sport leaders will treat every African American athlete in the same way as white athletes. Those who act responsibly will not tolerate racial slurs, exploitation of the athletic talents of African Americans, or discrimination in sport personnel decisions.

Summary

Historically, African Americans were excluded from sport competitions with white athletes because of the color of their skin and ignorance of whites concerning fair and just treatment. African Americans' physical abilities often were discounted as genetically based rather than developed through hard work; because of racial bias African Americans have been accused of being intellectually inferior. The media often has ridiculed, stereotyped, omitted, or shortchanged the achievements of African American athletes. African Americans have been hired into few management positions controlling athletics.

Significant progress has been noted as no longer must African Americans endure blatant discrimination in and exclusion from sport teams with whites. African American superstars enjoy huge salaries and the adoration of millions of fans; however, some African Americans believe full equity has not been achieved. Success will occur only when hiring decisions, team selection, media coverage, and other benefits associated with sports are equitable for all, regardless of race.

Although this section focuses on the discriminatory treatment experienced by African Americans and their progress toward racial equity in sport, it does not address the fact that many other ethnic minorities are involved in sport. Historically, ethnic groups including the Irish, Italians, and Jews used sports such as boxing for upward mobility. Many Latinos have contributed their talents in baseball and soccer. Asians, Native Americans, Hispanics, and other ethnic minorities had to combat subtle and overt racism and inequitable treatment, too. Racism remains a major problem in international soccer. With changing social attitudes and renewed emphasis on ethical conduct based on moral values, the future looks much more positive. It is hoped that all ethnic groups will compete side by side and against one another, with all individuals having the opportunity to display their athletic prowess while playing the game justly, honestly, responsibly, and beneficently.

The key to equity in society is education. Today, principle-centered leaders urge everyone to accept diversity on the moral principle that learning about and respecting the differences of each individual will lead to greater appreciation and acceptance, because it is the right thing to do. Shared values such as respect for self and others are essential for equitable treatment. Principle-centered leaders need to intentionally and continuously emphasize values as the foundation for eliminating injustices. This goal requires vigilant emphasis on teaching and reinforcing shared values as people learn to live by morally based principles.

Gender Equity in Sports

Societal expectations about appropriate feminine behavior and gender-bound roles curtailed women's active participation in sport until relatively recent times. Through the 1800s, the few females who pursued careers outside the home threatened the status quo of a woman's "true calling" as wife and mother. Early laws in the United States such as those prohibiting females from owning property or operating businesses verified the dominant position of males. Not until 1920 did females receive, through the 19th amendment, the right to vote.

While males were encouraged to engage in sporting activities, historically most females were excluded. In some sports, females were explicitly or implicitly banned. A few women disregarded disparaging comments and competed in a few sports. Notable among these have been Eleonora Sears in tennis, squash, and polo, Babe Didrikson in track and field, basketball, and golf, Billie Jean King in tennis, Joan Joyce in softball and golf, and Jackie Joyner-Kersee in basketball and track. But each of these female athletes had to endure innuendos about being a tomboy or less than feminine.

Historical Perspectives of Females in Sports

Despite dressing in restrictive feminine attire, some women in the early 1900s engaged in sports like archery and croquet, possibly because these sports emphasized gracefulness rather than assertiveness. When upper-class females began to participate in sports like golf and tennis, they were heavily influenced by a staunchly held belief in Victorianism. This dominant societal perspective dictated the boundaries of propriety for women's attire and behavior. Females were never to be seen sweating (they were supposed to glow). Any interest in sports was

Treating girls and women equitably is a continual issue in sport. Although access has increased for girls and women as athletes, males today are primarily the coaches and administrators of girls' and women's programs.

expected to remain frivolous as social encounters in sporting events always surpassed victories in importance.

During the latter years of the nineteenth century and well into the twentieth century, upper-class women in archery, golf, tennis, and equestrian events invariably stayed within societal norms. An exception occurred in 1926 when Gertrude Ederle accomplished the unthinkable for a woman by swimming the English Channel, shattering the record set by a man. Helen Wills in tennis, Glenda Collett Vare in golf, and Ethelda Bleibtrey in swimming were more respected for their participation in acceptable sports like tennis, golf, and swimming than for their outstanding achievements. Females playing in the All-American Girls Professional Baseball League (1943 to 1954) and with Hazel Walker's Arkansas Travelers professional basketball team (1949 to 1966) were always cognizant of appearing in feminine attire and behaving according to societal expectations, especially competing in these traditionally male sports. Why were there so few female athletes prior to the 1960s? Were females not interested in sports or were they discriminated against by not being allowed and encouraged to compete on sport teams? Box 6.5 provides some examples of noteworthy achievements or events for females in sports. Did these females succeed in sports despite limitations in their opportunities? What moral values may have been violated whenever females were prohibited from competing in sports or provided limited or fewer opportunities?

BOX 6.5 EXAMPLES OF FEMALES' ACHIEVEMENTS IN SPORTS

1879 Twenty females competed in the first National Archery Championship.

1887 The first women's national tennis championships were held in the United States.

1896 Stanford University played the University of California in the first women's intercollegiate basketball game.

1900 Females competed in the Paris Olympic Games in tennis and golf and with males in sailing, croquet, and equestrian, although females were not allowed in the inaugural Olympic Games in 1896.

1912 Females competed in aquatics for the first time in the Olympic Games.

1914 The Amateur Athletic Union held its first national swimming championships including females.

1917 Lucy Slowe became the first female African American national champion in any sport when she won the singles title in the American Tennis Association national tournament.

1924 In the first Winter Olympic Games, figure skating was the only event for females.

1924 The Amateur Athletic Union held the first national basketball tournament for women.

1928 First time females competed in athletics (track and field) and gymnastics in the Amsterdam Olympic Games.

1943–1954 Over 600 females played professional baseball in small Midwestern towns in the All-American Girls Professional Baseball League.

1944 Ann Curtis, a swimmer, became the first female to win the Amateur Athletic Union's Sullivan Award as the outstanding amateur athlete in the United States.

1944 Mary Garber began writing about sports for the *Winston-Salem Journal*. She is believed to be first female staff sports reporter for a daily newspaper.

1948 Alice Coachman became the first black African American female to win a gold medal (high jump) in the London Olympic Games.

1950 Patty Berg helped establish and served as the first president of the Ladies' Professional Golf Association.

1951 Althea Gibson became the first African American player to compete in the tennis championships at Wimbledon (England).

1953 Maureen Connolly became the first female to win the Grand Slam in tennis by winning the four major (United States; Wimbledon; French; and Australian) singles tennis titles in the same season.

1960 In the Rome Olympic Games, African American Wilma Rudolph became the first American female to win three gold medals in the 100-meter dash, 200-meter dash, and 400-meter relay.

1965 Donna de Varona, winner of gold medals in the 400-meter individual medley and 400-meter freestyle relay in the 1964 Tokyo Olympic Games, became the first female sports broadcaster on national television (ABC).

1972 Tennis champion Billie Jean King was named Sportswoman of the Year by *Sports Illustrated*, the first time a female received this "Sportsman of the Year" award.

1974 Little League Baseball admitted girls after losing a lawsuit challenging its refusal to allow girls to play.

1976 The National Junior College Athletic Association offered its first national championships for females. (It now offers 23 national championships in 13 sports for females.)

1976 Females competed in basketball for the first time in the Montreal Olympic Games.

1980 The National Association of Intercollegiate Athletics offered its first national championships for females. (It now offers 11 national championships in 10 sports for females.)

1981 The NCAA offered its first national championships for females. (It now offers 20 national championships in each of three divisions for females.)

1984 Joan Benoit wins the marathon, the first time females are allowed to compete in this event in the Los Angeles Olympic Games.

1991 The NCAA elects Judith Sweet as the first female president.

1992 The first two female players (Nera White and Lusia Harris-Stewart) are inducted into the Naismith Basketball Hall of Fame. (In 1985 Senda Berenson Abbott, who introduced the game to females, was the first female inductee.)

1996 Females competed in soccer and softball for the first time in the Atlanta Olympic Games.

1998 Females competed in ice hockey for the first time in the Winter Olympic Games.

1999 The United States won the Women's World Cup in soccer.

2003 Annika Sorenstam played in a PGA Tour event, the first time in more than half a century that a female competed against males in golf.

2003 Great Britain's Paula Radcliffe set the women's marathon world record of 2:15:25, proving that females were physiologically capable for running sub–2:20 marathons.

2006 Effa Manley, co-owner and business manager of the Newark Eagles in the Negro Leagues, became the first female elected in the National Baseball Hall of Fame.

2009 Pat Summitt, women's basketball coach at the University of Tennessee since 1974, became the first NCAA basketball coach to win 1,000 games.

2010 Kelly Kulick became the Professional Bowlers Association's first female champion by winning the Tournament of Champions.

The clothing worn by female athletes has constantly been a concern because of the fear that their garments would reveal too much flesh. Athletic attire gradually transformed from long dresses including yards of petticoats and corsets in the late 1800s to today's bikinis for beach volleyball. Are there any ethical concerns associated with the bikini uniform for this sport? Bloomers worn by the first females playing basketball when adopted by females in the 1890s gave way to the "scandalous" shiny, short uniforms worn by Babe Didrikson and the Golden Cyclones, the Amateur Athletic Union basketball champion in 1931. How may restrictive clothing worn by female athletes have contributed to their limited opportunities in sports?

It should be noted that males (with many females concurring) believed females and competitive sports were incompatible. Females were believed by most males to be naturally passive, nurturing, and submissive. As protectors of females as wives, mothers, and daughters, many men believed it was their responsibility to shield females from physical harm, including from competing in sports. Only gradually have males gained greater appreciation for females who eagerly, aggressively, and skillfully play sports.

It should be noted, however, that sometimes female athletes are sexualized, such as when the accepted (and expected) uniforms or costumes worn by female athletes emphasize their bodies. For example, in figure skating or ice dancing, female skaters often wear sexually revealing costumes that emphasize their femininity. In gymnastics, the always petite gymnasts choose costumes that emphasize their sexuality because this is the expectation. Female athletes in beach volleyball wear bikinis. Did the National Broadcasting Company feature the matches of Misty May-Treanor and Kerri Walsh because they were winning their second consecutive gold medal in beach volleyball in the Beijing Olympic Games in 2008 or did their feminine bodies attired in bikinis factor into this decision?

As sport opportunities for females increased in the late twentieth century, many males continued to discount females' athletic prowess. The media mostly ignored their accomplishments, with radio and television commentators only occasionally mentioning females' sport scores. With the exception of premier golf and tennis events and a few glamorous Olympic sports like figure skating, swimming, and gymnastics, most female athletes were perceived as inferior and their sport performances unimportant.

Legally, educationally, and socially, females' involvement in the world of work outside the home has been limited, as have their sport opportunities. This examination of gender equity in sports includes how and why discriminatory treatment historically, organizationally, and socially violated ethical standards. Although greater gender equity has been achieved, full acceptance of women as equal with males in sports has yet to be achieved. For example, the 90-game winning streak of the University of Connecticut women's basketball team received some media coverage, but nothing comparable to the hype that would have been given a men's basketball team winning this number of consecutive games.

Gender Inequity in Sports

Sports have historically and traditionally been a man's world. Males competed, coached, organized, publicized, owned, announced, wagered on, and watched sports in virtual exclusion from females. Religious, medical, and societal beliefs relegated females to the home as wives and mothers, although sometimes females watched or led cheers while males competed in sports. Assertiveness, dominance, toughness, tenacity, and leadership were viewed as masculine traits and inappropriate for women. Many males characterized females as too frail, slow, short, weak, or disinterested to become anything more than recreational players in sports.

History reveals, though, that attitudes excluding women from sports grew out of ignorance, societal misperceptions, and medical myths of the time. For example, many physicians claimed female athletes' internal organs might become incapacitated through excessive jumping and running, females might become sterile if they participated in vigorous sports, and female athletes risked using up their limited energy resources in sports, leaving them unprepared for the demands of childbearing. Limited medical knowledge contributed to perceptions that females were incapable of developing and challenging their bodies as males did. Many female physical educators in the early decades of the 1900s reinforced the notion that females should be encouraged to play games, but not compete in sports, because only moderate activity was healthy. Sport competition was considered unbecoming and non-feminine.

Sometimes by fiat, but mostly through societal constraints and norms, girls learned at early ages that their brothers and male classmates were encouraged to compete in sports, while they were discouraged. Boys' toys almost always were associated with assertive, vigorous, and competitive activities, while girls' toys reinforced passive, cooperative, and domestic play. Sometimes girls, disenchanted with inactivity, joined boys in their games and occasionally surpassed them in skills. Yet by the time they reached puberty, most girls faced the self-imposed, parentally imposed, or socially imposed expectation to drop out of competitive sports, although a few continued their sport involvement as fans or cheerleaders. A limited number participated in acceptable sports for females, such as tennis or golf, even though they might have preferred playing baseball. The choice of actively participating in an aggressive team sport like basketball carried the risk of being labeled a tomboy or having one's femininity questioned.

What seems remarkable in retrospect is that few people questioned this status quo. Did people actually believe that males possessed genetic or physiological rights to sports that females lacked? Given the valued outcomes thought to be associated with competitive sports, such as teamwork, fair play, cooperation, discipline, and self-control, why did society advocate the development of these positive outcomes only for males? In what ways did the exclusion of most girls from competitive sports violate the moral principles of justice, honesty, responsibility, and beneficence?

Limited Opportunities in Sports

Before the 1970s, few youth sport programs offered competitive sport opportunities for girls, as they did for boys, because parents and peers did not encourage girls to develop their sport skills. Maybe girls lacked interest, were disadvantaged physiologically in competing against boys, or realized sport competitions did not exist at higher levels and became discouraged about developing skills they would have limited opportunities to use. The few girls who successfully became youth sport athletes, usually in sports deemed appropriate for them, demonstrated self-confidence and determination in overcoming discouraging comments and societal limitations.

A lack of opportunities for girls certainly characterized interscholastic sports until the 1970s. Before this time, other than a small percentage of girls who played basketball, usually in rural, small-town settings, most girls were perceived to be uninterested in or not skilled enough to become serious athletes. Most schools sponsored no sport teams for females even though males had played on sport teams for decades. How and why did school administrators justify offering sport teams for male students only? How was this fair or beneficent?

Similarly, few competitive sport opportunities existed for college women as most female physical educators opposed the male model of highly competitive intercollegiate athletics. Instead, female physical educators claimed women's activity needs were best met through instructional physical education programs, intramurals, and occasional play days or sports days (where social interaction surpassed competition in importance). Gradually, beginning in the late 1960s, it became clear that women with higher levels of athletic skills wanted to compete. Within a decade, a new model for intercollegiate athletics for women that differed from the men's model would begin to challenge the exclusiveness of sport, as society questioned the moral basis for excluding females from sport competitions.

Governing Organizations for Women's Intercollegiate Sports

Building on efforts of preceding organizations, in 1971 the Association for Intercollegiate Athletics for Women (AIAW) emerged as the governing organization over women's sport competitions in colleges. Founded on an educational model that served female athletes, the AIAW expanded to offer 42 national championships in 19 sports for students attending its nearly 1,000 member institutions.

Early women's intercollegiate sport programs operated on shoestring budgets. Coaches initially volunteered their services, and athletes often bought and washed their own uniforms. Teams traveled in cars and vans, ate at fast-food restaurants, and stayed four to a room just so they could compete. Because these female athletes loved competitive sports, they endured difficulties in scheduling facilities, had little to no access to athletic trainers, publicity, and weight-training equipment, and seldom received grants-in-aid. What moral principles were violated when institutions failed to financially support sport teams for females although teams were provided and funded for males?

Some have advocated that the NCAA's decision to compete directly against AIAW championships in 1981–1982 was a power move. Given the AIAW's weak financial status and the NCAA's offer to provide more than $3 million in reimbursements for the expenses of competing institutions, the struggle for control over women's intercollegiate sports was short-lived. After the defection of 20 percent of its members during the 1981–1982 school year, the AIAW ceased to exist in 1982. The NCAA claimed to offer women's athletes greater opportunities through expanded programs, more financial support, and television coverage. Rather than seeing the end of the AIAW as an aggressive takeover, the NCAA viewed its actions positively and in the best interests of women's sports for member institutions. The NCAA alleged that a new federal law (Title IX) required it to sponsor women's championships (this law did not apply to the NCAA).

Title IX of the 1972 Education Amendments

The landmark event in equal educational opportunities for girls and women occurred when Congress passed the Education Amendments of 1972. Title IX of this legislation stipulated that schools and colleges could not discriminate in any of their educational programs, including athletics. The NCAA vigorously opposed Title IX from the outset, lobbying against its passage and repeatedly attempting to limit the scope of Title IX's application to athletics and especially football. Nonetheless, through the issuance of *A Policy Interpretation; Title IX and Intercollegiate Athletics*, the Department of Health, Education, and Welfare (HEW) explained the scope and application of this legislation. Box 6.6 provides an overview that describes the key features of this law.

BOX 6.6 OVERVIEW OF TITLE IX OF THE 1972 EDUCATION AMENDMENTS
- This law prohibits discrimination on the basis of sex in any federally funded education program or activity: "No person in the United States shall, on the basis of sex, be excluded from participation in, be denied the benefits of, or be subjected to discrimination under any educational program or activity receiving Federal financial assistance."
- Section 106.41 Athletics: "No person shall, on the basis of sex, be excluded from participation in, be denied the benefits of, be treated differently from another person or otherwise be discriminated against in any interscholastic, intercollegiate, club or intramural athletics offered by a recipient, or no recipient shall provide athletics separately on such basis."
- *A Policy Interpretation: Title IX and Intercollegiate Athletics*, issued in December 1979, provided guidance to educational institutions about how they must provide equal opportunity for all students. This law specifically requires equal opportunity in three areas:
   - Financial assistance (grants-in-aid) based on athletic ability must be available on a substantially proportional basis to the number of male and female participants in each institution's athletic program.
   - Male and female athletes must receive equivalent treatment, benefits, and opportunities in equipment and supplies, games and practice times, travel and per diem, coaching and academic tutoring, assignment and compensation of coaches and tutors, locker rooms, practice and competitive facilities, medical and training facilities, housing and dining facilities, and in publicity, recruitment, and support services.
   - "The regulation requires institutions to accommodate effectively the interests and abilities of students to the extent necessary to provide equal opportunity in the selec-

tion of sports and levels of competition available to members of both sexes." It may choose to do this in one of these three ways:

- – Participation opportunities are substantially proportionate to the undergraduate enrollment of females and males.
- – If members of one gender have historically been underrepresented among intercollegiate athletes, there must have been a continuing practice of program expansion to meet the interests and abilities of this group.
- – An institution could demonstrate that the interests and abilities of this gender have been fully and effectively accommodated.
- • In 1996, 1998, 2003, 2005, and 2008 the Office of Civil Rights issued letters of clarification that explained more fully, but did not change, the requirements for complying with Title IX.
- • The Equity in Athletics Disclosure Act, which went into effect in 1996, requires each institution receiving federal financial assistance to annually report specific financial and numerical information about its intercollegiate athletic programs.

Possibly because of the money required to provide equal opportunity in athletics or the extent of male dominance in existing sports, many athletic directors and institutions resisted complying with Title IX. What ethical issues emerge when administrators fail to comply with federal law? Are athletic directors acting based on fairness and beneficence when they fail to meet the requirements of Title IX? What moral values are being followed when equal opportunity in the selection of sports and levels of competition is not available to male and female students?

On behalf of its member institutions, the NCAA claimed that equal sharing of athletic funding, facilities, and services would threaten the viability of revenue-producing sports. That is, only an unequal distribution of financial resources and personnel would enable men's revenue-producing sports to earn the monies needed to support other men's sports and add sports for women. How was this argument flawed? Did the potential to earn revenue justify a moral injustice? No one knows what might happen with complete equity because in the four decades since enactment of Title IX, it has not been achieved. Does distributive justice dictate that inequality can never be legitimately defended or justified on the basis of scarcity of goods or an entitlement for those who earn revenues? Is who gets the most monies, facilities, and services more important than justice for all and how males and females are treated?

Although the NCAA failed to get football exempted from the requirements of Title IX, many institutions excluded football from their gender comparisons when reporting on progress in complying with Title IX, even though in violation of this law. Administrators in institutions that expanded their women's athletic programs claimed their actions were based more on a moral obligation of fairness and doing the right thing than fear of losing federal funding for non-compliance. As colleges slowly provided more equitable support for women's teams, they did avoid costly legal battles or negative publicity. Other colleges complied only under the threat of lawsuits alleging discrimination. A few females as a last resort filed lawsuits because they believed that decision makers in athletics (mostly males) violated moral principles and would only change if forced.

A few institutions refused to change. One college claimed Title IX did not apply to athletics because this program received no direct federal funding. The United States Supreme Court in 1984 agreed in *Grove City College v. Bell*. This court decision eliminated the application of Title IX to athletics, resulting in the withdrawal or the Office of Civil Rights' suspension of dozens of cases involving college athletics. Discrimination against women in intercollegiate athletics persisted and in certain instances increased until 1988, when the Civil Rights Restoration Act reapplied Title IX to all educational programs in all institutions receiving federal funds.

In 1992, the United States Supreme Court, in *Franklin v. Gwinnett County Public Schools*, strengthened the likelihood of compliance with Title IX by ruling that individuals discriminated against could receive punitive damages if institutions refused to abide by the law. That is, if females continued to suffer from discriminatory treatment after attempting to have violations of Title IX remediated, institutions found guilty would have to pay for losses suffered as well as their refusal to meet the requirements of this law. Several legal cases, most notably when the United States Supreme Court let stand in 1996 a lower court's ruling in *Cohen v. Brown University*, have consistently ruled that institutions must comply with Title IX. Why were congressional actions, judicial rulings, and threats of financial losses required before sport administrators were willing to treat female athletes equitably?

About a decade after the NCAA took over control of women's intercollegiate athletics, its Gender Equity Task Force released a status report to provide data about the financial support provided to women's intercollegiate sport programs. Table 6.1 provides the results of the initial and subsequent gender equity studies.

TABLE 6.1 NCAA GENDER EQUITY STUDIES
(NATIONAL COLLEGIATE ATHLETIC ASSOCIATION, 1993, 1999, 2006, 2008)

Funding for Female Athletes in NCAA Institutions

	1993	1997–98	2003–04	2005–06
Grants-in-Aid	30%	37.5%	45.1%	45.3%
Operating/Overall	23%	30.7%	36.5%	33.9%
Recruiting	17%	27.6%	32.3%	31.9%

Do these data indicate full compliance with Title IX regulations? It has been suggested that when the participants in men's and women's sports programs would accept as fair and equitable the overall financial support provided to the other gender, then equity has been achieved. Given the fact that this does not exist, what ethical principles are violated? What should be done to ameliorate this disparate treatment?

A few strategies to help with full compliance with Title IX might be: (1) urge the federal government to strictly and fully enforce Title IX; (2) reduce unnecessary expenses associated with men's revenue-producing sports, re-allocate these monies to women's sports, and aggressively seek new dollars to be used to eliminate gender discrimination in sports; (3) adopt the NCAA Division III non–grant-in-aid model with athletics conducted within a primarily academic, non-commercialized framework; and (4) accept the moral responsibility to treat males and females equitably by making athletics gender-blind.

Despite Title IX, in many institutions males continue to receive greater financial support for equipment, facilities, coaching, awards, and other program areas because by their actions athletic directors and their staffs suggest that male athletes deserve preferential treatment. If sport administrators acted justly, would they ensure that all athletes receive equal benefits? How can sport administrators develop their moral reasoning, leading to gender equity in sports?

Unintended Consequences of Changes in Sports for Females

With the NCAA in control of women's and men's intercollegiate sports, males today are the primary coaches and administrators for women's programs. Males predominantly coaching female athletes and administering programs for females may have occurred due to an increase in the number of teams, a lack of qualified female coaches and administrators, merged athletic programs in which males were more experienced, and males feeling more comfortable hiring male coaches and assistant athletic directors. According to Acosta and Carpenter (2010), since 1972 there has been a drop from more than 90 percent to 42.6 percent in the number of females' teams coached by women. The number of females presiding over intercollegiate sport programs for females (i.e., athletic directors) dropped from over 90 percent to 19.3 percent in 2010, with most of these employed at the NCAA Division III level rather than in larger institutions [see Table 6.2 for historical data from Acosta and Carpenter's (2010) longitudinal study]. Have discriminatory hiring practices resulted in over half of the intercollegiate sport teams for females in NCAA institutions being coached by males? Should sport teams for females be coached only by women? What ethical concerns might there be in the 2010 reduction in the percentage of females as head administrators over women's sport teams?

TABLE 6.2 WOMEN IN SPORTS IN NCAA INSTITUTIONS (ALL DIVISIONS)
(DATA FROM A STUDY BY VIVIAN ACOSTA AND LINDA CARPENTER,
"WOMEN IN INTERCOLLEGIATE SPORT — A LONGITUDINAL STUDY —
THIRTY THREE YEAR UPDATE")

Year	Average Number of Teams	Head Coaches of Women's Teams	Head Administrators over Women's Programs	Number of Athletic Directors Division I	Number of Athletic Directors Division II	Number of Athletic Directors Division III
1972	not avail.	Over 90%	Over 90%			
1978	5.61	58.2%	not avail.			
1982	6.59	52.4%	not avail.			
1986	7.15	50.6%	15.2%			
1990	7.24	47.3%	15.9%			
1992	7.09	48.3%	16.8%			
1996	7.53	47.7%	18.5%			
2000	8.14	45.6%	17.8%	27	45	99

Year	Average Number of Teams	Head Coaches of Women's Teams	Head Administrators over Women's Programs	Number of Athletic Directors Division I	Number of Athletic Directors Division II	Number of Athletic Directors Division III
2004	8.32	44.1%	18.5%	28	47	113
2006	8.45	42.4%	18.6%	31	50	110
2008	8.65	42.8%	21.3%	29	53	142
2010	8.64	42.6%	19.3%	30	43	128

Although the United States Department of Education considers the elimination of teams to achieve Title IX compliance as a disfavored practice, several institutions during the past several years have reduced the number of athletic teams for males and females or threatened to take this action. For example, in recent years, James Madison University stopped offering seven men's and three women's teams; Rutgers University dropped five teams for males and one team for females; and the University of California-Berkeley eliminated two men's teams and reduced one men's team to club status (although two women's teams were initially identified for elimination, this did not occur). Two reasons are typically given for the elimination of sport teams. When teams for both genders are dropped, the stated justification is inevitably the lack of financial resources to support them. If only teams for males are eliminated, athletic directors typically claim that this is only way to achieve proportionality in complying with the first option of the three-part test for measuring compliance with meeting the interests and abilities of the under-represented gender in athletics. This pitting of men against women leads to the question: what is the ethical basis for simultaneously claiming to do good to one gender while harming the other gender?

As female athletes began to specialize in one sport, train year-round, and sometimes prioritize athletics over academics, they were adopting the males' model for intercollegiate sports. As winning became all-important to female athletes, participation in sports was found to negatively influence females' moral reasoning levels in comparison with those of non-athletes. In addition, females' moral reasoning levels decrease the longer they participate in sport, an alarming trend also found for males. Female athletes' moral reasoning and development has been shown to be significantly higher than that of male athletes, although this gap is narrowing. Is there a connection between female athletes following the males' model for intercollegiate athletics and erosion in their moral reasoning?

Interscholastic Sport Changes for Girls

The National Federation of State High School Associations and its member (state) organizations historically focused on sports for boys. By assuming girls lacked interest or skills, administrators in most schools disregarded the activity and competitive needs of half of their students until the 1970s ushered in a new era in the treatment of aspiring female athletes.

The impact of Title IX, although gradual, was dramatic in most schools even though some school administrators were resistant to treating all athletes fairly and justly. Instead of relegating girls' sports to non-traditional seasons (e.g., basketball in the fall and soccer in the spring) under the guise of optimal use of facilities, these sports were returned to their traditional seasons that allowed the athletes to have equitable opportunities to be recruited to play on intercollegiate sport teams. Girls and boys in the 1980s began to share more equitably the use of practice and competitive facilities, athletic trainers, and weight rooms. Gymnasiums and fields were shared more equally between teams for both genders. Females were given access to weight-training rooms and athletic trainers.

Interscholastic sport teams for girls have increased since the 1970s with the number of girls competing growing from 294,015 in 1971–1972 to 3,172,637 in 2009–2010 (National Federation of State High School Associations, 2010). Because of a lack of females prepared for or interested in coaching, the increased number of teams, greater equity in coaching stipends, and male athletic directors hiring the coaches for girls' teams, more male coaches were hired. These hiring practices may be attributable in part to the fact that most high school athletic directors have been and continue to be men, who frequently consider males more qualified to coach than females.

Title IX has been unquestionably important in the elimination of gender-based discrimination in sports. This federal legislation would have been unnecessary had people truly valued females' right to sports competition. Why did male decision makers value the educational experiences of sports for males but not for females? Was it fair and just to refuse to fund competitive opportunities for females? Why did the legal system have to mandate compliance and threaten financial losses for those who refused? Did the possible loss of federal funding and the negative media attention lead to greater compliance than did the belief that gender equity in sports is a moral issue? The establishment and growth of the AIAW primed the pump by offering opportunities to women to develop their sport skills. Title IX's mandate for the elimination of inequities in financial support, access to facilities, and overall athletic opportunities led to significant increases in the quality and quantity of sport programs for girls and women. Have principle-centered leaders achieved equity in sports for females or does some inequity persist? If inequity still persists, why does it?

Societal Attitudes

One illustration of societal or psychological pressure placed on females is the emphasis on participating in what some label as feminine sports. Many people, for example, believe that females should not play baseball or football, box, race cars or horses, play rugby, pole vault, wrestle, or ride rodeo bulls. Is it permissible to play basketball, softball, volleyball, soccer, or run track but without risking how others view athletes' femininity? Do some females choose tennis, golf, swimming, figure skating, and gymnastics because they are more likely to receive media attention and societal approval for their achievements in sports which are viewed as more feminine?

As discussed in the historical section, societal attitudes in the past constrained and today continue to limit competitive sport opportunities for females. Individuals with preconceived ideas and maybe stereotypical biases believe and advocate that females should not be assertive, independent, or tough, although success in sport demands each of these traits as well as other so-called masculine characteristics. Society heaps praise and rewards on males who achieve in sports. To a much lesser extent, females receive accolades, trophies, and other awards for their sports achievements. Do the media largely ignore sportswomen, giving most of its print, broadcast, and electronic coverage to males? Why is or is this not ethical? Often when females' sports accomplishments are publicized, the media depicts them in sexist ways that undermine their seriousness as athletes. Does the media's image of female professional athletes trivialize their accomplishments as athletes? Do male sports stars receive praise for their physical prowess and skillful performances, while the coverage of female athletes emphasizes clothing, hair styles, and mannerisms?

Although males in general possess physiological advantages in sport, whenever females succeed in competing on equal terms with males — that is, at similar elite levels or as opponents — often their femininity is questioned or they are derided as being somewhat less of a woman. For example, Babe Didrikson, who was named the greatest female athlete of the first half of the twentieth century by the Associated Press, had to endure numerous disparaging comments because of her prowess in several sports. Even today female athletes are subjected to stereotypical put-downs and prejudicial treatment whenever they step outside others' perceived boundaries of propriety.

Often, attempts to put women in their place demonstrate ignorance of physiological facts about females' abilities to compete in sports. Will the limitations of discrimination change only if values are challenged through education, dialogue, and debate? How can moral reasoning challenge those in charge who hold to unfair and immoral practices?

Another societal issue that affects females and males in competitive sports is homophobia, which is characterized by negative attitudes and feelings toward lesbian, gay, bisexual, and transgender individuals. Homophobia may lead to fear of, discrimination against, and hostile behavior toward people who may choose partners of the same sex or a lifestyle differing from a heterosexual orientation. In the past, sometimes female athletes, especially those playing team sports, were labeled as lesbian, gay, or queer as a negative put-down and a way to demean or devalue their athletic achievements. Like racism and other forms of bigotry, homophobic rhetoric sought to dehumanize or demean the accused. While incidents of homophobia have lessened because of greater acceptance of individual rights and legal threats against discriminatory treatment, residual homophobia exists, and especially in sports because of the prevalence of locker room interactions among athletes.

Continuing Questions

Females do not suffer from total exclusion from sports or have to endure many of the discriminatory practices of the past. But, even though four decades have passed since Title IX banned gender discrimination in athletic programs offered by educational institutions receiving federal funding, full equity for females in sports remains elusive. Does insidious discrimination, advancements occurring only because of lawsuits or threats of lawsuits, and continued under-representation of females in coaching, athletic training, officiating, sport administration, and the sport media persist? Several problem areas are identified below, with alternatives to consider for each.

Issue 1: Who should coach female sport teams, and who should administer their programs?

Discussion: Who should coach and manage sport teams for males of all ages? Nearly 100 percent of the responses would affirm males. However, relative to the gender of the coach or administrator for females' teams of all ages, opinions are sharply divided. This ongoing issue is based on the hegemonic status of males in their domination of sports based on physical advantages, historic precedence, or prejudicial practices. Societal restrictions on the proper roles of females also have affected the domination of males in sports. Arguments persist that males know more about sports and thereby are better qualified than females to coach and lead sport programs. So, as the number of female sport teams at all competitive levels grew along with increased salaries for coaches of these teams, more males chose to coach females. These males were also more likely to be hired by male athletic directors.

Lacking sufficient female role models as coaches and sport administrators, many females, even those with highly successful competitive experiences, choose other careers. A lack of sufficient female applicants made it easier for males to hire males. One reason is that societal attitudes continue to expect females to fulfill most of the duties associated with home and children, thus making it more challenging for females to balance these responsibilities with the time and travel demands of coaching.

Does society value and appreciate the contributions that females can make as coaches and sport administrators? To facilitate a change in attitudes, females need a mentoring system to provide them with opportunities to develop knowledge and skills for success. Because role modeling helps teach values and develop a moral reasoning process, principle-centered leaders should hire qualified female coaches and sport administrators to provide athletes with same-gender teachers of ethical principles.

Issue 2: Does financial support for sport programs at all levels of competition inequitably favor males? If so, what ethical action might be required?

Discussion: Although equal opportunity, as required by Title IX, does not stipulate the expenditure of equal dollars for male and female teams, it does mandate equal opportunities in sports. Despite repeated threatened and actual lawsuits during the past four decades, the treatment of female athletes, while significantly enhanced, has yet to fully equal that enjoyed by males. More than half of the undergraduate students in colleges are females, yet they receive 40 percent or less of the athletic departments' financial resources for grants-in-aid, recruiting, and operational expenses. Most colleges expend huge sums of money on their football programs, regardless of whether they are producing revenue or not, and claim that equity exists in their sport programs as long as football is omitted from any comparisons.

Principle-centered leaders in sports should allocate equitable funding for males and females on the basis of participation numbers. A quota system is not necessarily fair because it assumes that a 50/50 split is the answer to a challenge that cannot be addressed so simplistically. Such an arbitrary decision, allegedly required by Title IX, could be unfair to males. Moral reasoning demands that one examines what is just, honest, and beneficent. For example, is it honest to claim that revenues from football finance all other sports and thus this team deserves a larger budget, when in reality most football teams lose money? Is it just to perpetuate traditional practices of preferentially treating programs for males? Is it responsible to provide teams for males with better facilities, certified athletic trainers, plush travel accommodations, and highly qualified coaches, while females' teams experience few of these program support services? Is it beneficent to fail to promote, fund, or expand females' competitive sport opportunities? Greater opportunities for females demand increased funding. If males should not receive special treatment, as reasoned thinking leads one to conclude, principle-centered leaders are needed to treat male and female athletes equitably. Another alternative obligates administrators to raise more money.

Issue 3: Should more college grants-in-aid be awarded to male athletes?

Discussion: An argument for favoring males in the awarding of grants-in-aid is that males are more highly skilled, more interested in sports, and more willing to work harder to enhance their athletic skills. Some vocal advocates for preferentially treating male athletes argue that since they bring in revenue, it should be theirs to spend. Conversely, those who support the equitable distribution of grant-in-aid funds state that discriminating against females is illegal and immoral, because once funds are available in athletic departments each student-athlete should be treated similarly. Providing financial assistance to only males or only males playing in revenue-producing sports denies females sport opportunities to improve their skills and engage in school- or college-sponsored extracurricular activities. Moral reasoning calls for a distribution of grants-in-aid in ways that are ethically defensible. That is, what is fair (and legally compliant)?

Issue 4: Should males have a greater number of participation opportunities than females at all levels of sport?

Discussion: Society traditionally has encouraged boys to engage in sports while providing less encouragement to girls. As a result, many more teams were available for males while teams for females were not even formed because of lack of interest. Although in recent years more females have been eagerly seeking teams to play on, they are not always welcome, such as on baseball, wrestling, or football teams. Since females have been competing in sports for such a brief time, it is unknown the extent to which their interests and skills will grow. The important decision that recreation departments, private clubs, schools, colleges, professional leagues, and the public must make is to what degree each entity should finance teams for females. Principle-centered leaders will determine whether to permit combined teams of girls and boys, how many different competitive levels of teams can be financed for each gender, and what sports should be offered to each gender separately or together. The challenge is to ensure that every child, student, and adult has opportunities in sports that she and he deserves and desires.

Related to this issue is whether females should be on the same teams with males or compete only against each other. There is ample evidence that prior to puberty there is little physiological advantage enjoyed by males. While sometimes in T-ball, soccer, and other sports boys and girls are on the same teams, this quickly changes when coaches (usually male) and sport administrators argue (and typically establish the rules) that boys will not learn to compete as aggressively or develop their sport skills as rapidly as long as the genders are combined. Inevitably, this skews the number of teams heavily in favor of boys, as girls begin to drop out when discouraged from playing on teams with boys. Exceptions occur when a few occasional highly skilled females play on teams comprised predominantly of boys or when females are allowed to compete for spots on wrestling or football teams. Title IX does not require that females be allowed to compete with males in contact sports. Post-puberty, males have decided advantages in strength and height, although given the short time that females have competed at the highest levels in sports, their potential is not yet fully known.

Issue 5: Should men control all levels of sport, with only a few women holding administrative positions in sport?

Discussion: Principle-centered leaders who hire athletic directors and their assistants, sports information and marketing directors, athletic trainers, and other sport administrators need to seek qualified women for these positions. They also should try to attract women for internships and assistants' positions to prepare them to become coaches and sport administrators because of the unique skills, perspectives, and styles these females would contribute to sport. No longer will only the autocratic, command-control management style of the male ex-coach work in sports. Rather, the building of relationships through encouragement, flexibility, and nurturing—traits more characteristic of females—will enhance performance in the sport setting as they have in the corporate world.

Moral Education

An overarching resolution to each of these issues requires moral education. Principle-centered leaders in sports need to model their personal values like integrity and respect. An athletic department's mission statement and purposes, as reflective of values and beliefs of principle-centered leaders, should match a philosophy that encompasses moral knowing, moral valuing, and moral acting.

The ethical issues pervading gender equity in sports remain, as does the importance of justice, honesty, and beneficence. Justice requires that female athletes receive fair treatment. This encompasses all the financially supported services associated with sports. Is it fair or just to fly the men's basketball team to a competition 250 miles away while expecting the women's basketball team to travel in vans? Would you reverse your response if you were a member of the women's basketball team? Does distributive justice demand equitable treatment regardless of skill level or fan popularity?

Are athletic directors, who are mostly men, honest when they state or demonstrate through their hiring practices that women are not interested in or qualified for coaching or athletic administration positions? Admitting to past discriminatory hiring practices and aggressively seeking to rectify them verifies that one believes in the importance and right of females serving as leaders in sport. Given the discussion about moral reasoning and moral development in the preceding chapters, it appears one effective strategy could be an educational intervention that helps individuals analyze what they value and why.

Responsibility governs how sport leaders and athletes deal with each other. Both should demonstrate a commitment to making things work for the greater good. If principle-centered leaders act responsibly on the basis of their beliefs and values, the existing system will enact change and promote gender equity in sport.

Based on this historical, organizational, and societal analysis of women in sport, have the characteristics of beneficence been achieved? Principle-centered leaders who believe in beneficence will work tirelessly to remove and prevent discrimination based on gender in sport. Beneficence leads to kind words and deeds. Sport administrators and media personnel who act upon ethical principles will stop demeaning, stereotyping, or ignoring female athletes. Kindness would lead to acceptance of females as equals in management positions in sports. Beneficent individuals will encourage females to achieve their athletic potentials through increased participation and competitive opportunities in the absence of discriminatory treatment.

Summary

Historically, females' opportunities have been limited because of societal perceptions of their lack of interest and ability, physiological myths, and discriminatory exclusion. Athletic programs for females remain unequal, even after being combined with existing men's governance structures. Title IX has helped females achieve greater equity, but full equality remains somewhat elusive because too many people do not value the right of women to equitable treatment within sports. Females also have not achieved significant movement into the power positions controlling sport. However, each new head coach of a female team or female sport administrator hired signals another victory in the battle for gender equity in sport. Many more are needed, along with equitable treatment, before discrimination in competitive sports will be fully eradicated.

Megan, Micah, Jeremy, and Jareem have discovered that the issue of racism and sexism is not simple or easily solvable. Some have suggested that discrimination and prejudice may always exist. With power comes corruption, and it doesn't matter what race or gender you are, you will be tempted to use that power. The real test of a principle-centered leader is to use that power to create equity and to break down the barriers of our own prejudice. You have the opportunity to make a difference and one of the most important things you can do is to enter into discussions with your peers and professors.

References

Acosta, R. V., and L. J. Carpenter (2010). *Women in Intercollegiate Sport: A Longitudinal Study—Thirty Three Year Update.* Retrieved from http://www.acostacarpenter.org/.

Lapchick, R., A. D. Calderon, C. Harless, and A. Turner (2010). *The 2009 Racial and Gender Report Card: College Sport.* Retrieved from http://web.bus.ucf.edu/documents/sport/2009_College_Sport_RGRC.pdf.

Lapchick, R., C. Kaiser, D. Caudy, and W. Wang (2010). *The 2010 Racial and Gender Report Card: Major League Baseball.* Retrieved from http://web.bus.ucf.edu/documents/sport/2010_MLB_RGRC.pdf.

Lapchick, R., C. Kaiser, C. Russell, and N. Welch (2010). *The 2010 Racial and Gender Report Card: National Basketball Association.* Retrieved from http://web.bus.ucf.edu/documents/sport/2010_NBA_RGRC.pdf.

Lapchick, R., J. M. Kitnurse, and A. Moss II (2010). *The 2010 Racial and Gender Report Card: National Football League.* Retrieved from http://web.bus.ucf.edu/documents/sport/2010-NFL-Racial-and-Gender-Report-Card.pdf.

National Collegiate Athletic Association. (1993). *Final Report of the NCAA Gender-Equity Task Force.* Retrieved from http://web1.ncaa.org/web_files/gender_equity/resource_materials/Historical/Task_Force_Report.pdf.

National Collegiate Athletic Association. (1999). *1997–98 NCAA Gender-Equity Report.* Retrieved from http://web1.ncaa.org/web_files/library/research/gender_equity_study/1997-98/index.html.

National Collegiate Athletic Association. (2006). *2003–04 NCAA Gender-Equity Report.* Retrieved from http://web1.ncaa.org/web_files/library/research/gender_equity_study/2003-04/2003-04_gender_equity_report.pdf.

National Collegiate Athletic Association. (2008). *2005–06 NCAA Gender-Equity Report.* Retrieved from http://www.ncaapublications.com/productdownloads/GER06.pdf.

National Federation of State High School Associations. (2010). 2009–10 High school athletics participation survey. Retrieved from http://www.nfhs.org/content.aspx?id=3282&linkidentifier=id&itemid=3282.

Additional Readings

Aaseng, N. (1993). *The Locker Room Mirror: How Sports Reflect Society.* New York: Walker.

Carpenter, L. J., and R. V. Acosta (2005). *Title IX.* Champaign, IL: Human Kinetics.

Coakley, J. J. (2009). *Sport in Society: Issues and Controversies* (10th ed.). Boston: McGraw-Hill.

Davis, T. (1995). "The Myth of the Superspade: The Persistence of Racism in College Athletics." *Fordham Urban Law Journal, 22,* 615–698.

Hoose, P. M. (1989). *Necessities: Racial Barriers in American Sports.* New York: Random House.

Lapchick, R. E. (1991). *Five Minutes to Midnight: Race and Sport in the 1990s.* Lanham, MD: Madison.

Lapchick, R. E. (2001). *Smashing Barriers: Race and Sports in the New Millennium.* Lanham, MD: Madison.

Lapchick, R. E. (2006). (Ed.). *New Game Plan for College Sport.* Westport, CT: Praeger.

Shropshire, K. L. (1998). *In Black and White: Race and Sports in America.* New York: University Press.

U.S. Department of Education. (1979, December 11). "A Policy Interpretation: Title IX and Intercollegiate Athletics." Retrieved from http://www.ed.gov/about/offices/list/ocr/docs/t9interp.html.

Zimbalist, A., and Hogshead-Makar, N. (2008). *Equal Play: Title IX and Social Change.* Philadelphia: Temple University Press.

CHAPTER 7

Competitive Advantages in Sports

- How do eligibility issues in all levels of competitive sports relate to moral values?
- Why have the number and specificity of eligibility regulations increased in all levels of competitive sports?
- How can ethical dilemmas associated with the breaking of eligibility rules in all levels of competitive sports be resolved?
- What are the ethical issues associated with the use of stimulants, depressants, anabolic steroids, and blood doping by athletes for enhancing their performances in competitive sports?
- What are the legal and moral issues surrounding drug testing in sports?
- What are the ethical issues associated with the use of legal drugs and genetic engineering in competitive sports?

You and your sport management peers have just finished a class in sport ethics focusing on the dilemma of gaining advantage through the use of performance-enhancing substances. The lecture focused on the problem of ingesting supplements to improve performance, and part of the lecture concerned the issue of ingesting supplements that could be tainted by unknown sources.

Micah, ever the disbeliever, starts the discussion. "You guys don't believe all of the stuff, do you? I am here to tell you I have been using XYZ products for years in my weight training and look at me, I'm a specimen of fitness and muscle."

Megan: "You do look good, but are you sure that what you are taking is okay?"

Micah: "Of course, it's okay. I bought it at XYZ and their products are advertised in all of the major fitness and muscle magazines. I'm taking a product now that really seems to be helping me and XYZ guarantees that it's a legal substance."

Jeremy: "Guaranteed? Aren't you a little worried about that—guaranteed? Aren't most of these products made in a foreign country and distributed in this country?"

Micah: "What's that have to do with it?"

Jeremy: "I read in our text that most of these supplements are not under the control of the United States Food and Drug Administration because the supplements are not considered food products so they are not monitored."

Micah: "I don't get what you are saying."

Jeremy: "What I am saying is that these supplements, like most vitamins and other drugs, really are not guaranteed to be what is advertised. In fact, the percentages of active ingredients in them may not be anywhere near what is advertised, and there may be other products included that aren't advertised to be in them, like anabolic steroids."

Micah: "So what? As long as it works, no harm, no foul."

Jareem: "No harm, no foul? Look, we are supposed to be future professionals in the field. Shouldn't we be concerned about this sort of thing because of all the performance-enhancing products out there and all the rules and regulations against using the stuff? Surely we should be concerned about what we take ourselves."

Micah: "So now you are telling me that I'm supposed to be some sort of role model? Look, I take vitamins and supplements. I know that Megan takes supplements because she's worried about bone loss. So what's the big deal?"

Jareem: "The big deal is we should be very careful about what we are taking; we live in a time in which people think that everything physiological can be fixed by a pill."

Jeremy: "Jareem has a point here. We as sport managers should be supporting good nutrition rather than supporting quick fixes through chemistry. We should be very thoughtful about what we believe in and what we do."

Micah: "Don't you guys know that performance enhancement has been around forever?"

Jeremy: "Well, anabolic steroids have not been around forever. Actually, they date from about 1920 and got their real start during the Josef Mengele era of Nazi Germany. Adolf Hitler needed a super race of police troops, the SS, who would have no conscience. Hitler called on his physician to figure out how to accomplish the task. Mengele, through experimentation on Jewish concentration camp prisoners, figured out how to extract testosterone and use it as an injectable substance to overcome the conscience of the SS troops. When Germany fell in 1945, the Mengele labs were discovered by the Soviets, and by 1948, anabolic steroids were being used in the sporting community. One could make the argument that anabolic steroids are actually the result of evil chemistry by very evil people."

Micah: "Okay, so anabolic steroids may have started under evil conditions, but they are used today to treat all sorts of diseases."

Jeremy: "That may be true, but choosing to use a supplement to enhance performance probably is not the best choice. You are making a moral justification based on questionable facts. We aren't talking here about a drug to help a wasted, diseased child; we are talking about chemistry to improve performance. Don't the World Anti-Doping Agency, the United States Anti-Doping Agency, and most other competitive regulatory bodies ban these drugs?"

Micah: "Sure, but you all know that all of those beefed-up bodies didn't occur through eating steak. Not all of us got the great gene pool like Jeremy here. I come from a family of short un-athletic people. I want to get girls to look at me — the extra muscle gives me an extra competitive advantage."

Megan: "That's sad. What sort of woman do you want who only wants your body?"

Micah: "Give me a break, that's the way of the world. If you don't look good you aren't going to be competitive — in the babe competition and the job market. And if you don't have the size and bulk on the athletic field you don't have a chance. That's why performance sup-

plements exist — to give an advantage — and that's why they have always existed. Even the Greeks knew how to use products and training techniques to get an advantage."

Megan: "I don't think training should be compared to using performance-enhancing drugs."

Micah: "Oh, really? Why do we train? Why do we eat well? Isn't it all about getting an edge? Why not use the most current and best technologically advanced substances to get an advantage?"

Megan: "Well, for one reason, because most of the stuff is against the rules of fair play."

Micah: "Fair play, oh please! There is no such thing as fair play. It's always been about getting the advantage. Look, here in the U.S. and other leading countries we have the best technology, so why shouldn't we use it? Using performance-enhancing drugs is no different from using technology to gain advantage. It's no different from using a knee brace if I have a weak knee. It's all about overcoming a disadvantage — my genes are a disadvantage. If we have the technology, use it."

Megan: "In that case, it just becomes an arms race of who has the best equipment, the best drugs, the best technology. Shouldn't we really want having the best athletes perform?"

Jareem: "Yeah, wouldn't that be great. Let's take all the world's best athletes, put them in the same place with the same coaches, the same equipment, the same nutrition, let them train for a year and then see who the best athlete really is. Wouldn't that be great? It would really be about competition instead of equipment and technology."

Micah: "Right, like that's going to happen."

You jump into the conversation. "Well maybe it could happen — if more people like us worked for it when we become the sport managers in charge, maybe we could make a difference!"

This conversation continues because winning in competitive sports is so handsomely rewarded in the United States, as reported 24/7 through the electronic and print media. Athletes earn multi-million-dollar salaries because they help teams win. Young athletes on playgrounds and in schools and colleges spend countless thousands of hours honing their skills while dreaming of becoming the next wealthy superstar. Because sport stars are rewarded financially and held in such high esteem, often athletes (and coaches and sport administrators) will use every available ethical and unethical means to win.

Athletes learn from parents, coaches, and teammates about the importance of gaining every possible competitive advantage. Even though gaining competitive advantages in sports often occurs outside the rules, such as when eligibility regulations are disregarded or blatantly violated, this does not concern most people. As a result, in all levels of competitive sports, new rules and regulations are enacted to thwart the actions of coaches, parents, sport administrators, and athletes who find loopholes in eligibility and recruiting rules or find ways to circumvent written rules so the most talented athletes play with the best teams.

Another way to gain competitive advantages is through the use of performance-enhancing drugs to build strength, enhance speed, expand energy levels, control weight, and increase aggressiveness. When faced with drug tests intended to prevent the use of performance-enhancing drugs, many athletes find ways to cycle on and off these drugs without getting caught or change to new drugs that cannot be detected through existing drug tests.

The ethical issues associated with violations of eligibility and recruiting rules, and with prohibitions on the use of performance-enhancing drugs, will be discussed in this chapter. To address the morally bereft actions of those who choose to violate sport rules, principle-centered leaders are needed who will model values like honesty and fairness and facilitate the moral education of athletes, coaches, and sport administrators to preserve and enhance the integrity of competitive sports.

Eligibility and Recruiting Rules in Sports

Eligibility concerns pervade competitive sports because many athletes, coaches, and sport administrators try to gain advantages over their opponents by breaking written rules and violating the spirit of the rules. What is the right thing to do? Why is it right? What socio-moral perspective underlies the decision-making process? If the non-moral outcome of winning exceeds in importance playing fairly and according to the rules, some may choose to do whatever it takes to win. This is especially true when the likelihood of being penalized is unlikely or penalties are small in comparison to the risks of being caught.

Beginning with early Greek competitors, winners received lucrative rewards and acclaim, while non-winners were ignored or disdained. Since there were no silver, bronze, or other medals or ribbons, every athlete who did not win was considered a loser. Over the centuries, the importance placed on winning in competitive sports grew stronger. Since athletes vigorously pursued victors' prizes and coaches and athletes cleverly and creatively exploited eligibility and recruiting regulations to gain competitive advantages, rules were added, expanded, and made more specific. When seeking to win results in unethical actions involving who is eligible to compete against whom, the non-moral value of winning supersedes moral values like justice, honesty, and beneficence.

Eligibility Concerns in Youth Sports

The passion for winning, gaining a competitive advantage, and being number one begins at the youth sport level, often resulting in breaking the rules such as when parents falsify birth certificates and lie on participation forms so larger, older, and more skilled players can win against younger, lesser skilled players. For example, in 2001 the father of Danny Almonte falsified his son's birth certificate so that he could compete in a baseball league for younger players. Danny was 14 years old (two years overage) when his no-hitter and other pitching achievements helped his team place third in the Little League Baseball World Series. When the ruse was exposed, Almonte and his teammates were required to forfeit their victories and endure the hurt of having been pawns maneuvered by the unethical actions of adults. Instead of modeling honesty and integrity, Danny's father and coach showed how to cheat to win.

Sometimes winning for national pride leads to cheating. For example, Chinese officials have lied about the ages of gymnasts and skaters so athletes below the minimal eligible ages would qualify for international competitions, including the Olympic Games.

Parents may lie to get their sons or daughters signed up for sport programs when they are under the minimal age. Typically, this occurs because parents want to give their children a jump or head start on other children or because they believe their children are so talented that regardless of age, they can be successful. When lying results in gaining unfair advantages, this is a lesson learned by athletes at a very young age.

Eligibility rules in football and wrestling restrict players to certain weight classes to limit the injury potential of larger, heavier individuals competing against smaller, lighter players. Although scales monitor weights, ethical and health issues surface whenever athletes attempt to compete below their developmentally appropriate weights. Some parents and coaches encourage athletes to drop weight using the quickest ways, such as by severely reducing caloric intake, exercising in rubber suits or excessive clothing, and taking diuretics. Serious health problems due to dehydration and electrolyte imbalance, and even death, are possible consequences of such unprincipled behaviors. Despite sport governing organizations specifically prohibiting these approaches to weight loss, some athletes continue to engage in them because parents and coaches pressure them to lose weight. These young athletes have not been educated about the rules disallowing such practices, or parents, coaches, and athletes prioritize gaining competitive advantages. If wrestling in weight classes is about matching competitors, what does dropping weight through high-risk methods say about competing by the spirit of the rules and valuing the welfare of competitors?

Youth sport programs rely on voluntary compliance with eligibility rules. But when coaches and parents get their pride and egos too invested in winning, they begin to try to gain inappropriate and often unhealthy competitive advantages in children's sports. For example, some youth sport leagues establish rules for who can play on teams based on where children live. Yet some parents will do whatever it takes to get and keep their children playing on the best teams by lying about legal residences or legal guardians, actions that have happened on Little League Baseball teams. Without a formal enforcement mechanism, usually such actions go unquestioned as parents are praised for their subterfuge. Coaches may actively recruit these players or are complicit with parents, even though their actions violate league rules. Whenever any of these unethical actions are taken by parents and coaches, who irresponsibly demonstrate that eligibility rules are made to be broken rather than followed, young athletes are learning unethical lessons.

Eligibility Concerns in Interscholastic Sports

The purpose of interscholastic sports should be to enhance the overall experiences of athletes by contributing to their physical, mental, psychological, social, and emotional development. In addition to enhancing sport skills and physical fitness, it is claimed that high school athletes can develop character, build self-confidence and self-discipline, learn how to win and lose with class, learn about teamwork, and gain skills they can use later in their lives. Interscholastic sports are rallying symbols for communities where on Friday nights on rural fields and in local gymnasiums, teams and towns vie for bragging rights in football and basketball.

Abuses, however, creep into interscholastic sports whenever an overemphasis on winning becomes commonplace. To curb problems associated with playing ineligible players, eligibility rules were enacted by state athletic associations affiliated with the National Federation of State High School Associations. These rules address age, residence, amateur status and remuneration, and academics.

Age requirements stipulate both maximal age limits and the number of years athletes can compete, to prevent individuals who are older and more physically mature students from continuing to play on interscholastic sport teams. Occasionally, falsified birth certificates allow athletes to play when they are older than allowed. A similar eligibility rule associated with age specifies that students can compete for only three years between the 10th and 12th grades. State associations enacted this limitation to prevent parents from insisting that their children repeat a grade so they could play another year when they would have physiological advantages. To get around this rule and gain physiological and developmental advantages in sports, however, some parents will arrange to have their children repeat grades before the high school years. Seldom are children consulted about being held back a grade, although they might agree with actions that could enhance possibilities of excelling in sports and enjoying the prestige associated with winning. Although willing parties in ethically questionable practices at the time, these young athletes later may conclude they were manipulated, especially if they lose, drop out of competitive sport programs, and realize their educational advancement was needlessly delayed a year.

Public schools typically serve specific geographic areas with athletes eligible to attend classes and play on interscholastic sport teams only in school districts where they live. State athletic associations had to specify through eligibility rules that athletes attend schools where they lived because some parents chose to enroll their children in schools with the best sport teams. Given these rules, sometimes coaches openly or covertly recruited highly skilled athletes to move into their school districts. When other coaches or schools offer what are perceived as better opportunities for athletic success, many high school athletes, with their parents' encouragement or agreement, choose to transfer to the new schools. These moves comply with the written eligibility rule when legal guardians of athletes are changed or when athletes leave home to live with relatives or friends (and sometimes coaches). What lesson about ethical behavior are adolescents learning when coaches entice them to lie about or misrepresent where they live to circumvent residency rules? Are adolescents behaving ethically when they attend different high schools each year in search of better coaches, greater media exposure, or improved opportunities to win championships? For Michael Beasley, the second pick in the 2008 National Basketball Association draft, his high school odyssey included attending six schools in four states.

One way to work around limited geographic school boundaries occurs whenever public school systems offer unique academic programs to serve all students within a metropolitan area. Coaches of teams at these schools can openly recruit star athletes under the guise that these recruited athletes are interested in the unique academic programs these schools offer. Similarly, private schools have no geographic constraints as their coaches can recruit nationally for the most highly skilled players. For example, the boys on the basketball team at Oak Hill Academy in Virginia often transfer to this school from around the country so they can perennially contend for a mythical high school national championship. Oak Hill Academy has a reputation as a short-term stop for adolescents preparing for being recruited to the top-tier intercollegiate basketball teams. What are the ethical issues, if any, associated with recruiting high school athletes?

Schools control the financial benefits provided to interscholastic athletes by allowing them to receive uniforms, competitive expenses, and awards for athletic achievements like trophies and plaques. When adolescents compete on non-school teams, however, there are no rules regarding what benefits they can receive. Athletes on teams and in individual sports typically receive shoes, warm-ups, bags, and other sport clothing and equipment in addition to all-expenses-paid travel and competitive opportunities throughout the United States and sometimes to other countries.

Problems occur, however, when the financial benefits received by prospective athletes are judged by the National Collegiate Athletic Association (NCAA) as violations of its amateur policies and eligibility rules. If the NCAA Eligibility Center uncovers evidence that prospective intercollegiate athletes accepted money or other financial benefits such as travel expenses or clothing not directly associated with their teams, athletes may lose their eligibility to play on a college team (see example in Box 7.1).

BOX 7.1 JOSH SELBY CLEARED TO PLAY BASKETBALL FOR THE UNIVERSITY OF KANSAS

The NCAA's decision regarding Josh Selby's eligibility in 2010 required him to miss nine regular-season games and repay to a charity of his choice the value ($4,607.58) of impermissible benefits (clothes, transportation, meals, and lodging for Selby and his family) received prior to his signing a grant-in-aid to attend and play basketball at the University of Kansas. The NCAA does not allow an athlete attending and playing for a member institution to receive financial benefits provided because of this person's status as an athlete without the NCAA's approval and fulfillment of any penalty it assesses. For what purpose do such rules exist? What are the ethical implications of these rules?

Eligibility Concerns in Intercollegiate Sports

Recreational, interclass activities for male collegians were initiated in the late 1800s to offset the rigors of academic work and perceived oppression of faculty constraints on students' behaviors. Because no eligibility regulations existed during the early years of intercollegiate sport teams, collegians recruited non-students, townspeople, alumni, students from other colleges, and professional athletes for their teams. At that time, no student or faculty member advocated eligibility rules requiring enrollment at the college, a minimum time of enrollment at the institution, or a certain number of credit hours enrolled in at the college. As a result, sport teams, especially in football and baseball, often had limited relationships to the institutions these teams supposedly represented.

As intercollegiate sports developed, became more popular, and expanded in the late nineteenth century, faculties began to exert more control over them, integrate them better with educational goals, and try to prevent sport teams, athletes, and student supporters from debasing the reputations of institutions for the sake of victories.

Established in 1906, the NCAA began primarily to save football from its violence, which it accomplished through rule changes. As the NCAA grew to over a thousand members, it depended on faculty (institutional) control for enforcement of eligibility rules. Not until the start of national championships in the 1920s and more televised college sports in the 1950s did the NCAA begin to gain greater leverage over its members. Sport administrators and coaches increasingly agreed to comply with NCAA eligibility rules governing grants-in-aid and recruiting as long as their opponents were required to adhere to the same rules. Opportunities to win NCAA championships and share television revenues yielded benefits to institutions that adhered to the NCAA's extensive eligibility regulations. Banishment from championships and restrictions on playing appearances on television were enforced as punishments for non-compliance.

The NCAA is strongly committed to ensuring a significant distinction between college athletics and professional sports based on the premise that college athletes are unpaid (i.e., amateurs). However, an amateur is defined by whatever the NCAA says it is. Whereas for decades the NCAA emphasized college athletes could receive no financial remuneration and maintain their eligibility, many athletes benefited financially from their athletic abilities. For example, Wilt Chamberlain played two seasons (1956–1958) for the University of Kansas (freshmen were not eligible his first year). Yet, years later he claimed he took a pay cut when he left KU and became a professional basketball player with the Harlem Globetrotters. The NCAA allows athletes to receive financial aid that does not exceed the cost of education, limited to tuition, fees, room, board, and books from his or her institution based on athletic ability, without violating the principle of amateurism. Athletes who receive anything beyond these expenses violate the NCAA's eligibility rules.

Oftentimes, athletes claim ignorance of the rules as a justification for failure to comply with NCAA eligibility rules regarding receiving financial benefits. Athletes have been suspended for one or more games or seasons for receiving meals and travel expenses from impermissible sources such as sport agents or individuals representing an institution's athletic interests (boosters). In late 2010, five Ohio State University football players were suspended for the first five games of the 2011 season for receiving money for selling personal items associated with their football activities and achievements. However, this controversial NCAA ruling allowed these five players to play in the Allstate Sugar Bowl after their suspensions were handed down. Many people perceived the NCAA's ruling to be financially related to the success of this Bowl Championship Series game, while others criticized the institution for putting financial benefits ahead of moral values. Some people questioned the right of the NCAA to prohibit a college athlete from selling his personal property; others questioned the claim by representatives of Ohio State athletics that they failed to inform the athletes that such actions were impermissible and would result in loss of eligibility.

NCAA rules dictate what is permitted in amateur sport eligibility for playing on teams representing member institutions. Past rule violations by coaches and individuals interested in promoting their favorite college's athletic programs led to the development by the NCAA of more detailed and comprehensive eligibility regulations. That is, annually new rules had to be written to explicitly ban activities of coaches, sport administrators, athletes, and team supporters who exploited loopholes in the rules, thereby acting as if ethical conduct were synonymous with only the written rules, and the spirit of the rules did not exist. If a particular action was not directly addressed by an explicit rule, they considered it permissible regardless of whether or not it was ethical.

BOX 7.2 EXAMPLES OF VIOLATIONS OF NCAA ELIGIBILITY REGULATIONS
- Academic fraud
- Errors in designation of degree program
- Excessive financial aid and grants-in-aid
- Failure to earn minimum percentage of credits for satisfactory progress during academic year
- Impermissible extra benefits
- Impermissible tutoring and academic assistance
- Improper certification of eligibility
- Ineligible participation
- Violations of two-year college transfer regulations
- Violation of financial aid eligibility regulations

Is it problematic to place all ethical judgment on eligibility rules? What might be the ethical issues associated with these rules? Are all of the NCAA's eligibility rules fair? Do intercollegiate coaches, sport administrators, and athletes have the moral duty to play by the rules and honor their word?

Rampant violations of recruiting rules exist according to various media exposes and truthful reflections by individuals with first-hand knowledge. Coaches, especially of sport teams that compete at the highest level, incessantly recruit the most talented athletes. Because successfully recruiting highly skilled players is essential to winning, coaches bombard interscholastic athletes with letters, informational materials, telephone calls, and visits. In response, the NCAA limits the number and time of contacts by coaches with prospective athletes and restricts types of communicating (e.g., disallowing sending text messages). The NCAA also limits the number of paid campus visits and prohibits giving any gifts to athletes and their parents during the recruiting process. Even though coaches at NCAA member institutions annually must pass a test on recruiting rules, some coaches continue to violate recruiting rules, thereby placing their institutions and teams at risk for penalties, such as loss of grants-in-aid, prohibitions on post-season play, and loss of employment.

Prospective athletes who are offered impermissible financial inducements and exposed to rule-breaking actions by recruiters may lose respect for the integrity of eligibility and recruiting rules. Most adolescent sport stars know that coaches who offer inducements to sign letters of intent do so in violation of NCAA rules. Also, by accepting money, sport clothing, sport equipment, cars, and other financial benefits, athletes become culpable along with these coaches and, if their actions are discovered, athletes face loss of eligibility, temporarily or permanently. Individuals representing the sport interests of colleges, according to NCAA rules, cannot give gifts or promise money to lure athletes to their favorite institutions. The father of Cam Newton, Auburn University quarterback, in 2010 shopped his son to an athletic supporter of Mississippi State University in a pay-for-play scheme. The NCAA continues to pass new rules to close the loopholes that allow such actions as these, since Newton retained his eligibility at the time because no evidence was found that directly connected him to his father's actions.

Many times the receipt of financial benefits by college athletes from coaches, fans, and sport agents results in the loss of eligibility for players. Sometimes players are ignorant of impermissible activities, while at other times they are complicit in breaking eligibility rules. The NCAA also penalizes institutions if their athletes accept money or impermissible benefits. The NCAA's Committee on Infractions concluded that Reggie Bush and his family accepted money and other financial benefits from two sport agents during his junior and senior years at the University of Southern California (USC). While Bush as a professional football player could not be penalized, given how long the investigation took, the USC's football program was placed on probation for four years, banned from playing in bowl games for two years, and limited by 30 the number of grants-in-aid that could be awarded over three years. USC also forfeited all wins in the 2007–2008 basketball season for playing O. J. Mayo, who was ineligible because he received impermissible cash and gifts. In addition to no post-season play at the end of the 2010 season, USC curtailed allowable recruiting and grants-in-aid in basketball.

Sport agents often provide financial benefits to athletes in hopes of getting these outstanding players to sign with them for negotiating their professional contracts. While there are federal and state laws that govern the often unscrupulous behaviors of sport agents, seldom are they penalized for giving money, cars, clothing, jewelry, and other lucrative items to college athletes whose eligibility is governed by the NCAA. Athletes become ineligible upon receipt of any of these monetary items, even though frequently these violations are not disclosed until years later. Marcus Camby, a 15-year veteran in the National Basketball Association (NBA), admitted receiving financial benefits while a college athlete at the University of Massachusetts. This disclosure resulted in his former team having to vacate its NCAA Final Four appearance and the institution having to repay funds received for participating in that event. Because Chris Webber, another 15-year NBA veteran, and other University of Michigan basketball players received money from an athletic supporter while in college, the institution had to forfeit games and post-season victories from the years when these players were ineligible because they received money, and repay thousands of dollars in revenues.

Alleged and actual recruiting violations have occurred in luring international athletes to the United States. Sometimes these recruits are elite athletes in their countries who enroll in colleges in the United States to help win games. For example, Tanya Harding, an outstanding pitcher from Australia, enrolled at the University of California at Los Angeles in the spring of 1995 just in time to lead her new softball team to an NCAA championship. Many teams, especially in ice hockey, soccer, tennis, and track, are comprised of more international students than citizens of the United States. Some individuals have suggested that many international athletes follow a similar pathway to that taken by Harding, who returned home without a degree soon after accepting the championship trophy. A few international athletes use playing on intercollegiate sport teams as pathways into professional leagues in the United States. International athletes are eligible to play for colleges where they matriculate, but many people question whether these athletes (and the coaches who recruit them) are acting ethically if these international athletes are masquerading as students.

In trying to equalize competition and prevent gaining unfair competitive advantages, the NCAA specifies permissible and impermissible recruiting practices in minute detail. The legalese used in its policy manuals reflects this organization's overarching goal of preserving the perception of athletes as amateurs playing for the love of sports. The detailed language used in these manuals to specifically prohibit certain actions may actually contribute to widespread circumventions of recruiting and eligibility rules. There is little doubt that creative violations of recruiting rules are used to gain competitive advantages, as dishonesty, lying, deceit, or distrust characterize the actions of some coaches who choose to recruit in ways that not only break the rules but violate moral principles of honesty, respect, and justice.

Some coaches argue that no one can fully comply with myriad recruiting and eligibility rules because many are too nebulous. The fact that the NCAA primarily sanctions those institutions that repeatedly and flagrantly violate the rules reinforces this perception. Thus many coaches and sport administrators rationalize that when their actions and institutions are not penalized for non-compliance, then they are by default allowable, even if they are not honest, just, and fair. How might this rationalization be questionable morally?

The NCAA cannot legislate or require morality. Rather, this organization enforces eligibility and recruiting rules to try to facilitate equitable competitive opportunities among member institutions. However, its small enforcement staff attempting to police rule compliance can never ensure that hundreds of coaches, thousands of athletes, and millions of fans will play by the rules. Although many think that if institutions have not been penalized for violations of eligibility and recruiting rule they must be in compliance, there remains a high probability the culprits simply have not been caught.

In a cost-benefit analysis, some coaches weigh the anticipated benefits of enticing to their institutions, through rule-violating actions, the most talented athletes against the small likelihood of getting caught and being penalized. Coaches may conclude that the benefits exceed the costs, such as when a team wins a national championship with players recruited or kept eligible while breaking the rules. Many coaches claim every coach violates some of the rules, as if to justify similar unethical actions. This rationalization of "everyone does it" in the minds of some seems to justify immoral actions.

Ethical issues relative to academic eligibility and recruitment in intercollegiate sports persist. For example, the University of Memphis men's basketball team had to forfeit its entire 2007–2008 season and NCAA tournament victories through the Final Four because its star freshman guard Derrick Rose (now playing for the Chicago Bulls in the NBA) had someone else take his SAT that enabled him to become eligible to play in his one season of college basketball. If athletes know financial inducements are explicitly against the rules, should they lose eligibility to play if they accept these benefits?

Are the coaches and athletic supporters who offer these inducements behaving unethically? Because most violations of NCAA rules result in sanctions against current and future teams that were not culpable in the violations, what moral issues arise when these teams lose their eligibility for post-season play? If coaches, sport administrators, and athletic supporters are involved in violations of written eligibility and recruiting rules, what steps can be taken to reduce these infractions? Because many confuse the spirit of eligibility and recruiting rules with an argument that since everyone else violates eligibility rules, to remain competitive we must, too, is anyone morally or ethically bound to follow the rules?

Eligibility Concerns in the Olympic Games

In 1896, the first Olympians in the modern era had to verify their amateur status before they were allowed to compete. Consistent with the British Amateur Sport Ideal as propagated by Baron Pierre de Coubertin, the founder of the Olympic Games, only gentlemen athletes who played for the love of sport were eligible. The International Olympic Committee (IOC), which governs this event, initially prohibited athletes from receiving remuneration and advocated that true sportsmen play sports for the game's sake, not for financial gain, thus excluding many athletes from lower socioeconomic strata.

When athletes received money or other benefits in violation of amateur rules, the IOC seldom enforced its eligibility regulations. Some national governments, and especially nations in the former Soviet Union and Eastern Bloc, in seeking to promote their ideologies, trained, sponsored, and rewarded Olympic athletes. Some athletes trained for their sports full-time while serving in their nations' military forces. In many nations under-the-table (not permitted within the rules) payments used for training and competitive expenses became commonplace. Sporting event organizers paid appearance fees to the best athletes to entice them to participate in international competitions. Overt commercialization, such as skiers displaying corporate trademarks on their clothing and equipment and track athletes wearing their sponsors' shoes around their necks on the victory stand, abounded in the 1980s but began much earlier. It appeared the pursuit of gold medals swept aside ethical concerns about whether athletes met eligibility regulations. The Olympic Games survived numerous barrages directed against their eligibility regulations and rampant violations of these rules. Originally touted as competitions between amateurs, the Olympic Games have not hosted such idealized events for decades. Violations of eligibility regulations that prohibited athletes from receiving financial rewards for their prowess continued until the IOC changes its rules.

Another issue facing the Olympics has been determining the eligibility of athletes relative to their nationality. That is, some athletes choose to leave their native-born countries and become nationalized citizens in other countries primarily for athletic reasons. Sometimes these changes enabled athletes to earn places on their new countries' Olympic teams, and at other times an athlete's elite status may have resulted in preferential treatment in obtaining citizenship in another country. The controversy regarding South African Zola Budd, who was granted expedited citizenship in Great Britain through her British grandfather so she could compete in the 1984 Los Angeles Olympic Games, was one notable example. A quick glance at the place of birth of most international soccer, basketball, and ice hockey players highlights this eligibility/citizenship issue. For example, Becky Hammon, a United States citizen who failed to earn a roster spot on her nation's team in the 2008 Beijing Olympic Games, took her Olympic dream to Russia. Although she has no ancestral ties to that nation, under Russian rules she was able to become a naturalized citizen and compete for Russia internationally.

Sport mirrors society as values viewed as important in society pervade sports as well. Rules governing eligibility in sports, regardless of the level, will be followed only if participants respect moral values and principle-centered leaders help ensure compliance with rules, setting examples by operating values-based organizations. Violations of rules occur because parents, coaches, athletes, and sport administrators esteem the non-moral value of winning more highly than playing honestly, justly, and responsibly. In many cases, they do not even think about the ethical considerations or ramifications of what they are doing. Eligibility regulations governing interscholastic, intercollegiate, and Olympic sports will be disregarded or violated indiscriminately unless those subject to these rules value them. Principle-centered leaders who model honesty, justice, and beneficence need to intervene to prevent athletes, coaches, and sport administrators from lying, cheating, and deceiving to gain competitive advantages. Principle-centered leaders need to engage athletes and coaches in discussing the eligibility questions in Box 7.3 and resolving these based on moral values.

BOX 7.3 QUESTIONS ABOUT ETHICS IN ELIGIBILITY

1. What are youth and adolescent athletes being taught about moral values when they observe adults circumventing eligibility regulations?
2. When colleges allowed non-students to play on their sport teams, why was or was not this ethical?
3. When colleges paid students to play on their sport teams, why was or was not this ethical?
4. Why was or was not the establishment of eligibility rules essential for fair competition in intercollegiate sports?
5. Why do or do not those involved with sports at all competitive levels choose to comply with eligibility rules governing sports?
6. Does dishonest, unjust, and irresponsible behavior necessitate the establishment of specific rules and regulations governing eligibility? Do such rules and regulations governing eligibility in competitive sports make people honest, just, and responsible?
7. When intercollegiate coaches use financial inducements to recruit players, how are these coaches and athletes violating eligibility rules?
8. In what ways do athletes at all levels of competitive sports make moral and immoral decisions?
9. How do eligibility rules affect the honest or dishonest behaviors of coaches, athletes, and sport administrators?
10. Why are more eligibility rules necessary to prevent coaches, athletes, and sport administrators from using every imaginable tactic or strategy to gain competitive advantages?

11. Should there be a moral basis for the conduct of sport competitions at all levels? If so, what should it be? How should the moral basis for the conduct of sport competitions vary by level of sport?
12. How do the media affect responses to and perceptions about moral or immoral actions in sport competitions?
13. How have some elite athletes worked around eligibility rules so they could qualify for competition in the Olympic Games?
14. Does the absence of rules and penalties prohibiting a particular action in sports make that action morally right?
15. What are the determining factors in making an action in sports morally right?

Principle-centered leaders in sports should emphasize the importance of respecting and playing by the rules that govern eligibility. (It should be noted, however, that sometimes you may not agree with a rule. If you think a rule is immoral, are you duty-bound to follow that rule? Dissent can be good, especially against an immoral rule, but at the same time, a commitment was made to follow the rules. What are your ethical options?) Winning will assume a less dominant place in competitive sports whenever people remember these are only games.

Traditionally, sportsmanship characterized intercollegiate sports despite occasional scandals. Most everyone in schools and colleges initially classified sports as educationally focused extracurricular activities, so few eligibility rules existed. Seldom were inducements offered to athletes to change their actions or decisions. Once television revenues, status, and the potential for professional sports contracts became inextricably linked with winning, violations of eligibility and recruiting rules increased. Many argue that institutions in the NCAA Division III (non-scholarship programs), National Association of Intercollegiate Athletics, National Junior College Athletic Association, and National Christian College Athletic Association keep winning in perspective. Since the financial bonanzas associated with the business of sports are not present in these institutions, the need to violate eligibility rules to help win does not exist. Increasingly, though, athletes in all levels of competitive sports view winning as the only thing that matters, as more important than the values of honesty and justice or playing by the spirit of the rules. How are people who prioritize winning over values and playing according to the rules acting dishonestly and unfairly?

Eligibility and Moral Reasoning

The ability to reason morally can be taught, learned, and developed. Through education and living in a principled environment with role models who are living honorably, individuals learn how to make morally right decisions. Despite claims to the contrary, the structure of competitive sports does not usually support the moral development of athletes and coaches. For example, when children play on their own, they consider differences in players' abilities without any eligibility rules. Rarely do they argue about who can play, with "the more the merrier" making playing fun. Eligibility rules in youth sports are not written for children because they do not need rules. Eligibility rules are written to control or prevent the manipulative behaviors of coaches and parents used to gain competitive advantages.

Children seldom get to take responsibility for decisions in youth sport programs because adults make all the decisions, whether morally right or wrong. When adults make decisions for children in sports, it may negatively influence how these youth grow morally and develop their moral reasoning processes. This probably occurs as a direct result of the hyper-organized structure of competitive sport programs at all age levels. Through education and living in a world of sport led by principle-centered leaders, athletes can learn how to habitually make morally based decisions. Unfortunately, at times the absence of principle-centered leaders and structure of competitive sports does not support moral development and moral reasoning, resulting in some athletes not learning how to make good, sound, consistently moral decisions.

Ethical Questions Regarding Eligibility

Research (Beller & Stoll, 1992, 1995; Beller, Stoll, Burwell, & Cole, 1996; Krause & Priest, 1993) involving more than 90,000 sport participants from ninth-graders through college students found that the longer individuals participate in sports, the more morally calloused they become. Competitive sports today do not often teach and reinforce values like responsibility, honesty, fairness, or beneficence. Issues regarding eligibility challenge individuals involved in all levels of competitive sports. Principle-centered leaders should be guided by moral values as they lead values-based sport programs. When faced with ethical challenges, each individual should begin by establishing underlying values and finding resolutions and actions by determining how chosen actions are based on moral values and demonstrate these consistently and impartially. Box 7.4 presents a few challenges associated with moral values and eligibility. Select an alternative from each list below each question or suggest other possible responses.

BOX 7.4 ETHICAL QUESTIONS: YOU DECIDE WHAT TO DO

Question 1. *Does the absence of prohibitive rules governing eligibility give moral license to do anything else (i.e., no rule, no harm)?*
  What to Do
a. Actions should be based on personal moral values, not rules.
b. The absence of rules gives license to do whatever it takes to win.
c. The situation determines what is right or wrong.
d. Adhering to the spirit of the rules and playing in morally responsible ways should always occur.
e. A person has the right to dissent and seek to change the rules.

Question 2. *Are eligibility rules inherently honest?*
  What to Do
a. The existence of a rule does not necessarily make it honest. Civil disobedience calls for violating a rule if it is unjust.

b. Because a rule exists, it is honest and just.

c. Honesty requires compliance only with the letter of the rule, not necessarily with the spirit of the rule.

d. If a rule exists and everyone agrees to play by that rule, then everyone is obligated to follow it. If anyone disagrees, that person can refuse to play or initiate action to change the rule.

e. If a person believes that eligibility rules are dishonest, this person can work to change the rules.

Question 3. *What makes violating an eligibility rule dishonest?*
   What to Do

a. Dishonesty exists only if punishment or penalties result.

b. A fraudulent or dishonest act is immoral regardless of whether it is penalized.

c. Each situation and the associated circumstances determine independently whether an action is honest or dishonest.

d. If a person believes in the value of honesty, dishonesty is wrong.

Question 4. *Should interscholastic or intercollegiate athletes who receive money lose their eligibility to compete?*
   What to Do

a. Receiving money violates eligibility rules.

b. Rules that prohibit receiving money discriminate against the economically disadvantaged.

c. Athletes have earned whatever money they receive based on their athletic achievements.

d. It depends on why the money was accepted; if it is used to fly home to visit a sick parent, it is permissible, but using the money to buy the latest and best cell phone is not acceptable.

e. Athletes are entertainers and should be paid.

f. Athletes agree to follow the rules, but the eligibility rules need to be changed.

In responding to the questions in Box 7.4, note that the ethical principles in Box 7.5 provide guidance in making morally reasoned decisions.

BOX 7.5 ETHICAL PRINCIPLES FOR RESOLVING ELIGIBILITY CONCERNS IN SPORTS

1. Keep winning in perspective.

2. Educate coaches, athletes, and sport administrators about moral values like honesty, justice, and beneficence. This educational process should be a Socratic approach that is bounded in principles, mission, and focus.

3. Inform athletes, parents, coaches, and sport administrators about the importance of eligibility rules and the morally based spirit of these rules.

4. Develop and publicize codes of ethical conduct for coaches, parents, athletes, and sport administrators and require adherence to them.

5. Penalize consistently every dishonest action by an athlete, a coach, or a sport administrator who previously has been educated about morally based decision making.

6. Question and change eligibility rules and policies that are unjust, precipitate dishonest actions, or are irresponsible.

7. Hire and retain coaches based on their adherence to eligibility rules, not on won-lost records.

8. Reward coaches who help athletes achieve physically, mentally, socially, and emotionally.
9. Articulate specific eligibility rules for all levels of sport competitions and enforce them consistently and impartially.
10. Recognize and reward athletes, coaches, and sport administrators who teach and practice moral values like honesty, justice, and beneficence.

Is moral development a priority in society and sports? If so, then athletes must be educated about how to make morally reasoned decisions. What are some examples of values-based sport teams and coaches? Unless led by principle-centered coaches and sport administrators who act ethically, eligibility problems will worsen. Educational programs that teach athletes and coaches how to reason morally are needed. One teaching method could be discussing situations in sports and analyzing how and why athletes and coaches might choose to act in certain ways. Through open forums among teammates facilitated by principle-centered leaders who ask probing questions, athletes and coaches could begin to question whether their values are being developed or violated in sports. If values are being violated, change is required. It takes courage to affirm and live by one's values, so such actions should be continuously reinforced.

In contests between two teams or individuals who previously agreed to follow eligibility regulations, when athletes or coaches violate these rules, the equity of competitions is destroyed. Congruency and consistency with the purpose and conditions of sport competitions must exist if fairness counts. In order to attain the espoused values of sports, lying and other immoral behaviors must not be allowed. Morally based actions will not permit the perversion of potentially good sport competitions. Whenever eligibility and recruiting rules are complied with, the real winners are the athletes, regardless of the score. Ethical conduct is critical to eligibility in competitive sports at all levels. Ethical issues in sports can be resolved through moral education, legislation, enforcement, and commitment to playing the game by the letter and spirit of the rules.

Performance-Enhancing Drugs in Sports

Most people in sports enjoy competition and strive to win. Competition is an integral (and often healthy) part of our market-driven, capitalistic society. We seek to outperform the store next door in sales, a company across the country in product line, and an international corporation in our market niche. We strive to graduate at the top of our class, own the biggest house and car in the neighborhood, and join the most prestigious country club. Seemingly for many, our self-concept or status in society is based on extrinsic achievements and material benefits such as these.

Similarly, sports in the United States have been heavily influenced by the motive to succeed, get ahead of everyone else, and attain status and prestige. The result in competitive sports has been a disproportionate emphasis on outcome and the non-moral

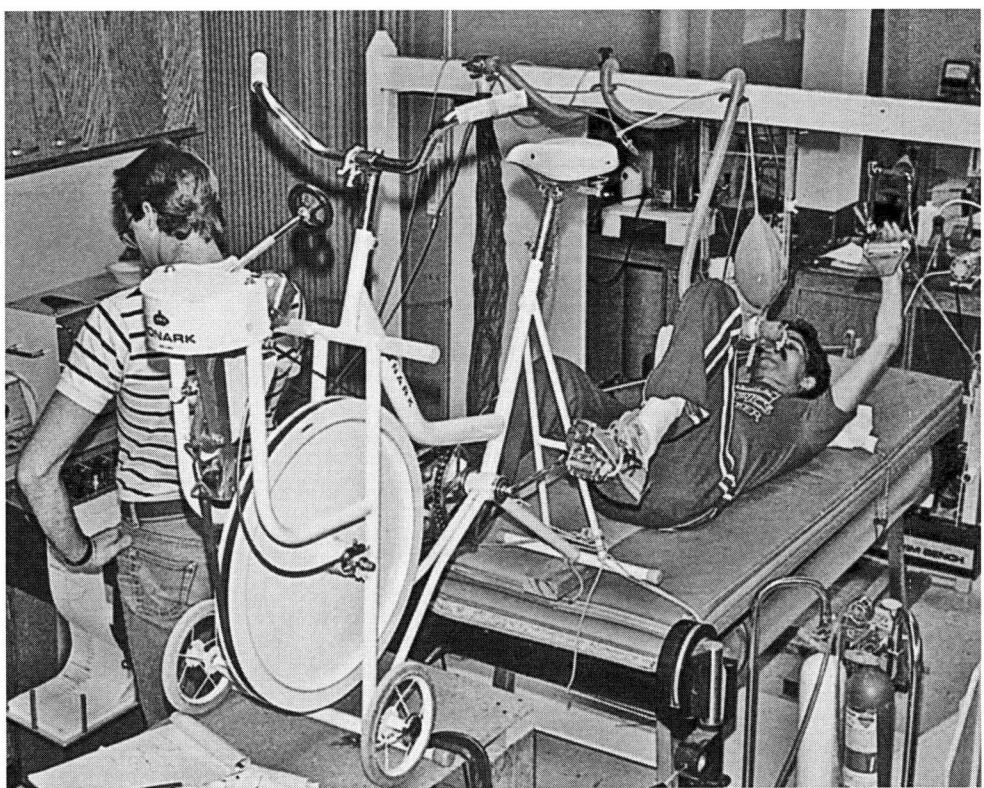

Because winning has become so financially lucrative, some participants and coaches will do anything to gain an advantage, including using performance enhancing drugs such as human growth hormone, steroids, blood doping, and other designer drugs. Because testing agencies can only test for drugs that are identified, some underground labs exist with a goal of designing performance enhancing drugs that are not on the banned substance list.

value of winning rather than on developing sport skills, developing as a person, and having fun. Because of fame and fortune, hero and heroine status, and special financial benefits, athletes realize early in their sport experiences that only winners receive multi-million-dollar contracts, endorsements, grants-in-aid, and free sport equipment and clothing. The drive to win dominates the thinking and actions of athletes, coaches, parents, and sport administrators. When the importance placed on winning supersedes all else, athletes may take drugs to enhance their performance and gain unfair advantages over opponents.

This section provides an examination of how the use of performance-enhancing drugs raises ethical issues for athletes and sports in general. It is suggested that the use of stimulants, depressants, anabolic steroids, and blood doping is morally wrong because it provides the user with unfair physical advantages (see Box 7.6). The legal and moral issues surrounding drug testing challenge the reader to determine whether such tests should be banned, optional, or mandated. Questions also will be raised about the appropriateness of legislating morality through sanctions associated with drug use in sport.

Box 7.6 Three Ethical Questions Associated with Use of Performance-Enhancing Drugs

Whether or not to use performance-enhancing drugs is a significant ethical issue facing athletes, especially because other athletes have chosen to use drugs to gain competitive advantages. If athletes believe that everybody else in sports uses drugs, they may conclude that to be competitive they must use performance-enhancing drugs, too. This argument, however, rests on the premise that ethical principles are guided by what others do. Ethical rules should be valued without regard to others because moral principles are inherently right. Three ethical questions merit close examination.

1. Is rule compliance only required if opponents follow the rules? When people enter sport competitions they explicitly or implicitly give their word they will follow the constitutive, proscriptive, and sportsmanship rules governing sports.
2. Do athletes have an obligation or responsibility to keep their promises? As members of a team, athletes accept the responsibility of following game rules that will treat all competitors fairly.
3. Do athletes have the responsibility to not intentionally harm their bodies or the bodies of their opponents? There is ample evidence that using performance-enhancing drugs places the athletes who use these drugs and sometimes opponents at risk physically.

Increasingly, athletes appear to seek ways to gain competitive advantages, often because obtaining the rewards of winning has become paramount. One way to improve the chances of winning is to use performance-enhancing drugs, defined as any aid, supplement, or ingested substance prohibited by the letter or spirit of the rules but used to garner advantages in sports. Depending on the drug, substance, or means chosen, enhanced endurance, strength, skill, and self-confidence may result. In other cases, performance-enhancing drugs alter athletes' perceptions so they see themselves competing at superior levels, when in reality their performances may remain the same or erode. Besides real or perceived improvements in performance that may lead athletes to use performance-enhancing drugs, there remains the drive to win, sometimes at all costs.

Stimulants

Central nervous system stimulants include amphetamines (speed), ephedrine (found in cold medications and nasal sprays), cocaine, nicotine, and caffeine. These drugs generally cause physiological and psychological responses such as increased alertness, reduced fatigue, heightened hostility and competitiveness, lessened fear and apprehension, and enhanced concentration, attention, arousal, drive, excitability, motivation, and self-confidence. Because these drugs affect the body so dramatically, and often dangerously, their use is prohibited or limited (see Box 7.7).

Box 7.7 Athlete Guide to the 2010 Prohibited List

Countries throughout the world have joined forces through the World Anti-Doping Agency (WADA) to eliminate the use of prohibited performance-enhancing drugs in sports. WADA's 2010 Prohibited List is available at http://www.usada.org/prohibited-list-2011/. The United States Anti-Doping Agency provides the *Athlete Guide to the 2010 Prohibited List* online at http://www.usada.org/files/active/athletes/Athlete%20Guide% 20to%202010%20Prohibited%20List.pdf to help athletes understand how use of prohibited drugs may affect them. This guide also provides information about how to apply for a therapeutic use exemption or to submit a declaration of use.

Physiologically, stimulants chemically induce the release of epinephrine, an adrenaline-like substance, into the bloodstream along with stress hormones. Amphetamines stimulate the release of epinephrine and nor-epinephrine from the adrenal glands and nervous system, thus increasing muscle tension, heart rate, and blood pressure. Increased blood flow from the heart to the muscles produces more free fatty acids and makes glucose more available. This may help the body use fats for energy instead of muscle glycogen, which may have a sparing effect on valuable body stores. Athletes who take large amounts of amphetamines may become overly hostile and aggressive because of their elevated moods, experience a reduction of fear, and demonstrate increased pain tolerance. Psychologically, athletes' perception and alertness are not as good as they think.

For a long time, endurance athletes have used caffeine and other stimulants to increase their performance levels. Gymnasts and wrestlers often choose to take amphetamines to help them lose weight because of their initial appetite-suppressing effects. A few athletes have become dependent on legally and illegally obtained dexedrine, benzedrine, and methedrine that they believe will help their performances. These drugs mask fatigue, giving the perception of endless energy. Cyclists, runners, and other endurance athletes have died of exhaustion because their bodies, under the influence of stimulants, were unable to naturally signal being overtaxed.

Cocaine, another stimulant drug, has become the drug of choice of some professional athletes, who typically use this drug recreationally and for relaxation, which may indirectly enhance performance. From the federal drug-trafficking trials that implicated players from several Major League Baseball (MLB) teams in the 1980s to the highly publicized death of Len Bias, the #2 pick in the 1986 NBA draft, sports fans have learned about the popularity of cocaine with some athletes. (Because of their salaries and star status, professional athletes can easily afford and obtain this expensive drug.) As an illegal substance, can cocaine use be condoned? Does its use violate moral principles if it gives the athlete a perceived or real competitive advantage? Gary McLain, who led Villanova University to the NCAA basketball championship in 1984, claimed he played most games his senior year on cocaine highs, obtaining this drug illegally and playing without being penalized.

The ethical issues associated with use of stimulants relate to whether drugs used to enhance performance, reduce or mask fatigue, or provide psychological advantages are morally defensible. If it is agreed that athletes competing against athletes is the essence of sport, is it honest or just to create an imbalance artificially by ingesting stimulants? Because several sport organizations have banned the use of many stimulants, do existing rules make the use of prohibited drugs unethical? If an athlete chooses to use a prohibited stimulant, is use of this drug fair or beneficent? Is an athlete who must compete against an opponent who takes stimulants justified in using similar drugs to level the playing field? What penalties, if any, should be assessed against athletes who take stimulants to gain competitive advantages?

Depressants

Although the intake of depressants may impair performance, athletes often consume alcohol as the drug of choice and develop a dependency on it. Professional athletes openly drink post-game alcoholic beverages during interviews with media representatives. These athletes and many younger ones relax with their favorite alcoholic drinks as they recover from the intense pressures and adrenaline flow brought on by competition. Some athletes have become dependent on drugs to cope with their demanding lifestyles. For example, a professional football player may drink several bottles of beer in the post-game celebration or drown his sorrows after a tough loss. These drinks may be followed by a few more alcoholic beverages at a restaurant during dinner or at home with friends as he unwinds from the game or numbs his aches and pains. A sleeping pill or tranquilizer may be needed to permit him to rest. The combination of these depressants and tough practices may leave him tired by midweek. So, in preparation for Sunday's game, he begins to take stimulants to offset the effect of these depressants. By kick-off time, he may be so pumped up with uppers that all he wants to do is hit somebody aggressively and even viciously. This cycle may repeat itself throughout the season. What moral responsibilities do sport teams and leagues have relative to issues such as drug use and drug dependency in sports?

Depressants typically are taken to calm feelings and dull one's sense of problems, but continued use may lead to rapid psychological and physiological addiction. Not only does the mind crave these drugs in increasing amounts, but so does the body. What ethical issues are associated with the use of depressants by athletes?

Anabolic Steroids

The male hormone testosterone contributes to the development of secondary sex characteristics including muscular strength. To increase strength more rapidly or in addition to what can be gained through training, many athletes ingest or inject synthetic varieties of testosterone called anabolic steroids. When taken in large dosages before intensive weight-training sessions, anabolic steroids cause males and females to achieve significant gains in muscular strength and bulk. Not only are there appearance changes, but significant performance improvements linked directly to steroid usage have been documented. Ben Johnson's muscular definition and his remarkable speed in the 1988 Seoul Olympic Games illustrated the effect of the anabolic steroid stanozolol. However, his appearance, athleticism, and world record did not prevent the IOC from stripping Johnson of his gold medal in the 100-meter dash because of his positive drug test.

Even though anabolic steroids can lead to increases in muscular strength, numerous adverse side effects accompany their use. Individuals who take 50 to 100 times the clinical dosage (as many athletes do) frequently experience life-threatening problems such as extreme psychoses, heart disease, liver and kidney damage, and cancer. Other negative side effects include severe facial and body acne, mood swings, and out-of-control aggression. Adolescents using anabolic steroids may experience premature closure of growth centers in the long bones, causing stunted growth. Males who use anabolic steroids risk impotence, development of breasts, shrinkage of the testicles, reduced sperm count, difficulty or pain in urination, and baldness. Female users risk growth of facial hair, deepened voices, breast reduction, and abnormal menstrual cycles.

Many trace the introduction of anabolic steroids in sports to the Soviets, who discovered that Nazi storm troopers had taken these drugs to heighten their aggression. Subsequently, medal-winning performances by Eastern Bloc athletes led to a proliferation in popularity of anabolic steroid use (see Box 7.8). The practice of taking anabolic steroids, however, was not restricted to any nation as athletes throughout the world used them.

BOX 7.8 STEROID USE IN INTERNATIONAL SPORT COMPETITIONS

It is unknown when steroids were first used by male and female athletes in international competitions including the Olympic Games. However, as national pride and seeking to prove the superiority of an ideology became increasingly pervasive after the end of World War II, athletes independently and those under the control of governmental officials used steroids. This practice was exacerbated because testing for steroids did not begin until 1983 at the Pan American Games. The use of steroids in the Olympic Games was banned beginning in 1974, but not until 1984 were athletes tested for steroid use. One egregious use of steroids characterized the women's swimming team from the German Democratic Republic. In the 1976 Montreal Olympic Games East Germany's women's swimming team won 11 out of 13 gold medals and continued to dominate in this sport for two decades. Years later, though, it was discovered the women on this team has been given steroids without their knowledge or permission. The steroids taken by former athletes resulted in serious health issues personally and in their giving birth to babies with genetic defects.

Even corticosteroids, medically used to reduce inflammatory conditions and pain, must be regulated because athletes have attempted to enhance performance through their use. The IOC, for example, bans orally, rectally, intramuscularly, or intravenously administered corticosteroids while permitting physicians to prescribe them topically through inhalation therapy or intra-articularly.

Weight lifters, track and field athletes, football players, bodybuilders, swimmers, and other athletes of all ages swallow or inject anabolic steroids. Box 7.9 provides information on the use of drugs including steroids by intercollegiate athletes. With the presumption that if a little is good, a lot must be better, many athletes have taken megadoses, thus increasing health risks. For most athletes, performance improves until side effects develop. What are the moral issues surrounding the use of performance-enhancing anabolic steroids in sport? Is it ethical to become bigger, stronger, and more aggressive through using steroids? What moral issues surface when athletes risk their health and lives by using anabolic steroids to seek fame and fortune?

BOX 7.9 NCAA STUDY OF SUBSTANCE USE BY INTERCOLLEGIATE ATHLETES
(DeHass, 2006)

This study, the sixth in a series that began in 1985, provides the NCAA information on the substance-use patterns of intercollegiate athletes. The major findings include the following:

1. Athletes' use of anabolic steroids decreased slightly since the 2001 study.
2. Athletes' use of amphetamines steadily increased since 1997 across all divisions, with the highest use reported in Division III.
3. Athletes' use of ephedrine remained stable in Divisions I and III and decreased in Division II since the 2001 study.
4. While athletes' use of alcohol decreased dramatically in all three divisions since the 2001 study, of the number of athletes who chose to drink alcohol, there was a significant increase in the number who drank more than five drinks in one sitting.
5. Most (about 60 percent) athletes stated that use of alcohol had no effect on athletic performance or health, although 30 percent admitted they had performed poorly in a game or practice due to alcohol or drug use.
6. While athletes' use of cigarettes decreased dramatically since the 2001 study, the number of athletes who smoked a pack or more a day increased.
7. Athletes' use of marijuana was at the lowest level since the studies began.
8. Athletes' use of cocaine increased slightly from the 2001 study in all three divisions.
9. Athletes' use of social drugs was highest in Division III.
10. White and African American athletes' use of amphetamines continued to increase. Among all of the racial and ethnic groups, African American athletes reported the lowest use of amphetamines and social drugs. White athletes' use of anabolic steroids was at its lowest level ever.
11. Athletes' use of amphetamines increased for most men's and women's sports, use of anabolic steroids decreased for most men's and women's sports, and use of social drugs decreased for males and females since the 2001 study.
12. Over half of the athletes who used amphetamines, ephedrine, anabolic steroids, and nutritional supplements began use of these drugs prior to college.
13. The majority of users of anabolic steroids said they used them to improve athletic performance.
14. Athletes' use of amphetamines to improve athletic performance decreased significantly from the 2001 study. The main two reasons for using ephedrine were to lose weight and improve athletic performance.
15. Student-athletes who used amphetamines or anabolic steroids most often obtained them through friends or relatives. Nutritional supplements were mainly purchased in retail stores.
16. Nearly two-thirds of the athletes supported drug testing of athletes as a deterrent to drug use.
17. Despite policies against hazing, some athletes (less than 10 percent) had been victims of hazing, with about 50 percent of the hazing incidents involving alcohol.

Although not an anabolic steroid, androstenedione, which is banned by the NCAA, should be mentioned because many athletes have used this over-the-counter muscle-enhancement drug. Risk factors associated with androstenedione, which was used by professional baseball player Mark McGwire and has been banned by WADA, are similar to those associated with the use of anabolic steroids.

Human Growth Hormone

When sport governing organizations banned the use of anabolic steroids, some physicians, pharmacologists, trainers, and athletes searched for new drugs to enhance performance in similar ways that would not be detected in drug tests. They found that the naturally occurring human growth hormone (HGH), which everyone produces in limited quantities, affects the body in a manner similar to testosterone, so some athletes began taking HGH.

Serious side effects occur from the use of HGH; most destructive are those associated with acromegalia (enlargement of the peripheral body appendages), gigantism (larger physical stature), and organomegaly, which can cause an increase in heart size leading to congestive heart failure. These irreversible changes may result in premature death, even though athletes have been led to believe taking HGH causes no side effects. Should an athlete take a drug to develop greater strength and bulk even if it is not banned? What moral issues exist when athletic accomplishments become more important than personal health?

Blood Doping

Blood doping involves withdrawing red blood cells six to eight weeks prior to competition and re-infusing these oxygen-carrying cells immediately before a competition. This re-infusion, also called blood packing, increases the number of red blood cells per volume of fluid and delivers more oxygen to exercising muscles to enhance performance. Athletes believe the reintroduction of packed cells plus their new production of red blood cells improves endurance and performance.

Erythropoietin (EPO) is a peptide hormone naturally produced by the kidneys that stimulates the bone marrow to produce more red blood cells. Some athletes inject additional EPO as another method of blood doping. This method comes with high risks because if the percentage of red blood cells (hematocrit) overshoots what is physiologically tolerable, heart failure, pulmonary edema, and death may result. Although not a drug, blood doping has been used to gain competitive advantages, which led WADA to prohibit its use. How is blood doping unethical?

Beta-Blockers

Beta-blockers dilate the blood vessels, resulting in relaxation of the nonvascular smooth muscle of the bronchioles and intestinal track. Beta-1 receptors affect the heart, kidneys, and adipose tissue, whereas beta-2 receptors specifically influence the arteries, liver, and bronchi. By blocking a specific type of receptor, a beta-blocker can decrease anxiety, heart rate, nervousness, and tachycardia or rapid heart rate. Beta-blockers have been used by athletes in biathlon, bobsled, luge, ski jumping, archery, diving, equestrian events, fencing, gymnastics, modern pentathlon, sailing, and shooting. The use of performance-enhancing drugs in sport raises questions such as those in Box 7.10.

BOX 7.10 QUESTIONS REGARDING THE USE OF PERFORMANCE-ENHANCING DRUGS IN SPORTS

1. Should athletes ever be allowed to use drugs obtained illegally to gain competitive advantages in sports?
2. If an athlete becomes stronger, faster, or more skilled in any way through the use of performance-enhancing drugs, should the drug, the athlete, or both be banned from sport competitions?
3. If an athlete gains a psychological advantage by using performance-enhancing drugs, how is or is not this cause for banning its use?
4. Should athletes be allowed to use drugs to relieve the pressures and demands of their sports?
5. Does the risk of negative side effects impact whether athletes should be allowed to use performance-enhancing drugs?
6. Should rules governing use of performance-enhancing drugs vary depending on the level of sport competition?
7. Why should or should not the use of human growth hormone, blood doping, or beta-blockers be permitted in sports?
8. How is or is not the statement "It is my own body, and what I take is my own business" morally suspect?

The use of stimulants, depressants, anabolic steroids, human growth hormones, blood doping, and beta-blockers has led sport governing organizations to prohibit their use. Rules have been enacted by principle-centered leaders to prevent athletes from gaining physiological and psychological advantages. To ensure that athletes comply with rules prohibiting the use of banned performance-enhancing drugs, drug testing began.

The Dilemmas of Drug Testing

As athletes increasingly pursue peak levels of performance and the non-moral value of winning, they frequently turn to performance-enhancing drugs in search of competitive advantages. Some Olympic, intercollegiate, and interscholastic athletes use stimulants, depressants, anabolic steroids, or other drugs they believe will improve their performances. For example, international cycling, and most notably the Tour de France, has been fraught almost yearly with cyclists being caught using performance-enhancing drugs. Contrastingly, principle-centered sport leaders suggest that the use of performance-enhancing drugs undermines the fairness of sport competitions.

Drug policies and drug tests for banned drugs have been implemented in most professional sport leagues for several reasons. Leagues are concerned about potential economic losses if players are perceived as cheating by gaining competitive advantages through the use of performance-enhancing drugs. This especially characterizes MLB. This league received unfavorable publicity when some players in testimonies during a

Congressional hearing in 2005 lied about their use of performance-enhancing drugs or refused to answer questions about drug use. Jose Canseco, the 1988 American League Most Valuable Player, who openly acknowledged his use of steroids while playing, implicated numerous other MLB players for their use of steroids in his book *Juiced*. Despite claiming that the players' union would not agree to drug testing protocol that would significantly reduce the use of steroids, amphetamines, and other drugs from baseball, under the pressure of Congress and public opinion, in 2005 MLB implemented a much more comprehensive and effective drug testing program. The NBA and NFL also have drug testing programs and penalties for players who violate their policies (see Box 7.11). Are fines and suspension for professional athletes who make millions of dollars really deterrents?

BOX 7.11 BRIEF OVERVIEWS OF DRUG TESTING POLICIES IN THREE PROFESSIONAL SPORTS

Major League Baseball
- Tests urine for performance-enhancing drugs and amphetamines.
- Tests players once in spring training and at least once during the regular season.
- Subjects players to year-round random testing.
- Mandates a 50-game suspension without pay for the first positive test for steroids.
- Mandates a 100-game suspension without pay for the second positive test for steroids.
- Mandates a lifetime suspension for the third positive test for steroids, although a player can seek reinstatement after two years.
- Requires counseling for the first positive test for the use of amphetamines plus six additional tests.
- Mandates a 25-game suspension without pay for the second positive test for the use of amphetamines.
- Mandates an 80-game suspension without pay for the third positive test for the use of amphetamines.

National Basketball Association
- Tests urine for performance-enhancing drugs and amphetamines.
- Tests each player randomly four times a season.
- Mandates a 10-game suspension without pay for the first steroids or performance-enhancing drugs offense.
- Mandates a 25-game suspension without pay for the second steroids or performance-enhancing drugs offense.
- Mandates a one-year suspension without pay for the third steroids or performance-enhancing drugs offense.
- Mandates disqualification for the fourth steroids or performance-enhancing drugs offense.

National Football League
- Mandates a four-game suspension without pay for the first steroids offense.
- Mandates a year-long suspension without pay for the second steroids offense.
- Requires the automatic forfeiture of a prorated portion of a player's signing bonus if he is suspended for violating the steroid or substance-abuse policy.
- Test randomly 10 (out of 53 players) players per team each week during the pre-season, regular season, and postseason (totaling around 12,000 tests a season).

- Enhances the unpredictability of the year-round testing schedule to address the perception of gaps in the testing periods.
- Test players for erythropoietin (EPO) through a urine specimen.
- Provides at least $500,000 to the UCLA Olympic testing lab and other researchers for the development of new testing methods for human growth hormone.
- Requires no suspension until the second violation for use of street drugs, such as marijuana or cocaine.

Opposition to Drug Testing

Many intercollegiate athletes have opposed mandatory drug testing on the basis of constitutional law. The Fourteenth Amendment to the United States constitution guarantees all citizen privileges and immunities of citizenship, due process, and equal protection. Based primarily on the equal protection guarantee, athletes argue they are singled out for drug testing from the student body, whose members do not have to be tested for drug use. A college as a state actor, if challenged in court for its mandatory

drug testing program of athletes, must establish a rational basis or compelling state interest for testing (e.g., equity in competition and protection of athletes from harmful side effects can be used as a defense). On the basis of the Fourth Amendment, which secures the rights of individuals against unreasonable searches, some athletes claim that taking their urine constitutes a search. Again, a college, if challenged, must show a compelling state interest for the search. Despite these constitutional guarantees, intercollegiate (and some interscholastic) athletes are required to submit to drug testing as a prerequisite to competing, thus waiving their Fourth and Fourteenth Amendment protection.

Many athletes oppose mandatory drug testing on the Constitutional basis of the Fourth Amendment (rights against unreasonable searches) and the Fourteenth Amendment (due process and equal protection), as well as on questions about invasion of privacy. A college, as a state actor, if challenged in court for its mandatory drug testing program of athletes, must establish a rational basis or compelling state interest for testing.

Another justification for resisting drug testing involves the issue of invasion of privacy. Some question the degree of intrusiveness that occurs when a urine sample is obtained. Because most people expect personal privacy during urination, this right must be balanced against the importance of securing a sample from the competing athlete, not a substitute's urine as has happened. Do the procedures used to obtain a urine sample humiliate athletes, impugn their motives, or show disrespect for human dignity? Because some deviant drug users have substituted others' urine through creative methods or diluted their samples, sport governing organizations usually require that athletes are visually monitored when they provide a urine sample. Many individuals resent being assumed guilty because of their status as athletes and strongly disagree with the indignities associated with the drug testing process. They also state that drug testing largely remains an ineffective deterrent without drug education.

Justifications for Drug Testing

Some individuals justify drug testing on the basis of the harm principle. The harm principle, a form of paternalism, states that the organization or authority, because of its knowledge, goodwill, and good intentions, knows what is best for others and society. The rules of sport organizations state that banned drugs place athletes at risk presently or in the future. Since athletes can be pressured by social conditions to make poor choices, especially when young, the principle-centered leader as a coach or sport administrators has a moral obligation and responsibility to make good decisions for athletes currently or in the future. Thus, drug testing removes the burden from athletes of having to choose whether or not to use performance-enhancing drugs. Therefore, when using the harm principle to justify drug testing, society obligates the governing authority to keep athletes from harming themselves.

Another justification for drug testing is to equalize competition. This rationale assumes that only by banning performance-enhancing drugs will competitions match athletes versus each other on a level playing field. Does this imposition of a rule eliminate the use of moral reasoning by athletes to decide whether or not it is ethical to use performance-enhancing drugs in sports? Is drug testing a violation of an athlete's ethical prerogatives or moral values?

Thwarting Drug Testing

Drug tests are able to detect only the specific chemical compounds banned. To avoid being caught, ingenious athletes, coaches, and trainers know how to cycle on and off prohibited drugs without being detected. Even heavy drug users can taper off before competitions and not test positive. Some athletes have learned to take drugs that mask banned performance-enhancing drugs. By the time existing drugs have been identified, banned, and tested for, athletes have started taking new performance-enhancing drugs. So even though drug testing has been touted as the way to impose ethical behavior on athletes, drug testing may deter only those athletes not clever enough to cycle-off or mask banned drugs before getting caught. Is drug testing the way to teach moral principles, or does it perpetuate a failure to educate morally?

Educating Against Drug Use in Sports

Moral education may provide the key to a fair and just playing field as principle-centered leaders guide athletes, coaches, and sport administrators in discussions about what is good, bad, right and wrong in sports. Just talking about the physiological and psychological side effects may not preclude drug use because young people believe in their invincibility and will often choose to take risks. Many elite athletes today would likely respond in the affirmative, as they did in the 1980s, to this question: *Would you take a drug that was guaranteed to kill you within five years if it would help you win a gold medal today?* Education can convince some athletes about the health risks associated with use of performance-enhancing drugs.

It should be noted, however, that some athletes with medical conditions, such as allergies, must use prescription drugs whether or not they are athletes. The IOC stripped swimmer Rick deMont of his gold medal in the 1976 Montreal Olympic Games because he tested positive for a stimulant taken through his asthma inhaler. Is it fair and just for the IOC to ban an athlete from the Olympic Games for taking medicine prescribed by a physician? (The IOC now allows the use of certain drugs, if approved in advance, for specific medical conditions.) However, is taking drugs for medical reasons ethical if these drugs result in competitive advantages?

Are athletes who replace lost fluids during competition or eat balanced and nutritious diets that positively impact their performances gaining unfair competitive advantages? If athletes gain advantages through non-drug-assisted weight training, aerobic conditioning, vitamin supplements, and various rehabilitation techniques acting ethically? Is it fair for athletes to use performance-enhancing surgeries to repair injured ligaments and tendons or eye surgeries to improve their vision? Is it fair for athletes to use drugs, treatment modalities, and rehabilitative exercises to hasten their recovery so they can return to sport competitions? Each of these questions is important to discuss to determine what is and is not ethical in sports.

Taking Performance-Enhancing Drugs That May Cause Health Problems

The concept that principle-centered coaches and sport administrators should teach values is certainly associated with the question of whether athletes should be permitted to use drugs known to be harmful to them. To some athletes, taking amphetamines, anabolic steroids, or other performance-enhancing drugs, even though these drugs might cause heart problems, sterility, or death, is worth the risk because financial benefits and celebrity status are more highly valued.

Athletes may discount future health risks because these have not been definitely proven or because of the dearth of research addressing whether or not performance-enhancing drugs can be taken safely. Some athletes may rationalize that any potential dangers will affect others, not them. The glamour of athletic stardom may overshadow for a brief time any potential long-term harm.

Another related issue is when athletes are encouraged by their coaches and trainers to take performance-enhancing drugs that may enhance their performances even though the risks associated with many of these substances have not yet been identified. What role does moral reasoning serve when athletes have to decide whether or not to take these performance-enhancing drugs whose side effects remain unknown? Do athletes act responsibly toward themselves when they ingest drugs without knowing with some degree of certainty the risks involved? Just because a drug is not banned or the risks associated with its use are unknown does not mean that taking this drug is fair, just, or beneficent in sports.

Using Performance-Enhancing Drugs for Weight Gain and Loss

Many athletes are expected to gain or lose weight according to the demands of their coaches and sports. Football players, for example, must add bulk and strength to gain starting positions or playing time and succeed against strong opponents. Stories abound about seniors (in high school and college) who use weight gains of 10 to 50 pounds to bench press and squat over 100 pounds more than they did as freshmen. Unfortunately, these large weight gains tax the heart and joints, leading to health problems immediately and in later years, as does the increased potential for obesity and weight fluctuations.

In contrast, many wrestlers are pressured to compete in weight classifications below their developmentally appropriate weights. As a result, these athletes exercise in rubber suits or layers of clothing, risk dehydration by refusing to drink fluids, and eat little or nothing prior to weigh-ins. These athletes then eat and drink to regain their ability to wrestle. This cycle of under- and over-eating continues throughout the season.

Female gymnasts are expected to reduce their caloric intake to near-starvation diets to ensure they maintain the petite size thought essential to optimal performance. Too often, these gymnasts and other female athletes who are pressured by their coaches to lose weight for competitive as well as aesthetic reasons battle anorexia, bulimia, and other eating disorders while trying to meet this unrealistic expectation. Maintaining an abnormally smaller intake of food often leads to amenorrhea and injuries associated with inadequate calcium intake that may lead to osteoporosis in later years. The female athletic triad of disordered eating (like anorexia and bulimia), amenorrhea (lack of a menstrual period), and osteoporosis (loss of bone mineral density) form an interrelated set of medical concerns that have adversely affected performance and can lead to serious health problems. Some athletes resort to taking drugs to help them lose or gain weight because they think there are more ideal weights at which they can perform more successfully. Diuretics and stimulants are favored choices for eliminating fluids and reducing appetites respectively. Is it ethical to take drugs to manage weight if the purpose is to enhance performance?

Possible Changes in How Drugs Are Viewed in Sports

Some performance-enhancing drugs used illegally by athletes in the United States are legal in Europe. This adds to the debate about whether such drugs should be decriminalized, thus potentially increasing the likelihood of their use by athletes to enhance performance. For example, if a professional athlete chooses to smoke marijuana after having previously been caught in this violation of a sport league's drug policy, the athlete may be suspended or banned, something that would not occur in many other nations. Possibly drugs currently banned in sports may one day be legalized, regardless of their impact on sport performance.

There is also the issue of athletes using drugs to enhance their performances that are not on the banned lists of the governing organizations of sports. Whenever a new elite level athlete emerges victorious, some members of the media immediately question what performance-enhancing drugs this person must have taken to suddenly win a gold medal or championship. Some argue that already sports have become contests between pharmacologists instead of between athletes.

Given genome and stem cell studies, the issue of genetically engineering superior athletes has become more likely. What are the ethical issues, if any, associated with breeding bigger, stronger, faster athletes? Integral to the concept of sports is the belief in equitable competition between opponents to determine who is superior. Is a contest fair if one or more of the athletes has been bred to benefit from a higher ability level, thus providing an artificial (or is it?) advantage (see Box 7.12).

BOX 7.12   USING SCIENCE TO BUILD A BETTER ATHLETE — IS THIS ETHICAL?

- The human genome is comprised of 100,000 genes that instruct the body's physical development through a chemical code known as deoxyribonucleic acid, or DNA. While humans share 99.8 percent of their DNA, the other .2 percent of these genetic building blocks makes a huge difference athletically.

- One gene, ACTN3, produces a protein that contributes to the ability to generate forceful, repetitive muscular contraction. Genetic Technologies of Melbourne, Australia, offers an ACTN3 Sports Gene Test that identifies whether a person is naturally predisposed toward sprint or power events or has endurance sporting ability. Since this test shows the types of sports or events in which a person is most likely to succeed, these results can be used by coaches and athletes to tailor training programs to help athletes realize their potential.

- One approach to talent detection uses the measurement of specific traits or abilities to identify those with favorable attributes. With the goal of developing the highest number of elite athletes using this approach, selected individuals are provided advanced training opportunities dedicated to the development of their skills. The Australian Institute of Sport (AIS) is an international leader in elite athlete development. Through its talent identification program based on the physical measurements of children, such as vertical jump or 40-meter sprint, AIS matches athletes with the right sports and coaches so nature can take its course. Given the narrow window of opportunity for athletes, the idea is for athletes to specialize in the sports in which they have the greatest potential for success.

- Elite athletes have genetic and natural advantages, because a person cannot buy or build in what nature did not supply. Physical characteristics are largely determined by genetics including 70 percent of height, bone structure, muscle fiber percentage, and body type, 75 percent of the ability to pull weights, and 66 percent of vertical jumping ability. Elite athletes are at the extreme end of the curve of physical characteristics. For example, men's basketball suffers from not having enough tall people, since only 3 percent of the grown men in the United States are taller than 6'3". The average height of players in the National Basketball Association is 6'7". To improve the sport of basketball with more tall players, is genetic engineering the key?
- What are the ethical issues associated with using science to build a better athlete?

Summary

Eligibility concerns pervade every level of competitive sports. Typically, eligibility regulations have been violated in order to gain competitive advantages. Many violations have been associated with age, residency requirements, and recruiting. Seemingly to get and keep athletes eligible, some coaches, athletes, and sport administrators advocate finding loopholes in complicated rules that can be exploited for competitive advantages.

Recruiting continues to be a major area of abuse as athletes are given monetary and other benefits in direct violation of eligibility rules. Impressionable athletes learn whether honesty, trust, and fairness are or are not valued, and if rules are being followed or ignored. When entertainment is prioritized over educational values by some coaches and athletes, the ideals of sports at these levels appear headed in a downward spiral relative to moral reasoning and morally based behavior. Principle-centered leaders can help reverse this trend by stressing moral education and the application of the moral reasoning process to decision making in sports.

The use of performance-enhancing drugs threatens equity and the concept of fair and just playing fields in sport. Because athletes believe they can become bigger, stronger, faster, and more skilled, and also can relax and recover from the pressures of competition, they may elect to use performance-enhancing drugs. In search of ever-improving performances and victories accompanied by media attention, awards, and monetary rewards, athletes may risk their current and future health. Drug testing and the risk of losing competitive opportunities have deterred some athletes from using banned drugs. Yet many question the legal and moral basis for drug testing. Athletes, coaches, and trainers need to examine their personal beliefs and values and determine what actions are fair, just, honest, and beneficent. Making drug testing mandatory should be the final, not the initial, step in a responsible educational system. Principle-centered leaders in sports have the obligation to educate themselves and their athletes morally and not to abdicate this responsibility to a governing body that may mandate drug testing but not provide moral education. The use of performance-enhancing drugs remains a question of responsibility and honor as well as fairness and justice.

Micah would argue that the choice of using performance enhancement is really about gaining advantage. Jareem would argue that it is an issue of fair play and following the rules that organizations develop and athletes should follow. Megan would argue that the issue is about personal responsibility, and every individual has a choice to make. Jeremy might say that it is really a case about making a promise to follow the rules, and perhaps more time should be given to the importance of promise keeping in organizational structures. What do you think?

References

Beller, J. M., and S. K. Stoll (1992, Spring). "A Moral Reasoning Intervention Program for Student-Athletes." *Academic Athletic Journal,* 43–57.

Beller, J. M., and S. K. Stoll (1995). "Moral Reasoning of High School Student-Athletes and General Students: An Empirical Study versus Personal Testimony." *Pediatric Exercise Science, 7,* 352–363.

Beller, J. M., S. K. Stoll, B. Burwell, and J. Cole (1996). "The Relationship of Competition and a Christian Liberal Arts Education on Moral Reasoning of College Student Athletes." *Research on Christian Higher Education, 3,* 99–114.

DeHass, D. M. (2006). "NCAA Study of Substance Use of College Student-Athletes." Retrieved from http://www.ncaa.org/wps/wcm/connect/007d81004e0dabfe9f3afflad6fc8b25/2006_substance_use_report.pdf?MOD=AJPERES&CACHEID=007d81004e0dabfe9f3afflad6fc8b25

Krause, J., and R. F. Priest (1993). "Sport Values Choices of United States Military Academy Cadets: A Longitudinal Study of the Class of 1993." Unpublished manuscript, Office of Institutional Research, United States Military Academy.

Additional Readings

Bahrke, M. S., and C. Yesalis (2002). *Performance-Enhancing Substances in Sport and Exercise.* Champaign, IL: Human Kinetics.

Engh, F. (1999). *Why Johnny Hates Sports: Why Organized Youth Sports Are Failing Our Children and What We Can Do About It.* New York: Penguin Putnam.

CHAPTER 8

Youth Sport Issues

- What is the general history and purpose of youth sport and character development?
- What are the ethical issues of having youth athletes specialize at early ages in highly organized sports?
- What are the ethical issues of the emphasis on winning on the development of character in youth sport? How do we determine the balance between moral character development and motor skill development?
- What principles can help guide principle-centered leadership in youth sport?
- How, as a principle-centered leader, do you balance the needs of the sport programs, the participants, and the parents?

You and your sport marketing peers are given an assignment to return to the days of your youth — not literally but figuratively — to recount the problems that might be encountered as a director of a "pay for play" youth sport program in a large urban area. The program is located in an upscale west coast neighborhood which is largely inhabited by upper-middle managers of Microsoft Corporation. The starting salary for youth coaches is around $60K a year. The program has been highly successful in offering year-round competitive experiences for the participants. In fact, the program is so financially flush that weekend competitions often are scheduled in Los Angeles, Portland, San Francisco, San Diego, Denver, and Salt Lake City. The head coach of the program is a former European national star as well as a former Olympian. The assistant coaches are also Europeans with impressive credentials as players in their own rights. The scenario that you and your sport marketing peers are to solve is the following: You are hired as the director of the program. Historically, the program has been exceptional in quality of play and expertise of the coaches, however, the program has also been known for its poor sportsmanship. Players who come from wealthy families often are difficult to deal with. The coaches have continually lamented their arrogance. The players' families are equally disagreeable. They are rude to the coaches, rude to the opponents, and rude to the director. They demand respect, but seldom give respect to anyone else. Support staff to the program is impossible to keep because the conditions are obnoxious. To compound the problems, the parents often get into shouting matches with each other and with opposing players' parents.

You and your sport marketing peers are supposed to come up with a solution to (1) help the youth sport director educate or at least cope with the parents, and (2) guide the coaches in their quest to not only teach motor skills but also to instill some notion of character into their charges. The dialogue begins:

Micah: "Personally I think this assignment is sort of like trying to get the wild horse in the barn—the horse doesn't know what a barn is, is too stubborn to go into the barn, and generally just likes being wild. I think we should just say, you get what you get. If you want to work with wild horses you've got to expect some real issues. Wild horses have their own specialness, so let them alone."

Megan: "That's an interesting philosophy. Just let the wild horses destroy the surrounding area. Let them trample down others. Let them do whatever they want. Let them be wild."

Jareem: "I don't know that the analogy is that great. There probably is a very good place for wild horses where they do pretty well—but not necessary in a farmer's barn without some serious training. Maybe that's the point of Micah's comments. Maybe to change the culture and climate of this organization there will have to be some serious training to make any kind of difference."

Jeremy: "You know, I spent my summers on my grandpa's ranch out in Idaho, and we often trained horses. Grandpa every once in a while would buy one of the wild mustangs at auction and bring them home to the ranch. He would introduce them to the herd of tame horses, and after a couple days of establishing hierarchy, the horses would adjust, and the wild mustang would become a part of the herd. It wasn't always a pretty thing to watch."

Megan: "What do you mean?"

Jeremy: "When you bring in a different horse to a herd, the herd by instinct establishes who is in charge. There is a pecking order of which horse is dominant. It's always a dominant mare—not the stallion. In order to establish that system, there is a lot of kicking and biting and fighting until order is established. We would have to stay out of it or we would get kicked also."

Megan: "Well, why do that, why not just keep them separate?"

Jeremy: "Since on a working ranch in the west, the horses are on the range during the winter—they need an established hierarchy to lead them and control them. They learn to work as a team to fight off the predators."

Megan: "They wouldn't just get use to each other if they were in separate pens?"

Jeremy: "No, they would still do the hierarchical, territorial thing when they were introduced together."

Micah: "So you agree there isn't much we can do with these youth sport people. They obviously have a lot of money and are used to having things their way. You can't force them into the sportsmanship barn."

Jeremy: "I do agree you can't force them into the concept of playing nicely with others. You have to get them to want to play nicely."

Micah: "Right, like the wild horses. Don't they have to break them? Doesn't sound like a real pleasant thing."

Jeremy: "Well, there are people who believe you have to establish dominance through physical force. But my grandpa always broke his mustangs through trust. He would spend time in getting to know the horse. He would then separate the mustang from the herd and use specific, for lack of a better term, horse whisper techniques that work. My point here is that within a relatively short period of time, the horse wanted to do what grandpa asked of him. It wasn't overnight. It took time."

Micah: "So you are saying we have to come with a strategy to help the director and coaches persuade the parents and athletes to want to 'play nice.'"

Jeremy: "That's the idea."

Micah: "Well, good luck with that one! These aren't wild mustangs. They are human beings and appear to be rather arrogant."

Jareem: "I'm interested in how it would work. How could we apply the concepts to help our director and coaches?"

Megan: "Wouldn't it depend a great deal on the environment that the director sets up?"

Jeremy: "Perhaps it starts even earlier. The director has to have certain character traits. He/she must want to make a difference."

Jareem: "So we want to be careful who is hired to be the director."

Jeremy: "Yes, we do want to be careful. It's not that an old dog can't be taught new tricks, but it is very difficult if everyone in the organization has the same character flaws. Then our suggestions may not help. But the scenario states that we are to help the director, so we have to assume that the director and the coaches are not happy with what they are dealing with and want to make a difference."

Jareem: "Okay, so let's assume that they are individuals of character. What's the next step?"

Megan: "I guess they would have to establish what the organization should be about. What is the mission of the youth sport organization? We already know that about missions, but this group of parents doesn't seem to want anything but playing time for their kids and 'wins.'"

Jeremy: "It does seem so, but don't you think that all parents want their kids to be taught and coached by honorable people?"

Micah: "Maybe, but maybe not."

Jeremy: "If we can't assume that, we will have difficulty changing the environment. If the parents are totally consumed with the outcomes, then perhaps the director and coaches need to find a better place. Sometimes it is better to fire the organization than to wither in an environment of oppression."

Micah: "You are such a bleeding-heart liberal—'environment of oppression?'"

Jeremy: "Sorry, Micah, but if the scenario teaches us anything, these parents are abusing everyone around them. Maybe the big bucks are not as wonderful as it sounds. It sounds rather oppressive to me."

Megan: "Okay, so we argue in our response to the scenario that if there is no hope for change, then the director and coaches should fold their tents. But let's assume there is hope for change. What would we recommend?"

Jeremy: "I think after establishing the mission and having frank talks with the parents, you then work with the parents to establish two things: (1) a code of conduct for the players and fans (including the parents); and (2) an educational component in sportsmanship for both the parents and the players."

Micah: "Like they are going to want to sit down and be 'educated.'"

Jareem: "Actually there are many programs around the country that demand that parents attend an educational session, and they have to sign a code of conduct promise. Sounds like a good idea."

Micah: "Like how are you going to get them to do that?"

Jeremy: "In establishing the mission statement and the rules of conduct, a child can't play until the parents attend the meeting and sign the pledge."

Megan: "Do you make the kids sign the same thing?"

Jeremy: "Maybe, but perhaps a better educational tool is using practice and play to teach the rules of etiquette and sportsmanship."

Megan: "Like what?"

Jeremy: "John Wooden (1988) once said that the best teaching tool that a coach utilizes to teach respect for the coach, the game, and the opponent is the bench. Of course, how the player is sent to the bench and what occurs while on that bench is also important."

Megan: "Meaning?"

Jeremy: "If the coach pulls a player out and tells them to go to the bench and wait until he/she can talk with them, it gives the player some time to wonder why they are there. After a few minutes, the coach can take the time to talk with the player. For example, he/she could ask what happened out on the field. Listen to the response and then say, 'I know you want to win and so do I, but that's not the way we play the game. Our team is better than this.' This should be said in such a way as to instruct, not to demean or to yell or embarrass. Wooden also argues that this is a most powerful means to get a point across. 'The coach is the greatest role model and he/she is also the greatest teacher of sportsmanship.'"

Micah: "I don't remember anyone ever teaching me any of this stuff."

Jareem: "I'm not surprised at that. I would guess most of us were never taught like that."

Jeremy: "Of course there are a lot of variables to teaching character. One of the most powerful ways is through the role model (coach) working with the players during practice and play, but there is also the opportunity for more education that the program director might consider."

Micah: "Oh, oh ... here it comes."

Jeremy: "It doesn't have to be like what you are assuming. I read somewhere that there are educational programs that actually use a question and answer approach to help improve moral reasoning. Some of them have been very successful. In general, a curriculum is developed based on the values of the program. Coaches who believe in the program teach the curriculum, and outcome is measured as to success in change of reasoning. It works. The key is having role models who believe in it, live it, and teach it" (Winning with Character, 2011).

Megan: "So that's how we are going to address this scenario. There are programs that can help, if and only if you have people who really want to make a difference."

Jareem: "Right— we need to have principled-center leaders in youth sport programs."

One of the more difficult areas for sport leaders is in using principle-centered leadership strategies in youth sport programs and activities. Working as a leader in this role brings with it many challenges, especially in today's sport climate, because leaders must balance the needs of organizations and programs with the psychological, social, physical, and developmental needs of children and youth. Unlike collegiate and professional sport arenas, complicating the picture of youth sport are the needs of parents and guardians who often do not have the best interest of either the program or their children in mind. Understanding the history and purpose of youth sport programs, however, will help aspiring sport managers to better implement a principle-centered leadership strategy within their programs.

This chapter will focus on several keys issues related to your role as a leader of youth sport programs. In particular, this chapter will focus on perceptions about competition, the principles of beneficence and responsibility, and balance between motor skill and character development inherent to youth sport participation.

Youth Sport and Character Development

In the early 1920s, business people saw a need and began providing financial support for organized sport leagues for boys. In 1929, Joseph T. Tomlin started a four-team league, Junior Football Conference, later changed to Pop Warner Football after Glenn "Pop" Warner. The initial goals were to use sport more altruistically as a means to develop one's character, values, and skills, which they argued would directly reduce juvenile delinquency. As the program grew to include not only football but cheerleading and dance as well, leaders kept the same basic mission, which is to increase participation levels, provide safe and positive playing environments, and instill values such as teamwork, dedication, and work ethic both within and outside sport, all values central to a democratic nation (Pop Warner Football, 2011). From these early beginnings, programs in other sports for boys were developed. By the late 1930s, Carl Stotz of Williamsport, Pennsylvania, founded Little League Baseball with very similar character and skill-related goals in mind to teach the ideals of sportsmanship, fair play and teamwork that would help boys become good citizens (Little League, 2011). By the 1960s local, regional, state, and national programs were available in many sports for boys, with missions clearly similar to these early programs. In 1964 the American Youth Soccer Organization (AYSO) was started by Hans Stierle with the expressed mission to provide positive coaching, skill development, and sportsmanship in a fun and family friendly atmosphere (American Youth Soccer Organization, 2011). The values of the National Alliance for Youth Sports (NAYS), one of the largest youth sport organizations in North America, are very similar to AYSO in that they support using sport and physical activities to enhance participants' emotional, psychological, physical, mental, and moral character in a safe, fun, and healthy environment, thereby instilling lifelong values important throughout an individual's life (National Alliance for Youth Sports, 2011).

By the early 1970s, the leaders of the Women's Movement took to task educational entities offering sport for boys. Through Title IX legislation girls were integrated to varying degrees into organized sport programs within schools. Because Title IX only applied to educational programs receiving federal financial support, this legislation did not directly cause youth sport organizations to open their programs to girls. Public pressure, court cases, and other social forces arguing from the perspective of the equal protection clause were successful in causing doors to open for girls to participate in organized, competitive youth sport activities. By 1973 girls were playing Little League Baseball, with the opportunities to play organized mixed and gender specific competitive sport open across all levels and most sports by the 1990s.

By 1999, USA Junior Hockey was organized with a major goal of helping male players improve skills, continue their education, and grow socially (USA Junior Hockey, 2011). While USA Junior Hockey is designed specifically for males who have a goal of collegiate or elite competition, a strong girls' and women's program has seen membership soar to levels of approximately 59,500 (USA Junior Hockey, 2011). In these organizations as well as with many current sport programs, organizers clearly state missions of teaching skills, fair play, teamwork, and the ideals of competition, and advocates tout that participation increases one's self esteem, discipline, motivation, dedication, sacrifice, accountability, physical fitness, motor skills, and game strategies, all important contributions to a quality life.

Historically, however, it did not take long for businesses to advertise on tee shirts, ballpark signs, and uniforms (Eitzen & Sage, 2003). As the number of sport programs increased, the number and type of sponsors also increased, each with their own particular philosophies and goals, thus raising more potentially difficult questions for sport leaders in balancing the mission of the program, needs of youth participants, and commercialization. Communities invested large sums of money in ballparks, gymnasiums, tracks, and fields all in the name of providing opportunities for youth. During tournaments and championships, money was made through ticket and tee shirt sales, programs, and concessions.

While sport programs for youth began in small, isolated areas, it did not take long for teams and programs to spread across communities, regions, and states (Eitzen & Sage, 2003). Non-school-sponsored sport programs are now organized by over 25 different agencies, while local, regional, and national organizations have grown to include Babe Ruth and Cal Ripken Baseball, USA Swimming, YMCAs, and the United States Tennis Association to name a few. Currently, over 46 million American children and youth participate in organized sport of which 40 percent are girls and women (American Council of Youth Sports; Fergusson, 1999). It is estimated that over 65 percent of all households (four of five households with children) in North American have at least one child participating in organized sport activities. With 17.5 million youth players, soccer has the highest participation levels, while Little League Baseball accounts for approximately three million youth participants. Over 3,000 YMCAs offer youth organized sport activities, with 21 different sports competitions at the local, state, regional, and national levels offered through the Junior Olympic Sports Program.

Ethical Issues in Youth Sport

Although businesses, organizations, communities, and parents have missions with very altruistic goals for youth sport programs, many ethical issues surface daily that you as a sport leader will face. The key to resolving these conflicts will be how you develop your principle-centered leadership strategies and how much courage you have in holding to these principles in the face of many conflicting non-moral values and interests held by relevant stakeholders within your organizations and communities.

The ethical issues in youth sport are many and varied, although in general they can be categorized into the following areas: (1) age/size/height-appropriate equipment, fields, courts, and arenas; (2) developmental motor skills and physical fitness; (3) appropriate training of coaches and officials; (4) injury recognition and care; and (5) parental interest and control versus program goals.

Because sports were originally developed and played by adults, equipment for children and youth was non-existent. Children and youth played with hand-me-down balls and equipment that were ill-fitting, often leading to unsafe play and many injuries. While equipment today is more age-specific, in many communities, children and youth still play with hand-me-down equipment that does not fit properly, sporting implements that do not match the size and skill level of the participants, and rules designed for adult play. While the exact cause is unclear, the current youth sport environment has seen an exponential increase in youth sport injuries (Patel & Nelson, 2000). According to a recent study, over 8,000 youth sport participants are treated in emergency rooms each day (Satlof & Waxenberg, 2010). While the majority of injuries (approximately 65 percent) are minor, the expanded level and intensity of play as well as the number of hours spent practicing and competing has led to a marked

Equipment for youth sport is oftentimes handed down from high school and adult teams. Face guard bars cover a child's eyes, making it difficult to see, chest protectors do not cover the upper chest, and helmets fit loosely, leading to potentially unsafe play.

increase in chronic injuries as well as catastrophic injuries that sideline children for multiple games, the season, and even a lifetime (Albohm, 2010). The increase in concussions, sudden cardiac arrest, exertional heat illness, and other conditions has led state legislatures and national organizations such as the National Athletic Trainers' Association, the American Medical Association, and the American Academy of Pediatrics to develop guidelines for education and expectations for care by coaches and parents relative to youth participants and their returning to play.

While the majority of injuries remain chronic, meaning that they occur from overuse and are preventable, there were 115 sport-related deaths in 33 different states from 2008–2010 and a significant increase in concussions and traumatic brain injuries, leaving many athletes with long-term and lifelong problems (National Athletic Trainers' Association, 2010). The problem with injuries is also exacerbated in that few if any trained medical personnel are present at games and/or practices. Few coaches hold first aid certifications, and because youth sport is typically coached by parent volunteers with little to no formal training or education in sport and sport-related training and injury recognition, injuries go undiagnosed and children are allowed to play when it is not in their best interest. While teachers spend four to six years preparing to teach, parents or other volunteers typically attend one evening or maybe one day-long workshop, if any time is spent at all, becoming familiar with the program before taking charge. Most of this training time is spent with managerial tasks, team rosters, and equipment assignment, with little on developmental tasks. Thus is it not surprising that few parents have a good understanding of the physical, developmental, social, and emotional well-being of children engaged in sporting activities.

Not only are there ethical problems related to equipment, fields, and rules, but many ethical questions arise from a lack of knowledge about developmental sequences in children. Without thinking, many programs, while touting safe and developmental skill missions, in practice provide environments that treat children and youth as though they are mini-adults. For example, elementary-aged children typically play on basketball courts, football fields or ice hockey arenas. While it is well-known that the more children train, the greater their physiological improvement, they are pushed to exhaustion due to their smaller total lung volumes much sooner when compared to adults. The more exhausted a child, the greater the incidence of both minor and serious injury (National Athletic Trainers' Association, 2010).

In another example, most children play basketball with a full-height basket, even though they are typically around four feet tall in elementary school. Many mistakenly believe that if a child is challenged to shoot, throw, and hit on adult-sized baskets, fields, and arenas that they will be better prepared. The result is often poorly executed skills and well-developed bad habits. After many bad habits have been ingrained, skills then have to be re-taught and re-learned. Parents become frustrated, yelling and chastising their children; coaches lose patience which leads to much frustration and anger on the part of the child (Weinberg & Gould, 2007). The more frustrated they become, the lower the self-esteem and feelings of competency, and the less fun they experience. Those few who excel move on while those who have not matured as quickly become frustrated, lose interest, and become a part of the 70 percent of youth that drop out of sport every year by age 13 (Eitzen & Sage, 2003). It has been found, however, that young athletes' perceptions of competence or ability were keys in helping children enjoy and remain in sports. In other words, children persisted in sports more when they felt that they had developed a skill and game competency (Weiss & Ferrer-Caja, 2002). It would appear then that to increase participation levels and decrease potential dropout, a major goal of any youth sport program should be to help children feel competent. One way a sport leader can help children gain that feeling of competency can be as easy as adapting the adult game to a more age/size/height appropriate arena.

Parental involvement is probably the single area that will challenge your resources and patience as a principle-centered leader in youth sports. Before age eight, most children enter sports because of parental influence; after age eight, peers become more powerful as socializing agents to sport participation (Eitzen & Sage, 2003). Parents, however, still have a major influence on a child's motivation about participation, perceived competence, and enjoyment of sport (Brustad, Babkes, & Smith, 2001). How parents emphasize what they believe and value as important about sport participation (i.e., winning and skill acquisition) and their actions before, during, and after a game (yelling, cajoling, belittling, encouraging, and congratulating) radically affects how a child perceives personal competency, enjoyment, and persistence in the activity. While both parents influence a child, it has been found that fathers have a greater influence on both girls' and boys' enjoyment and persistence in sport (Greendorfer, Lewko, & Rosengren, 1996). Moreover, the lower the perceived parental pressure, the greater is the child's enjoyment (Brustad, 1988). While the majority of research has examined how parental expectations and behaviors influence sport involvement, more recently researchers have examined problems created by parents (arguing, fighting, belittling, and confronting) and the concomitant effect on participants, coaches, officials, and sport leaders and increase in sportsmanship rules. Leaders and sponsoring organizations have found that problems with parents before, during, and after practices and games are the most frequently cited issues they face (Cumming & Ewing, 2002; Enigk, 2002; Herbert, 2000; Nack & Munson, 2000; Randall & McKenzie, 1987).

Frankl (2011) believes that youth sport would not exist today if it were not for the well-meaning intentions and sacrifices of millions of parents; however, the influence of parental involvement cannot be underestimated and may radically affect why many children and youth drop out of sport. In a nationwide study of youth, the top reasons to enter sport were having fun, improving skills, and enjoying the excitement of competition, while the major reasons they left sport were because they were not having fun, lost interest, and felt it took up too much time (Ewing & Seefeldt, 1990). Winning was toward the bottom of the list for boys and did not even make the top ten reasons for girls. While few if any researchers have examined parents' view about why children enter and drop out of sport or how they view the impact of their own actions and involvement on their child, many argue that parents place far too much emphasis on winning. Perhaps this view exists because of the negative actions of parents at practices and games or living vicariously through their own children (Eitzen & Sage, 2003).

Adding to the ethical mix is the push by parents, coaches, and others for children to specialize at a very early age. While originally parents enrolled their children in a variety of different sports throughout the year, depending on the season, parents can now enroll their children in gymnastics and swimming programs at age three and ice hockey, soccer, football, t-ball, and many other sports by age four (Eitzen & Sage, 2003). Coaches and sport leaders encourage parents to sign their children up for off-season sport-specific camps as well as extra clinics on weekends. The result is that many children specialize in a sport before entering elementary school and by the time they enter their teens they have upwards of eight years of competitive experience in just one sport. The goal oftentimes is to gain the elusive college sports scholarship (less than 1 percent), national rankings, Olympic participation, or professional contracts (less than 1 percent of college athletes). Parents spend thousands of dollars, enroll their child in continual sports camps, and even send them to sport academies such as IMG Sport Academies, where children as young as preschool and as old as high school are trained in a specific sport and also receive a general K–12 education. The popular press and research literature, however, are replete with example after example of the psychological,

Children begin competitive play in many sports by as early as age three. They are pushed to attend camps and workshops, leading to specialization at an early age. By specializing early, many children experience overuse injuries and no longer find the sport fun. By age 13 as many as 70 percent of children drop out of sport.

social, emotional, and physical problems children and youth face after such intensive years of training (see Anderson's *Will You Still Love Me if I Don't Win?*, Ryan's *Little Girls in Pretty Boxes: The Making and Breaking of Elite Gymnasts and Figure Skaters*, Wertheim's *Venus Envy: A Sensational Season inside the Women's Tennis Tour*, Engh's *Why Johnny Hates Sport*).

With parents engaging their children in competitive sports as early as three years old, and specializing by the time they are five, sport managers walk a difficult line between parental involvement and engagement and what is developmentally good for the child. Whatever the reason, the balance between what is in the child's best interests, the parents' interests, and the program's mission and goal does not appear in sync and does seem to cause undue ethical issues for sport leaders and participants.

Principle-Centered Leadership and Youth Sport

Given the issues we have discussed in youth sport as well as the many others seen daily, how do you as a sport leader lead with principles and have the courage to stand by those principles in the face of many conflicting interests (parent goals, youth goals, program goals, character development, skill development, and safe environments)? At first glance it may appear that the task is insurmountable, that you are in a no-win situation. There are some steps, however, that will help you in your quest to provide strong programming and principle-centered leadership.

Tackling such difficult ethical issues requires us to think about what philosophers call the metaphysical questions. Metaphysics is a branch of philosophy that asks weighty questions about what is the nature of something, such as "What is the nature of mankind?" and "What is my purpose in the world?" In sport, however, we ask what Kretchmar (2005) calls the "soft" metaphysical questions such as "What is the purpose of sport?" and "What is the purpose of competition?" For us as sport managers we must first ask "What is the nature and purpose of youth sport competition?" In other words, what are the mission and purpose of our programs? Is what we do only about the development of physical skills? Do we have a purpose of developing and shaping a person's values — in other words, moral character? How much of each is important? Answering these questions allows us to build a foundation to support what it is we do and how we should carry out this sport endeavor with young athletes. Once we have a strong "soft" metaphysical foundation, it becomes easier to identify whether a moral issue has surfaced, whether individuals are being violated, and how to resolve the ethical conflict.

Most sport governing bodies have developed well-articulated mission statements and goals which provide the foundation to address the "noble goals" of what we are about and help guide us in our day-to-day responsibilities. Mission statements make it clear to all involved (parents, coaches, referees, and participants) what the organization is about, where we are going, and how we will go about doing it. Strong mission statements clearly articulate and help communicate the organization's core values and provide a starting point for leaders to address ambiguous and unclear situations. This mission statement provides the basic "soft metaphysical" frame in which to teach, model, and work with the relevant stakeholders in your youth sport programs. It requires, however, more than just handing out the mission statement and having parents, coaches, and participants sign that they understand the values. Rather, the mission must be taught, emphasized, and lived throughout the course of participation, as individuals often have very different interpretations of the stated values relative to competition. Moreover, these mission statements most often state principles in general terms. For example, many organizations state that sportsmanship and fair play are central. The organizations assume that we truly know and understand what constitutes fair play and sportsmanship. However, what is sportsmanship exactly? Fair Play? Most of us know when we see poor sportsmanship and unfair play, but do we have a good understanding on what comprises good sportsmanship and fair play beyond shaking hands at the end of a game?

This mission provides a starting point for all involved to have continual conversations about the program/league's values and behaviors and holds the organizations and its people accountable to the core values and its ideal self. It clearly states that sport participation develops positive character traits and values that are important and imperative to individuals throughout their lives.

As a principle-centered leader you must develop a strong understanding of values such as honesty, justice, and beneficence and attempt to lead using those values. Probably the most important value to principle-centered leadership in youth sport is beneficence. As discussed before, beneficence (benefiting others) has four conditions: (1) not doing harm; (2) preventing harm; (3) removing harm; and (4) doing good. Beneficence has a long tradition that dates back to Socrates and the Hippocratic Oath and was traditionally a part of the nature of being a professional (Kitchener, 1985). In other words, being a professional was considered a vocation or calling, with a professional's major goal service to others. Applied to principle-centered leadership, a sport manager would be a professional whose vocation or calling is in the service to others. These professionals would seek to benefit, or do good, to those whom they serve directly and those in a broader societal context.

In our world today, it is probably a hard sell to argue for beneficence as part of principle-centered leadership, especially in sport. The environment of gamesmanship, "doing unto others before they do unto you," "I'm not doing anything to help the other guy" and "my sole goal and purpose is to take the other guy out of the game so I can play number two," takes precedence over beneficence. Moreover, it is difficult, if not impossible to ferret out what "good" is derived from competition, especially at early ages (Slentz & Krogh, 2001). While some athletes, coaches, and sport managers might concede that they should not do any harm and that they should remove harm, few agree that they have a role in either preventing harm and almost no one will argue that "doing good" has any place in sport competition. These thoughts are not surprising in that debates have existed in society in general as to whether people have an actual obligation to do good. Individuals typically argue from a perspective of non-maleficence: "first, do no harm," or in the Latin, *primum non nocere*, primum meaning primary. The argument becomes that our primary interest is to do no harm, rather than to think about actually doing good. Most people in sports, however, would argue that they have no obligation to do good, just support non-maleficence. Their ethical arguments are more focused towards avoiding harm or not violating others' rights rather than on what good can or should be done in and through sport. While this debate has existed in society and sport in general, we argue that given the mission and purposes of most youth sport programs, the value of beneficence should be central to any principled leadership strategy. We only need to look back to the mission and its "soft" metaphysical positions to determine what we should do.

For example, if we know an action will cause something bad to happen, do we have a duty to prevent it? Since we know that the waving of signs and other materials distracts players during play, do we continue to hand these materials out to fans as they arrive, as others do, or do we take a stand and ask fans to refrain from such acts? Given that these youth programs support character development in a safe, fair, and family friendly atmosphere, do we allow aggressive and physical play because everyone else is doing it, or do we set the stage at the beginning of the game for self-control and skill? If we know that specializing in a sport at an early age is developmentally questionable and actually physically, mentally, and psychologically hurts young athletes, do we have an obligation or duty to remove that harm by not providing workshops and clinics for the very young, even though we know parents and coaches want them and much revenue is raised? If we know that pitching curve balls increases the likelihood of permanent elbow problems, do we develop rules eliminating these pitches? If we know that playing on shorter baskets with young athletes increases their success and feelings of competence, do we ensure that baskets are lowered to appropriate heights or do we continue to use adult-sized goals? If we know that sport-specific competition is not developmentally appropriate for children under the ages of seven, do we continue to offer such activities just because there is a demand? If we know that negative parental involvement such as belittling, arguing, pushing, and fighting negatively impacts self-esteem and persistence to sport, do we keep our mouths shut and walk away, or have the courage to teach, model, and expect the positive program values and remove parents, coaches, parents, and officials who violate such values?

Having the courage to take a stand as a principle-centered leader is not easy, especially in a society and sport environment that appears more morally calloused than beneficent. Moral calluses are the hardening around our hearts similar to calluses, the tough skin that we build upon our hands and feet (Kretchmar, 2005). We become morally calloused when we are unable to recognize or to care that a moral issue exists or that a moral conflict has surfaced. Moral calluses manifest themselves in moral insensitivity. Kretchmar argues that moral insensitivity is socialized in many different ways in our society today, especially in sports. He believes that young athletes develop these calluses at a very early age because they look up to highly skilled athletes who are splashed across the television screen, newspaper, and internet in an almost non-stop fashion, playing out acts that inside sport appear accepted, yet many would argue are unacceptable outside sport. These acts of callousness play continually on YouTube and receive thousands of hits within minutes of posting, causing many to become desensitized or morally calloused to the act. Calluses begin to develop and harden in many different ways. The hardening increases when we believe that certain actions are acceptable just because everyone else is doing them, that competition is amoral and therefore gamesmanship (pushing rules to the limit by dubious means) is the name of the game, that it is only unethical if we get caught, and that it is only the officials' responsibility to ensure ethical play (Kretchmar, 2005). Where will you stand? What values will guide your leadership style as you work with youth and parents? How will you develop the courage to take a stand on the difficult ethical issues you face in youth sport?

While you have gained knowledge about the values that underlie youth sport and have begun to develop principle-leadership strategies, read the following real-life scenario and see if you can put into play some of what you have learned.

Beneficence in Practice

You and a couple of your sport management peers are interning at a local park and recreation department where you are in charge of managing the youth basketball league with teams of 3rd, 4th, 5th, and 6th grade girls' teams. Your immediate Parks & Recreation supervisor oversees your work and takes input from other individuals who supervise you. One of your first responsibilities in your internship was reading the program mission statement and goals and providing copies for all participants, coaches, and parents to sign. Among other things, the mission states that the major goals of the program are "to develop and deliver quality youth basketball programs which promote a fun, safe, family environment that teaches skills, fair play, and teamwork."

Besides setting up the local schedule, your teams also play in the surrounding regional areas, so you work with supervisors from other Parks & Recreation programs in other local towns. In some cases, the managers are also coaches and/or referees. It's a Saturday morning and you and your program's 5th grade girls' basketball team is preparing for the championship game. When you arrive at the gymnasium you check the facilities, make sure the referees have arrived, check for potential safety issues, and ensure other general pre-competition responsibilities have been met. A lot is riding on this championship game, and the teams have split two previous games. As the teams warm up, parents, grandparents, and friends pour into the gym and take their seats. While noisy, no one appears out-of-line and it appears that the competition should go off without a hitch. One of your last-minute responsibilities is to talk with the referees about the game rules, and you let them know that if they have any concerns or questions that you are available for help and advice. Again, you are not concerned about the game as the two officials have officiated in the past, and one is also your immediate supervisor at the recreation facility.

Warm-up has concluded, the "Star-Spangled Banner" was sung, and the game begins. While these two teams are the top in the league, they are still 5th graders learning basic basketball skills and strategies. The ball changes hands several times, and the girls race back and forth before the first basket is shot. For the first five minutes of the game, all is well and the score is 10–6 with your team in the lead. Then your team steals the ball and races down the court on a breakaway. Coaches and parents from both teams are yelling and cheering on their respective girls. As your team's girl starts her lay-up move, a girl from the opposing team slams into her from behind, knocking her headlong into the mat against the wall. She is hit hard enough that it takes her a moment to get up and head back to the court. Parents are out of their seats, yelling at the officials to call a foul; your team's coach jumps up and is hollering at the officials, yet no whistle is blown. Neither coach steps onto the playing floor. The officials signal that the play was "incidental contact," give the ball to your town's team, and play resumes. Parents and your team's coach are visibly upset, but the girls continue to play.

From that point on, play become noticeably rougher between the girls, and the coach of the opposing team even yells at his girls to "knock it off," although he does not remove anyone from the game. At half-time you talk with the referees and ask them to call a tighter game so that no one gets hurt and better sportsmanship can be expected. It crosses your mind that the lead referee is your supervisor, and so you are pretty careful not to say or do anything that might affect her evaluation of your work. You also speak with both coaches and ask them to talk with their girls about self-control and sportsmanship. The second half begins and while play appears a little more under control, you realize that the referees are not calling blatant fouls and the game is starting to get out of hand. Your team is behind 17– 15. Another breakaway happens and another girl is knocked hard into the wall as she attempts her lay-up. Your team's girl gets up more shakily this time and is visibly upset. At this point both coaches jump from their seats but do not enter the court. Parents are going nuts, and it looks as though the gymnasium crowd is going to come from their seats. Things are quickly getting out of hand. The opposing coach again yells at his girls to knock it off but leaves them in the game. The lead official tells both coaches to sit down or she will kick them out of the gym. The opposing coach sits while your coach stands with his hands to his sides and talks non-threateningly to the official. He wants things under control, and he wants fouls called. The official turns to your coach, gets right in his face, calls a technical foul and kicks him out of the gym. Your coach says nothing other than "play a fair game and have fun" to his girls and then walks toward the locker room, hands to his sides, shoulders bent. From out of nowhere the official runs up behind your coach and pushes him as hard as she can, whereby he stumbles toward the door. He still does not bring up his hands or speak poorly toward the officials. The crowd goes ballistic. The girls begin to cry. Your assistant coach is looking on in disbelief. Five minutes remain in the game. The opposing coach is just sitting there. What do you do? You know that what is going on is completely wrong and against anything you know about competition, fair play, and sportsmanship—the mission of the organization. On the other hand, the lead official who appears to be causing most of the problems is your immediate supervisor and writes the evaluation for your internship, your last requirement to graduate. You also realize that the 6th grade game follows this one, using the same referees. What do you do?

Making decisions in the heat of the moment is difficult if not impossible, especially if one has not thought through the program's mission and developed a well-thought-out, principle-centered leadership strategy. In this case it is probably too late to change the current game in any meaningful way, as the problem has gone on too long in the game, emotions are way too high, and trying to get nine sobbing 5th grade girls back to playing the game is probably not going to happen. However, you do have some obligations to the athletes, the organization and its mission, as well as other stakeholders. First you need to remember that your personal interests (i.e., internship recommendation) are of no concern to the ethical dilemma. It is not about what you need or want, but rather about what are the interests and needs of the program and its participants, as you are the professional and leader of the overall program. That is a tough one for any of us to swallow as it is generally very difficult to separate our wants, needs, and desires from that which we are charged to do as professionals.

Once we set aside our personal interests, it becomes a bit more clear where the true ethical issues are and how to begin resolving the conflict. The mission clearly states that this program will be conducted in a safe, family-friendly environment. Clearly the environment is not safe, the official is adding to the hostility, and the opposing coach is taking no direct actions to control his players. As we have discussed in previous chapters, a moral dilemma occurs when two values are in conflict. It is not completely clear why the officials were not calling fouls to curtail rough play and reduce injury potential even after you spoke with them. It is a bit clearer about the opposing coaches' interests in that he appeared to support rough play as a means to help ensure a win. Although he appeared to stand against rough play by yelling at his players to knock it off, his actions spoke louder in that he did not remove the offending player(s) from the game, a clear violation of one of the tenets of beneficence — removing harm. Both the officials and the opposing coach appear to be morally calloused and do not appear to believe or follow the program's mission.

At this juncture, as a principle-centered leader you are obligated to step in and take immediate action. While it would have been best to remove the offending official early on in the game when she refused to call fouls and support your request that the game be more under control, you have no choice but to remove her from the current as well as following game, knowing that you will probably have to officiate yourself. To do otherwise is to violate the tenets of beneficence. By removing her from these games, you have removed harm and potentially set the stage to do good.

Finally, to remove callousness that develops over time is not a simple task. Kretch-mar (2005) argues that we must first make certain promises, that of honoring both the letter and intent of the rules and keeping the interests of the youth participants foremost in our thoughts. Second, we must be vigilant for harm. If we follow beneficence, it is more than just identifying harm; it is about removing that harm, not only physical, but emotional, psychological, and social as well. More importantly it is about actually choosing to do good. To what extent have we taken the time to identify what are developmentally and morally appropriate actions in sport and remove those activities and actions that are not consistent with our program purpose and goals? Third, Kretchmar argues that as professionals we often forget or underestimate the importance of ourselves in the ethical equation, in other words loving our profession and taking pride in our work as professionals. Essentially, being ethically responsible as a principle-centered leader is about keeping control, respecting ourselves, and placing our needs and wants in proper perspective relative to the program and our professional responsibilities. Fourth, he states that some of the most difficult ethical questions arise in highly emotional and charged states such as the current basketball scenario. In highly emotional exchanges that often happen in sports, it is difficult, if not impossible, to step back and identify the true moral issue, reflect on the program's mission and purpose, and identify rational options that ensure a moral climate. At this point addressing these issues requires a cooling-off phase. Perhaps in the basketball scenario the second game should be rescheduled to a different time, in a different venue, with different officials. In the ensuing cooling-off phase coaches, officials, players, and parents could revisit the mission and purpose of why they are playing and competing, and cooler heads with a better perspective would prevail.

More importantly, though, parents, coaches, officials and participants would probably benefit from ongoing education about their roles and importance in the development of youth through sport. Few if any individuals would argue that they have a goal to make children's lives miserable or to cause them to drop out of sports. In most cases, all involved have their hearts in the right place. They want what is best for their children; they have often had wonderful and life-changing experiences through sports and want their children to benefit from and gain the same. Through their over-zealousness and enthusiasm, the ethical questions arise; more is better ... more practices, more games, and more workshops. They become caught up in the frenzy, and that which is good often leads to questionable actions and behavior.

While the discussion about mission could be seen as theoretical, how then could we practically apply these principles to helping fans, parents, coaches, officials, and participants actually learn to "live" the program's mission? One of the more powerful ways of mentoring (helping others to be the best they can be and rise above expectations) is to lead by example. John Wooden talks of walking into locker rooms, picking up trash off the floor and putting it into waste baskets, picking up towels and placing them in dirty clothes bins, and realizing that by the simple act of respecting place and space that his players would quickly do the same without ever being asked (Wooden, 2009). This respect for others' places and spaces increases self-respect, which in turn increases respect for others and a more cohesive concept of who we are, what we are about, and the road map of how we are going to get there. If we respect others, we are less likely to violate others and more likely to see a purpose greater than our own personal wants and needs. An example of this idea can be seen in a practice started by a group of basketball teams that was committed to living the ideals of their program through the sport experience. The sport leaders knew that changing the current climate and environment of this particular program was an uphill battle. So they decided to enlist the help of the each team's young athletes. Before warm-ups, players from each team were matched by position and introduced to each other. They each had to learn the other's name and a little about that person they could share with the other members of each team. After getting to know each other they went about their warm-ups, sometimes warming up together and sometimes as separate teams. Before the game actually started, one player from each team stood in front of the crowd of parents and fans and introduced his "new friend." He would say something like "This is my new friend Jamal. He and I play the same position; we both have worked really hard for this game. Please encourage us to play hard, compete to the best of our ability, and cheer our good plays. Please cheer our successes and encourage us when we make mistakes. Let's all have fun." Some might argue that this kind of action is "hokey," that competition would somehow be less intense, or that such thoughts and statements have no place in sports. Leaders in youth sport, however, must set the stage for the ideal sport competition; the ideal holds that sport competition is a moral endeavor. It requires that each of us play and challenge each other to do our very best, thus causing excellence in competition. With this perspective, when someone wins, they know they have beaten the best (Simon, 1985). Knowing each other as people helps set an expectation for a different kind of competitive experience.

The challenge for leaders committed to the ideals of their program is to honestly and compassionately educate, reflect, model, and mentor all stakeholders to the program's ideals throughout the program, not just when problems or issues arise. This reflection and mentoring requires setting the stage for individuals to examine purpose and meaning relative to beliefs and actions. It is easy for leaders in sport to say, "But there isn't time for that"; or "No one is interested in that — we are about basketball, football, volleyball and other sports." Wooden (2009) would argue that there is value in principled leadership. Principle-centered leaders lead by example and believe that character development is imperative to youth sport. The more we lead with principles, the more participants and others benefit from a kind of "osmosis," learning the values and goals through proximity with individuals practicing and living those values and goals (Wooden, 2009). We argue that while mentoring and modeling are important, everyone must also be engaged in dialogue and reflection about the mission, values, and purpose relative to what is in the best interests of our children. Moreover, parents, coaches, and officials may benefit from a series of thoughts posed by Al Rosen, a former major league baseball player (Frankl, 2004). These questions are a good starting point to reflect on the balance between skill development, character development and competition, and help ensure that what we do benefits our children and youth in sport (see Box 8.1).

BOX 8.1 REFLECTION QUESTIONS FOR SPORT LEADERS, PARENTS, COACHES, AND OFFICIALS ENGAGED IN YOUTH SPORT PROGRAMS

- Can we listen to our child and support their choice to play or not play sport?
- Can we expect our program to be led by competent coaches and entrust our children to these coaches without interfering?
- Can we let our children experience both success and failure and love them for both?
- Can we invest the time to learn everything we can about the developmental, social, emotional, physical, psychological, and mental aspects of our child's sport?
- Can we help our child set realistic goals and can we hold expectations that are consistent with where he/she is developmentally without comparison to others?
- Can we hold emotions in check and avoid becoming fanatical about our child's participation?

NOTE: Adapted from questions posed by Al Rosen, a former major league baseball player (cited in Frankl, 2004).

As principle-centered leaders we must love what we do, our "craft," and place our needs and interests in proper perspective (Kretchmar, 2005). This loving of our craft should support a beneficent leadership style that is not only about skill development but about actually doing good in the support of our children and youth's social, emotional, psychological, and moral character development through play.

Jareem: "So our key here is the development of principled-centered leaders who really care about youth sport."

Micah: "Care—don't most people care?"

Jeremy: "I think most people care, but that most people perhaps get caught up in the 'winning' rather than in the development of youth for sportsmanship. It takes more than kicking a soccer ball to learn sportsmanship. There has to be a concerted effort by everyone involved in youth sport, from the parent, the coach, the administrators, and the fans. And there has to be a commitment by all of these 'stakeholders' that character development is more than just saying sports build character. It takes a community with a vision, a mission, and a plan to make it happen."

References

Albohm, M. J. (2010, January 8). "National Athletic Trainers' Association Alliance to Address the Youth Sports Safety Issues in America." Sacramento, CA. Retrieved from http://www.nata.org/NR01112010.

American Youth Soccer Organization (2011). Organization mission statement. Retrieved from http://soccer.org/AboutAYSO/mission.aspx.

Brustad, R. (1988). "Affective Outcomes in Competitive Youth Sport: The Influence of Intrapersonal and Socialization Factors." *Journal of Sport and Exercise Psychology*, 10, 307–321.

Brustad, R., M. Babkes, and A. Smith (2001). Youth in Sport: Psychological Considerations. In R. Singer, H. Hausenblas, and C. Jenelle (Eds.). *Handbook of Sport Psychology*. New York: Wiley.

Cumming, S. P., and M. E. Ewing (2002). "Parental Involvement in Youth Sports: The Good the Bad and the Ugly!" *Spotlight on Youth Sports*, 26(1), 1–5.

Eitzen, D. S., and G. H. Sage (2003). *Sociology of North American Sport* (7th ed.). Boston: McGraw-Hill.

Enigk, M. E. (2002). "A Study on the Nature and Frequency of Adult Comments at Little League Baseball Games." Eugene, OR, Microform Publications, University of Oregon.

Ewing, M. E., and V. Seefeldt (1990). "American Youth and Sports Participation: A Study of 10,000 Students and Their Feelings About Sport." North Palm Beach, FL: Athletic Footwear Association.

Fergusson, A. (1999). "Inside the Crazy World of Kids' Sports." *Time*, 1–8.

Frankl, D. (2004). "Taming the Beast: Excessive Parental Involvement in Youth Sports." Retrieved from http://www.sports-media.org/sportapolisnewsletter24newlook.htm

Greendorfer, S. L., J. H. Lewko, and K. S. Rosengren (1996). "Family Influence in Sport Socialization: Sociocultural Perspectives." In F. Smoll and R. Smith (Eds.). *Children and Youth in Sport* (pp. 89–111). Dubuque, IA: Brown and Benchmark.

Herbert, D. L. (2000). "Youth Sports and Parental Violence: Is There a Solution?" *Sports, Parks, and Recreation Law Reporter*, 14(1), 7–9.

Kitchener, K. S. (1985). "Ethical Principles and Ethical Decisions in Student Affairs." In H. J. Canon and R. D. Brown (Eds.) *Applied Ethics in Student Affairs* (pp. 17–30). San Francisco: Jossey-Bass.

Kretchmar, R. S. (2005). *Practical Philosophy of Sport* (2nd ed.). Champaign: IL. Human Kinetics Press.

Little League (2011). History of little league. Retrieved from http://www.littleleague.org/learn/about/history-andmission.htm

Nack, W., and L. Munson (2000). "Out of Control: This Rising Tide of Violence and Verbal Abuse by Adults at Youth Sports Events Reached Its Terrible Peak This Month When One Hockey Father Killed Another." *Sports Illustrated*, 93(4), 86–94.

National Alliance for Youth Sports. (2001). History and mission statement. Retrieved from http://www.nays.org/who_we_are/mission_and_history.cfm.

Patel, D. R., and M. A. Nelson (2000). "Sports Injuries in Adolescents." *Medical Clinics of North America*, 84, 983–1007.

Pop Warner Football (2011). Organization mission statement. Retrieved from http://www.popwarner.com/aboutus/mission.asp.

Randall, L. E., and T. L. McKenzie (1987). "Spectator Verbal Behavior in Organized Youth Soccer: A Descriptive Analysis." *Journal of Sport Behavior*, 10, 200–211.

Satlof, E., and R. Waxenberg (2010). Alliance to address the youth sports safety issues in America, Sacramento, CA. Retrieved from http://www.nata.org/NR01112010.

Simon, R. L. (1985). *Sport and Social Values.* Englewood Cliffs, NJ: Prentice-Hall.

Slentz, K., and S. Krogh (2001). *Early Childhood Development and Its Variations.* Florence, KY: Lawrence Erlbaum Associates.

USA Junior Hockey. (2011). Purpose statement. Retrieved from http://www.usahockey.com//Template_Usahockey.aspx?NAV=PL_07&ID=176314.

Weinberg, R., and D. Gould (2007). *Foundations of Sport Psychology and Exercise Psychology* (4th ed.). Champaign, IL: Human Kinetics.

Weiss, M. R., and E. Ferrer-Caja (2002). "Motivational Orientations in Youth Sports." In T. Horn (Ed.). *Advances in Sport Psychology* (2nd ed.) (pp. 101–183). Champaign, IL: Human Kinetics.

Wooden, J., and D. Yaeger (2009). *A Game Plan for Life: The Power of Mentoring.* New York: Bloomsberry.

Additional Readings

Anderson, C. (2000). *Will You Still Love Me If I Don't Win?* Dallas, TX: Taylor.

Engh, F. (2002). *Why Johnny Hates Sport.* New York: Square One.

Ryan, J. (2000). *Little Girls in Pretty Boxes: The Making and Breaking of Elite Gymnasts and Figure Skaters.* New York: Warner.

Wertheim, L. J. (2002). *Venus Envy: A Sensational Season Inside the Women's Tennis Tour.* New York: Harper Collins.

CHAPTER 9

Academics for Athletes in Colleges

- What should be the primary focus of intercollegiate athletic programs for coaches and athletes?
- What are preferred admissions, and why should or should not they be allowed?
- What are the ethical issues surrounding athletes emphasizing academic achievement or athletic achievement?
- Why is or is it not important to play by the academic rules of the NCAA and institutions?
- Why does the NCAA enforce rules dealing with academic progress and expectations for athletes earning degrees?
- Why should or should not freshmen athletes be eligible to compete?
- What are the issues associated with the length of practice and competitive seasons in intercollegiate athletics?
- Why should or should not academic support services be provided for athletes?
- Should coaches be held accountable for the academic achievement of their athletes?

You and your sport management peers are just returning from one of your required sport sociology classes in which the discussion centered on some research that argued that perhaps athletes and athletics don't really belong in the academic arena of the university. The argument focused on the commercialization of athletics and the concomitant ethical issues that arise: academics versus athletics; amateurism versus professionalism; coaching salaries versus professorial salaries.

Micah: "You know, I'm a little tired of Professor Jones beating up on athletics. If athletics are so bad, how come we have them?"

Jareem: "Well, he did say that athletics as it is now practiced is more about selling a product than educating athletes."

Megan: "I agree with him. I'm so tired of athletes in my classes missing class and only occasionally showing up. I think they get too much recognition and too much support. If you look at the amount of money that athletics and the university provides for support services, shouldn't all of those athletes graduate?"

Micah: "Look, as a former athlete, I think athletes should get all of that support. Do you have any idea how much time is put into practice, weight lifting, watching film, travel, and training room preparation? We like live at the gym."

Megan: "Isn't that your choice?"

Micah: "I wasn't born with a silver spoon in my mouth. I'm only here because of that athletic grant-in-aid I received. I want a chance to get an education and athletics was a way to do it. The NCAA has really cracked down on graduation rates. Programs are graduating their athletes. At most of the big schools, athletes are enrolled in classes year-round and many finish their course work by December of their senior years."

Jareem: "If you had put as much effort into your high school education as you did in practicing athletics, you could have had an academic scholarship. I heard you say once that you started competition in your sport at age five and practiced year-round for the next 12 years. If you had put that much time in creative writing, you'd have a book on the market by now."

Megan: "Right!"

Micah: "Creative writing? So my work in athletics doesn't translate into what is considered academic—but creative writing does? You are missing the point. There should be some appreciation for what athletes do at the university. Everyone seems to benefit but the athletes. Sure we get scholarships, but we do all of this work and none of it applies to our degrees. I remember reading that athletes are really just a part of a plantation system. They are the slaves who do all the work, and the coaches and universities get all the money."

Jareem: "Oh pl … ease! Athletes do pretty well, and they are getting the opportunity of a world class education at our university."

Micah: "Maybe so, but none of you know the time we put into athletics, and we get a little bit of money and our scholarships. But I have even a better question: how come all of my work in athletics never counted for any credit in academics?"

Jareem: "Academic credit for what—playing a game?"

Jeremy: "You know, Micah has a good question. What is it about athletics that the athlete can't get a major in playing a game but could get a major in playing a flute?"

Micah: "Yeah? Why is that? I should have been able to get a degree in playing football."

Jareem: "What? A major in football, like what would you do with that degree? Wouldn't that make all the institutions look like jock factories? A degree should be useful—a degree should open doors to a job."

Jeremy: "Do all degrees have to be put to work? I mean, is a degree about knowledge or about a vocation? I think a degree should be about knowledge. Many people get degrees and never use them: for example, someone who gets a degree in history, but then decides to go to law school. Or maybe a degree in English and then becomes a stock broker."

Megan: "Okay, but your point is?"

Jeremy: "I have a friend who is a dance major. She is getting a degree in dance. All of her technique classes count toward her degree. All of her performances count toward her degree. But if Micah is a football player, none of his experience counts toward a degree; it's all extracurricular."

Micah: "Right! I think that's a great idea."

Jeremy: "I don't know if it's the right idea, but it should merit some consideration in that so many other motor-skilled activities on campus are actually majors. For example, I have another friend who is getting a major in piano; another who is getting a major in clarinet; another who is getting a degree in organ. If these fine motor skills are worthy of a degree, why aren't gross motor skills worthy of a degree?"

Megan: *"Jeremy, I always thought you were smart. Those fine motor-skilled activities are art."*

Jeremy: *"Okay, then how is dance different? There are only eight locomotor skills: walking, running, skipping, hopping, galloping, jumping, leaping, and sliding. Dancers get credit for putting them into a combination to music. Football players get no credit for putting them into a combination with only the rhythm of the skill. Doesn't seem fair to me."*

Megan: *"But dancers are graceful!"*

Jeremy: *"Football players aren't graceful when they catch a pass or evade a blocker? It's all a matter of perspective."*

Jareem: *"Dance has an importance in our culture."*

Jeremy: *"Really. Super Bowl Sunday, the bowl games, the fall season—those aren't important in our culture?"*

Micah: *"This is so cool! For once, someone agrees with me!"*

Megan: *"Dance is an art form. Football is not."*

Jeremy: *"Again, I think that has to do with perspective. Any movement has a degree of art to it including football."*

Megan: *"No one is going to make a major for football. No one."*

Jeremy: *"That's so funny. Did you know that it is possible to get a Ph.D. in specific sports in other countries of the world? They seem not to be so biased about athletics."*

Megan: *"I'm not biased, I just don't see the worth of it or how it could possibly work."*

Jeremy: *"Perhaps if we took athletics a little more seriously we could see the possibilities."*

Jareem: *"I don't understand what you mean—more seriously? Millions and millions of dollars are spent on athletics, and you don't think that's serious?"*

Jeremy: *"Look, athletics in both high school and college are extracurricular, except the time spent in preparation exceeds all sensible notions of what extracurricular is. Micah started in his sport at five and played and practiced almost four hours a day for 12 years. However, in the training and preparation the focus is almost entirely on the motor-skill acquisition and not on the science, the art, the history, or the culture of the activity."*

Micah: *"What? What are you talking about?"*

Jeremy: *"Dancers don't just dance to get that degree. They study dance—all aspects of dance from composition, choreography, mechanics, physiology, injury prevention, movement science, and so forth. We don't seem to value athletics except for what it brings the university—fame and fortune."*

Micah: *"I knew there was something wrong. I knew it was too good to be true. You aren't really on my side at all. This is crazy."*

Jareem: *"What's so crazy about it? I totally get it. Maybe if athletics were valued more for how the athlete grows and learns within the experience, we would have fewer problems with all of the ethical issues that occur in athletics."*

Jeremy: *"Right, if athletics were a part of the academic mission, maybe the athletic experience would have fewer ethical issues. If a major were offered in football, the football coaches would have to have advanced degrees. If a major were offered, the university would be overseeing the quality of the instruction. Unfortunately, athletics are not valued as a part of the academic mission. Instead, athletics doesn't really match the mission of most institutions—well, not really."*

Micah: "Of course athletics are a part of the institution."

Jeremy: "Oh really? Perhaps athletic programs write mission statements about how they are a part of the institution, but if you start to peel back the layers all is not so clear. Whether it is at the high school or collegiate level, ethical issues abound because of the very nature of athletics being extracurricular. Many institutions have permitted their athletic programs to be their own incorporated status and as such they are the 'beast in the corner.'"

This chapter will focus on the "beast in the corner." Bailey and Littleton (1998) noted the dilemmas and problems of big-time sport and the ethical issues that it brings to the university. As they noted, most university presidents try to control "the beast," feed it, care for it, sell it, but are always worried about how to control it, because the beast has the potential to do great ethical harm to the institution. Maintaining the beast is costly.

Higher education administrators and athletic directors pride themselves on providing academic support programs for athletes, often at a cost of hundreds of thousands of dollars. Plush study facilities equipped with the latest technologies, dozens of paid tutors, and advisors committed to assisting athletes make progress toward their degrees are among the services provided. Advocates heap praise upon sport administrators for giving high levels of academic support to athletes because of the time athletes spend with their sports. Critics argue that these academic support services illustrate preferential treatment of pampered athletes and express displeasure that compliance with National Collegiate Athletic Association (NCAA) regulations contributes to erosion in the academic integrity of institutions of higher education. This chapter will examine the ethical issues associated with the incessant tug between the academic performance of intercollegiate athletes and the time and physical demands placed on athletes.

While the overarching mission of higher education from a student's perspective remains earning a college degree, there are significant differences in the philosophies of athletic programs depending on institutional choice. In the past few decades, divisional membership reflects how educational outcomes are positioned relative to business goals. Institutions in Division I sponsor more teams, award more grants-in-aid, recruit and compete nationally, must meet minimal attendance standards for their football teams, and generate millions of dollars in ticket sales and donations. Division II institutions offer fewer sports and grants-in-aid, are state and regionally focused, and depend extensively on institutional financing of their athletic programs. Institutions in Division III are more closely aligned with the historical ideal associated with the early years of the NCAA. That is, no grants-in-aid are awarded, few distinctions exist between athletes and students, and competitions are viewed mostly by friends and family (Crowley, 2006).

The NCAA has long claimed that athletes only play for the love of their sports, although pundits argue this no longer characterizes athletes in Division I institutions. While certainly many of the approximately 400,000 college athletes playing in NCAA-member institutions would choose to play their sports without any remuneration, many others use their athletic talents to earn partial or full grants-in-aid and gain admission into highly selective or not-so selective institutions of their choice. Not always, however, are the outcomes positive, as the research reported on in Box 9.1 highlights.

BOX 9.1 ACADEMICS AND ATHLETICS

Shulman and Bowen (2001) studied these colleges and universities: Pennsylvania State; Michigan; Duke; Northwestern; Notre Dame; Stanford; Tulane; Vanderbilt; Columbia; Princeton; Pennsylvania; Yale; Denison; Kenyon; Hamilton; Oberlin; Swarthmore; Wesleyan; Williams; Washington in St. Louis; Emory; and Tufts. These were among their key empirical findings:

- Athletes comprised a sizable portion of the undergraduate student population at these institutions.
- Male athletes in recent years were more intensely recruited than they were previously.
- Since 1989, the recruitment of female athletes followed a similar model to the one characterizing male athletes.
- Recruited male and female athletes had a huge advantage in the admissions process (i.e., if listed as coaches' preferred admissions, athletes were likely to be admitted). These advantages continued to increase.
- The preferred admission of recruited athletes resulted in admitting students who had considerably lower SAT scores than did their classmates.
- Athletes developed an athletic culture that differentiated them from their classmates.
- The recruitment of athletes did not markedly affect the socioeconomic composition or racial diversity of these institutions.
- Based on their grades, the academic standing of athletes relative to their classmates has deteriorated in recent years.
- After controlling for appropriate variables like standardized test scores, the authors concluded that athletes under-performed academically. The authors also suggested this under-performance began in high school because of prioritizing athletes over academics.
- Male athletes and more recently female athletes were more likely to select majors in certain fields of study, and especially in the social sciences.

Bowen and Levin (2003) studied these colleges and universities: Ivy League institutions Brown, Columbia, Cornell, Dartmouth, Harvard, Princeton, Pennsylvania, and Yale; University Athletic Association institutions Carnegie Mellon, Emory, Chicago, and Washington in St. Louis; and New England Small College Athletic Conference members Amherst, Bates, Bowdoin, Colby, Connecticut, Hamilton, Middlebury, Trinity, Tufts, Wesleyan, and Williams. They reported these key findings:

- Athletes comprised between a third and half of the student bodies in these institutions with the percentage for male athletes 5–10 percent higher than for female athletes.
- Recruited athletes that coaches identified for preferred admissions were up to four times more likely to be admitted than were other applicants.
- Recruited athletes had substantially lower SAT scores than did other athletes and students. The most dramatic gap (more than 100 points below those of other students) occurred for males playing football, basketball, and ice hockey. Although not as large, gaps also were noted between students and athletes in other sports for both genders.

- Athletes reported spending large amounts of time with teammates outside of their sports, limited their extracurricular activities to their sports, and mostly majored in social science or business fields.
- Recruited athletes earned far lower grades than did other athletes and students.
- Recruited athletes under-performed academically based on their credentials at admission, a finding unrelated to time commitments (this pattern continued when they were not participating in athletics), differences in race or socioeconomic status, and field of study.
- A trend of increased intensity and specialization continued unabated as recruited athletes focused more on their sports at the expense of academics.
- Athletes in the four institutions in the University Athletic Association were more like their classmates than were athletes in institutions in the Ivy League and New England Small College Athletic Conference. Contributing factors could have been the limited emphasis on athletics, less formalized recruiting, greater monitoring of academic performance, and stronger presidential control of athletic programs.

These studies and other research (Byers & Hammer, 1995; Duderstadt, 2000; Gerdy, 2006; Sack & Staurowsky, 1998; Sperber, 2000; Thelin, 1996; Yost, 2010) offer evidence that athletics often surpass academics in importance to many athletes. Coaches' emphasis on athletics is not lost on athletes as they adopt a similar priority. Since coaches' jobs depend on winning, some may exploit loopholes in the written rules and violate the spirit of the rules dealing with academics to help win. As discussed in other chapters, principle-centered sport administrators are vitally important to preventing unethical actions and ensuring that core values like integrity and honesty will prevent violations of academic rules. These principle-centered leaders may choose to take some or all of the following actions to help eradicate violations, each of which will be more fully discussed.

- Make explicit statements about the educational purposes of intercollegiate athletics and hire only coaches who clearly understand and are committed to achieving these potential educational outcomes.
- Eliminate preferred admissions for athletes.
- Emphasize the academic achievement of students as more important than athletic achievement.
- Ensure that coaches play by the intent and spirit of academic rules.
- Structure intercollegiate athletic programs in ways that facilitate athletes who are interested in learning and earning their degrees.

Focus on Educational Purposes

For decades NCAA personnel and intercollegiate sport administrators have claimed that college athletes were motivated primarily by educational purposes and received physical, mental, and social benefits through their participation on sport teams (Crowley, 2006; National Collegiate Athletic Association, 2010). Thousands of adolescents have envisioned themselves earning grants-in-aid to fully or partially pay for their college education and enhance their collegiate experiences. They believed the athletic abilities they honed through tireless efforts would lead to opportunities to compete in the sports they loved, make lifelong friendships, and broaden their experiences while earning a college degree. For many athletes, this is exactly what happened.

For others, the passion for their sports at times resulted in disproportionate allocations of time and effort to their sports to increase the likelihood of success. Because the athletic role trumped the academic role, athletes focused primarily on conditioning, practicing, and competing, while viewing attending classes and completing required class assignments as distractions and a means only to maintain eligibility. This prioritization may have been continuously reinforced by coaches who dictated most aspects of the lives of recruited athletes receiving grants-in-aid.

Coaches, academic advisors, and faculty should encourage athletes to take advantage of their educational opportunities and create a culture where learning is important and fun. While most coaches, when recruiting prospective athletes, stress their colleges' academic programs and the benefits of earning college degrees, does this message remain the same after athletes enroll and begin playing their sports? Coaches who support athletes' academic achievement, progress toward degrees, and graduation potentially can serve as principle-centered leaders who have their priorities right, because coaches know that very few college athletes will play their sports professionally. Since former inter-

Thousands of adolescents have envisioned themselves earning grants-in-aid to fully or partially pay for their college education. Even though rules exist to limit time for athletics, the athlete role typically trumps the academic role with athletes often disproportionately spending more time on developing their athletic prowess than their academic abilities.

collegiate athletes will spend all or almost all of their lives working, the financial, psychological, intellectual, and emotional benefits of a college degree should be stressed and continually reinforced.

Athletic directors can show their commitment to the educational benefits of intercollegiate academics by hiring only coaches who can understand, articulate, and share a commitment to academic achievement. Rather than writing into coaches' contracts an expectation for winning games and championships, the prioritized expectation should be academics first and athletics second. Holding coaches accountable to this standard might send shock waves throughout intercollegiate athletics, but it is a necessity if what is espoused by the NCAA and institutional leaders is what is actually sought. Coaches and athletes, like all other humans, will respond to what is expected and rewarded. If sport administrators reward coaches for educating athletes for life and positively reinforce athletes for focusing on achieving academically, then coaches and athletes will emphasize these factors.

Historically, educational purposes associated with playing sports in college included learning virtues like commitment, fair play, self-control, self-discipline, sportsmanship, teamwork, and work ethic, and values like respect and responsibility. While learning to subjugate individual glory to achieving team goals, athletes were taught how to win and lose with grace and humility. Potentially, intercollegiate athletics can be enriching extracurricular activities, teaching life lessons transferable to work environments and applicable to interpersonal relationships. The commitment to physical development and fitness can bode well for athletes who continue to live healthy lives when their competitive sport careers are over. Psychological benefits, such as using feedback to enhance performance and demonstrating mental toughness and resilience when overcoming daily challenges and setbacks, represent transferable skills. The social benefits from making life-long friends with teammates or networking through sports leading to employment opportunities are just a few outcomes that often accrue to former intercollegiate athletes. Added to these are the academic knowledge, skills, and abilities learned in classes from professors and classmates that reinforce the importance of earning a college degree. Achieving all of these, however, is dependent on principle-centered coaches and sport administrators who focus on teaching, modeling, and reinforcing values while keeping athletics as a balanced part of athletes' lives.

No Preferred Admissions

Decades ago athletes on intercollegiate sport teams represented student bodies in their demographic characteristics because they and their classmates chose colleges based on similar reasons. This ceases to be true when coaches recruit the best athletes regionally, nationally, and internationally, and the non-recruited athlete is the exception rather than the norm. While outstanding athletes occasionally were recruited in the early decades of intercollegiate sport teams, this practice grew in practice and importance after the NCAA changed its rules in 1956 to permit the awarding of grants-in-aid. Since then, coaches have awarded grants-in-aid to attract highly skilled athletes to attend institutions that they would not have chosen to attend except for the promised financial aid and potential competitive sport opportunities.

Top athletes narrow their choices of institutions they consider attending to the ones with national reputations (and rankings) and those offering the best opportunities to develop their skills and gain exposure to possibly play professionally. Coaches with the best reputations for developing and expanding the skills of adolescents often deliver national media exposure as well as provide the most luxurious practice and competitive facilities. Many highly recruited athletes, however, lack the academic skills, background, and abilities to meet institutional admission standards.

Private and more academically elite public institutions admit a fraction of the applicants who have achieved significantly above the national average SAT or ACT scores. Recruited athletes whom coaches want for their teams often meet only the minimum SAT or ACT and grade point averages required by the NCAA. These recruited athletes may be insufficiently prepared to meet academic standards because of poor educational opportunities in schools or because they failed to take their academic work seriously enough in high school. Barely qualifying for eligibility in intercollegiate athletics is insufficient preparation for many athletes for the colleges they attend and may set up them up to fail, especially in comparison with classmates who have been admitted because they met or exceeded institutional admission standards.

Several ethical questions emerge when this occurs. First, is it fair to expect athletes who are academically less prepared to succeed in classes with students who are much stronger academically? Second, is it fair to allocate limited admission slots to less academically prepared students while denying admission to students who meet and exceed institutional admission criteria? Third, in trying to help less academically prepared athletes to catch up or offset the number of hours committed to their sports, is it ethical to provide tutors, note takers, tutors who sometimes complete homework and assignments for athletes, and academic support personnel who schedule their classes, select easier classes with athlete-friendly instructors, monitor their class attendance, and periodically check with instructors on athletes' academic work? Fourth, at what point, if any, do the academic support services act paternalistically toward athletes by delaying their acceptance of responsibility or accountability for their own academic work?

Providing preferred admissions has been a volatile issue on many college campuses when athletes with marginal and even poor academic preparation are admitted. Despite conflicting viewpoints, coaches at all competitive levels send lists to admissions office personnel with the names of highly skilled athletes they expect to be admitted regardless of SAT or ACT scores or high school grade point averages. As long as these athletes meet the NCAA's minimum scores on its sliding scale (as shown in Box 9.2), coaches argue that these athletes are no different from highly skilled musicians or other individuals with unique talents. There is a difference, however. A musician's talent is in an academic area in which a degree can be earned. Playing an intercollegiate sport is an extracurricular activity. Another important difference is that while highly talented musicians spend numerous hours increasing their skills, they also can be paid for their entertaining performances. Athletes develop their skills, and football and men's basketball players at many institutions entertain thousands, but they are not permitted to receive money or other financial benefits associated with their athletic talents, other than the NCAA-stipulated grant-in-aid.

BOX 9.2 SELECTED EXAMPLES OF THE NCAA DIVISION I SLIDING SCALE FOR ACADEMIC ELIGIBILITY		
Core Grade Point Average	SAT Reasoning Test (combined verbal and mathematics scores)	ACT (sum of English, mathematics, reading and science reasoning tests)
3.550 and above	400	37
3.400	460	42
3.300	500	44
3.200	540	47
3.100	580	49
3.000	620	52
2.900	660	54
2.800	700	57
2.700	730	60
2.600	760	62
2.500	820	68
2.400	860	71
2.300	900	75
2.200	940	79
2.100	970	82
2.000	1010	86

A negative association with preferred admissions of athletes is the stereotypical labeling of all athletes as special admits despite the fact that many recruited athletes meet and exceed institutional admission standards. Athletes often resent being perceived as less capable academically even though they are excellent, high-achieving students. One contributing factor to the ease of singling out athletes occurs at institutions with contracts with shoe and clothing companies like Nike and Adidas that outfit athletes in attire often worn to classes, making athletes easy to identify.

By eliminating preferred admission of athletes and requiring each athlete to meet institutional admission requirements, this stereotyping would cease. Eliminating preferred admissions would send a clear message to prospective athletes that no matter how great their athletic skills may be, these talents will not compensate for inadequate academic preparation in high school.

Academic versus Athletic Achievement

Most people do not know the origin of the term student-athlete even though its use is ubiquitous in intercollegiate athletics (and increasingly in interscholastic sports).

Walter Byers, former executive director of the NCAA, was the individual who crafted this term, mandated its use throughout all NCAA rules, and fostered its use by the media as the descriptor for college athletes (Byers & Hammer, 1995). The intentional choice to place student before athlete was to subconsciously and overtly elevate the NCAA's claim that the academic role was more important than the athletic role in the 1950s, when the NCAA began to allow the awarding of grants-in-aid to male athletes. The use of the term student-athlete was emphasized to support the claim of NCAA personnel and intercollegiate sport administrators that college athletes played for the love of the game while pursuing their college degrees. This made them different from professional athletes and thwarted any claims that athletes who received grants-in-aid were employees and eligible for workers' compensation benefits.

Fast-forward half a century, and this claim at times rang hollow. The Knight Commission on Intercollegiate Athletics (2010), in *Restoring the Balance: Dollars, Values, and the Future of College Sports*, called for treating college athletes as students first. This commission expressed concern that academic responsibilities of students had been supplanted by placing more importance on their roles as athletes. At all competitive levels, many intercollegiate athletes acted as if the primary reason for attending college was enhancing athletic skills and participating in sports, not earning college degrees. A high percentage of athletes spent the equivalent of a full-time job (i.e., 40 hours minimum) on their sports each week, taxed their bodies physically through training, practicing, and competing, and drained themselves emotionally leaving little time and energy to complete their academic work. Some athletes who had intended to use their grants-in-aid to earn degrees in academically rigorous and time-demanding majors, such as engineering or pre-medicine, quickly realized the time demands of their sports simply precluded this from happening. Many athletes failed to achieve their potential academically because they had little time or energy left to focus on their academic work.

The NCAA tried to address the time demands of playing sports in college when it established 20 hours per week and four hours per day as the maximum amounts of time athletes could spend in countable athletics-related activities during their seasons. In addition, the NCAA prohibited athletes from engaging in countable athletically related activities during one calendar day per week in-season. However, excluded from the 20-hour limit was the time for travel associated with competitions (which also could occur on the required day off) and the length of most competitions (each counted three hours regardless of the actual time spent).

The NCAA also permitted athletes to spend any number of additional hours practicing their skills, studying films, and conditioning as long as these were not coach-mandated hours. Athletes have readily admitted that vying for starting positions and playing time, further developing their skills to help them succeed in competitions, and sending messages to coaches about their commitment to their teams and sports meant they really had little choice but to regularly exceed the NCAA weekly and daily maximum number of hours. Not surprisingly, when involvement with sports exceeded 20 hours a week, athletes' priorities were on their sports, with much less time left for academics. How have pressures from coaches violated the letter and spirit of the hour limitation rule for athletes playing in NCAA-member institutions? Have athletes made

When athletes with poor and marginal academic skills and preparation are admitted, providing preferred admissions has been a volatile issue on many college campuses. Because these athletes often do not succeed academically, it leads to a perception that most athletes are less capable academically, even though many are high-achieving students.

wise and well-reasoned choices by dedicating themselves more to athletics than to academics?

A similar issue associated with time spent on their sports existed during non-playing seasons because the NCAA limited athletes to spending eight hours in countable athletics-related activities and required that athletes have two days off per week. During the off-season, athletes regularly train more than eight hours per week while claiming that any hours beyond eight are voluntary. Since coaches have instilled in athletes the importance of enhancing their sport skills, is it ethical for coaches to not-so-subtly suggest that athletes must work on their skills and conditioning on a year-round basis to enhance their skills? Is it ethical for coaches to expect athletes not to take time off from their sports?

Is it ethical for coaches and sport administrators to require athletes to sign statements that they are complying with the NCAA's in-season and off-season hour limitations when in reality they are lying because these limits are regularly violated? What effect does the number of hours dedicated to one's sport have on an athlete's academic performance?

Not surprisingly, because of the huge number of hours athletes dedicate to their sports, they often struggle to keep up with their academic work. This challenge is further exacerbated because of the number of classes that athletes miss. Given the number of allowable competitions (see some examples in selected sports in Box 9.3), travel, and coach-mandated practices associated with competitions, it is not unusual for some athletes to miss nearly one-third of the class sessions in each course they are taking. For example, for a class that meets on Monday, Wednesday, and Friday, an athlete might miss 10–15 classes during the regular season plus conference tournaments and other post-season play. Since most sports compete during two academic semesters or trimesters, the negative impact on academic work potentially can be continual.

Box 9.3 Allowable Number of Competitions in Selected Sports in NCAA Divisions			
	Division I	**Division II**	**Division III**
Basketball	27 or 29	26	25
Baseball	56	50	40
Football	12 Football Bowl Subdivision; 11 Football Championship Subdivision	11	10
Golf	24	21	20
Ice Hockey	34	32 men; 34 women	25
Soccer	20	20	20
Softball	56	56	40
Swimming	20	16	16
Tennis	25 team + 7 singles and doubles events	25 team + 7 singles and doubles events	20
Volleyball	28	28 men; 26 women	28 men; 22 women

While athletes who miss classes while participating in institution-approved activities are excused from classes, they are responsible for all missed work. Sometimes this may mean turning in assignments in advance or late and making arrangements to compete tests in advance, while traveling, or late. Making arrangements to get class notes and catching up with missed homework or class work is the responsibility of the athlete. Not surprisingly, it challenges athletes to complete missed assignments, find the time to study, complete scheduled homework and other written assignments on time, and perform academically to the best of their abilities. When athletes play in the number of competitions listed in Box 9.3, the message sent, whether intended or not, is that athletics is more important that academics. If the priority was truly on academics, why are Division I athletic teams permitted to play in so many competitions? Do athletes need the number of competitions listed in Box 9.3 to reap the potential educational benefits of playing sports in college, or has the commercialized business model that will be discussed in Chapter 10 become the primary focus, especially in Division I? Is this good or bad?

What is being prioritized when college basketball players are required to miss classes for a shoot-around or walk-through practice on the date of a home game? What is being prioritized when golfers are required to miss classes for practice rounds played before the actual competition begins? Are academics or athletics being prioritized when football or men's basketball games are scheduled or rescheduled to accommodate television even if this means that athletes (and managers, student athletic trainers, and band members) will miss one or more days of classes? Were academics or athletics prioritized when the University of Alabama canceled the first three days of classes for the spring semester of 2010 so students could attend, watch, and celebrate their team in the national championship football game? What message was being communicated to University of Alabama students with this decision?

Playing by the Academic Rules

For nearly six decades, the NCAA operated with the understanding that home rule or institutional control over the interface between athletics and academics was preferred. This existed because the faculty members (e.g., Faculty Athletic Representatives) who led and served on NCAA committees advocated this approach. After recruiting and awarding grants-in-aid to athletes were allowed beginning in 1956, these faculty representatives realized a lack of consistency among athletic programs that threatened level playing fields in all sports. Sometimes athletes were less than serious students and prioritized athletics over academics. Subsequent academic regulations passed by the NCAA (see Box 9.4) attempted to ensure that the academic preparation of prospective athletes met minimal standards and to prevent athletes from majoring in eligibility or managing to stay eligible while making little or no progress toward earning college degrees.

BOX 9.4 NCAA MINIMUM ACADEMIC STANDARDS FOR INITIAL ELIGIBILITY (Crowley, 2006)

Year	Rule	Description
1965	1.600 GPA	A prospective athlete had to be predicted to maintain a 1.600 grade point average (GPA) for initial and continuing eligibility in intercollegiate athletics. Each prospective athlete's GPA was calculated based on his high school GPA along with his SAT or ACT score.
1973	2.00 GPA	This replaced the 1.600 rule, so a prospective athlete had to earn at least a 2.00 high school GPA to be eligible for intercollegiate athletics.
1984	Proposition 48	A prospective athlete had to earn at least a 2.00 GPA on 11 specified (core) courses or earn 700 combined on the verbal and mathematics sections of the SAT or a 15 composite score on the ACT. A prospective athlete was classified as a partial qualifier if he or she failed to meet one of these alternatives. An athlete, who could receive a grant-on-aid but not play, had three years of eligibility remaining and could play his or her second year if a 2.00 GPA in 24 credit hours was earned.
1992	Proposition 42	The number of core courses used in calculating the GPA was raised to 13 in Division I. (The current regulation requires 16 core courses in Division I and 14 core courses in Division II. There are no initial eligibility requirements in Division III.)

1992	Degree completion	• By the start of the third year, an athlete had to have completed 25 percent of the degree requirements and earned 95 percent of the GPA required to graduate.
		• By the start of the fourth year, an athlete had to have completed 50 percent of the degree requirements and earned 100 percent of the GPA required to graduate.
		• By the start of the fifth year, an athlete had to have completed 75 percent of the degree requirements and earned 100 percent of the GPA required to graduate.
1992	Proposition 16	A prospective athlete could establish initial eligibility by meeting any of the standards for GPA and standardized test score, using a sliding scale (see Box 9.2). The use of a sliding score allowed a prospective athlete to meet eligibility requirements by having a lower GPA or test score offset by a higher score on the other standard.

The sliding scale in Proposition 16 was eventually implemented in 1996 following extended discussions, including with vocal critics who argued that the use of standardized tests (e.g., SAT and ACT) was racially biased against African Americans. Some African American coaches protested that the NCAA's academic standards discriminated against athletes of color by limiting the number of African Americans qualifying for grants-in-aid. Other African American leaders argued that the NCAA's academic standards remained too low, suggesting that if requirements were raised athletes would achieve at higher levels academically. Although a higher percentage of African Americans have been denied eligibility and grants-in-aid to compete for NCAA member institutions because of academic eligibility requirements, college presidents and athletic directors claimed higher standards were enacted to improve the image and integrity of intercollegiate athletics, not discriminate against African Americans. Coaches continued to recruit African Americans athletes, especially for their football and basketball teams, often increasing the percentage of African Americans on some campuses. Are some college coaches recruiting these athletes simply to help them win games, or is the primary goal to give these athletes opportunities to obtain college educations and play intercollegiate sports?

Principle-centered sport administrators require coaches to understand and comply with institutional and NCAA rules dealing with academics. This commitment is undermined whenever recruited athletes are ill-prepared for the rigors of collegiate study. Those who advocate preferred admissions of athletes state that institutions are morally obligated to provide extensive support services, such as tutors, required class attendance, and athletic academic advisors who schedule athletes' classes and continually monitor their academic performances. Learning study skills, attending hours of study hall each week, and reporting on their class work to academic advisors hired by athletic departments are among the services provided to athletes. Some athletes, however, resent the assumption that they will be academically irresponsible. Many instructors oppose giving preferential or different treatment to athletes, while others fear that individuals on athletic department payrolls may complete homework or other assignments for athletes to help them earn grades and maintain eligibility.

An illustration of the abuse in keeping athletes eligible was exposed by Jan Kemp at the University of Georgia. This case was adjudicated in 1986 when she received an award of over $2.5 million (later reduced to $1.1 million) for lost wages, mental anguish, and punitive damages from the institution. This judgment was rendered because the University of Georgia had wrongfully fired Kemp after she exposed the practice of enrolling athletes in its developmental studies program and keeping academically eligible athletes who could barely read and write. University of Tennessee (UT) English professor Linda Bensel-Meyers in 2000 alleged that the UT football program was involved in serious academic fraud, including abuse of academic probation rules, grade changing, plagiarism, and directing athletes into certain majors. Although she claimed to have damaging academic records showing the alleged misconduct, she was not allowed to share these with an NCAA investigator who found no reason to punish the institution. An academic misconduct case involving an online course during the 2006–2007 academic year involved at least one athletic department staff member at Florida State University and 61 athletes who played 10 sports. While the institution imposed reductions in grants-in-aid, the NCAA ordered it to vacate all wins in which these athletes participated during the time they were involved in the academic fraud. Sometimes coaches condone or facilitate keeping athletes eligible to compete rather than helping them achieve their best in their academic work, as the two examples in Box 9.5 illustrate.

BOX 9.5 COACH-ABETTED ACADEMIC ABUSES

- In 1999, the NCAA penalized the University of Minnesota with probation for four years and reduced grants-in-aid, official visits, and evaluation opportunities due to serious academic fraud. With the full knowledge and support of men's basketball coach Clem Haskins, a team tutor (Jan Gangelhoff) wrote hundreds for papers for numerous basketball players over a five-year period. In addition, the violations involved extra benefits, academic eligibility, unethical conduct, and lack of institutional control. Haskins resigned under pressure, and the NCAA show-cause requirements applied to him, which meant no NCAA institution could hire him to coach basketball for a designated period of time without permission of the Infractions Committee.
- After Jim Harrick coached the University of California at Los Angeles (UCLA) men's basketball team to the 1995 NCAA men's basketball championship, UCLA fired him for lying on an expense report. The University of Rhode Island (URI) hired Harrick as its basketball coach in 1997. Christine King, a secretary in the basketball office, alleged that Harrick harassed her, changed some players' grades, had term papers written for players, and gave players improper benefits. After moving to the University of Georgia in 1999, Harrick subsequently resigned under pressure in 2003 due to academic improprieties, including the travesty of grades given to basketball players in a basketball class taught by his son, an assistant coach.

Focus Athletes on Earning their Degrees

Many athletes enter college with the belief that they will earn college degrees, but before the end of their first season, they have become more realistic about their meager chances, at least in four years, of successfully combining athletics and academics due to the time demands of each. Taking five or more years to earn degrees was not what most athletes planned for, especially if their grants-in-aid ended after four years. Athletes, especially those playing football and men's basketball in Football Bowl Subdivision (FBS) institutions, may feel exploited because they have given maximally to their sports, thus fulfilling their part of the agreement associated with receiving grants-in-aid. Have coaches and sport administrators fulfilled their part of this agreement when they do not renew grants-in-aid to athletes whose talents do not contribute to team success? Does this suggest that athletics is more important than academics? Some sport administrators provide little academic support to help academically ill-prepared athletes succeed in their classes, often resulting in the loss of grants-in-aid if these athletes fail to remain academic eligible. Box 9.6 examines whether a grant-in-aid is a business contract or an educational opportunity. Who is benefiting from the awarding of grants-in-aid to athletes?

BOX 9.6 ATHLETIC GRANT-IN-AID: A BUSINESS CONTRACT OR AN EDUCATIONAL OPPORTUNITY

Perception of right and wrong may become murky for some college coaches and athletic directors who sometimes lose sight of moral values when faced with ethical dilemmas. One ethical issue revolves around whether the purpose of an athletic grant-in-aid is to help an athlete earn a college degree. Ethical dilemmas occur when actions do not match the stated motive and intention. The usual justification for unethical actions when faced with ethical issues and dilemmas is a form of palliative comparison using business as the backdrop. Everyone else puts athletics before academics, so we have to do the same thing to stay competitive. For example, if people measure the rightness or wrongness of what they do by what others do, no integrity exists except in relation to social expectation. Situational ethics, in which existing circumstances influence what is considered right or wrong, becomes the norm. When recruiting, coaches often promise a prospective athlete the opportunity to earn a degree in exchange for performing in a sport. While athletes most often have fulfilled their part of this agreement, are institutions of higher education failing to fulfill their obligation? Is it morally wrong to promise a college degree from an institution when academically a marginal student is unlikely to succeed in achieving this goal?

Because so many athletes focus only on maintaining eligibility to compete in their sports until they declare for professional drafts or exhaust their four years of eligibility, the NCAA strengthened academic standards to force athletes to get more serious about their studies. The NCAA's current requirements for making progress toward earning a degree are listed in Box 9.7.

BOX 9.7 CURRENT NCAA REQUIREMENTS FOR MAKING PROGRESS TOWARD A DEGREE IN DIVISION I (NCAA, 2010)

• After the first year in college, an athlete must have completed 24 credit hours and earned 90 percent of the GPA required to graduate.
• After the second year in college, an athlete must have declared a major, earned 95 percent of the GPA required to graduate, and completed 40 percent of degree requirements.

- After the third year in college, an athlete must have earned 100 percent of the GPA required to graduate and completed 60 percent of degree requirements.
- After the fourth year in college, an athlete must have earned 100 percent of the GPA required to graduate and completed 80 percent of degree requirements.

To address athletes' failure to graduate in Division I, in 2003 the NCAA established the Academic Progress Rate (APR) to measure the academic performance of all athletes on intercollegiate sport teams on a term-by-term basis. The APR, which equals roughly 50 percent of the NCAA's Graduation Success Rate, set the expectation that within six years every athlete would graduate. Box 9.8 explains this policy and the sanctions on teams whose athletes fail to graduate. In 2005, Division II institutions adopted the APR and also included athletes who do not receive grants-in-aid.

BOX 9.8 CALCULATION OF THE ACADEMIC PROGRESS RATE AND SANCTIONS

The APR is calculated for teams in Division I using data for a four-year rolling period as follows: the number of players who were eligible for the next term plus the number of players who returned to college for the next term or graduated divided by the number of players on grants-in-aid or who were recruited times 1,000. Teams scoring below 925 and having a student-athlete who fails academically and leaves college can lose grants-in-aid (up to 10 percent each year) as an immediate penalty. If a team's APR falls below 900, it faces sanctions that increase in severity for each consecutive year failing to meet the standard. For the first failure, there is a public warning letter for poor performance. For the second failure, there are restrictions placed on the team's practice time and awarding of grants-in-aid. For the third year of failing to meet the standard, the team is banned from post-season competition. For the fourth year of failure, the NCAA restricts the institution's membership status (i.e., the entire athletic program is penalized and it is no longer considered a part of Division I).

To further re-emphasize the importance of earning degrees, coaches should prioritize athletes making progress toward their degrees and graduating in a timely manner. Athletic directors should evaluate coaches based on these expectations. Principle-centered sport administrators should not allow coaches to award new grants-in-aid until current athletes have earned their degrees.

Outside of the NCAA, other groups have expressed concerns about the undermining of the academic integrity of higher education because of an overemphasis on athletics. For example, in 1929, the Carnegie Foundation for the Advancement of Teaching in *American College Athletics* reported that 81 of 112 colleges subsidized athletes, a practice not then permitted by NCAA rules (Savage, Bentley, McGovern, & Smiley, 1929). This report concluded that the two major problems in intercollegiate athletics were commercialism and loss of educational values. In 1952 the American Council on Education (ACE) established a Special Committee on Academic Policy that found serious violations of sound academic policies as well as violations of good moral conduct. This committee recommended the movement of athletic departments into academic units, no participation by freshmen on athletic teams, and no financial aid earmarked just for athletes (Crowley, 2006). In 1974, ACE again commissioned a study of intercollegiate athletics, looking specifically at commercialization and ethical shortcomings with the goal of strengthening the connection between athletics and higher education. Nothing came of the recommendations of either ACE report (Crowley, 2006).

In more recent years, two independent groups have been working to emphasize achieving educational outcomes by intercollegiate athletes. Since 1999, the Drake Group has been working to improve academic integrity due to the widening gap between the educational purposes of higher education and the commercialized emphasis on winning in intercollegiate athletics. The Drake Group proposals call for academic transparency, academic priority, and academic-based participation. Academic transparency should include providing composite data about athletes' majors, GPAs, standardized tests scores used to establish eligibility, missed classes due to athletics, and other related academic data to help encourage athletes to earn college degrees and to hold athletes and those who support them accountable. To further demonstrate a priority on academics, athletes should be required to maintain a cumulative GPA of 2.0 for eligibility, receive academic counseling from the same personnel as all other students, and not be permitted to miss classes for athletic competitions. To further emphasize academic-based participation, the current one-year, renewable grants-in-aid should be replaced with need-based financial aid or multi-year grants-in-aid, and one year residency would be required prior to athletic eligibility to participate (Drake Group, 2010).

The Coalition on Intercollegiate Athletics (COIA), representing 57 faculty senates in many of the larger institutions, has spoken out on intercollegiate sport issues and especially about conflicts between athletics and academics on their campuses. This alliance in 2007 issued its fourth policy paper, *Framing the Future: Reforming Intercollegiate Athletic,* that advocates a greater alignment of intercollegiate athletics with the academic mission and aims of higher education. Specifically, COIA offered 28 proposals dealing with academic integrity and quality, student-athlete welfare, campus governance of intercollegiate athletics, and fiscal responsibility that it hoped would lead to dialogue and adoption of its proposed policies and practices (Coalition on Intercollegiate Athletics, 2007).

Excelling in intercollegiate athletics vies for primacy with taking advantage of educational opportunities for many athletes. At the FBS level, academic abuses threaten the integrity and purpose of higher education. Despite efforts by the NCAA to strengthen and enforce its rules regarding academics, some athletes continue to masquerade as students while often chasing the elusive dream of playing professionally. Some coaches, athletes, sport administrators, and presidents lie, use deceit, and break academic rules to get and keep athletes competing. These ethical violations may have occurred because after the NCAA Clearinghouse (in 2006), today NCAA Eligibility Center, established the initial eligibility of a prospective athlete, the institution was responsible for ensuring that each athlete makes progress toward earning a degree and is eligible to compete. Because of numerous incidents of ineligible athletes being allowed to compete, the process on many campuses for clearing athletes to play has been removed from athletic department employees. Now faculty and staff under the oversight of the chief academic officer on most campuses are charged with ensuring adherence with NCAA and institutional academic rules for each athlete's continuing eligibility.

Principle-centered leaders are needed to educate coaches and athletes about the underlying principles and values that should guide their actions. These leaders must impress upon the minds of athletes that most will not play professionally (fewer than 2 percent of them will play football and basketball professionally), and then for only a short period of time. In preparation for the remaining years of their lives, taking advantage of learning opportunities and earning college degrees will prepare them for more fulfilling lives after their athletic careers end.

Principle-centered leaders can help enact specific measures to reduce ethical abuses associated with academics and intercollegiate athletics. Some suggested actions include the following, each of which will be more fully discussed.

- Eliminate freshman eligibility.
- Shorten practice and competitive seasons.
- Eliminate athlete-only academic support services to athletes.
- Hold coaches accountable for athletes' academic achievement.

Eliminate Freshman Eligibility

For decades freshmen were ineligible to compete on varsity teams in colleges, although sometimes they were allowed to play on freshmen teams that competed in restricted schedules or were allowed to further develop their abilities while practicing with upperclassmen. Proponents of freshmen ineligibility believed adolescents were ill-prepared physically, emotionally, and psychologically for the demands of intercollegiate athletics. They also believed adolescents benefited from having one year to adjust to college life academically and socially while adapting to the demands of their sports physically and psychologically. This also enabled athletes to earn their eligibility to compete by achieving academically in college.

This changed in the 1970s when NCAA member institutions voted to make freshmen eligible, claiming this was a necessary cost-cutting measure because eliminating freshmen teams would lessen the number of grants-in-aid required to field varsity teams. Associated with this change were myriad problems and potentially unethical actions associated with determining the academic eligibility of prospective athletes using high school grades and standardized test scores. Freshman eligibility required young athletes to adjust to the independence of college life while juggling the time and physical demands of their sports and facing the higher academic requirements of college courses. Most coaches supported freshman eligibility because it gave them more athletes to choose from for their varsity teams. If athletes needed time to grow or develop physically, coaches redshirted them, knowing that these athletes still had four years of playing eligibility remaining. Those freshman athletes who were ready to contribute immediately earned playing time and even starting positions. The pressures on mostly 18-year-old athletes were less likely to negatively affect them physically than academically because these athletes often emphasized their sports. Their lives often revolved around their sports, teammates, and coaches.

The recommendation to eliminate freshman eligibility seeks to emphasize the primacy of academics, which characterized intercollegiate athletics for over a century, for several reasons. First, adolescents typically face major challenges in learning how to study and achieve to their potential because of the higher standards and requirements of college courses. They have to learn the self-discipline and importance of attending class, taking notes, completing demanding assignments on time, and studying for tests. Second, first-year students should be expected to earn the privilege of playing on sport teams by completing 24 semester credit hours with GPAs of at least 2.0, rather than relying on high school grades or standardized test scores. Third, one year in college without the time and physical demands of intercollegiate athletics would allow first-year students to get involved with other campus activities and develop social networks outside of their teammates and other athletes.

Opponents of freshman ineligibility claim that today's freshmen are physically prepared to compete immediately because of their extensive sport experiences, so they should not be denied the opportunity. They also state that freshmen are significant contributors to the entertaining quality of intercollegiate athletics. While these two arguments may be true, does this justify allowing freshmen to be eligible? Does freshman eligibility contribute to a greater emphasis on athletics with lesser importance accorded academics? If the purpose of intercollegiate athletics is to provide educational opportunities to athletes, should athletes be required to earn their way onto teams through their academic performances? Is academic achievement of athletes more or less important that entertaining fans or fielding teams of specified sizes?

Shorten Practice and Competitive Seasons

As discussed previously, the time demands on athletes often conflict with their academic work, especially when they are prioritizing their sports or simply not having enough time to complete assigned readings, homework, class projects, and research papers. To be eligible, an athlete must be enrolled in a minimum of 12 semester hours (or the equivalent in quarter hours). Athletes who are trying to graduate in four years must take 15 or more credit hours, depending on the major and institutional requirements. Assuming an athlete takes the minimum academic load and combines it with 20 hours in countable athletics-related activities, time management abilities remain crucial to juggling these demands along with sleeping, eating, and caring for personal needs. This does not include travel time to away competitions, which is not included in the maximum 20 hours, the time over three hours associated with home competitions, and any time for social activities. Since something has to give or be left out, it is easy to understand how academic work may be the first thing to go. This choice often leads to lower academic achievement than an athlete is capable of achieving and sometimes to failing grades.

To give athletes a better chance of achieving their potential in classes, they should not be expected to dedicate the time and physical energy required for a large number of competitions. That is, the NCAA should enact a rule restricting all sports to no more than one competition or day of competition per week while classes are in session. A related rule should be passed by the NCAA and enforced on each campus that would permit athletes to miss no more than five days of classes per academic term for travel and competitions, and no classes should be permitted to be missed for on-campus practices and competitions. Institutions could easily apply these same rules to students engaged in activities associated with athletic teams such as band members, team managers, and student athletic trainers.

If intercollegiate athletes are really students first and athletes second as the NCAA claims, it should revise its rules about maximum hours. The 20-hour-per-week limit should include all hours associated with athletically related activities, including physical conditioning, studying game videos, practices, competitions, and travel time. A person not on the payroll of the athletic department should be assigned responsibility for monitoring athletes' reporting of the hours spent on athletic activities.

In addition to needing the time to dedicate to their academic work, athletes also need to have the physical energy required to perform academically to their potential. Cutting down the hours associated with their sports during their seasons will definitely help the body recover physically. Eliminating off-season, coach-organized practices and competitions in non-traditional seasons would as well. In addition, the NCAA should legislate and enforce that athletes in all sports must have at least one month off each year from training and competitions.

While fans, including students, who want to be entertained at football, basketball, and other sport competitions may think these recommended reductions in the emphasis on intercollegiate athletics seem radical, is it morally wrong to re-prioritize academics by giving athletes more realistic opportunities to succeed in the classroom? Since most intercollegiate athletic programs have limited fans, these reductions in hours spent dedicated to competitions, practices, and other related activities will primarily impact athletes and their coaches. The athletes will receive a resounding message that attending college is more about earning a degree and preparing for the future and less about having the privilege of playing sports. This also will help coaches realize that the individuals they are coaching are students, not athletes, first.

Eliminate Athlete-Only Academic Support Services to Athletes

Oftentimes faculty members, such as those involved with the Drake Group and COIA, have expressed concerns about how athletes are treated differently from other students relative to academic support services. These concerns are exacerbated whenever academic misconduct or fraud is alleged, as previously described within a few institutions. It could be argued that athletes need and deserve separate study facilities, tutors, advisors, and individuals to monitor and support their academic work because of the time demands of their sports. Conversely, it could be perceived that these unique services are provided primarily to help keep athletes eligible rather than with a focus on helping athletes earn their degrees. If the recommendations just described to limit the time and physical demands on athletes were enacted, the case could be made that academic support services provided within athletic departments would no long be necessary. Would it be morally wrong to provide academic support services to athletes in the same ways as provided to all other students if the time demands on athletes were reduced as proposed? Would it be just to treat all students the same by expecting them to avail themselves of tutors, academic advisors, and learning resources in the same way?

Hold Coaches Accountable for Athletes' Academic Achievement

Before discussing the topical heading, it should be stated that intercollegiate athletes, who are adults, are ultimately responsible for their decisions, including how much they emphasize earning a college degree. The college years comprise a transitional time between adolescence and adulthood for athletes and non-athletes, all of whom are expected to assume responsibility for their choices and actions. If less time and energy were dedicated to sports, athletes would face the similar time management challenges as other students do. This would be especially true if preferred admissions were eliminated so that all athletes would be as prepared to meet academic expectations as their classmates.

Coaches hold partial responsibilities to help the athletes they recruit and include on their teams achieve their academic potential. Even if the hour commitment to an athlete's sport were 20 hours, this still represents a significant reduction in the time available each week to be a full-time student. It seems reasonable to require coaches to instill in their athletes a commitment to make annual progress toward earning their degrees. If coaches are hired with the expectation that they will continually reinforce this priority, they would accept inclusion in their contracts of the requirement that their athletes achieve a minimum of 925 on the APR within four years of employment. Once attained, this level would be maintained. If their athletes do not achieve and maintain this minimal score, the contracts of each team's head and assistant coaches would be terminated.

Assuming coaches are meeting this expectation, the next logical extension is to include in the contract of each head and assistant coach the requirement that their athletes must graduate. While the NCAA's GSR is based on graduating within six years, this standard seems too low if combined with no preferred admissions for athletes, fewer hours permitted in athletics-related activities, and restrictions on the number of competitions. Would it be morally right and just to expect athletes to graduate at or above the institution's five-year graduation rate? If so, coaches should be hired with the expectation that their athletes graduate at or above the institution's five-year graduation rate, and once achieved this level must be maintained or the coaches' contracts will be terminated.

To further emphasize the importance of athletes earning their degrees, the opportunity to qualify for post-season play, including conference tournaments, should be based on a team's academic performance. That is, post-season play would be earned by the collaborative priority placed on athletes' academic performance, rather than being an automatic right that potentially could negatively affect academic work. Earning the privilege of post-season play should be based on a team having achieved at least 925 on the APR the preceding academic term and on athletes on a team graduating at or above the institution's five-year graduation rate the preceding year.

Principle-centered leaders with the moral courage to enact these recommended changes are needed if academics are to become the central focus of athletes, coaches, and sport administrators. While many people may perceive these as radical changes, in reality these specific measures will help reduce the ethical abuses too often associated with intercollegiate athletics. Returning athletics to its rightful place as an extracurricular activity will enable it to remain important and valued rather than over-emphasized and at times a detractor from the academic mission of higher education.

Summary

Educational exploitation in colleges may take many forms. Lowering admissions standards to allow academically unprepared students into college may set them up for failure. Tutoring, close monitoring of progress, personal advising, and minimal course schedules filled with non-rigorous classes may not bridge the gap for marginally prepared student-athletes. Despite such help, to prevent failure, these students may be tempted to cheat on tests, let others write their papers, or expect good grades to be given because they are athletes. Others may major in eligibility, with or without their coaches' encouragement, doing whatever it takes to stay eligible to play. While all these occur, most often in football and men's basketball, most athletes take advantage of educational opportunities made possible through their athletic prowess by earning their degrees.

Several specific recommendations offer concrete strategies for regaining a balance between intercollegiate athletics and academics. The educational purposes of higher education must become central, continuously stated and reinforced as a basis for hiring and retaining coaches. The elimination of preferred admissions for athletes will mean that each recruited athlete will have met at least minimal admission standards and be much more likely to earn college degrees. Everything espoused by institutional and athletic administrators and coaches should emphasize and prioritize the academic achievement of students over athletic performance. Coaches' contracts should require adherence to NCAA and institutional academic rules as a condition for continued employment. First-year students should not be eligible to play on athletic teams so they can develop socially, focus on their academic work, and earn the privilege to play. The practice and competitive seasons in all sports should be shortened so athletes have the time and energy to achieve academically. With these changes in place, athlete-only academic support services could be eliminated and coaches would be more willing to be held accountable for athletes' academic achievement.

Jeremy: "And just maybe if we were truly serious about athletics as a part of the academic mission of the university, maybe we could see play in its motor form just as important as play in its fine motor form. If gross motor-skilled activity were taught like the fine motor skills, maybe we wouldn't have that 'beast in the corner.'"

Micah: "Yeah, and then I could have gotten a degree in football."

Jeremy: "Yes, you could have—but it wouldn't look like the football that you know. It would be football that is taught as it should be taught and valued as it should be valued, and the athlete would be valued as an artist. The athletic department would be an academic unit, coaches would have advanced degrees, and courses would span the complete gamut of what an academic unit would. It would be a different world."

References

Bailey, W. S., and T. Littleton (1998). *Athletics and Academe: An Anatomy of Abuses and a Prescription for Reform.* New York: American Council on Education.

Bowen, W. G., and S. A. Levin (2003). *Reclaiming the Game: College Sports and Educational Values.* Princeton, NJ: Princeton University Press.

Byers, W., and C. Hammer (1995). *Unsportsmanlike Conduct: Exploiting College Athletes.* Ann Arbor: University of Michigan Press.

Coalition on Intercollegiate Athletics. (2007). "Framing the Future: Reforming Intercollegiate Athletics." Retrieved from http://coia.comm.psu.edu/FTF/FTFsummary.pdf.

Crowley, J. N. (2006). *In the Arena: The NCAA's First Century.* Indianapolis: National Collegiate Athletic Association.

Drake Group. (2010). Drake Group proposals. Retrieved from http://www.thedrakegroup.org/.

Duderstadt, J. J. (2000). *Intercollegiate Athletics and the American University.* Ann Arbor: University of Michigan Press.

Gerdy, J. R. (2006). *Air Ball: American Education's Failed Experiment with Elite Athletics.* Jackson: University Press of Mississippi.

Knight Commission on Intercollegiate Athletics. (2010). *Restoring the Balance: Dollars, Values, and the Future of College Sports.* Retrieved from http://www.knightcommission.org/index.php?option=com_content&view=article&id=507&Itemid=176.

National Collegiate Athletic Association. (2010). *2010–11 NCAA Division I Manual.* Retrieved from http://www.ncaapublications.com/productdownloads/D111.pdf.

Sack, A. L., and E. J. Staurowsky (1998). *College Athletes for Hire: The Evolution and Legacy of the NCAA's Amateur Myth.* Westport, CT: Praeger.

Savage, H. J., H. W. Bentley, J. T. McGovern, and D. F. Smiley (1929). *American College Athletes.* New York: Carnegie Foundation for the Advancement of Teaching.

Shulman, J. L., and W. G. Bowen (2001). *The Game of Life: College Sports and Educational Values.* Princeton, NJ: Princeton University Press.

Sperber, M. (2000). *Beer and Circus: How Big-Time College Sports Is Crippling Undergraduate Education.* New York: Henry Holt.

Thelin, J. R. (1996). *Games Colleges Play: Scandal and Reform in Intercollegiate Athletics.* Baltimore: Johns Hopkins University Press.

Yost, M. (2010). *Varsity Green: A Behind the Scenes Look at Culture and Corruption in College Athletics.* Stanford, CA: Stanford University Press.

CHAPTER 10

Commercialized Sports in Schools and Colleges

- Is the sponsorship of commercialized sports in educational institutions an ethical issue?
- What ethical issues have emerged because of increasing commercialization in interscholastic and intercollegiate sports?
- What are the ethical issues associated with the use of interscholastic and intercollegiate sports for purposes of public relations and promotions?
- Have commercialized sports exploited athletes in schools and colleges? If so, how?
- What moral dilemmas have arisen when sports in educational institutions are used for entertainment?
- Have sports in schools and colleges been used to promulgate economic purposes to the detriment of ethical values? If so, how?
- What steps could be taken to rectify any erosion of moral values in commercialized sports in schools and colleges?

You and your sport marketing peers are on the way to watch the big game of the week at the local sports bar, when the discussion begins to center on "making money" in big-time sports.

Micah: "Did you see the payout for the bowl game? If our team wins the game this week, we probably will get a bowl bid and the payout is something like $750,000. Man, that is a pretty neat chunk of change."

Jareem: "The university will never see a dime of it."

Micah: "What are you talking about? Of course the university will get the money. Who do you think gets it?"

Jareem: "As I understand it, once the money is split between the colleges in the conference and all the bills are paid to go to the bowl game, there won't be much left."

Micah: "What bills?"

Jareem: "Costs like transporting the team, the coaches, the families, the staff, and the band, plus the hotel costs and per diem."

Megan: "Families? What families?"

Jareem: "Well, these bowl games usually occur during a holiday season, so the athletic department gives a perk to the coaches who would miss the holiday with their families."

Micah: "A perk?"

Jareem: "You know, an incentive. It's a benefit that is offered to employees because, well, they are employees."

Megan: "Sounds like a really big perk to me. Aren't those teams traveling for at least a week or more. I mean, I have seen news clips of the week before the Rose Bowl, and there is a lot of partying going on before the game. The players are hosted about every day."

Jareem: "Right, as well as practicing at the game site."

Megan: "I was just thinking about the magnitude of this—and with just some quick math, it looks like an outlay of anywhere between 400 to 500K to put up this many people. Is that right?"

Jareem: "I think so. I remember at my old college, our team went to the Humanitarian Bowl. The payout was $380K—they spent it all. The president wrote a letter to the university community and argued that even though they spent it all, they intended to because there was no better advertisement of what the university did or what the university was."

Megan: "So it's all a hoax? They don't make any money, they just spend it!"

Jareem: "Yes, I also remember reading that the hotel bill for one of the competing coaches at the Rose Bowl a few years back was $64,000. The university thought it was money well spent. The coach took his wife, children, and grandchildren, and they were all in a rather nice suite."

Megan: "Again, it's a hoax!"

Jareem: "Maybe that language is a bit strong. The universities see the games as a selling point—great advertisement. No other part of the university gets the university in the newspaper daily more than the athletic department. It's a trade-off."

Micah: "So what? We still get to go to the bowl game."

Megan: "Wait a minute. You were arguing that a reason for the bowl game is the payout to the university, meaning we should be going to a bowl game for the big bucks."

Micah: "Right, I mean the amount of money that the university brings in for the big games more than justifies having the 'big game' even if they do spend most of it."

Jeremy: "Perhaps, but if the costs outweigh the burden, should we have the 'big game' or any big games?"

Micah: "What are you talking about? Every time we get into one of these discussions, you go off on some philosophical tirade."

Jareem: "Maybe if you paid more attention in philosophy class, you wouldn't think it was a tirade. What is your point, Jeremy?"

Jeremy: "I believe we learned in our marketing and finance classes that most of the big-time programs in the U.S. are subsidized by the university in some manner. At our institution, the coaches' salaries are paid through state funding, and in many universities student fees are paid to athletics. In most universities, the land that the facilities sit upon is owned by the state and thus land taxes are not assessed. The benefits by the state for the programs are really rather large, and if we did an assessment of how much money that is, most of these big-time programs really don't make money."

Micah: "Wait a minute. I once heard you say that athletics shouldn't have to make money. Didn't you say that?"

Jeremy: "Yes, I did. I don't agree that athletics should be a business and that it should make a profit. Just like any other program on campus, I'm not sure that the English department should make money, or the chemistry department, or history. Unfortunately in the 21st century, it seems that athletics are supposed to make money. I just don't think it's for the best."

Megan: "Wait, wait, wait... you aren't comparing the purpose of athletics to the purpose of academics, are you?"

Jeremy: "Yes, I am. I think that one of the basic problems with athletics is that it's supposed to make money. Why? I believe that athletics shouldn't be different from any other program on campus. It should have an academic mission just like any other program, and it should have merit like any other program. Unfortunately, athletics seemed to have lost its way many generations ago. Once upon a time, athletic programs were part of the academic programs on campus. In some institutions, athletics and physical education were combined into one unit, and in some colleges a degree was offered through athletics and physical education. Classes about athletics were taught by coaches who were skilled and educated. The first physical educators were often physicians, and the first coaches were a part of the physical education academic program... but then someone figured out that you could sell tickets to watch students play — and thus began the downward spiral."

Micah: "Really? When was that?"

Jeremy: "Mid– to late 1800s. Actually the first truly commercialized athletic event dated from 1852. It was a competition between Harvard and Yale, only it wasn't football, it was a rowing event. Held at a resort; tickets were sold; players were transported to the event by train; lots of brew was sold. Interestingly, even cheating occurred. Some of the players — oarsmen — were ringers; they weren't even students at either school" (Smith, 1990).

Jareem: "So there was always a problem with commercialization in athletics."

Jeremy: "Yes, there has always been trouble with commercialization. When we all wish for the good old days, there probably were not many of those good old days."

Jareem: "Right. It becomes very difficult to handle the different values and the push and pull from those values."

Micah: "You guys are losing me again. What values?"

Megan: "You really do need to study more in class instead of texting and keeping track of sports scores on your handheld."

Micah: "Nag, nag... don't I keep you all up to speed on what's happening? It's me who is able to keep the discussions going with what's happening in the game today."

Megan: "That's true, you are a sports encyclopedia."

Jeremy: "That's what is really interesting about commercialization of sport and athletics — we all want to know the scores. We all want to know the latest that is happening. We all want to keep track of the big game. People love to follow sports and there is money attached — big bucks attached."

Micah: "So what are the different values?"

Megan: "The non-moral values of money versus the moral values of integrity, justice, fair play, honesty, and respect."

Micah: "Meaning?"

Jeremy: "Commercialization places great stress on the college or high school when administrators choose to sell the products of education. If it's about making money, people sometimes get blurred about what is right and what is wrong. The temptations mount as the money pressures decision making. Unfortunately, the result isn't always very pretty."

Micah: "Yeah, but as I have heard you say, sports can build character."

Jeremy: "Right, sports can build character, but sports often do not build character. When athletics is about making money, it's kind of hard to focus on building character. The tension between moral values and non-moral values is so great that moral values usually are forgotten, even though we hear the mythical version that sports build character."

Sports in the United States are praised for promoting character development, dedication, self-control, discipline, fair play, and moral values like integrity and justice. For decades, school and college administrators have trumpeted an idyllic image of sports as positive components of extracurricular experiences of athletes and students. Viewed in this way, sports have grown and thrived while enjoying enormously increasing levels of support. However, popularity, potential revenues, and excessive pressures on coaches and athletes to win have tainted the purity of this image, as a commercialized business model of sports emphasizing winning is replacing a values-based educational model.

Differentiating between educational sports and commercialized sports is an important place to begin this discussion. Educational sports are competitions between individuals enrolled in schools and colleges that are of interest primarily to the athletes, friends, and family because the outcome, while diligently sought, is secondary to the sporting experiences mostly characterized by fair play, teamwork, and cooperation. Educational sports are extracurricular activities designed to enrich and expand the enjoyment of school and college years as well as provide settings in which athletes and students can learn, grow, and demonstrate moral values. Commercialized sports are organized competitions advertised and promoted for entertainment, financial gains and status. While some high schools have commercialized their sport programs, all football and basketball teams at top-tier colleges competing in the National Collegiate Athletic Association (NCAA) Football Bowl Subdivision (FBS) and other programs operate as entertainment businesses.

Commercialized sports (see Box 10.1) and the associated pressures to win often negatively affect ethical choices. An ethical dilemma occurs when two goods such as honesty and responsibility are rubbing against each other. Is it possible that the good of integrity is rubbing against the good of money? Is it fair or just if one group of students receives more benefits than another group of students? If commercialization is a good thing, should benefits be distributed equally? Or are only coaches, athletes, and ardent fans benefiting? When sport competitors harm each other physically or psychologically to gain competitive advantages, moral values are sacrificed. This chapter presents an analysis of commercialized interscholastic and intercollegiate sports with specific reference to the use of sports for public relations and promotions, for entertainment, and as a transmitter of economic outcomes rather than for developmental and educational purposes and for ethical values.

BOX 10.1 SHOULD SPORTS BE COMMERCIALIZED

Making money is not immoral; commercialization is not immoral. When sports become overly commercialized, however, athletes, coaches, and sport administrators may let the non-moral values of money, success, or fame influence ethical decisions. If these non-moral values become the primary foci, immoral actions such as cheating and a disregard for the welfare of opponents may result. How are honesty, justice, responsibility, and civility affected when sports become commercialized?

To discuss ethical issues in sports in relation to money always raises the question of whether participants and administrators of educational sports in schools and colleges should market their games as commercial enterprises. Principle-centered leaders in sports say the purpose of sport at these levels is to develop character traits such as dedication, sacrifice, responsibility, and esprit de corps (group spirit). But commercialization may thwart achieving these goals by emphasizing winning-at-all-costs to make more money. Is the power of greed affecting individuals? The more power we give to non-moral values, the more those values will affect our reasoning. That is, non-moral values may drive us to immoral decision making. As commercialization increases and becomes the primary goal, the purpose often becomes selling or marketing entertainment rather than facilitating individual and team spirit. In what ways does the emphasis on making money contribute to erosion in moral values? What might lead to unethical practices when educational sports are replaced by commercialized sports?

Intercollegiate sport administrators in FBS institutions admit they operate commercialized businesses. The economic realities of their sports programs require them to maximize consistent and significant revenue streams from television rights fees, ticket sales, advertising, sponsorships, licensing contracts, and conference revenue sharing to pay the huge salaries of coaches and operational expenses for comprehensive sport programs. To earn revenues in football and men's basketball, athletes and coaches in these sports must win.

One reason why commercialized sports have become so popular is the economic impact on college towns. In some cases, income from the sale of team-related licensed clothing and merchandise and purchases in restaurants and hotels increases greatly on game days. This is not hard to understand when a sold-out football stadium includes more people than live in most towns in a state. To these fans, each game and its outcome is all-important as they return to college towns and enjoy relaxing in social settings with like-minded fans dressed in team-licensed clothing.

The true ethical dilemma in the commercialization of sports is not the money or the promotion but what occurs in moral decision making when money and winning become more important than shaping sports through morally based decisions. Sports can be commercialized and moral, but this will only occur when principle-centered leaders in sports establish and follow moral values in making business decisions. In top-tier athletic departments, the task gets trickier because not all athletes, coaches, and athletic supporters will choose to live by moral values like integrity, respect, and justice. What usually occurs is a form of moral justification.

Interscholastic Sports

Sports for Public Relations and Promotions

When you ask a football fan to tell you where the best high school football is played, he will inevitably identify in varying order the states of California, Florida, Ohio, Pennsylvania, and Texas. While certainly population influences this domination, so does the emphasis many cities and communities place on their teams. For example, in *Friday Night Lights* Buzz Bissinger tells the story of football at Permian High School in Odessa, Texas, in the late 1980s and concludes that this town, team, and dream are symbolic of what is wrong in high school football. His riveting story describes how football in this and other towns has careened out of control due to excesses perpetrated by adults on adolescents. Rather than eliminating these abuses and returning interscholastic sports to (maybe) idealized games where character is taught and expected, the realities described in *Friday Night Lights* led to its release as a movie in 2000, followed by an Emmy-winning television series beginning in 2006; *Friday Night Lights* returned for its fifth season in 2010. Maybe the popularity of this series resonates with viewers because of its realistic portrayal of high school football through which adults and students live vicariously.

For decades sports have been used to promote cities, businesses, schools, geographic regions, and products. Because of their visibility, entertainment value, and association with educational institutions, several sports have historically and socially been publicized positively. Realizing the increased popularity of interscholastic sports, some corporate sponsors have chosen to provide money in exchange for the generation of fan enthusiasm for their services and products and interest in making purchases.

Most schools help finance interscholastic sport programs through booster clubs that conduct fund-raising activities and solicit donations from individuals and businesses. Booster clubs also garner revenues from selling sweatshirts, banners, caps, and other merchandise sporting team logos. Taken positively, this financial support for interscholastic sports is provided because it contributes to educational experiences. But negatively, because of their contributions to interscholastic sports, some boosters may seek to influence decisions (such as who should coach teams and which players should play) and to expect (demand?) winning teams. When schools' budgetary allocations pay the bills, school administrators and athletic directors seldom experience interference from boosters. With greater dependency on external revenue sources, school administrators at times struggle to retain an educational rather than commercial focus for interscholastic sport programs.

Because funding for public education has been unable to keep pace with costs, financing interscholastic sport programs for boys and girls increasingly relies on external revenue sources. In addition to booster clubs and fund-raising events, many schools have resorted to charging athletes fees to play on teams (i.e., pay to play) to help defray the cost of uniforms, equipment, and travel expenses. Most parents support this alternative in lieu of eliminating varsity teams because of shortfalls in state educational funding. In some instances, schools and booster clubs make provisions for economically disadvantaged students who cannot afford to pay these fees. If this does not occur, what moral concerns exist when students are excluded from playing on interscholastic sports teams if they cannot pay participation fees?

The potential for corporate sponsorships and television revenues may be viewed as the panacea for the challenges of financing interscholastic sports teams. In the struggle to maintain increased opportunities for boys and girls, schools face difficult decisions. Commercial sponsors, including those selling alcohol, tobacco, and non-nutritional food products, may be solicited to pay for advertisements in game programs and on sport facility scoreboards and walls. The ethical issue is deciding whether or not schools should permit advertisements in gymnasiums and on fields for companies promoting tobacco and alcohol products when adolescents are involved in these sport programs. If the answer involves the importance of health and wellness or social responsibility, then the school should have a moral duty to support good health practices. Tobacco use is a known health hazard, the promotion of the consumption of alcohol to adolescents is unacceptable, and use of tobacco products and drinking of alcoholic beverages by adolescents is illegal. If a school accepts money for advertising a beer company, it could be argued that the school is promoting underage drinking. Are school administrators acting in ethically and socially responsible ways when they accept money to support interscholastic sport teams from alcohol and tobacco companies? What if the corporate partner is a clothing and shoe company like Nike, Adidas, and Under Armour that offers to provide their products to teams if they are granted exclusivity? Should athletes be forced to wear a specific brand of shoes when these shoes are uncomfortable or even cause harm to the wearer? Should public schools enter into contracts for branded products and thereby rely on a company seeking to gain entrée into an impressionable market of adolescents to sell them other merchandise? Is it ethical if clothing and shoe companies pay high school coaches for granting permission to outfit their teams in a popular brand?

Commercialized Sports as Entertainment

Although modeled after collegiate and professional programs, sports for adolescents remain somewhat insulated from the potentially negative side of entertainment emphasizing winning. Nonetheless, parents, coaches, and sometimes overly enthusiastic fans expect adult-level entertainment from adolescents. Pressures to win have led some coaches of interscholastic sports to use overage players or recruit athletes from other school districts.

A handful or a few hundred fans may boo and berate adolescent athletes who do not win championships or play at an expected level. Family, school, and community pride may rest on the narrow shoulders of adolescents who feel heavy burdens both to entertain and win. Failure to perform up to the standard demanded may lead to disparaging comments and abandonment of support. When the pressures become too intense, adolescent athletes may violate rules to help them win games, praise, and awards. If sport spectators pay the price of admission, do they expect to be entertained, even when the athletes are adolescents? Is this morally defensible? Additionally, much of the data on why adolescents drop out of sports indicate that two of the primary reasons are intense pressure to win and unrealistic expectations.

Intercollegiate Sports

Sports for Public Relations and Promotions

As early as the 1890s, college presidents realized that the popularity of successful football teams could enhance the prestige of and perceptions about their institutions. Fast forward over a century and this phenomenon, now including men's basketball, continues to thrive. Some colleges find that donations to athletic departments and admissions applications increase after winning national championships. If you question whether winning promotes an institution, just ask an Ohio State University football fan or University of Kansas men's basketball fan and hear a resounding "yes, it does."

College presidents, who are ultimately responsible for the conduct of all programs in their institutions, often emphasize athletics as the most visible public relations tool at their disposal. College administrators nurture alumni involvement through athletics-related social events and make appeals for their support and money through these events. What are the risks to educational values when a college is recognized more for sports achievements than for the quality of its educational programs? Is the high visibility of a commercialized intercollegiate sport program in any way detrimental to a college's educational mission? To what extent do coaches, sport administrators, and college presidents use sports to promote themselves, their institutions, and their teams?

Integrally linked with public relations and promotions are four revenue sources in intercollegiate athletics: donations, ticket sales, sponsorships and advertising, and television rights fees including conference revenue sharing, which are briefly discussed in the following paragraphs. Donations have become a vitally important source of financial support for intercollegiate sport programs as fans love to bask in the reflected glory of their favorite teams and are more likely to financially support teams that win conference and national championships. This is especially true for intercollegiate sports programs in the top tier that receive over 90 percent of all donations. Most evidence suggests that when donations increase because of athletic successes, these increases are small and transitory. However, non-alumni are much more likely to donate to athletic departments based on the level of success on the field and court and are more likely to give to athletic department than academic departments. Since donations to athletic departments have been found to negatively affect (decrease) donations to academic programs, what are the associated ethical issues, if any?

Having athletic supporters and donors is not an ethical problem if they follow the expressed purpose and goals of institutions of higher education. But, what is they only support the athletics mission or try to subjugate the mission of the institution for selfish purposes? Athletic supporters can positively support athletic programs and institutions but only by following rules and adhering to values espoused by principle-centered leaders in institutions and athletics. If these athletic supporters become a power unto themselves with their own agendas that violate college, conference, or NCAA rules, (both the written rules and spirit of the rules), impermissible and unethical actions of these athletic supporters often become problematic. What happens to ethical values if individuals and groups representing an institution's athletic interests violate the stated purposes of the intercollegiate athletic program?

The number of tickets sold reflects the success of athletic teams. At small colleges, this may mean only a few dozen, hundred, or thousand buy tickets. Big-time colleges attract 50,000 to 100,000 fans to their football stadiums and more than 10,000 spectators to their basketball arenas. The sizes of these crowds heighten expectations that victories must exceed losses to maintain fan support.

Most intercollegiate sport programs depend on corporate sponsorships as advertisements in game programs, on scoreboards, and on uniforms are ubiquitous. Fans are bombarded by commercialized ads on video boards, virtual messages on television, and an incessant stream of corporate messages trying to elicit purchases from consumers. When corporate sponsors pay millions of dollars, they expect intercollegiate sport programs to deliver highly vested fans for increased sales, brand image enhancement, and awareness, even if this means many teams are expected to pursue victories by every means possible. Because many football and men's basketball teams enjoy intense loyal from alumni and other fans, intercollegiate sport administrators are able to provide a positive return on investment for sponsors. Intercollegiate sport programs benefit from tax-exempt status, so all sponsorship and advertising revenues are retained for defraying expenses. Questions arise, however, when the corporation is associated with products that could be viewed as conflicting with educational goals. For example, with binge drinking a major problem on many college campuses, should an intercollegiate sport administrator sign a contract with a sponsor that allows signage at games promoting consumption of alcoholic beverages? Should an intercollegiate sport administrator accept thousands of dollars from a beer distributor or tobacco company for advertisements in its programs or on its scoreboard? Do institutional or sport administrators need to establish ethical limits for what components of their sport programs they will market to the highest bidder regardless of the products or services being promoted?

In our capitalistic society, the commercialization of sports is inescapable. If sponsors pay enough money, their companies become the names of football bowl games (e.g., Allstate Sugar Bowl, Discover Orange Bowl, Tostitos Fiesta Bowl). Television inserts "brought to you by…" companies that provide game statistics and replays of scores; outstanding player recognitions and championship trophies often carry the names of sponsors. Have sport administrators sold out to the highest bidder? If so, how? Are there any ethical concerns when the chief executives of non-profit bowl games earn hundreds of thousands of dollars in salaries? Is it ethical for bowl games to have successfully thwarted efforts to make the naming rights and television rights fees for these games taxable, claiming their revenues are used for educational purposes (i.e., pay-outs to conferences/teams) while taking Bowl Championship Series (BCS) conference commissioners and teams' athletic directors on all-expense-paid cruises?

Nike and Adidas pay millions of dollars to colleges and provide clothing and shoes

Four revenue sources are typical in intercollegiate sports: donations, ticket sales, sponsorships, and advertising. Having sponsors and receiving donations is not an ethical problem as long as they follow the expressed purpose and goals of the organization.

for athletes, coaches, and other athletic personnel. For example, the largest exclusive shoe and clothing contracts as of the end of 2010 were Adidas paying the University of Michigan $60,000,000 over eight years and the University of Alabama receiving $30,000,000 over eight years from Nike. Should institutions provide athletes with an extensive assortment of clothing items and shoes to wear around campus as walking advertisements for a company? Should athletes be required to wear only branded clothing items and shoes as stipulated in an institution's exclusive shoe and clothing contract and be forbidden to wear anything else when practicing, while competing, and in association with team activities? Another ethical issue facing colleges is deciding whether to sell licensed tee shirts, sweatshirts, and other clothing items with team logos manufactured in international locations where companies have been shown to exploit workers. Should corporations that do not protect the rights of workers be boycotted, even if this means risking a reduction in revenue for athletic departments?

Television may lead to erosion in moral values because of the huge potential revenues associated with telecasts. For example, because of the large sums of money national, regional, and cable networks wield, colleges readily agree to allow their teams to be scheduled at any time, regardless of the effect on athletes' academic schedules as the day of the week, time of day, and place often are dictated by television. When television-dictated game schedules adversely affect the sleep and academic work of athletes, have commercialized sports surpassed educational outcomes in importance? Is it ethical for television to manipulate game schedules to maximize viewership and revenues despite the effect on athletes? For example, how can a men's basketball player finish an ESPN-televised game at 11 P.M., be expected to respond to questions from the media, recover from the game physically while showering and dressing, eat dinner, return to campus from four states away, and be awake and ready to participate and learn in an 8 am class? How and why do colleges use athletics for public relations and promotions? What are the ethical issues, if any, of colleges using athletes and teams to promote their institutions to fans? Is this use (abuse?) of athletes worth the national publicity or 30-second advertisement of the institution during a televised game? Has a commercialized sport enterprise become more important than the academic mission? What are some of the positive outcomes of the commercialized sport enterprise for an intercollegiate athlete and the college?

Commercialized Sports as Entertainment

The media's 24/7 coverage of intercollegiate teams places sports continuously before the public; a symbiotic relationship links print and electronic media promoting sports while sports help sell newspapers, advertisements, and products. Office conversations, game-viewing parties at sports bars, ubiquitous information about sports on cell phones, and *USA Today* sports sections are examples illustrating the pervasiveness of sports.

The president of the University of San Francisco eliminated its men's basketball program during the 1980s because of NCAA sanctions for abuses. He questioned how educational institutions could allow their integrity, principles, and students to be prostituted for the purposes of winning and achieving ill-gotten recognition and financial gain. Colleges today face an ethical quandary of trying to preserve their academic credibility when their highly visible sport programs are multi-million-dollar entertainment businesses. The tough question remains: Should colleges sponsor sport teams that are more commercialized than they are extracurricular educational programs? Is there an appropriate and healthy balance between the purpose of educational institutions and the commercialization of sports? If so, what is that balance? Does the fact that these commercialized programs have existed for decades automatically exclude them from ethical scrutiny?

Many people say that college athletes across NCAA Division I programs are exploited financially. In exchange for grants-in-aid worth between $5,000 and $50,000, depending on the institution, some athletes may help their colleges collect millions of dollars in ticket sales, television rights fees, and NCAA championship revenues. Is this situation an exploitation of athletes playing on teams that bring in these revenues? When coaches and athletic directors receive million-dollar salaries from the economic rent not paid to athletes, how is this ethical? Is it ethical for a college to receive huge revenues and yet not give spending money to the athletes who help earn these revenues?

The NCAA regulates the mobility and duration of intercollegiate sport careers, collects and distributes profits (to and from its members), and polices its members by levying penalties as it deems appropriate. For example, if an athlete signs a national letter of intent to play for a particular college and later decides to transfer to an institution at the same competitive level for academic or athletic reasons, the athlete is not allowed to compete in the same sport for one year at the new institution. Does this rule violate the moral principle of justice, since coaches regularly break their contracts, move to colleges offering more lucrative salaries, and immediately coach without penalty? A coach can drop or reduce an athlete's grant-in-aid at will with no due process accorded the athlete. Is this ethical? Have the moral principles of honesty and beneficence been violated by NCAA policies and coaches' actions?

The NCAA and its FBS member institutions are in the entertainment business. Fans value, as indicated by their willingness to purchase tickets, the entertainment provided by intercollegiate athletes. The fact that these athletes are students is secondary in importance to most fans, if relevant at all. The coach has one primary responsibility: to provide the most enjoyable entertainment possible (i.e., to win). Many myths surround the economics of big-time intercollegiate sports. Box 10.2 lists some of these myths and explains what is really true.

Box 10.2 Myths and Realities in Commercialized Intercollegiate Sports

Myths	Realities
1. Intercollegiate athletics is an integral part of the educational mission of American colleges.	1. A primary purpose of sports in FBS institutions is to provide commercialized entertainment. At lower competitive levels, there is less commercialization and a closer connection between educational values and sports. But the commercialized model is increasing at all competitive levels in colleges.
2. Many alumni and most non-alumni demand and financially support successful intercollegiate sport programs more than strong academic programs at their alma maters.	2. Many alumni contribute to the athletic and academic units of their colleges. Research also indicates that many donors to intercollegiate sport programs never attended the college, but give money to athletics primarily in proportion to the successes of football and to a lesser extent men's basketball teams, and are less likely to contribute to academic programs.
3. Intercollegiate sport programs are profitable, earning huge sums of money in FBS institutions, and are self-supporting in all others.	3. Almost all intercollegiate sport programs spend significantly more money than they earn in revenues.
4. Colleges earn millions of dollars when their teams play in post-season football bowl games.	4. Teams are expected to spend their payouts from bowl games in cities hosting games and bring thousands of others with them to spend more money. After expenses (including the requirement to pay for — whether sold or not — thousands of game tickets) and conference sharing, most colleges participating in bowl games do not make money but run a deficit.

Myths	Realities
5. The money earned from inter-collegiate athletics helps support academic programs.	5. Because athletic department expenses exceed revenues, most money earned by intercollegiate sport programs remains in the athletic department. Rarely have athletic departments allocated some revenues for student scholarships, library support, or academic purposes.
6. College head and assistant coaches deserve high annual salaries, bonuses, and other incomes because they generate huge profits for their athletic programs.	6. Most teams' expenses exceed their revenues. Past winning records lead to coaches' higher salaries.

Top-tier intercollegiate sport programs depend heavily upon television revenues. In football, since the NCAA was ruled in violation of antitrust law in 1984, first the College Football Association and subsequently conferences have controlled televising regular season games. While other bowl games proliferated (there were 35 at the end of the 2010 season), the premier bowls (Fiesta, Orange, Rose, and Sugar) were controlled by the BCS, along with the Tostitos BCS National Championship Game. The BCS, which replaced an unstructured system, the Bowl Coalition, and the Bowl Alliance, was begun in 1998 among teams in six dominant conferences: Big Ten, Pac Ten, Big East, Big 12, Southeastern, and Atlantic Coast. How dominant, you might ask? Each conference received over $17 million in 2010, plus the Big Ten and SEC each got an additional $4.5 million for having a second team in BCS bowl games. While the BCS shares some of its windfall revenues with smaller conferences (and three independent teams) in the FBS, the NCAA receives no funds from bowl games. Controversies continue to swirl around the BCS because some people question whether it is morally (or economically) right to exclude an undefeated team, like Texas Christian University at the end of the 2010 season, from playing the BCS National Championship Game, or if anything other than determining a champion on the field is ethically defensible. Is it ethical for the 73 institutions holding membership in the BCS conferences to control the process for selecting (and the teams invited to compete for) the national championship in a NCAA division that includes 126 institutions? Since the BCS conferences are in the entertainment business, how can sport administrators and coaches morally justify not paying the athletes who play the games, yet require these athletes to be students and demand that they dedicate huge amounts of time to their sports while alleging that they are amateurs, not professionals?

While conferences and institutions reap the financial rewards from contracts with networks and cable companies to televise regular season games, the NCAA controls the major revenue source in the men's basketball championship (i.e., "March Madness"). In 2010 the NCAA extended and increased its agreement (14 years for $10.8 billion) to broadcast on CBS, TBS, TNT, and truTV all games in the 68-team tournament. (The NCAA in 2010 paid out over $700 million annually to conferences/colleges for academic enhancement, basketball funds, conference grants, grants-in-aid, sports sponsorship, and student assistance funds.) What ethical issues, if any, are associated with how these revenues are distributed (as well as the millions retained by the NCAA)? Is it ethical for intercollegiate men's basketball players to subsidize the operations of the NCAA while being denied opportunities to reap the benefits of their performances personally? Why do the National Football League (NFL) and the National Basketball Association (NBA) not seek to encroach on the millions in revenues earned by the BCS and March Madness?

Each athlete, coach, and sport administrator must choose whether providing entertainment supersedes an emphasis on ethical values like justice, honesty, and beneficence. Box 10.3 offers a few questions to challenge your thinking about the ethical questions associated with commercialized sports. Alternative responses are suggested, but you are encouraged to propose other resolutions.

BOX 10.3 ETHICAL QUESTIONS IN COMMERCIALIZED INTERCOLLEGIATE SPORTS

Questions

1. Is a primary purpose of intercollegiate sports the promotion of a city, educational institution, or product?

2. Should intercollegiate sports be used for public relations purposes?

3. Does the winning-at-all-costs mentality in intercollegiate sports lead to the exploitation of athletes?

4. When should intercollegiate sports exist for the entertainment of fans?

Alternatives to Consider

1.
   a. Using sports for promotional purposes is acceptable whenever cities, colleges, and sponsors provide funding for sports.
   b. Colleges should not use sports for public relations or promotional purposes.
   c. Sports are extracurricular activities, not promotional units for institutions of higher education.
   d. Because corporate sponsors help fund sport programs, they deserve any and all associated promotional benefits.

2.
   a. Colleges should build their reputations and status on academic, not athletic, programs.
   b. Colleges should seek to benefit from the popularity and success of their sports teams.

3.
   a. Coaches have the right to use athletes in any way necessary to help win (and possibly save their jobs).
   b. Winning is never more important than the physical, psychological, emotional, social, and academic well-being of athletes.
   c. Often athletes are exploited and ethical principles violated when winning-at-all-costs is the goal.

4.
   a. Most intercollegiate sport programs provide football and men's basketball teams that enrich the collegiate experiences of participants as well as provide entertainment for students and other fans.

Questions	Alternatives to Consider
	b. Because football and men's basketball teams at many colleges attract huge crowds, these teams are rightfully in the entertainment business.
5. Do economic purposes and ethical values conflict in intercollegiate sports?	a. When money and other financial inducements become paramount, ethical values often are violated.
	b. Seldom are intercollegiate athletes lured by money or other benefits to break sport rules.
	c. Only males on football and basketball team in FBS institutions are faced with ethical dilemmas regarding economic issues.
6. How has increasing commercialization impacted intercollegiate sports?	a. Positively, because athletes are treated better by receiving more grants-in-aid, enjoying better facilities, and having increased media coverage.
	b. Negatively, because money influences so much that happens in sports such as when and where to play.
	c. Positively, because sports have become more important in the lives of most Americans.
	d. Negatively, because getting more money has replaced the teaching and reinforcing of values.

Point shaving and gambling have become a part of commercialized intercollegiate sports because of the money associated with these activities. Point shaving in sports is described as gamblers paying athletes on the team favored to win not by less than the published point spread. This yields profits for gamblers who bet on the losing team. Several point-shaving incidents, which are highly unethical, have occurred in intercollegiate athletics (see examples in Box 10.4). Some players may justify shaving points by claiming there is no harm done since the outcome of the game is not affected. A few basketball and football players may attempt to rationalize shaving points because they feel exploited by the current system limiting the amount of the grants-in-aid they receive. What is the ethical difference, if any, between receiving money for agreeing to attend a particular college and receiving money for shaving points in a game?

BOX 10.4 POINT-SHAVING IN INTERCOLLEGIATE ATHLETICS

• In 1951, the first reported cases, involving male basketball players from City College of New York (CCNY) and the University of Kentucky who shaved points in 49 games, were exposed. CCNY, the 1950 National Invitational Tournament and NCAA champion, de-emphasized basketball after their players were implicated in these scandals. Kentucky, the 1948, 1949, and 1951 NCAA men's basketball champion, cancelled its 1952–1953 season after the Southeastern Conference banned the team and, under NCAA pressure, other teams refused to play Kentucky.

• In 1961, gamblers and fixers enticed 37 players from 22 colleges to alter point spreads in 44 basketball games. The players on teams representing Brooklyn College, Columbia

University, La Salle University, Mississippi State University, New York University, North Carolina State University, Seton Hall University, St. John's University, St. Joseph's University, University of North Carolina, University of Tennessee and 11 others were involved in point-shaving schemes.
- In 1978–1979, three Boston College basketball players consorted to shave points in nine games.
- In 1994, two Arizona State University basketball players accepted bribes to shave points.
- In 1995, two Northwestern University basketball players were indicted for fixing the outcome of three games.
- In 2010, seven University of Toledo basketball and football players admitted to or entered into plea bargains for point shaving and fixing games over several years.

Gambling can be defined as one person placing a wager (stakes) on whether a future event will occur. Sports and gambling are inseparable in the minds of many because they believe gambling heightens interest in the outcomes of games. The publication of betting lines or point spreads in newspapers and online appears to legitimize gambling in intercollegiate sports, especially at the popular FBS level. Incidents of gambling by college athletes have led to heated discussions about whether Congress should make gambling on intercollegiate sports illegal. However, it should be noted that the number of legal sports bets in Nevada and via the Internet pales in comparison to the wagers among friends and on the office pools during March Madness (estimated to be over $2 billion dollars annually). Under what circumstances would sport gambling be considered unethical? Should athletes be permitted to bet on the outcome or point spread of a game in which they could have an influence on its outcome or score? Why or why not? Should athletes be allowed to place bets on any intercollegiate sports competition? Why or why not? The prevalence of gambling by intercollegiate athletes is described in Box 10.5.

BOX 10.5 GAMBLING BY INTERCOLLEGIATE ATHLETES (Cross & Vollano, 1998–1999)
- Most athletes (72 percent) and males (80 percent) gambled in some way since entering college.
- Nearly half (48.2 percent) of all athletes wagered at a casino while in college.
- Over 45 percent of male athletes (and nearly 35 percent overall) gambled on sports while in college.
- Over 5 percent of male athletes provided inside information for gambling purposes, bet on a game in which they played, or accepted money for performing poorly in a game.
- The mean amount of money wagered by athletes on a single sport bet through a bookmaker was $57.25. For the athletes who gambled on sports with bookmakers, they averaged wagering $225 each month.

The Professional and Amateur Sports Protection Act of 1992 prohibits gambling on sports except for existing sport gambling in Delaware, Montana, Nevada, and Oregon, where it was grandfathered. This law specifically makes it unlawful for a person to bet, gamble, or wager on one or more competitive games in which amateur athletes participate or on one or more performances of athletes in such games. Given this law, what are the ethical issues associated with gambling on intercollegiate sports for fans and athletes? The ethical dilemma of sports gambling occurs when moral values like honesty, justice, and responsibility are violated and other individuals suffer because of unethical acts. In sports gambling, the issue is the effect of the gambling on the individual and the integrity of the game. Because people are highly affected by the power of money, and gambling usually uses money as the stakes, gambling often becomes questionable moral behavior.

Sports potentially can teach teamwork, yet many athletes injure themselves through overuse while teammates languish on the bench. Sports potentially can teach self-control; still, basketball coaches and players are cited for technical fouls, abusive language, and on-the-court fighting. Sports potentially can teach discipline; however, college athletes are often arrested for driving while intoxicated, using illegal drugs, and assaulting someone sexually. Sometimes coaches and sport administrators disregard athletes' behaviors as frivolous or mischievous; sometimes these athletes are aided in avoiding arrest and punishment for their actions. Sports potentially can teach fair play, but only if athletes learn to obey the letter and spirit of game rules. Sports potentially can teach that the athlete's well-being as a person is foremost, yet many coaches treat athletes as expendable commodities. Has the pursuit of profits resulted in a widespread erosion of ethical values? If so, how? Are actions and behaviors in sports like these influenced by how they will benefit a team or individual, regardless of right and wrong or potential harm to others?

Perhaps no ethical boundaries exist for sports used as entertainment, at least not as long as sanctions are ineffective deterrents. This is even truer when we realize that many interpret the rules to their institutions' benefit and push the rules to the limit and beyond. Whether athletic programs are conducted honestly, justly, responsibly, and beneficently depends on the ethical values of principle-centered leaders and their modeling of moral principles. Principle-centered leaders need to ensure that adhering to moral values is central to the mission of intercollegiate sport teams. Striving and competing to win and winning in the right way are not mutually exclusive, as many people in and around sports know.

Although presidential and institutional control are pivotal factors that can lead to reforms in intercollegiate athletics, many college presidents have found out the hard way that controlling the policies, personnel decisions, and actions of sport administrators on their campuses is challenging. In fact, some question whether integrity is compatible with intercollegiate sports used for entertainment. As discussed in Box 10.6, one outside group has repeatedly called for reforms in intercollegiate athletics to preserve the integrity of higher education.

BOX 10.6 REPORTS FROM THE KNIGHT FOUNDATION COMMISSION ON INTERCOLLEGIATE ATHLETICS

In 1989, the trustees of the Knight Foundation created the Knight Commission on Intercollegiate Athletics and asked it to propose a reform agenda for intercollegiate athletics because abuses associated with athletics were threatening the integrity of higher education. Brief summaries of each of the commission's reports follow.

Keeping the Faith with the Student-Athlete: A New Model for Intercollegiate Athletics (1991). The commission identified problems in the areas of recruiting, unending efforts to maximize revenue, and an overemphasis on entertainment. These ends seemed to be outweighing the means and were reported as deep-rooted and long-standing, thus resulting in a loss of focus on why intercollegiate athletics should exist, which is for students and their educational development.

The commission recommended a *one-plus-three* model for reform. Presidential control, the one, included the call for trustees to reaffirm the president's authority over all aspects of intercollegiate athletes and presidents to exert control over conferences, the NCAA, and television interests associated with their athletic programs. In the first of three, academic integrity, the commission recommended strengthening eligibility requirements for, academic progress by, and graduation rates of athletes. The second of the three, financial integrity, included controlling costs, increasing grants-in-aid to cover the full cost of attending college, curbing the independence of athletic foundations, providing greater oversight over coaches' non-institutional income, and supporting intercollegiate athletics financially. The last of the three was the call for independent authentication by an outside body of the integrity of each institution's sport program.

A Solid Start: A Report on Reform of Intercollegiate Athletics (1992). One year after its initial call for reform, the commission reported on progress made and especially changes in rules proposed by the NCAA Presidents Commission and adopted during the 1992 NCAA convention. Among the measures enacted to reshape intercollegiate athletics were: require satisfactory progress in degree requirements, grade point average, and satisfactory annual progress academically; presidential approval of coaches' income; limitations on official visits by prospective athletes; and higher initial eligibility standards.

A New Beginning for a New Century: Intercollegiate Athletics in the United States (1993). Over the next year, the commission continued to discuss the issues of cost containment and gender equity. The commission again advocated its one-plus-three model and called for continuing vigilance in reforming intercollegiate athletics. Specifically, the commission emphasized the importance of presidents fulfilling their responsibilities to defend the academic and financial integrity of higher education as verified through an independent certification process.

A Call to Action: Reconnecting College Sports and Higher Education (2001). A decade after the initial call for reform, the commission found that the problems in big-time college sports had grown rather than diminished. The commission stated that major college sports damaged the reputation and credibility of institutions because of academic abuses, a financial arms race, and commercialization causing an increasing chasm between educational values and intercollegiate sports played at the highest level. It concluded that an overemphasis on winning, permitting potential revenue sources such as television and corporate interests to dictate actions, illicit payments to athletes, sport for entertainment and gambling, and the denigration of the ideals of higher education littered the landscape of major college sports in the twenty-first century. The commission noted, however, that despite this problematic environment, some major colleges operated their programs without sacrificing academic integrity and ethical standards.

This report did not paint a pretty picture when it characterized intercollegiate sports as corrupt, thoroughly professionalized and commercialized, and replete with deplorable sportsmanship and misconduct. Some former college presidents, such as James Duderstadt of the University of Michigan told the commission that if left unchecked intercollegiate athletics would continue to damage the reputation of colleges as the sideshow of sport engulfed higher education and displaced its academic integrity. The commission also heard from James Shulman and William Bowen, authors of *The Game of Life*, who reported that even in academically selective institutions core educational values were threatened by intercollegiate athletics. The commission recommended academic reforms, de-escalation in the athletic arms race, de-emphasis in commercialization of intercollegiate athletics, and restoration of athletics to a more balanced role alongside the academic mission of colleges.

Restoring the Balance: Dollars, Values, and the Future of College Sports (2010). The latest report of the commission challenged colleges to focus on greater accountability through transparency in reporting better assessment measures of finances, to reward making academic values a priority, and to treat athletes as students first, not as if they were professionals. Athletic departments were encouraged to make financial reports public, publish information about capital spending and debt, and report on growth rates in spending. In strengthening institutional oversight over athletics, the commission called for reform in the NCAA Division I certification process. In the realm of academics, the commission called for strengthened eligibility standards for participation in championships and changes in the distribution process of revenues based on educational values and priorities. Relative to students, the commission encouraged institutions to ensure athletes were allowed to be students first by limiting intrusions on their academic responsibilities, reducing commercial activities, curbing trends toward professionalization of athletic staffing devoted to athlete development, and reducing grant-in-aid offerings without adversely affecting equitable participation opportunities for males and females.

Sports as Transmitters of Economic Values

Early in an athlete's career, economic values may exceed ethical values because the former are rewarded while the latter may be faintly praised. Financial benefits are so important that many athletes, coaches, and sport administrators have redefined sportsmanship as pushing rules to the limit without getting caught. Fans enthusiastically support a redefinition of sportsmanship as effective strategies used to help win.

Sport competitions require rules and participants' respect for them. A direct result of the importance of economic values occurs when the spirit of the rules dies. Constitutive rules give boundaries to sport. If a player commits an act outside these boundaries, then a violation has occurred. Sometimes players violate rules unwittingly; other times they do so intentionally to help win and attain the associated benefits. Two kinds of intentional violations are frequently observed. First, a player may consciously violate a rule, expecting to be caught, yet willingly accept the penalty in order to attain some tactical advantage that the violation affords. Second, a player may intentionally violate a rule, hoping to avoid getting caught and benefiting from breaking a rule. To what extent are these rule violations ethical? Do rule violations occur because the economic rewards for winning outweigh ethical behavior such as honesty and development of principled behavior like sportsmanship?

Although the NCAA limits the number of hours in a week that athletes can spend practicing and competing in their sports, the time demands on these athletes are excessive. Because compliance with maximal competition and practice time rules is based on the head coach's integrity to document hours spent in required activities, many hours go unreported. Allegedly in some programs athletes sign blank forms and coaches fill in the maximum allowable times, even though the athletes regularly spend more hours engaged with their sports than NCAA rules permit. When coaches pressure and expect athletes to focus primarily on their sports, is this ethical?

Athletic commitments also often detract from opportunities for athletes to enlarge their social contacts and participate in service organizations and other activities during their years in college. Proponents for the ineligibility of freshmen cite the importance of achieving academic success and participating in social and extracurricular activities before focusing on athletic competition. But freshmen were made eligible in the 1970s because institutions claimed eliminating freshmen teams was an essential cost-cutting measure.

Psychological pressures may exceed academic and social demands, especially on first-year athletes. Because almost all FBS athletes receive grants-in-aid, they are expected to perform at high levels. Pressure to win exerted by coaches, fans, and teammates, if allowed to become excessive, may hamper performance. Overemphasis on one's sport may lead to a reduction in social development because no person or thing is as important as winning. Other areas of psychological exploitation include pressures to maintain coach-imposed weights (possibly leading to eating disorders) and the under-development of athletes' decision-making skills and mature and responsible actions because of the extensive control coaches exert over the lives of athletes on their teams. How can an unethical overemphasis on performance and winning lead to psychological harm to athletes?

In 2007, the Knight Commission on Intercollegiate Athletics commissioned a survey of faculty members in FBS institutions to assess their perceptions of intercollegiate athletics. A few of their shared beliefs (see Box 10.7) shed light on how intercollegiate sport programs, sport administrators, and intercollegiate athletes are perceived.

BOX 10.7 PERCEPTIONS OF INTERCOLLEGIATE ATHLETICS OF FACULTY IN FBS INSTITUTIONS (Knight Commission on Intercollegiate Athletics, 2007)
• Intercollegiate athletics focus on entertainment with little regard for academics.
• Intercollegiate athletes overall are serious about their academic work and earning their degrees; however, faculty members are less satisfied with the academic performance of football and basketball players.
• Nearly one-third believe academic standards have to be compromised to achieve success in athletics.
• Nearly three-quarters believe salaries of head coaches of football and basketball teams are excessive.
• Nearly one-half believe that football and basketball players are not fairly compensated for their contributions.

These findings suggest many faculty members consider the economic values so prevalent in intercollegiate athletics that they have some negative consequences on their institutions and athletes.

Athletic departments operate as unique commercial businesses because their affiliation with non-profit educational institutions shelters them from having to pay taxes on any of their commercial activities. While the top-tier athletic departments raise millions of dollars from stadium and arena naming rights, corporate sponsorships and advertising, and licensed merchandise sales, none of these revenues are taxed. Athletic departments also benefit from tax laws that allow donors to report 100 percent of their donations to athletics if no benefits are received. Donors are allowed to report 80 percent of their donations if they get opportunities to purchase choice tickets, receive preferential parking, and attend social events with athletes and coaches. These donations to athletic departments are often associated with membership in elite clubs that become status symbols with social affiliation perks received in exchange for lucrative donations. Another financial windfall occurs because intercollegiate athletes are amateurs who may only receive tuition, fees, room, board, and books; in effect, intercollegiate sport programs operate with a salary cap. This enables athletic directors and coaches to maximize their own compensation. Even though sport administrators and coaches of professional teams manage much larger operations and budgets, many college coaches are paid significantly higher salaries than coaches with professional teams receive. Since athletic directors hire and supervise coaches with higher salaries, their salaries go up proportionately.

Some of the arguments against paying college athletes merit examination. First, it is claimed there is not enough money in athletic department budgets to pay athletes in revenue-producing sports. In response, money currently expended for sport administrators' salaries, coaches' salaries, recruiting, and facilities could be redirected to pay at least the full cost of attending college for athletes. Second, it is argued that non-revenue sports and especially women's sports would be harmed if athletes in revenue-producing sports were paid. In response, pitting pay for athletes playing football and men's basketball against other men's and all women's sports is incorrect, as pay for the athletes who help bring in revenues could come from reductions in the salaries of coaches and sport administrators. Third, it is claimed that wealthy programs would buy all the best players. In response, the invariance principle reaffirms that the distribution of talent would be unchanged, although the salaries of sport administrators and coaches would decrease. Fourth, it is argued that some athletes would receive greater financial benefits than others. This is true and reflects the reality of the world of sports.

Football and men's basketball coaches and athletic directors often argue that football and men's basketball teams should be preferentially treated because they generate the monies that support the entire athletic program. Would it be ethical to eliminate men's sport teams or fail to fund women's teams adequately if this claim were true? What if this argument were flawed? Fulks (2010) states that only 14 FBS programs reported positive net generated revenues in 2009. The median net generated deficits for each of the other FBS athletic programs were $11,267,000 in 2009. Since expenses must be paid, Fulks provides data to show that allocated revenues, which include student fees, direct and indirect institutional support, and governmental support, provide the remaining 28 percent of financing. These findings debunk the myth that colleges competing at the highest level depend exclusively on revenues from football and men's basketball to subsidize all other aspects of athletic programs.

Television may lead to erosion in moral values because of the huge revenues associated with telecasts. The large sums of revenue produced by telecasting these competitions may lead to scheduling games at any time that may conflict with athletes' academic schedules.

No athletic programs in the Football Championship Subdivision (FCS) generate enough revenue to cover their expenses, with the median negative net generated revenues of $8,643,000 per institution in 2009 (Fulks, 2010). FCS programs depend on allocated revenues for 72 percent of their funding. Division I institutions without a football team in 2009 had a median negative net generated revenue of $8,340,000, with allocated revenues paying 76 percent of athletic program expenses (Fulks, 2010).

In examining operational revenues and expenses in FBS institutions, Orszag and Orszag (2005) made several conclusions about intercollegiate sport programs, a few of which can inform this discussion about economic outcomes versus ethical values. First, increased operating expenditures in football and men's basketball on average do not result in net operating revenues. Second, increased operating expenditures in football and men's basketball are not associated with higher winning percentages. Third, increased operating expenditures in football and men's basketball do not measurably affect the academic quality of students or alumni giving. These are significant conclusions because they provide evidence that arguments favoring spending more on athletics are not supported by the data. In fact, it has been suggested that the only (ideal?) way to significantly reduce commercialized intercollegiate sport programs would be a 100 percent agreement by all college presidents in FBS institutions to cut in half the budgets for these programs. This proposal will only be effective if everyone agrees to reduce the perceived out-of-control emphasis on using intercollegiate sports to make money. If this were to occur, it is suggested that the entertainment value of sports would remain the same and ethical values would trump economic goals.

Every director of intercollegiate athletics acknowledges that winning = fans = money = winning = fans = money. This upwardly spiraling cycle brings in much-needed revenue that must be reinvested to produce more victories. This never-ending cycle is explained more fully in Box 10.8. How are moral values violated when making more money and gaining more victories become the primary goals for athletic departments?

BOX 10.8 THE ENTRAPMENT GAME APPLIED TO INTERCOLLEGIATE ATHLETICS

Intercollegiate athletics operates in a winner-take-all market in which participants as a whole and the majority overall will suffer financial losses because once committed there is no other choice than to continue to spend more in chasing the elusive goal of trying to win (Frank, 2004). Here is how this entrapment game works in intercollegiate athletics. When an athletic director seeks to launch a big-time program, such as through reclassification to a more highly competitive NCAA division, or to achieve higher rankings through winning more games in an existing program, he will overstate the odds of being successful or potential for financial benefits in order to gain presidential or institutional support. While overestimating the positives, the athletic director inevitably underestimates the costs required to initiate and maintain a top-tier program. Once expenditures begin, however, these will always increase because every athletic director assumes that by spending more money than opposing athletic departments, the odds of winning more games and advancing in national rankings will go up. What is inevitably overlooked, however, is that every game won or higher ranking achieved leads to rivals increasing their levels of spending to recapture their former positions. That is, each institution's increased spending become self-canceling. The result of this entrapment game to intercollegiate athletes is an ever-escalating arms race.

The arms race exists because institutions continually build bigger and better facilities to attract blue-chip athletes who help in making more money; it also includes paying huge salaries to celebrity coaches to win games. The arms race in intercollegiate sport programs often benefits from the use of governmental tax-exempt bonds in construction projects for practice, competitive, and training facilities. What are the costs and benefits of participating in the arms race? What are the ethical issues associated with the arms race? What happens to athletic development and teaching and reinforcing character development through sports when intercollegiate sport programs pursue the arms race? Possible ways to reduce the ethical abuses associated with the arms race are provided in Box 10.9.

BOX 10.9 REDUCING ETHICAL ABUSES DEALING WITH THE ARMS RACE

1. Require that teams compete only against teams from institutions of similar size and philosophy (i.e., prohibit buying wins by paying guarantees to lower-tier teams).
2. Reduce the soaring expenditures in football and men's basketball by limiting squad sizes and number of grants-in-aid awarded in football.
3. Compensate coaches with salaries commensurate with other educators within the institution and insist that coaches focus on achieving educational, not entertainment goals.

4. Revise the distribution of revenues from television so these revenues are based on the overall educational development of athletes and their ethical conduct, not on winning.
5. Eliminate advertisements of beer during televised games of intercollegiate athletics.
6. Eliminate corporate signage and advertising from intercollegiate sport facilities and sports equipment.
7. Prohibit athletes from wearing corporate trademarks and logos on uniforms and other issued clothing.
8. Reclaim from commercial interests control over when and where games are played.
9. Encourage the professional leagues to sponsor developmental leagues for athletes who are not interested in taking advantage of the opportunity to get a college education.
10. Provide institutional support to sport programs but require that they operate within institutional guidelines and values, follow NCAA regulations governing recruiting, and limit and make more transparent operational revenues and expenses.

Another issue potentially associated with economic versus ethical values deals with gender equity. As discussed in Chapter 6, federal law (Title IX of the Education Amendments of 1972) prohibits discrimination against either gender in the provision of educational programs. While this law does not require equal expenditures for both genders, it does mandate equitable treatment in the areas of participation opportunities, financial aid, and other program support areas. In an analysis of data for 2008 reported by intercollegiate sport programs in compliance with the Equity in Athletics Disclosure Act (shown in Box 10.10), enrollment of female undergraduate students exceeds male undergraduate students at each competitive level within the NCAA. FBS institutions financially support sports teams for females at a higher level than institutions sponsoring football teams at lower competitive levels. At the Division II and III levels, females are the highest percentage of athletes in institutions that sponsor no football teams and the lowest percentage that sponsor football teams. These data suggest that full compliance with Title IX has not been achieved.

Box 10.10 Financial Support for Female Athletes in NCAA-Member Institutions in 2008					
NCAA Division (number of institutions)	Female Students	Female Athletes	Grants-in-Aid	Operating Expenses	Recruiting Expenses
Football Bowl Subdivision (126)	54.1%	45.9%	43.1%	29.2%	31.1%
Football Championship Subdivision (121)	53.9%	42.8%	44.3%	38.1%	34.1%
Division I without football teams (97)	56.4%	51.2%	56.8%	45.4%	42.8%
Division II with football teams (152)	54.9%	36.2%	37.9%	39.8%	34.0%
Division II without football teams (133)	58.6%	47.7%	52.0%	48.2%	47.2%
Division III with football teams (234)	53.2%	37.6%	N/A	40.5%	33.1%
Division III without football teams (183)	58.7%	48.7%	N/A	49.6%	N/A

Those who claim that males earn all the revenues, are more interested in participating in sports, or are more highly skilled may be reflecting economic rather than ethical values. When institutions are providing 28 percent, 72 percent, and 76 percent of the financing for intercollegiate sport programs in NCAA Divisions I, II, and III respectively, the claim that males bring in all the revenues cannot be supported. The percentages of females in colleges (and schools) who have eagerly joined teams debunk the myth that females are not interested in competing on sports teams. Are educational organizations as morally required to treat all students equally by providing them opportunities to participate in engineering or nursing classes as they are to sponsor sports teams for both genders? The athletic achievements of females, while not yet as appealing to fans or earning millions in revenues, are nonetheless outstanding.

Summary

The abuses in intercollegiate sport programs that were prevalent in previous years continue to expand and are spreading downward into interscholastic sport programs. Through televised sport, a school, college, or city can promote itself, but only if teams win. The cycle of winning = fans = money = winning = fans = money is thriving and appears to be getting worse each year. Exploitation occurs when what is best for athletes physically, educationally, psychologically and emotionally is replaced by what has to be done to win and make more money. Too many people seem to believe it is permissible to break any rule necessary to ensure more victories. Athletes and coaches can win and still live according to moral values. The challenge is how to balance winning and gaining lucrative benefits to behaving in morally responsible ways and playing fairly. Exploitation occurs when winning surpasses in importance obtaining an education and developing values. Exploitation is felt when athletes are manipulated and used for the benefit of others.

Athletes learn early in their careers that they are entertainers even though sport administrators and organizations still hide behind the myth of the amateur athlete. The higher many athletes climb on the elite sport ladder, the more they realize they are being used for making money and entertaining others. Around the world, sports have become businesses and transmitters of economic outcomes more than ethical values. Although sport can teach virtues like loyalty, dedication, sacrifice, and teamwork, and moral values such as justice, honesty, and beneficence, these will only be lived when principle-centered leaders such as those described in Box 10.11 and those they influence prioritize these values.

Box 10.11 Examples of Principle-Centered Leaders in Sports

- **Arthur Ashe**, winner of the 1965 NCAA singles tennis title and NCAA team championship at the University of California at Los Angeles (UCLA) and winner of three major tournament singles titles (U.S. Open in 1968; Australian Open in 1970; and Wimbledon in 1975), was a vocal opponent of apartheid, an author of a three-volume book on the history of African Americans in sports, and a person known for his sportsmanship, courtesy, and graciousness on and off the court.

- **Bill Bradley** was a three-time All-American at Princeton University, 1965 National Player of the Year, captain of the gold-medal winning basketball team in the 1964

Tokyo Olympic Games, ten-year NBA player, two-time NBA champion (1970; 1973), and United States Senator, and wrote *Values of the Game* in which he described how the values of courage, discipline, passion, respect, responsibility, resilience and teamwork have importance in basketball and life.

- **Anita DeFrantz**, Connecticut College rower who won a bronze medal in the women's eight at the 1976 Montreal Olympic Games, president of the Amateur Athletic Foundation in Los Angeles, and fifth woman appointed to the International Olympic Committee, is a principled advocate for athletes, children, women, and minorities.

- **Tony Dungy**, University of Minnesota quarterback, three-year NFL defensive back, assistant coach, and head coach of the Super Bowl–winning Indianapolis Colts in 2007, stressed family values and responsibilities and the non-abusive and respectful development and importance of each player.

- **Grant Hill**, winner of the NCAA men's basketball championship in 1991 and 1992 while at Duke University, a gold medal in the 1996 Atlanta Olympic Games, and a seven-time NBA All-Star in 16 seasons, has received the NBA Sportsmanship Award for his ethical behavior, fair play, outstanding sportsmanship, and integrity an unprecedented three times (2005; 2008; and 2010).

- **Mike Krzyzewski**, basketball player at the United States Military Academy under Coach Bobby Knight and his assistant coach at Indiana University, coach of the gold medal-winning men's basketball team in the 2008 Beijing Olympic Games, and winner of over 800 games at Duke University, in his books has emphasized principle-centered leadership and the application of commitment, integrity, respect, and selflessness to life.

- **John Wooden**, a three-time All-American in basketball at Purdue University and 27-season coach at UCLA where his basketball teams had a 620–147 record, including winning ten NCAA championships, in his ten books taught the moral values and characteristics of character that he modeled throughout his life and described how these values were applicable to basketball and more importantly to life.

Micah: "So can sports build character while we still have commercialization in athletics?"

Jeremy: "Well, maybe, but an awful lot depends on us as future professionals to get it right. There are some role models out there to follow, but even the best of people are always torn by the challenges of those non-moral values: fame, fortune, success, and money versus the moral values of honesty, justice, beneficence, respect, and responsibility."

Micah: "I can be humble and rich."

Jeremy: "Maybe… but it's more about keeping the values in line. What exactly is the purpose of athletics? It should not be about making money and winning—the purpose of athletics should be about the education of the athlete and the role of athletics in the academic role of the college and high school."

References

Cross, M. E., and A. G. Vollano (1998–1999). "The Extent and Nature of Gambling Among College Student Athletes." Retrieved from http://www.umich.edu/~mgoblue/compliance/gambling/study.html.

Frank, R. H. (2004). "Challenging the Myth: A Review of the Links Among College Athletic Success,

Student Quality, and Donations." Retrieved from http://www.knightcommission.org/index.php?option =com_content&view=article&id=73%3Achallenging-the-myth-a-review-of-the-links-among-college-athletic-success-student-quality-and-donations&catid=8%3Afiscal-integrity&Itemid=36.

Fulks, D. L. (2010). *Revenues and Expenses 2004–2009, NCAA Division I Intercollegiate Athletics Programs Report.* Retrieved from http://www.ncaapublications.com/productdownloads/REV_EXP_2010.pdf.

Knight Commission on Intercollegiate Athletics. (1991). *Keeping Faith with the Student Athlete.* Retrieved from http://www.knightcommission.org/images/pdfs/1991–93_KCIA_report.pdf.

Knight Commission on Intercollegiate Athletics. (1992). *A Solid Start: A Report on Reform of Intercollegiate Athletics.* Retrieved from http://www.knightcommission.org/images/pdfs/1991–93_KCIA_report.pdf.

Knight Commission on Intercollegiate Athletics. (1993). *A New Beginning for a New Century: Intercollegiate Athletics in the United States.* Retrieved from http://www.knightcommission.org/images/pdfs/1991–93_ KCIA_report.pdf.

Knight Commission on Intercollegiate Athletics. (2001). *A Call to Action: Reconnecting College Sports and Higher Education.* Retrieved from http://www.knightcommission.org/images/pdfs/2001_knight_report. pdf.

Knight Commission on Intercollegiate Athletics. (2007). *Faculty Perceptions of Intercollegiate Athletics Survey.* Retrieved from http://www.knightcommission.org/images/pdfs/Knight_ExecSum_FINAL100907.pdf.

Knight Commission on Intercollegiate Athletics. (2010). *Restoring the Balance. Dollars, Values and the Future of College Sports.* Retrieved from http://www.knightcommission.org/index.php?option=com_content& view=article&id=503&Itemid=166.

Orszag, J. M., and P. R. Orszag (2005). "The Empirical Effects of Collegiate Athletics: An Update." Indianapolis, IN: National Collegiate Athletic Association.

Smith, R. (1988). *Sports and Freedom: The Rise of Big-Time College Athletics.* New York: Oxford University Press.

Additional Readings

Byers, W., and C. Hammer (1995). *Unsportsmanlike Conduct: Exploiting College Athletes.* Ann Arbor: University of Michigan Press.

Duderstadt, J. J. (2000). *Intercollegiate Athletics and the American University: A University President's Perspective.* Ann Arbor: University of Michigan Press.

Gems, G. R. (2000). *For Pride, Profit, and Patriarchy: Football and the Incorporation of American Cultural Values.* Lanham, MD: Scarecrow.

Gerdy, J. R. (2006). *Air Ball: American Education's Failed Experiment with Elite Athletics.* Jackson: University Press of Mississippi.

Quinn, K. G. (2009). *Sports and Their Fans: The History, Economics and Culture of the Relationship Between Spectator and Sport.* Jefferson, NC: McFarland.

Smith, R. A. (2011). *Pay for Play: A History of Big-Time College Athletic Reform.* Urbana: University of Illinois Press.

Thelin, J. R. (1996). *Games Colleges Play: Scandal and Reform in Intercollegiate Athletics.* Baltimore, MD: Johns Hopkins University Press.

Yost, M. (2010). *Varsity Green: A Behind the Scenes Look at Culture and Corruption in College Athletics.* Stanford, CA: Stanford University Press.

Zimbalist, A. (2001). *Unpaid Professionals: Commercialism and Conflict in Big-Time College Sports.* Princeton, NJ: Princeton University Press.

CHAPTER 11

Principle-Centered Leadership, Morality, and Ethical Decision-Making in Sports

- What is the relationship of follower to leader?
- What advice can be offered to help in the role of principled leadership?
- How can one develop a clear vision of leadership?

Leadership is presently in vogue and a common quest for college students in America. Leadership is the Mecca in which all students are to drink, sojourn at, and then soldier on and show others the way to riches and possibly enlightenment. Unfortunately, the result is usually the former and seldom the latter — riches rather than enlightenment. Apparently everyone should be a leader, but the reality is not always the case. There are times and places in which we are not leaders, we are followers. There are times and places in which we may never be a leader nor will we want to be. There are times and places where we have a moral duty to be a leader (see Box 11.1), and other times and places where we have a moral duty not to be a leader. The tricky part of all of this is to know the difference and to know when to be a leader and when to be a follower.

BOX 11.1 DUTIES AND OBLIGATIONS

Moral duties and obligations are the responsibilities that we hold as moral agents in our motives, intentions, and actions as directed toward others. Our motives are what drive us to do a moral action, and our intentions are our plan of how we are going to do the action. Motives and intentions are usually described as good and bad, while actions are described as right and wrong. An individual could have a good motive, a bad intention, and a right action. Or an individual could have a bad motive, a bad intention, and a right action. The words of duty and obligation have to do with our relationship to others. We have a duty to care for our families. We have a moral obligation to follow our mission. We have a duty not to do harm. We have a moral obligation to honor our promises. Usually a duty is the more personal action, whereas an obligation is the "ought" of our behavior. I ought not to tell a lie because I believe it is wrong to lie. I have a duty to care for my children because they rely on me to care for them. When do we have a duty to be a moral leader? We have a moral duty when we are in the role of leader.

Unfortunately, seldom do colleges note that being a follower (see Box 11.2) is just as important as being a leader, and in most cases there are manifest, important obligations and pressures to be a discerning follower. There is a story told by an admissions group that in the essay required of student applicants, the question was, "How are you a leader?" When one young applicant began to write her essay, she felt challenged by the question, and upon reflection wrote back, "I am not a leader. I try to be a good follower and try to find the right people to follow both in class, in groups, and organizations. I look for places where I can follow and do 'good' for others. I know that's probably not what you are seeking at your university, but I believe I need to tell you the truth of who I am." Many weeks later, she received a response from the admissions office: "We are pleased to inform you that you have been accepted. We accepted 4,000 leaders and you, the one follower. We are looking forward to meeting you — you have much to offer us on the notion of humility." It is at this junction that you, as a future leader and sport management professional, will be challenged to know when to lead and when to follow in a humble, ethical, and moral fashion.

BOX 11.2 BEING A FOLLOWER

Contrary to popular opinion in leadership studies, not everyone can be a leader. The reality is that every leader at one time or another was a follower. President Dwight David Eisenhower was once a second lieutenant. Abraham Lincoln worked as an apprentice to learn the law. No coach in America becomes the head coach first; all learn how to be a coach from other coaches. No *Fortune* 500 company executive gets the job as boss without first paying his or her dues. Every leader was first a follower. Followers are just as important or maybe more so — for without the follower how could one lead.

Interestingly, as a follower we learn much about principled leadership. In other words, we learn by watching others — we learn what works and what does not work. We, as followers, also learn through mentorship. If we are fortunate enough to be a follower of a principled leader, we learn the value of hard and honest work. We learn that fair play is important, giving one's word is imperative to trust, and being respectful and responsible is essential to a good work climate. The opposite is also true — we as a follower can learn to violate others and to be disrespectful.

Perhaps a follower learns to lead others — perhaps not.

But what does it mean to be a follower? A follower actually learns the importance of following honorable pursuits by learning from an honorable leader. The reverse is also true; a follower can also learn dishonorable behavior by following a dishonorable leader. If that is so, then how does a future principled leader, an emerging principled leader, know if the leader they are following is honorable? What are the benchmarks to consider? Said another way, as a follower, how do we evaluate an honorable leader? When is an honorable leader in an honorable pursuit? Here are some questions that a follower should ask when joining any organization to ferret out the honorable ends of the leader in charge and the organization which you are considering joining. What is the purpose of the organization? What has been its track record? To what honorable ends is the organization directed? What sorts of individuals are parts of this organization? Do the individuals who lead the organization live by honorable goals and pursuits? Do these individuals have a tradition and history of honorable behavior? When should one be loyal and when should one challenge authority? What are your duties to yourself and your principles if the leader does not follow honorable action? What is your responsibility to the organization when you give your word to support its mission and goal? What does it mean to be an honorable member? What responsibilities and duties exist when one gives one's word?

Obviously it might be hard to find the answers to all these questions, but there are possibilities. Talk with other followers in the organization. What is their take on the culture and climate? Do they feel safe? Do they feel that they are treated well? Do they think they are evaluated fairly? Do they believe they have a future in the organization? What is the climate? Do people look like they enjoy what they are doing? Is there any sense of humor or joy in the building? Are people upbeat? Do they like their work? Don't be pulled into the false sense of success because the salary is great or the organization is famous.

In this chapter we will discuss:

- The magnitude of mission in where you are going both as a leader and a follower. We will discuss, explore and reflect on values and attitudes of self in relation to leadership.
- The process needed to reflect on personal growth as a servant leader.
- How to demonstrate servant leadership and develop strategies to cope with situations that arise from conflicting values and beliefs.
- The need to develop a clear vision of leadership style and commitment to principled leadership.

Be Careful What You Wish For

What is it to be a principled leader? Soon you will be selected to do a sport management internship, and if you are lucky, the stars align correctly, and the cards are dealt in your favor, you will get an internship that favors you being hired at your dream job. You will be assigned various duties in which your good education will act as a cushion of knowing what to do. But be careful of what you wish for; sometimes all that glitters is not gold.

You and your sport management friends are sitting down for a brew when Jareem informs all of you about a common contact you all consider a friend, Josiah. You all know Josiah; he was one of the blessed sport management seniors who seemed to have a Midas touch. He was the leader of the student sport management group, he did a research practicum with your favorite sport philosophy professor and was published, he did an internship at the coveted XYZ professional team in sunny Florida, and then he won an entry-level job with the same team. XYZ is owned by one of the wealthiest men in America, and Josiah was blessed again by being noticed and taken on as one of the wealthy owner's protégés. Josiah again soared and scored. He married his college sweetheart, rose quickly in the organization, had two kids along the way, and all of you were seriously jealous of his high six-figure salary — all in a span of less than five years. Josiah was a great human being and whenever he was in town, he would drop in and speak to sport management classes. He always had time to lend a hand. You all went to dinner with him numerous times and got to know him in a one-on-one fashion. Many of your peers were able to get an internship with XYZ because of his contacts.

Jareem: "Did you guys hear about Josiah?"

Micah: "What? He got another raise? He divorced his college sweetheart and married the centerfold of Playboy?"

Jareem: "Not exactly. He quit his job!"

Micah: "What? What did he do, sleep with the boss's wife? No one quits a job like his unless there was some illicit behavior."

Megan: "Micah, you are such a pessimist—maybe it's something else. Is he sick? His wife, the kids?"

Jareem: "None of that. He quit because he didn't find the job fulfilling."

Micah: "Fulfilling—the guy is making close to three quarters of a million a year, and it's not fulfilling? I'll take his job. That would fulfill me plenty!"

Jeremy: "What happened?"

Jareem: "I saw Josiah at our last holiday when I went home. You know, he's from my home town. He came over to see me one night and told me that he decided to go back to school."

Micah: "Whatever for?"

Jareem: "He said that he didn't like what he was doing at XYZ. There was no meaning to it. He was managing people and programs, but he never felt like he made a difference in anyone's life."

Micah: "Give me a break, that $750,000 did a lot of good in his family's life. The last time I saw him, he told me he had a membership at one of the exclusive golf clubs in town, and his wife belonged to the accompanying country clubs, and didn't he tell us that they had a full-time nanny who they took along with them when they traveled to Hawaii on vacation? Sounds like a whole lot of good to me!"

Jeremy: "Rich doesn't always mean money. I remember a quote about never mistaking wealth with money—maybe Josiah is seeking a different kind of wealth."

Jareem: "You hit on it! Josiah is going to Union Seminary to study religion. He wants to become a pastor."

Micah: "Oh, please! What sort of salary is that going to be?"

Jareem: "He said that one of his colleagues just signed a letter of intent to serve a parish for $12,000 a year—someplace in Arkansas. Of course they will provide a home, cost of living allowance, car, and retirement."

Micah: "There is no way he can make it on that."

Jareem: "I said the same thing. He said he wasn't worried about it—things would work out."

Micah: "What in the world? How did he get to this place in his thinking?"

Jareem: "He said he felt called. Actually, he said that his family—his mom and dad— were always devout Lutherans and once upon a time he had considered serving others. He originally wanted to be a teacher, but his family would not permit it. Teachers don't make enough money and they have no power. So Josiah was pressured to 'make money.' First he was majoring in business and then transferred over to sport management. I think his dad *knew some corporate types in sport and they made big bucks. His dad really pressured him to get connected with the power groups in sport. When he got the job with XYZ, his family was overjoyed. His father and mother really were into the benefits of Josiah's job. They loved those box seats at the big games."*

Micah: "Who wouldn't love that?"

Megan: "So what happened?"

Jareem: "Well, Josiah didn't feel that life had much meaning. He started to wonder and doubt what he did; it wasn't long until he was telling his wife he hated his job. He kept asking, 'Is this it?' I guess he said it so much and so often, she asked him what he wanted to do. He said that he always wanted to teach."

Micah: "He wanted to become a teacher?"

Jareem: "Yes, but he didn't think anyone would believe him, especially his dad, so he contemplated it, thought about it, meditated on it, and finally said he felt called to the ministry to serve others."

Micah: "That's a bit of a jump from being a teacher."

Jareem: "I made that same comment. Josiah said he knew that, but he felt called because his dad and mom could understand a call to service through the ministry which they never would through teaching. He thought about taking his wife and children to Africa to teach the poorest of the poor, but realized this decision was his and he had a responsibility not to foist his call on everyone."

Micah: "Sounds to me that giving up a $750,000 salary is foisting a lot on a family."

Jeremy: "Maybe there is more to living than making a lot of money."

Jareem: "That's the message Josiah wanted me to send to all of you. He said, 'Be careful of what you wish for. All the money and position didn't make his life better. He said he wished he had taken more time to figure out who he was and then evaluate that in relation to XYZ. He thought if he had done that, maybe he would have figured out that XYZ was not a place for him."

Micah: "And how are we supposed to do this? How do you know if you are a match for an organization? Josiah looked like the perfect match—the owner of XYZ thought he was the perfect match. I watched on TV numerous times and saw old Josiah right up there in the owner's sky box, holding a drink, and the owner having his arm around Josiah's shoulder. If that isn't a match, what is?"

Megan: "But you are assuming that what you want is what all of us want. I have a friend who worked for a for-profit organization. She made rather good money, but then she abruptly quit and went to work for a non-profit organization for about half the salary. She said she didn't care for the constant grind of 'making money.' She wanted to do something to make a difference."

Micah: "Are you saying you can't make a difference by making a good salary? Come on, we can make good money and still make a difference. You don't have to be poor to make a difference."

Megan: "That's not what I am saying. I think each of us is different and each of us should have a clear picture of what we want and who we are. That might take us a lifetime to figure out, but it might be very helpful to consider all of this and reflect on it as we go through our college experience."

Jeremy: "Maybe that's the moral of Josiah's story—what is our purpose as people and what is our purpose in sport management? Perhaps there are many different sorts of places that we can work or serve or maybe work/serve as one component. I get the feeling that many of us are marking time and running on a treadmill. I see some of our peers on campus who are just going through the motions. Why are we here? If we can answer that question, maybe we might have a better understanding of what we are doing in sport management."

In Parker Palmer's work (see Box 11.3), this author, educator, and activist focuses on issues in education, community, leadership, spirituality, and social change and argues that purpose should be thoughtful, directive, and

As a sport manager, your ability to make ethical decisions will have a direct bearing on almost every action you take. A principle-centered leader makes decisions based on the mission and values of the organization and has courage to act on these values even when others do not. Using the mission and values as guides allows sport managers the greatest potential to maximize sport's many positive benefits.

intentional. We agree there should be great thought and reflection put into what we do. Principled leaders are those who have taken the time to figure out who they are before they begin the process of becoming the principled leader that they want to become. All of this is a process, a thoughtful process that takes some time and energy. We will offer some ways of doing this in a thematic principled, thoughtful, moral way in this our concluding chapter on principled leadership.

BOX 11.3 PARKER PALMER

Parker Palmer for 15 years was the senior associate of the American Association for Higher Education, which today is the American Association for Higher Education and Accreditation. The association has literally set the standards in higher education in the United States for over 140 years through research, publications, conferences, and partnerships. Palmer is considered one of this country's best examples of an individual of principled leadership who inspires others to be better than what they think they can be. His books (*A Hidden Wholeness: The Journey Toward an Undivided Life*; *Let Your Life*

Speak: Listening for the Voice of Vocation; *To Know As We Are Known: Education As a Spiritual Journey*) are dedicated to inspiring the best within us to lead others to be the best they can be. Who are you? What do you believe? What do you aspire to be? These questions should always and continually direct each individual as he/she quests for a place in life that is meaningful and inspiring.

The goal of this process is four-fold:

- Explore and reflect on values and attitudes of self in relation to leadership.
- Reflect on personal growth as a servant leader.
- Demonstrate servant leadership and develop strategies to cope with situations that arise from conflicting values and beliefs.
- Develop a clear vision of leadership style and commitment to principled leadership.

Explore and Reflect on Values and Attitudes of Self in Relation to Leadership

In the study of philosophy, one of the basic questions is who are you? What sort of person are you? We can guess a few things about you. You must be a person who wants to work with others, for this field that you have chosen is about people. As such, who are you in relation to other people? In a principle-centered approach to leadership, we must consider the importance of compassion when working with others. The environment you set as a leader will help others flourish only if there is a purposeful commitment to helping others become better. If your followers get to be better, stronger individuals and learn as they follow you, you will have succeeded greatly in your role as leader. People only get better in an environment in which compassion is the fertile soil. We are not saying that compassion forgets the flaws, inadequacies, or the limitations of the people you serve. However, we are saying that compassionate leadership understands these issues and works to help individuals become better. Are you a person who truly cares about the success of the people who follow you?

Presently we live in a consumer culture in which our values are often informed by material goods and gain. Yes, your followers will want to be monetarily rewarded and rewarded fairly, but they also need to be cared for and cared about. A principled leader cares for followers as people and cares about their growth. As Greenleaf (2002) said in *Servant Leadership*, one of the markers of true servant leadership is that the followers get better, and he wasn't talking about their ability to be better at producing products, he meant that they got better as people. This same concept was noted in Dupree (2004), who argued in *Leadership Is an Art* that leadership is more about caring than it is about doing. How does one care for and care about others? Basic philosophical questions to use are: "How would I want to be treated? How would I want my boss to treat me? How would I want my peers to be treated?" Most of us want to be treated with compassion — for others to care for us and to care about us. We want to know that our lives have meaning and that we make a difference by being here and being heard. It is especially true in the workplace. Reflect for yourself on how you can manifest caring for and caring about in your actions toward the people with whom you work. In colleges, the environment is often one of distance and closeness. Youth life centers around a daily schedule in which you sit approximately in the same seats in the same classes, in the same buildings, taught by the same instructors for approximately 16 weeks. However, most students, even though they are close in proximity to others in this environment, are really very distant from the experience. For example, can you give the full name of all of your instructors or professors? Can you give the full name of more than five people in any of your classes? Do you know the full name of any of the support staff who work in your building?

The distance and close relationship often also flows out into our everyday lives. We are members of teams, families, and organizations, but often forget the power of the relationships that make a difference. For example, have you ever thanked the important people in your life who have made a difference for you? Did you ever take the time to write a "real" note or letter to a former coach, teacher, or friend who made a difference in your life?

We will not become principled leaders who care about others until we take that first step to notice others, break down those walls of distance, and listen to the voices of those around us. We can't make a difference until we listen. Pay attention to those people, learn from them, share with them — that is a beginning point of making a difference. Chelladurai and Saleh (1980) label this sort of caring social support. All of us need the support of our leadership and in the social environment in which we work daily. This is not to say that leadership should be blind; rather leadership should be informed about the needs of the followers in order to support them to grow and be better at what they do.

Reflect on Personal Growth as a Principled Leader

A principled leader does not just spring out of the academic world — rather, it would be unusual for such a principled leader to even blossom in our academic world today. Unfortunately, our colleges on the whole have succumbed to the belief that the worth of a college education is the vocational final product that it provides. Our academic majors often are inundated with courses that help us be better managers but not necessarily better leaders. We learn how to do budgets, build spreadsheets, balance ledgers, manage people, and generally answer to the bottom line. Thus our general skills and tools do not necessarily focus on compassion and caring. Rather, each of us needs to spend some serious thought and reflection on what it means to be a compassionate principled leader to make a difference in the lives of others. Parker Palmer (Personal communication, 2011) argues that we have to purposefully cultivate an environment of culture that expedites opportunities. What opportunities will you seek? How will you use the opportunities and how will you be thoughtful about those opportunities?

In what volunteer organizations are you involved? How are you involved in your family as a leader? How are you involved in your community as a leader? These experiences will be helpful when you get to the work stage of your life. Of course, many of you have had part-time jobs. In this day and age, most young people have had some experience in making money. However, in all of those roles you will play a follower. You will serve at the whim and leisure of your superiors. In these roles, what values will you display as a follower? How will you lead as a follower? The reflection that you do now on who you are as a follower will pay you dividends when you become a leader.

Demonstrate Principled Leadership and Develop Strategies to Cope with Situations That Arise from Conflicting Values and Beliefs

Talking about it and studying about it does not always make the personal, meaningful connection; we actually have to get our hands dirty and get out there and lead. As we started this chapter, we noted that there are seasons and times to be a leader and seasons and times to be a follower. In your life presently, you may have some limited opportunities to be a principled leader — but most of your time presently will be about following, and that in and of itself is problematic. We seldom ask important leadership questions of the person who leads us. Rather, we ask about the non-moral values that we will reap by being in this program. What percentage of this program's graduates get good jobs? What percentage of this program's student get good internships? Where do students do internships? How famous is the faculty? Is this program one of the best? However, "the best" is never really defined in moral values but in the social values of success and acquiring a position. Knowing who you are and what you are is the first step in demonstrating your principled leadership. Be clear about who you are and what values describe and define your life. These values should carry you through the dark hours of life.

Megan, Jareem, and Jeremy, in discussing their friend Josiah, noted that wealth probably should not be measured by money but by the qualities that make us successful as people. There is a wonderfully thoughtful text written by Robert I. Sutton (2010) called *The No Asshole Rule*. Sutton is a professor of management science and engineering at Stanford University and was approached by *Harvard Business Review (HBR)* to write an article on incivility in the business world. Sutton said he would, but only on condition that he could title the article what he wanted to title it. HBR agreed, and thus the title, "The No Asshole Rule." The article grew into a book and today there is an active online site for this same title. Sutton argues that individuals who only care about themselves, who use others to get ahead, who abuse others, and do whatever they will do to get ahead are not people whom others want to work with. He mentioned in his work that a Nobel Prize winner was being considered for a teaching position at Stanford. There was no doubt that this individual would bring great notoriety and academic respect to their program, however, the program faculty said no way. In fact, one of the professors said "I quit if you bring that fellow in, he is a real asshole" — and thus the title of Sutton's work. It makes a difference in leadership of who you are and what you are. Leadership is where you find it. You might not be a leader in the classroom, but you can be a leader in your home. You might not be a leader in group organizations, but you can be a leader as a volunteer in the community. We become leaders by getting involved. Incidentally, the most important leadership role you will ever have is in being a strong leader and advocate for the values that describe you. How you manifest these values in your everyday life defines you as a leader.

Develop a Clear Vision of Leadership Style and Commitment to Principled Leadership

A leadership style is the actual way you manifest what you believe, what you do and how you follow through. Ethical study clearly informs us that few people have the commitment to follow through on what they believe when things get tough or even follow through on somewhat mundane issues.

In psychology, the Abilene Paradox (Harvey, 1988) features the story of group-think. A paradox is a seeming contradiction. In this case, a family was sitting on a hot, sweltering porch many miles from Abilene and pretty much being miserable, when one of them came up with the idea of driving to Abilene to get an ice cream cone. No one spoke up to say anything about how this might not be the best thing to do. Even though some of them considered the distance, the condition of the car with no air conditioning, or the problems that would occur with too many people packed into the car, none spoke up because they didn't want to rock the boat. When they got back from Abilene, they all noted that it was a pretty unpleasant thing to do and no one really wanted to go there in the first place. Interestingly, the majority of people with whom you will work will be pulled to group-think and will not challenge being a victim of the Abilene paradox. Group-think can be a dangerous state of affairs, because it always rests on the notion that someone else will speak up or someone else will intervene. Numerous examples of this sort of thinking occur in daily life. We do not turn in a cheater in the classroom because we do not want to get involved. We do not step in when we see questionable behavior because it does not involve us. We do not volunteer because it is not convenient and someone else will do it.

What is also interesting about group-think is that often just one person intervening, one person speaking up, one person questioning, or one person volunteering leads others to get involved. As an emerging leader in sport management, this is the time for you to watch for opportunities to speak up and to make a difference. Get out of your comfort zone to volunteer and to make a difference. Be clear about why you are doing this leadership and be clear that it has to do with what you believe. In Chapters 2 and 3 we discussed the importance of mission. Hopefully you have considered your mission and have reflected on what sort of leader you are and want to be.

Leadership in Application to Moral and Ethical Issues in Sport Management

Moral issues abound in sport. This text only addresses a few of a multitude of problems that can and do exist. Boxhill (2005) wrote passionately about the moral significance of sport. Her point was that sport and athletics occur in a flood of interpersonal relationships. As we learned in Chapter 1, morality is the interaction of person meeting person. Besides, determining the moral duty and obligation we have based on the promises that we make is not easy because we also have the difficulty of discovering these moral issues in an environment in which gaining advantage and gamesmanship flavors, defines, and potentially can corrupt the fair play experience. The moral issues abound outside of play activity, affecting interpersonal human actions in leadership roles as coach, assistant coach, athletic director, associate or assistant athletic director, marketing director, or finance director. In each of these leadership roles, the moral interaction occurs when the tension between non-moral values challenges the moral motive, intention, and action of one human being to another. This is highly messy business — there are no fail-safe rules or road maps to finding the approved and proper solution. All that we can offer you are some basic skills and tools that you should consider in developing your principled leadership style. Let us consider a few of the conflicts of social values in college athletics in relation to the general university community.

As a future principled leader, if you choose the university athletic environment consider the following situations into which you shall be thrust:

1. Few places on college campuses display an extreme level of tension between ethics and social values. Athletics is the beast in the corner, as the late Wilford Bailey (Bailey & Littleton, 1991), former NCAA president and president of Auburn University, said. Athletics is measured and rewarded for the social values of winning, gaining advantage, and exclusionary practices; we call it competition.

2. Few places in colleges exist where we find student behavior which borders on crude, uncivil, and disrespectful, yet is often glorified; we call them fans.

3. Few events on campus support an environment where heavy drinking and brutish drunkenness is commonplace; we call it tailgating.

4. Few places in colleges exist where revenue, costs, and salaries are blatantly obscene. Salaries of big-time coaches are often more than the president of the university or even the governor of the state, and many times more than the President of the United States. Most of the individuals who receive these salaries are employed at state-funded universities which make them state government workers; we call it hiring good coaches based on market factors.

5. Probably the only place on campus where a highly competitive environment exists and ethics are never taught as subject matter is athletics. Study of ethics is mandated in business, law, engineering, and business, but not in athletics. Rather, ethics are usually dismissed in the name of gaining advantage. Clever comments such as "If you aren't cheating, you aren't trying" are often found in locker rooms; we call it motivation.

6. Few places on campus exist where administrators continually hire individuals who have questionable ethical practices. However, a coach can be fired for violating NCAA rules one day at institution A and be hired a few days later at institution B with little concern about the former behavior. Rather, the moral justification offered by the coach is believed and the moral responsibility is

Many fans believe they have the right and obligation to influence the outcome of the game. Many sport managers hand out noise-making sticks that fans wave and bang together during opposing team play, making it difficult for players to hear and concentrate, thus negatively influencing play.

usually placed on University A — they were non-compliant. The belief is that institution B can control the behavior of the coach in question. The NCAA has begun to respond to this problem but not to the degree that it should; we call it a good hire.

7. Probably the only place on campus in which the hiring process doesn't follow the rule or norm of hiring as ascribed by the Human Resources Department of the university is athletics. Rules don't seem to apply to athletic departments. Instead the practice is justified by the argument that coaches need to be hired; this hiring is an emergency, rules are suspended. Such practice flies in the face of ethical practice and principled leadership; we call it common practice.

8. Probably the only place on campus in which salaries are neither equitable nor justified is athletics. Coaches of women's sports are paid less than coaches of men's sports; coaches of Olympic sports are paid markedly less than the coaches of revenue-producing sports. In many universities, assistant coaches of male revenue-producing sports make a higher wage than the head coach of a women's team; we call it the competitive marketplace.

9. Probably the only place on campus where students are treated inequitably is athletics. The athletes in the revenue sports have more resources, more coaches, more support, more adulation, more fans, and more perks than other students in the same department; we call it just the tough breaks.

10. Probably athletics is the only place on campus where the sacred cow — the revenue-producing sports — never have funding cuts. Instead other sports are cut and the blame is laid to rest on the women; we call it the pitfalls of Title IX.

11. Probably athletics is the only place on campus where revenue-producing activities really don't pay for themselves. instead the programs spend more than they make; we call it "big-time sports."

This is the place in which you, the sport management professional, will spend your future. It will tax you, stress you and demand of you difficult decision making. It is easy to tell you that you will need principled leadership; it is another case for you actually to do it.

Conclusion and Summary

In this book we have discussed the necessary ingredients of moral and principled leadership. We recommend four specific practices that may further help you as you become a principled leader in the field.

- Explore and reflect on values and attitudes of self in relation to leadership.
- Reflect on personal growth as a servant leader.
- Demonstrate servant leadership and develop strategies to cope with situations that arise from conflicting values and beliefs.

• Develop a clear vision of leadership style and a commitment to principled leadership.

As we have discussed in this text, there are many other variables that affect leadership style and action, including role modeling, the environment in which you live and from which you learn, and your own reasoning and education about principled living.

If you truly want to be a principled leader, you will need to find a place in which, as a follower, you will learn from ethical role models in an ethical environment, and where discussions of moral dilemmas are part of the management style of the leader and part of the practices of the program (Stoll & Beller, 2006). It will not be an easy task to find such an environment. More likely most of you will find yourselves in places that may not match who and what you are. Be advised that the majority of people who are in management and leadership positions think they are doing "good." They are not bad people, but they are not necessarily principled leaders. You will have an interesting journey if you stay in the profession; we hope that when you assume your leadership role, you are able to practice principled leadership. We wish you good luck and good fortune.

Micah: "Well, maybe there is something more to leadership than just being in charge. Maybe we all need to consider how well we lead?"

Jeremy: "Yes, Micah, maybe we should all ask some pretty simple questions of ourselves in our leadership roles, Do our followers grow? Do our followers get better in their leadership abilities?"

Micah: "I'm still not sure of what that means."

Jareem: "I know what it means; I can feel it when it happens to me."

Micah: "Oh, great, it's like some cosmic force that none of us really know but it just happens. Sounds like Rudy Giuliani's book on 'Leadership'—maybe it's mystical."

Jeremy: "Perhaps it is. But Micah, maybe we should all remember this basic question: how would I feel as a follower if I were treated this way? That's pretty simple. The basic question of what is known as reversibility really works for followers and leaders. How would I feel is an important point."

Megan: "Yes, that is simple, but from what we have learned in this journey there are other things to consider. For example, principled leadership occurs from the basic beginning stages of being a follower."

Jeremy: "Yes, and we have also learned that we should be asking important questions about the mission of any organization in which we become involved. Are the core values of the organization values that we can share? Is the business of the organization honorable?"

Jareem: "We should also determine if the leaders of the organization show through their actions these same important core values. Do these leaders have a history in which their followers grow into leaders? Do these leaders support the mission of the organization and try to live their personal and professional lives accordingly?"

Micah: "Isn't that asking too much?"

Jareem: "I don't think so—our reach should be beyond our grasp. We should be challenged to be more than what we think we can be."

Micah: "*That's a lot to consider. Don't you also think that we have to make sure that we are informed about the issues? That means we have to do some research and make sure we have selected the best sources to learn about the issues.*"

Jeremy: "*Right, and those social and ethical issues will change over time as we go through our careers. What we know today about the issues may change during our professional life.*"

Micah: "*You mean what we have studied thus far may not be the final answer—maybe there is more out there than what we have covered in this text?*"

Jeremy: "*Yes, there are many, many more issues.*"

Micah: "*I guess that means that I can't quit studying the issues. I hope we are up to the task.*"

Megan: "*I think we can do it. We just need to stay focused on an honorable approach and ask the tough questions of ourselves: What is the right thing to do? Why is it right? And what historical, social, and cultural experience and wisdom helps us answer these questions?*"

Micah: "*Might be a tough thing to accomplish, but even I think I can do it!*"

References

Bailey, W. S., and T. D. Littleton (1991). *Athletics and Academe: An Anatomy of Abuses and a Prescription for Reform.* Washington, D.C.: American Council on Education.

Boxhill, J. (2005). "The Moral Significance of Sport." Retrieved from http://www.ncssm.edu/ethics/sessions.

Chelladurai, P., and S. Saleh (1980). Dimension of Leader Behavior in Sports: Development of a Leadership Scale. *Journal of Sport Psychology, 2,* 34–35.

Dupree, M. (2004). *Leadership Is an Art.* Moberly, MO: Crown.

Greenleaf, R. (2002). *Servant Leadership: A Journey Into the Nature of Legitimate Power and Greatness.* Mahwah, NJ: Paulist.

Guiliani, R. (2007). *Leadership.* Long Island, NY: Miramax.

Harvey, J. B. (1988). *The Abilene Paradox and Other Meditations on Management.* New York: Jossey-Bass.

Palmer, P. (2004). *A Hidden Wholeness: The Journey Toward an Undivided Life.* New York: Jossey-Bass.

Palmer, P. (1999). *Let Your Life Speak: Listening for the Voice of Vocation.* New York: Jossey-Bass.

Palmer, P. (1993). *To Know as We Are Known: Education as a Spiritual Journey.* San Francisco, CA: Harper One.

Stoll, S. K., and J. M. Beller (2004). "Ethical Dilemmas in College Sport." In R. Lapchick, *New Game Plan for College Sport* (pp. 75–90). Westport, CT: Praeger.

Sutton, R. I. (2010). *The No Asshole Rule: Building a Civilized Workplace and Surviving One That Isn't.* New York: Business Plus.

Index